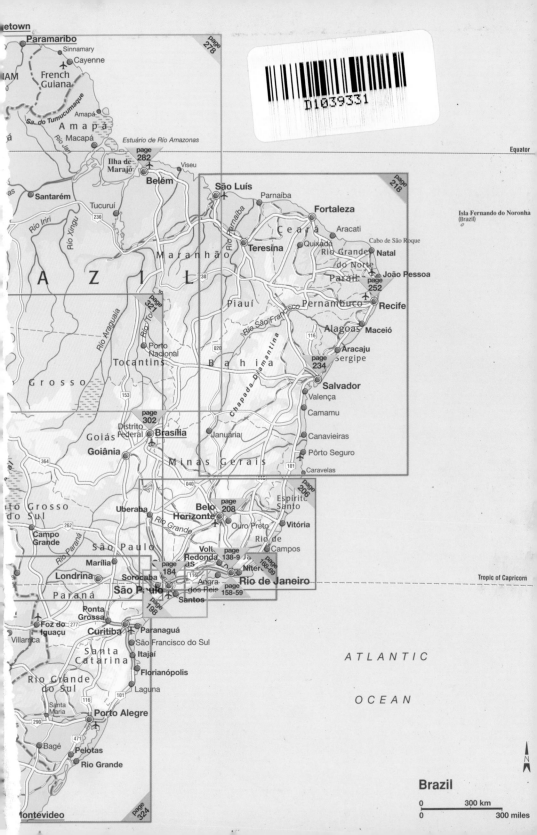

Brazil

page 278
page 282
page 218
page 321
page 252
page 234
page 302
page 206
page 208
page 184
page 138-9
page 166-69
page 158-59
page 198
page 324

etown

Paramaribo
Sinnamary
Cayenne

French Guiana

NAM

Amapá

Macapá
Río Jari
Estuário de Río Amazonas

Ilha de Marajó

Belém
Viseu

Santarém

Tucuruí
Río Iriri
Río Xingu
230

B R A Z I L

M a r a n h ã o

São Luís
Río Parnaíba
Parnaíba

Fortaleza

Teresina
C e a r á
Aracati
Quixadá
Cabo de São Roque
Rio Grande do Norte
Natal
Paraíba
João Pessoa
30

Piauí
Pernambuco
Río São Francisco
Recife

Alagoas
Maceió
116
Aracaju
Sergipe

B a h i a
Chapada Diamantina
020

Salvador
Valença
Camamu
Canavieiras
Januária
Pôrto Seguro
101
Caravelas

Río Araguaia
Río Tocantins
321

Porto Nacional

T o c a n t i n s

G r o s s o
153

Goiás
Distrito Federal
Brasília
Goiânia
364

M i n a s   G e r a i s
040
Espírito Santo

Uberaba
Río Grande

Belo Horizonte
Ouro Preto
Vitória
Río de Campos

to Grosso do Sul
262

Campo Grande
São Paulo
Río Paraná

Marília
Londrina
Volt. Redonda
Niterói
Rio de Janeiro
Angra dos Reis
Sorocaba
São Paulo
Santos

P a r a n á

Ponta Grossa
Foz do Iguaçu
277
Villarrica
Curitiba
Paranaguá
São Francisco do Sul
Itajaí

S a n t a
C a t a r i n a
Florianópolis
Laguna

Río Grande do Sul
116
101
Santa Maria

Porto Alegre
290
Bagé
471
Pelotas
Rio Grande

Montevideo

Equator

Isla Fernando do Noronha
(Brazil)

Tropic of Capricorn

A T L A N T I C

O C E A N

N

0   300 km
0   300 miles

INSIGHT GUIDES

BRAZIL

APA PUBLICATIONS

Part of the Langenscheidt Publishing Group

※ INSIGHT GUIDE

BRAZIL

Editorial
Project Editor
Pam Barrett
Managing Editor
Alyse Dar
Editorial Director
Brian Bell

Distribution
United States
Langenscheidt Publishers, Inc.
36–36 33rd Street, 4th Floor
Long Island City, New York 11106
Fax: (1) 718 784 0640

UK & Ireland
GeoCenter International Ltd
Meridian House, Churchill Way West
Basingstoke, Hampshire RG21 6YR
Fax: (44) 1256 817988

Australia
Universal Publishers
1 Waterloo Road
Macquarie Park, NSW 2113
Fax: (61) 2 9888 9074

New Zealand
Hema Maps New Zealand Ltd (HNZ)
Unit D, 24 Ra ORA Drive
East Tamaki, Auckland
Fax: (64) 9 273 6479

Worldwide
**Apa Publications GmbH & Co.
Verlag KG (Singapore branch)**
38 Joo Koon Road, Singapore 628990
Tel: (65) 6865 1600. Fax: (65) 6861 6438

Printing
Insight Print Services (Pte) Ltd
38 Joo Koon Road, Singapore 628990
Tel: (65) 6865 1600. Fax: (65) 6861 6438

©2008 Apa Publications GmbH & Co.
Verlag KG (Singapore branch)
All Rights Reserved
First Edition 1988
Sixth Edition 2007
Reprinted 2008

CONTACTING THE EDITORS
We would appreciate it if readers
would alert us to errors or out-
dated information by writing to:
**Insight Guides, P.O. Box 7910,
London SE1 1WE, England.
Fax: (44) 20 7403 0290.**
insight@apaguide.co.uk

www.insightguides.com
In North America:
www.insighttravelguides.com

ABOUT THIS BOOK

The first Insight Guide pioneered the use of creative full-color photography in travel guides in 1970. Since then, we have expanded our range to cater for our readers' need not only for reliable information about their chosen des-tination but also for a real under-standing of the culture and workings of that destination. Now, when the internet can supply inexhaustible (but not always reliable) facts, our books marry text and pictures to provide those much more elusive qualities: knowledge and discern-ment. To achieve this, they rely heavily on the authority of locally based writers and photographers.

How to use this book
Insight Guide: Brazil is carefully structured to convey an understand-ing of the country and its culture and to guide readers through its sights and activities:

◆ The **Best of Brazil** at the front of the guide helps you to prioritize what you want to do.

◆ The **Features** section, indicated by a yellow bar at the top of each page, covers the country's history, culture, and people in a series of informative essays.

◆ The main **Places** section, indi-cated by a blue bar, is a complete guide to all the sights and areas worth visiting. Places of special inter-

we had to rewrite and re-photograph large portions of it. This major new edition brings together a team of experts from all over Brazil who have pooled their invaluable knowledge.

Hugh O'Shaughnessy brought his expertise to features on the History and Economy of Brazil, and contributed to the Amazon chapter. **Bruna Rocha** shared her enthusiasm for Brazil's traditions when she revamped the feature on saints and idols. **Tom Murphy** updated his earlier features on the Brazilian people, carnival, and festivals. Rio resident **Steve Yolen** brought his passion for soccer to a feature of that name, and covered changes in Rio State. Music writer **Sue Steward** gave us a new slant on Brazil's vibrant music scene; and **Christopher Pickard** wrote features on cinema and TV, and updated the chapter on Rio de Janeiro. London-based Brazilian national **Jorge Mendez** brought the chapters on Bahia, Salvador, and Pernambuco up to date. **Karinna Damo** gave new insights on São Paulo, and on the Southern States. **Ricardo Mendonça** covered the changing face of Brasília; **Michael Clifford** looked at life in the Far Northeast, Sergipe and Alagoas; **Joby Williams** wrote about the Pantanal and Iguaçu Falls; and the Travel Tips section at the end of the book was updated by **Brian Nicholson**.

These writers built on earlier contributions by **Edwin Taylor**, **Richard House**, **Elizabeth Herrington**, **Moyra Ashford**, **Sol Biderman**, **Michael Small**, **Patrick Cunningham**, **Daniela Hart**, **Ricardo Buckup**, **Sue Branford**, and **Richard Ladle**.

Neil Titman proofread the text, **Penny Phenix** compiled the index, and picture research was carried out by **Hilary Genin** and **Jenny Krautz**.

est are coordinated by number with the maps. Restaurant listings are included at the end of the chapters.
◆ The **Travel Tips** listings section, with an orange bar, provides a handy point of reference for information on travel, hotels, shops, restaurants, and more.
◆ The **Photographs** are chosen not only to illustrate the Brazilian landscape, and the beauty of its cities, nature reserves, and beaches, but also to convey its cultural diversity.

The contributors

Brazil has changed in many ways over the past few years, so it was not enough simply to update the guide –

Map Legend

— ·· —	International Boundary
– – – –	State Boundary
– · – · –	National Park/Reserve
– – – –	Ferry Route
Ⓜ	Metro
✈ ✈	Airport: International/Regional
🚌	Bus Station
🅿	Parking
❶	Tourist Information
✉	Post Office
✝ ✝	Church / Ruins
✝	Monastery
☾	Mosque
✡	Synagogue
🏰	Castle / Ruins
∴	Archeological Site
∩	Cave
⚊	Statue/Monument
★	Place of Interest

The main places of interest in the Places section are coordinated by number with a full-color map (e.g. ❶), and a symbol at the top of every right-hand page tells you where to find the map.

LEFT: Fisherman on a tributary of the São Francisco River, Pernambuco.

Contents

The historic quarter
of São Luís in the
northeast of Brazil

Travel Tips

THE BEST OF BRAZIL

Breathtaking views, glorious tropical beaches, historic colonial towns, a vast array of wildlife, a tempting selection of restaurants, and a calendar of festivals that would be hard to beat anywhere in the world. Brazil has it all, and these essential tips reveal where you can find the best of everything

TOP VIEWS

● **Corcovado, Rio de Janeiro**
You can't go to Rio without taking the train to the top of Corcovado, where the statue of Christ spreads its arms over the city, and the views are phenomenal. *See page 155.*

● **Sugar Loaf, Rio de Janeiro**
There are those who claim the views of Rio and the bay are even better from the top of Sugar Loaf mountain than from Corcovado. It's a hard one to decide. *See page 150.*

● **Pai Inácio Mountain**
There are stunning view of the Chapada Diamantina region, one of the most beautiful in Bahia, from the top of the mountain, where a host of exotic plants thrive. *See page 227*

● **Paranapiacaba**
The name means "Sea View" in the Tupi-Guarani language, and you get a spectacular view of the sea and the Santos lowlands. *See page 197.*

● **Curitiba to Morretes**
Fascinating views of the best-preserved section of Brazil's Atlantic rainforest during this three-hour old-fashioned train ride in Paraná state. *See page 326.*

HISTORY AND CULTURE

● **Pelhourino, Salvador**
According to UNESCO this is the most important grouping of 17th- and 18th-century colonial architecture in the Americas. *See page 234.*

● **Belém**
This *belle époque* Amazon city grew rich on the proceeds of the rubber industry in the 19th century, and still has a lot of style. *See page 280.*

● **Parati**
One of the world's newest but most prestigious literary festivals is held every August in this pretty little colonial town. *See page 177.*

● **Petrópolis**
Founded by Emperor Pedro II in the 1840s as a summer refuge from the heat of Rio, Petrópolis takes you a step back in time. *See page 167.*

● **Ouro Preto**
Gold and diamonds made Ouro Preto rich, and financed the baroque architecture and sculpture that led UNESCO to declare it a World Cultural Monument. *See page 208.*

● **Congonhas do Campo**
The town is the site of the two greatest works of the 18th-century sculptor Aleijadinho. *See page 212.*

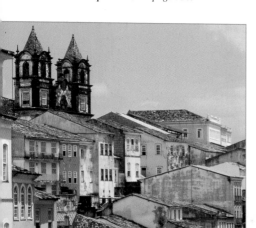

LEFT: colonial Salvador. **ABOVE:** view over Rio.

SPECTACULAR WILDLIFE

● **The Pantanal**
Home to around 650 bird species, the majority of which are wading birds such as the graceful jabiru stork, and the roseate spoonbill. Lots of mammals, too, including the capybara, the world's largest rodent, caiman, marsh deer, and armadillos. *See page 312.*

ABOVE: Capybara.

● **Amazon**
Amazonia supports 30 percent of all known plant and animal species, including 2,500 fish species, 50,000 higher plant species and millions of insects. *See page 280.*
● **Sooretama Biological Reserve**
Protects the rainforest and an incredible variety of plants, birds, and other wildlife. More than 370 species of birds have been recorded, including the red-billed curassow. *See page 215.*
● **Fernado de Noronha**
Its waters ares home to dolphins, sharks, and a myriad multi-colored fish. *See page 260.*

ABOVE: one of Brazil's idyllic beaches.

TOP SHOPPING TIPS

● **Barra Shopping**
Latin America's largest shopping center, in Barra da Tijuca, Rio. Everything a dedicated shoppper could want, and in air-conditioned comfort.
See page 164.
● **Jewelry**
You can buy delicate and innovative designs from craftsman Pepe Torras at Avenida Ataúlfo de Paiva 135, Rio. *See page 356.*
● **Handicrafts**
Fabulous collection of Indian handicrafts, plus

RIGHT: designer jewelry.

CDs of Indian music from Amoa Konoya Arte Indígena, Rua João Moura 1002, São Paulo. *See page 357.*
● **Livraria Cultura Editora**
Stocks a wide selection of books, including many about Brazil; the best in Latin America (Avenida Paulista 2073, Conjunto Nacional, São Paulo). *See page 357*

BEST BEACHES

● **Búzios**
Splendor in the tropics – white-sand beaches, crystalline water, palm trees, and coconuts. *See page 172.*
● **Lopes Mendes, Ilha Grande, Rio State**
A glorious stretch of beach where the fine white sand squeaks beneath your feet. *See page 176.*
● **São Paulo State**
The Rio–Santos Highway passes more than 400 km (240 miles) of glorious beaches. *See page 198*
● **Taipús de Fora, Bahia State**
On the remote Maraú Peninsula, this is considered by many to be one of the finest beaches in Brazil. *See page 223.*
● **Praia do Forte**
Thousands of coconut palms stand on 12 km (7 miles) of white sandy beach, some 85 km (53 miles) from Salvador. It is protected by a private foundation. *See page 224.*
● **Praia Pajuçara, Maceió, Alagoas State**
Maceió beaches are famous for the transparent, bright emerald green of the water. Praia Pajuçara, which becomes an enormous wading pool at lowtide, is a prime example. *See page 248.*
● **Jericoacoara, Ceará State**
Ceará has innumerable beautiful beaches, but perhaps the finest is the remote Jericoacoara. Declared a national park in 2002, it is a magical spot, that has been described as "one of the 10 most beautiful on the planet." *See page 270.*

BEST FESTIVALS

● **Rio Carnival**
Rio de Janeiro is famous for its huge, exuberant pre-Lent Carnival, the biggest and brashest in the world. *See page 81.*

● **Salvador, Bahia**
Carnival in Salvador is quite a different thing. The centerpiece is a glittering music festival on wheels called *Trio Elétrico. See page 85.*

● **Boi-Bumba**
The last 3 days of June mark the Parintins Folk Festival in Amazonia, a huge street festival centered on the Amerindian Boi-Bumba fable. A rival to Carnival, it is the most complete mixture of Amerindian, European, and African cultural elements in Brazil. *See page 91.*

● **June Festivals**
Celebrating the feast days of St John (June 23–24), and St Peter (June 28–29) they are characterized by brightly illuminated balloons, and bonfires blazing through the night; and by fireworks, food and drink, and folk music. *See page 87.*

● **Bom Jesus dos Navegantes**
Celebrated at New Year in Salvador. A procession of small craft decked with streamers and flags carries a statue of the Lord of Seafarers from the harbor to the Boa Viagem church. *See page 88.*

● **Círio de Nazaré**
A four-hour procession on the second Sunday of October, centered on a colorfully decorated carriage bearing the image of Our Lady of Nazareth. *See page 90.*

● **New Year's Eve**
The most popular celebration is in Rio, where there's an elaborate firework display. On Copacabana beach, white-robed priestesses of Brazil's African religions launch miniature wooden boats, filled with flowers and gifts for Iemanjá, Queen of the Seas. *See page 90.*

ABOVE: celebrating Carnival in Rio

OUTDOOR ADVENTURE

● **Fernando de Noronha**
Scuba diving and snorkeling are popular activities here. There are wrecks of sunken ships to visit; and the possibility of meeting sharks on a night dive. *See page 260.*

● **Iguaçu Falls**
Aboard sturdy, 20-seater inflatable boats you are able to see up close the incredible power of the water from the base of the falls. *See page 320.*

● **Amazon**
Take treks into the forest, canoe trips, or go piranha-fishing or torchlight caiman-spotting. *See page 290.*

● **Ilha do Mel, Paranaguá**
The island is a nature reserve with natural pools, grottos, deserted beaches, and no vehicles. Its primitive, unspoiled nature makes it a popular spot for campers. *See page 327.*

● **Parque Nacional de Brasília**
An area of savanna and low forest where birds, wolves, monkeys, and armadillos find refuge. There are forest trails, and natural swimming pools. *See page 308.*

LEFT: taking a trip up the Amazon.

WINING AND DINING

● **Gero, Rio**
Opened in 2002, Gero soon became one of the hot spots on Rio's gastronomic map, with its sophisticated Italian cuisine. *See page 165.*

● **Locanda della Mimosa, Petrópolis**
Danio Braga is rated as one of Brazil's best chefs, with good reason. The fact that he's off the beaten track doesn't deter his many fans. *See page 179.*

● **Banana da Terra, Parati**
Seafood partnered with local ingredients. Brave combinations make for memorable meals. *See page 179.*

● **Cantaloup, São Paulo**
A real favorite: serves creative contemporary food in a beautifully refurbished old bread factory. *See page 201.*

● **Sorriso da Dadá, Salvador**
Great Bahian food in lovely surroundings. *See page 201.*

● **Famiglia Giuliano, Recife**
In a replica medieval castle, and particularly famous for its *feijoada*. *See page 201.*

● **Alice, Brasília**
A French bistro that is considered by many to be the best restaurant in Brasília. *See page 309.*

ABOVE: Museu de Arte Contemporânea.

TOP MUSEUMS

● **Museu Nacional das Belas Artes, Rio**
Houses one of Latin America's finest art collections, including works by the great 20th-century Cândido Portinari. *See page 146.*

● **Museu de Arte Contemporânea, Rio**
Designed by Oscar Niemeyer, the sinuous building maybe more of an attraction than the exhibits, but it shouldn't be missed. *See page 150.*

● **Museu Afro-Brasileiro, Salvador**
A fascinating collection of objects that highlight the strong African influence on Bahian culture. *See page 234.*

● **Museu do Homem do Nordeste, Recife**
The museum is a tribute to the cultural history of this fascinating region. *See page 253.*

● **MASP, the Museu de Arte de São Paulo**
Rembrandt, Goya, and Monet are just a few of the European artists represented here. There's also a sweeping survey of Brazilian art. *See page 192.*

ABOVE: caipirinha, the national drink.

MONEY-SAVING TIPS

● **Air Passes**
A good idea if you are going to travel around the country a great deal, but they must be purchased outside Brazil. Cost depends on the number of flights, the season, and the region they cover. They are valid for 21 days and allow you to visit four or five cities (not including your starting point in Brazil). Passes can only be used on flights of the issuing airline.

● **Kilo restaurants**
Pile your plate up high in one of the many kilo restaurants, or self-service eateries, which provide excellent value for money. As the name suggests, your food is priced by weight rather than by content.

● **Free Events Listings**
The daily newspaper *O Globo* produces a Friday insert, a useful source of information and listings for Rio; and the Friday edition of the *Folha de São Paulo* has a handy booklet covering the week ahead. *Veja* is a national weekly news magazine that also publishes regional Friday entertainment inserts, called *Vejinha*.

● **Churches**
Admission is free to nearly all Brazil's churches, which often allows you to admire some good, representative art and architecture for nothing.

A LAND WITHOUT FRONTIERS

Visitors have always been slightly dazed by
the sheer size of the country and its hidden
riches. Brazilians are no less captivated

Since its colonization by the Portuguese in the 16th
century, Brazil has held a constant fascination for foreigners. First it was gold, then rubber and coffee, and
more recently the exotic sights and sounds of the nation.
For Brazilians, too, it is an intriguing land. There is a feeling that, hidden in some far corner of this great nation, there
may be an immense treasure just waiting to be discovered.
The main problem lies in identifying the corner.

Brazilians and foreigners alike have been gradually occupying the enormous empty spaces of this continent-sized country ever since the 16th
century. They have populated them with some 175 million souls, composing one of the world's most heterogeneous populations.
They live amid modern splendor in sprawling cities and in
squalid deprivation in rural backwaters. They work in high-
tech industries and push wooden plows behind laboring
beasts. Within the confines of this country live indigenous
people in near Stone Age conditions, semi-feudal peasants
and landlords, pioneers hacking out jungle settlements, and
wealthy entrepreneurs and business people.

Perhaps nowhere on earth is the process of development as
tangible as in Brazil. The dynamism of the country is its
greatest achievement. Even in periods of stagnation, Brazilians continue to get on with the process of nation-building. The once
impregnable Amazon rainforest is being opened up quickly – many say too
quickly – and is the last great frontier that is still not fully explored.

Brazilians are united by a common language, Portuguese; a common
religion, Catholicism (though mixed with indigenous faiths); and a common dream, that some day Brazil will be a great nation. Despite enormous social and economic difficulties, Brazilians are a remarkably
spontaneous, enthusiastic and high-spirited people, who tend to live in
the moment. After all, at any moment, you may just find treasure. ❏

PRECEDING PAGES: the great swoop of the Amazon; looking down on Rio de Janeiro;
a new day dawns on Copacabana beach.
LEFT AND ABOVE: Brazil has one of the world's most heterogeneous populations.

FROM SANDY BEACHES TO AMAZON JUNGLE

Brazil occupies such a large landmass, and is so diverse topographically, socially, and economically, that it is hard to consider it as a single entity

Although Brazil is the fifth-largest nation on the planet, four times the size of Mexico and more than twice that of India, the Brazil where most people live forms only a small fraction of the country's total landmass of 8,509,711 sq. km (3,285,618 sq. miles). One in four people crowds into five metropolitan areas in the southern part of the country. Together, the southern and southeastern states contain more than 60 percent of Brazil's population yet account for only 16 percent of the country's geographical area. More than 100 million Brazilians live in an area slightly smaller than Alaska, while another 72 million populate an area the size of the continental US, minus Texas. What Brazil has is space – enormous regions of vast, empty space.

A regional structure

For administrative purposes, Brazil's 26 states and one federal district are divided into five regions; north, northeast, center-west, southeast and south. The two largest regions are also its least populated. The north, home to the mighty Amazon basin rainforest, occupies 42 percent of Brazil, a country large enough to accommodate all Western Europe, yet its population is smaller than that of New York.

Located just south of the Amazon is the center-west, dominated by a vast elevated plateau, and covering 22 percent of Brazil's territory. The population here has doubled since the 1970s and now represents 15 percent of the country as a whole. These two great landmasses, which together are larger than most of the world's nations, are both the promise and challenge of Brazil's future.

LEFT: a dream beach in Salvador, Bahia.
RIGHT: lush vegetation in the Pantanal.

The north's living enigma

The Amazon is one of the planet's last unsolved mysteries. The world's largest river basin, it contains not only one-fifth of all the fresh water on earth, but also the planet's greatest rainforest, a teeming biological storehouse whose true potential remains largely unknown and untapped.

Despite the encroaching devastation along the forest's frontiers, it is still possible to fly for hours over the Amazon and see no break in the carpet of greenery except for the sinuous curves of the region's rivers. On boat journeys, the wall of vegetation at the river's edge rolls by for days on end, broken only by the occasional wooden hut.

These huts, however, are clues to a fact that has been largely ignored both by Brazil's development planners and by many of the ecologists who campaign to protect the forest as the "lungs of the world" – the Amazon is no empty wilderness. Aside from the remnants of the Amerindian nations who once ruled the jungle, an estimated 3 million people are scattered over this huge area, eking out a living as their forefathers have for generations. Known as *caboclos*, these true Amazonians are rubber-tappers, Brazil-nut gatherers, fishermen and subsistence farmers.

More recently, cattle ranchers, land speculators and small farmers were encouraged to move into the area by government incentives, the promise of free land and the scent of quick profits. Cattle barons and land speculators carved up swathes of virgin forest, employing unscrupulous methods, and gangs of gunmen, to intimidate anyone who stood in their way. The main victims, along with the trees, plants, and wildlife, were the *caboclos*, many of whom were driven off the land into shanty towns on the margins of the cities. However, as the government starts to take the forest loss seriously *(see below)*, there is cause for some optimism. Substantial investment has been poured into the education of settlers, teaching them appropriate forms of agriculture and encouraging them to

CHICO MENDES

Chico Mendes (1944–88) was a rubber-tapper and environmental activist, who led the first grass-roots organization against logging and forest clearance when he and his followers resisted the loggers' bulldozers in what were known as *empates* – stand-offs. In 1985 he founded the Xapuri Rural Workers' Union, a national union of rubber-tappers.

In 1988 Mendes was murdered, and a local rancher and his father were sentenced to 19 years' imprisonment for the killing. International media pressure resulted in the creation of the Chico Mendes Extractive Reserve, and there are now some 20 such reserves scattered around the Amazon region.

adopt sustainable extractive techniques.

The wealth of the Amazon is not restricted to its huge land area. Below the surface lie untold riches. In the Serra dos Carajás, 880 km (546 miles) southwest of Belém, there is enough iron ore to keep the entire world supplied for 500 years, while elsewhere gold, tin, rare metals and oil have been found. Carefully exploited, these valuable commodities are capable of bringing development to the region without the need to destroy the forest.

The center-west

In Brazil's other great void, the center-west, the pace of development has slowed after a quick burst in the 1970s. The planned capital of Brasília was placed in the central plateau so that it would act as a magnet for settlers and integrate this region with the coastal areas. But while Brasília has matured into a city with a population of more than 2.1 million, it has failed to spawn the growth hoped for by its planners.

In terms of its geography, the center-west offers none of the natural barriers of the Amazon. An elevated plateau 1,000 meters (3,300 ft) above sea level, the Planalto Central is divided into two kinds of area – forest and woodland savanna known as *cerrado*.

Made up of stunted trees and grasslands, the *cerrado* appears to be a scrubland with little

The northeast

Brazil's third-largest region, the northeast, occupying 18 percent of the country, is the nation's poorest. Although sugar plantations made it the original economic and political center in colonial times, the northeast has not developed as fast as the southern and southeastern states. Unlike the north and center-west, the northeast is neither isolated nor underpopulated. Its fatal flaw has been its climate.

The region is divided into four zones: its northernmost state, Maranhão, combines characteristics of the northeast and the Amazon; along the coast from the state of Rio Grande do Norte to

value. Experience has shown, however, that once cleared, the *cerrado* land is extremely fertile. Farmers from southern Brazil have turned areas of the *cerrado* into sprawling farms and ranches, including the world's largest soybean farm. Roads and bridges have been built, corn and cotton production improved, and an increasing number of qualified people have moved into the area. The grasslands of the southern part of the region have also been adapted to pasture, and some of Brazil's largest cattle herds now graze there.

LEFT: ferries docked in the port at Manaus, in the Amazon.
ABOVE: the frothing red waters of the Iguaçu Falls.

Bahia runs a narrow 100–200-km (60–120-mile) strip of fertile land known as the *zona da mata*; just west of this strip begins a transition zone of semi-fertile land called the *agreste*; the final zone occupies the bulk of the interior of the northeast's states, a dry, arid region known as the *sertão*.

It is the *sertão* that has given Brazil its most devastating poverty. It is an area of periodic drought, of parched earth, of temporary rivers that swell to flood stage in times of rain, of a thorny scrub called *caatinga*; and it is an area of widespread human suffering.

One drought ended in 1984 after five years. Another – a result of El Niño in 1998 – caused massive destruction, while in 2000, one of the worst droughts in more than 70 years struck the

The Disappearing Rainforest

Being in the rainforest at dusk is an almost spiritual experience. As darkness falls, frogs and cicadas begin their chorus, while the eerie call of red howler monkeys echoes through the stillness of the twilight forest. But the next generation may not have the opportunity to experience this, because evolution's grandest experiment is in danger of coming to a premature end, as the rainforest is burned and hacked to death for the sake of short-term gain.

When the first Europeans arrived in Brazil, it was blanketed with a rainforest that stretched along the Atlantic coast from Recife south to Florianópolis. Covering 1 million sq. km (386,000 sq. miles), it held the most diverse communities of plants and animals on the planet.

The shrinkage of the forest is a direct consequence of Brazil's ever-expanding population, particularly along its Atlantic fringes, now densely populated due to the productive soil. Moreover, fires started by farmers to clear the land of fallen trees and brush often rage out of control, destroying huge tracts of virgin forest. The most damaging recorded blaze, in 1998, was described by the United Nations as "an environmental disaster without precedent on this planet".

Once, 200 species of mammal roamed or swung through the glades of the Brazilian forest. One thousand butterfly species fluttered through the forest canopy. Eight hundred species of trees, more than in the whole of North America, could be found in locations ranging from the Amazon river mouth to the highest mountain.

Amazingly, in view of the widespread destruction, Amazonia still tenaciously holds onto most of its plants and animals – and its secrets. Many of the species here are found nowhere else in the world. The rainforest canopy is one of the last great unexplored regions of the world, and there may be anything from 10 to 30 million species of insects alone that are currently unknown to science. It is still the case that a scientist may stumble upon a new species within days or even hours of arrival in the forest.

But a huge loss of biological diversity is happening right now, and deforestation is the chief cause. No animal or plant can live in a void, and the rate of destruction of their forest habitat is staggering. Between 1995 and 2000, 2 million hectares (4,942 million acres) were cut down each year. Overall, 51 million hectares (127 million acres) have been deforested, mostly during the 1980s. And in the mid-1990s, an area equivalent to over 11 percent of the extent of the original rainforest was lost.

One sad result of this wholesale destruction is that the Amazon may soon lose some of its most distinguished denizens. The giant otter, for example, which was overhunted in the 1950s and 1960s, now clings to survival in rapidly shrinking habitats. The pet trade has driven several species of blue macaw close to extinction. Other endangered animals include the jaguar and black caiman.

Although reforestation programs are in place, the rate of growth is still far exceeded by the rate of destruction. But there is some cause for hope. It was reported in October 2006 that rainforest loss over the previous 12 months was 13,100 sq. km (5,057 sq. miles). This is a lot, but less than 40 percent of the loss in 2004, and the lowest figure since 1991. There are a number of reasons for this, including falling commodity prices, but government conservation initiatives and enforcement laws must also be credited. "We increased enforcement of environmental laws... and it has worked," João Paulo Capobianco, Minister of Biodiversity and Forests, told a press conference. ❏

LEFT: flooded rainforest on the Rio Negro.

region, propelling millions of the *sertão*'s residents to the urban centers of the southeast, mainly to São Paulo and Rio de Janeiro.

Sparkling beaches

Just a few hours from the despair of the *sertão* is the beautiful coastal zone where white sandy beaches sparkle beneath the tropical sun. It is here that Brazil's famed coastal beaches begin, and stretch the length of the country from Maranhão to the southernmost state of Rio Grande do Sul. Altogether, Brazil's coastline encompasses 7,700 km (4,600 miles) – the longest continuous coastline in the world.

Beginning in the central plateau, the river flows east for over 3,000 km (1,865 miles), reaching into the northeast at its southernmost state, Bahia, and providing a link between the northeast and central Brazil. In addition, the São Francisco has provided a reliable source of water for the interior through which it passes, creating a narrow belt of productive farmland for a region that has never been able to feed itself.

The southeast

At the other end of the development scale from the northeast is the southeast region, comprises only 11 percent of the national territory but

Blessed with adequate rainfall, the northeast coast is the site of the bulk of the region's agricultural production, concentrated in sugar and cocoa, and home to a constantly increasing percentage of the region's population. Lacking investment capital, the economy of the northeast has remained dominated by farming, with a few isolated pockets of industry. Tourism, however, may yet prove to be the northeast's real saviour.

The São Francisco River

Running along the southern edge of the northeast is the São Francisco River, the second of Brazil's main river systems *(see page 247)*.

ABOVE: cattle slow down traffic in the center-west.

which is home to Brazil's three largest cities, São Paulo, Rio de Janeiro and Belo Horizonte, and 45 percent of the country's population. The region is divided between a narrow coastal zone and an elevated plateau, with a coastal mountain region (the Escarpment) beginning in Bahia and running the length of the coast south to Rio Grande do Sul.

The dense tropical foliage of the *mata atlântica* has wrapped the coastal mountains in a rich, deep cloak of green. But, ironically, the very development that has brought prosperity to the southeast of the country is threatening the survival of this tropical vegetation. In many parts of the state of São Paulo, the forest has been destroyed by pollutants in the air, a by-product of the state's industrial park, the largest in Latin America. The best-preserved example of Brazil's coastal tropical forest is in the southern state of Paraná.

With the exception of the coastal cities of Rio and Santos (two of Brazil's busiest ports), the southeast's main population centers are on the plateau at an average altitude of 700 meters (2,300 ft). This area of rolling hills and temperate climate, where there is a clear distinction between winter and summer, has been the center of Brazil's economic growth since the 1800s.

Minas Gerais, the only state in the region that does not have a sea coast, owes its early development to its mineral wealth. The red earth of Minas Gerais provides graphic testimony to its iron-ore deposits. Part of Brazil's mammoth Precambrian shield area, Minas was the world's leading gold producer in the 18th century. In modern times, it has made Brazil a chief producer of iron ore and gemstones.

The south

The south is the smallest of Brazil's regions, accounting for only 7 percent of the total national territory. Like the southeast, it was blessed with rapid development in the second half of the 20th century, and today is home to 15 percent of the nation's population. Located below the Tropic of Capricorn, the south is the only region of Brazil with a subtropical climate and four distinct seasons, including frosts and occasional snowfall in winter.

It was in part due to its climate that the three states of the southern region attracted large numbers of immigrants from Italy, Germany, Poland and Russia in the early years of the 20th century. The rolling farmlands of Paraná and Rio Grande do Sul have made these states, along with São Paulo, the breadbasket of Brazil, growing primarily wheat, corn, soybeans and rice.

The region is also Brazil's traditional cattle producer, although it has been losing ground to the center-west. In the western half of Rio Grande, pampas grasslands, or prairies, are home to many of Brazil's largest farms and cattle ranches. The eastern half of the state is marked by mountainous terrain with deep, forested valleys where Italian and German immigrants have established Brazil's wine and grape industries *(see page 331).*

Besides its rich farmlands, the state of Paraná has benefited from its vast pine forests, which have been a primary source of lumber for Brazil's construction industry, although they are now being rapidly depleted. Marking the state's western border is the Paraná River which, together with the Paraguay farther to the west, forms the country's third great river system. The force of these rivers has been harnessed to produce energy for the industries of the south and southeast, particularly the Paraná, where Brazil (in collaboration with neighboring Paraguay) has built the world's largest hydroelectric project, the Itaipú Dam *(see page 321).* ❏

GRAZING THE PRAIRIES

The prairies of Rio Grande do Sul are the grazing grounds of nearly 14 million head of cattle and 10 million head of sheep, which means they produce an awful lot of meat. The excellence of its beef is recognized throughout the country, and abroad – rightly so, as anyone who eats at a Brazilian *rodizio (see page 94)* will agree. Leather and footwear industries are obvious spin-offs from cattle production. Some of the sheep are of the Karakul breed, originally from Turkestan, introduced to Brazil in the 1980s. They have long fleece – some black, some brown, some gray and some a distinctive pinkish shade. Their broad tails store fat, a source of nourishment, rather like a camel's hump.

LEFT: harvesting coffee, still a crucial crop.
RIGHT: colonial Ouro Preto in Minas Gerais state.

DECISIVE DATES

Colonial Era (1500–1822)

1409
The Treaty of Tordesillas divides the non-European world between Portugal and Spain. Portugal gets present-day Brazil.

1500
Portuguese explorer Pedro Álvares Cabral is the first European to set foot in Brazil, which he names Ilha de Vera Cruz.

1501–2
Amerigo Vespucci sails along the Brazilian coast, naming places after the saints on whose days they were discovered.

1533
The colony is divided into 15 *capitanias* (captaincies), each governed by a Portuguese courtier.

1549
A central administration based in Salvador is put in place to oversee the capitanias. Colonists and Jesuit missionaries argue about the treatment of Amerindians.

1549
A royal decree gives Jesuits control over Christianised Amerindians, while colonists are allowed to enslave those captured in warfare. Colonists import African slaves to boost workforce.

1555
The French build a garrison on the site of present-day Rio de Janeiro, but are driven out in 1565 by governor general Mem de Sá, who founds a city there.

1550–1800
Sugar cane, grown on huge plantations worked by African slaves, is the colony's most important crop, supplemented by tobacco, cattle and, in the 18th century, cotton and coffee.

1580–1640
Portugal and Spain are united.

1600s
Expeditions *(bandeiras)* of settlers delve into the interior in search of gold and slaves. Many Amerindians are wiped out by enslavement, massacres and European diseases.

1624–54
The Dutch West India Company conquers much of the northeast. A Dutch prince, Maurice of Nassau, rules Pernambuco, in the heart of the sugar cane-growing region, 1637–44.

1695
Discovery of gold in Minas Gerais leads to the growth

PRECEDING PAGES: a naive painting of Salvador by Calixto Sales.

of gold rush towns in the country's interior.

1759
After years of disputes with colonists and Portuguese government, the Jesuits are expelled.

1763
Rio de Janeiro becomes the capital city.

1789
An independence movement, the Inconfidência Mineira, springs up in Ouro Preto. In 1792 its leader, Joaquim José da Silva Xavier (Tiradentes) is hanged and the movement collapses soon afterwards.

1807
King João VI of Portugal flees to escape Napoleon and establishes his court, with all its customary ceremonials, in Rio. He introduces many reforms; Brazil is allowed to trade freely.

1821
João returns to Portugal and names his son, Pedro, as prince regent and governor of Brazil.

The Empire (1822–89)

1822
Pedro I *(above)* proclaims independence from Portugal, and establishes the Brazilian Empire, which is recognized by the US and, in 1825, by Portugal.

1831
Pedro I abdicates in favour of his five-year-old son (also Pedro). Political leaders run the country, and face revolts and army rebellions.

1840–89
Reign of Pedro II sees the population increase from 4 million to 14 million. Wars with neighboring countries strengthen the status of the military, while the emperor's opposition to slavery makes him enemies among the landowning class.

1853
The importation of slaves is brought to an end.

1870–1914
Manaus becomes prosperous from the Amazonian rubber trade, but declines when Asia starts producing the crop, using seeds being smuggled out of Brazil by an English botanist.

1871
All children born to slaves are declared free.

1888
The last slaves are freed.

Republican Brazil (1889–1963)

1889
Pedro II overthrown by the military and sent into exile.

1890s
Coffee makes São Paulo the country's commercial center and dominant power base.

1894
Prudente de Morais becomes the first elected civilian president.

1898–1902
President Manuel Ferraz de Campos Salles renegotiates Brazil's foreign debt.

1930–45
After riots *(above)*, the army installs Getúlio Vargas as president. He assumes total power, brings in social security and minimum wage.

1942
Brazil declares war on Germany – the only Latin American country to take an active part in World War II.

1950–4
Vargas again made president – this time in a democratic election. In 1954, on the brink of a military coup, he commits suicide.

1953
Founding of national oil company, Petrobras.

1954
With Pelé *(above)* in its side, Brazil wins the World Cup in Stockholm.

1956
President Juscelino Kubitschek unveils a five-year plan aiming to achieve rapid industrialization.

1960
The new capital city, Brasília, is inaugurated.

1961
President Jânio Quadros resigns, after only seven months in office.

Military Dictatorship (1964–84)

1964–7
General Humberto de Alencar Castelo Branco rules as president after a successful military coup.

1968
General Arthur da Costa e Silva closes Congress and institutes a program of repression.

1969–74
Under General Emílio Garrastazu Medici, state terrorism is used against insurgents, but the economy soars. A massive road construction program is undertaken in Amazonia to facilitate settlement.

1974–9
General Ernesto Geisel begins a gradual relaxation of the military regime.

1977
First national conference of Amerindians.

1979
João Baptista Figueiredo becomes military president. Political rights restored to the opposition.

1982
Latin American debt crisis – Brazil has the largest national debt in the Third World.

1985–Present

1985
Tancredo Neves becomes president, but dies six weeks later. José Sarney *(below)* succeeds him.

1986
Sarney's economic package, the Cruzado Plan, attempts unsuccessfully to curb inflation, running at 300 percent.

1988
A new constitution is introduced, but without the long-hoped-for land reform. Amerindians are granted full civil rights. Chico Mendes,

defender of the rainforest, is murdered.

1989
Fernando Collor de Mello is elected president.

1992
UN Earth Summit is held in Rio, the largest ever gathering of heads of state and government.

1992
Collor resigns amid corruption scandals.

1994
Racing driver and national hero Ayrton Senna dies after a crash at the San Marino Grand Prix.

1994
Brazil wins the World Cup.

1994
Fernando Henrique Cardoso is elected president. His Plano Real brings inflation under control.

2000
Brazil's 500th anniversary as a country.

2002
Brazil wins the World Cup for a record fifth time.

Financial markets in Brazil and abroad panic at the prospect of victory of Luiz Inácio Lula da Silva, in the presidential elections in October. He becomes the country's first left-wing president for 40 years – and the first president ever from a working-class family.

2003
At his inauguration in Brasília in January Lula announces his pledge for "Zero Fome", the eradication of hunger. 21 people illed when space satellite explodes at the Alcântara space centre.

2004
Brazil, in company with Germany, Japan and India, launches a formal bid to become a permanent member of the United Nations Security Council. Brazil's first space rocket launched.

2005
Murder of Dorothy Stang, 73-year-old US-born nun and champion of peasants' rights, highlights bitter contest over the encroachment of

loggers and soya-growers in Amazonia. Senior figures in Lula's Workers' Party resign after serious allegations of corruption.

2006
Strained relations with Bolivia after it announces the nationalization of the country's oil and gas, including Brazilian interests. In the second round of voting in the presidential elections Lula *(below)* is re-elected to a second four-year term.

2007
A small plane with four people and $2.6 million of newly minted currency on board crashes in Bahia. The people die and looters make off with the money.

THE MAKING OF BRAZIL

The only Portuguese-speaking country in Latin America, Brazil became an empire in the 19th century. Throughout the centuries, however, it played only a minor role in shaping the world – but that is now changing fast

Brazil has often avoided the kind of violent upheavals that have occurred so frequently elsewhere in Latin America. Brazilians feel they have a way of resolving their disputes through compromise rather than confrontation.

Brazil's history sets it apart from the rest of South America. In addition to its size, which dwarfs that of its neighbors, Brazil stands out because of its language, Portuguese; its colonial period, in which it became the seat of government of the mother country; its mostly bloodless path towards independence and its largely peaceful relations with its neighbors.

Discovery and colonization

The discovery of Brazil in 1500 by Pedro Álvares Cabral occurred during a series of voyages launched by the great Portuguese navigators in the 15th and 16th centuries. Cabral, sailing to India via the Cape of Good Hope, was blown off course. At first he thought he had discovered an island, and named it Ilha de Vera Cruz. When it became obvious that it was the east coast of a continent, it was renamed Terra de Santa Cruz, but eventually became Brazil after one of the colony's primary products, *pau brasil* or brazilwood, highly valued in Europe for red dye extract.

In 1533 the Portuguese crown made its first determined effort to organize the colonization of Brazil. The coastline, the only area that had been explored, was divided into 15 captaincies, given to Portuguese noblemen who received hereditary rights. They were expected to settle

and develop them, using their own resources in order to spare the crown this expense. The two most important captaincies were São Vicente in the southeast (now the state of São Paulo) and Pernambuco in the northeast, where the introduction of sugar plantations quickly made the area the economic center of the colony.

The captaincies, however, couldn't satisfy the needs of either the colonists or Portugal. Left to the whims and financial means of their owners, some were simply abandoned. Furthermore, there was no coordination, so Brazil's coastline fell prey to constant attacks by French pirates. In 1549 King João III finally lost patience with the captaincy system and imposed a centralized colonial government on top of the existing divi-

LEFT: funeral cortège of Pedro II, 1891.
RIGHT: a depiction of the founding of São Paulo, 1554.

sions. The northeastern city of Salvador became the first capital of Brazil, a status it maintained for 214 years. Tomé de Sousa was installed as the colony's first governor general.

With this administrative reform, colonization again picked up. From 1549 until the end of the century, a variety of colonists arrived – mostly noblemen, adventurers, and Jesuit missionaries, charged with converting the Amerindians to Christianity. Several leading Jesuits, such as Father José de Anchieta in São Paulo, declared that Amerindians were to be protected, not enslaved, which put them in direct conflict with the interests of the colonizers. The Jesuits built

schools and missions, around which Amerindian villages sprang up, in an effort to protect them from slave traders. It was because of the Jesuits' initial success in preventing enslavement of the Amerindians that the colony looked elsewhere for manpower. Soon, slave ships were unloading slaves taken from the west coast of Africa.

French and Dutch occupations

In 1555 the French occupied what is now Rio de Janeiro, the first step towards a major French colony in South America. But they were unable to attract European colonists to the area, and in 1565 the Portuguese drove them out. Two years later, the city of São Sebastião do Rio de Janeiro was founded by the Portuguese.

This would be the last challenge to Portuguese control until the Dutch West India Company sent a fleet, which, in 1630, conquered the economically important sugar-growing region of Pernambuco. This followed Portugal's alliance with Spain (1580–1640), which brought Brazil under fire from Spain's enemies, Holland included. The Dutch established a well-functioning colony in Pernambuco and remained there until 1654, when they were driven out by a rebellion led by the colonists themselves.

The adventurers

In the same period, in the south of Brazil, bands of adventurers called *bandeirantes* (flag carriers) began to march out from their base in São Paulo in search of Amerindian slaves and gold. The great marches *(bandeiras)* took them west, south and north into the hinterlands. Some of these treks lasted for years. Through the *bandeirantes*, the colony launched its first effort to define its frontiers. The adventurers clashed with the Jesuits, but there was nothing the missionaries could do to stop the great *bandeiras*, which reached south to Uruguay and Argentina, west to Peru and Bolivia and northwest to Colombia. In the process, the *bandeirantes* crossed the imaginary line of the Treaty of Tordesillas, which carved up South America into two empires. At the time, this had little significance, since Portugal and Spain were united, but after 1640, when Portugal again became an independent nation, the conquests of the *bandeirantes* were incorporated into Brazil against the protests of Spain.

As part of this period of nation-building, Jesuit missionaries moved into the Amazon, and the powerful landholders of the northeast expanded their influence and control into the arid backlands of this region. Uniting this huge colony was the Portuguese language and culture, which underlined the distinction between Brazil and Spanish South America. The Treaty of Madrid with Spain in 1750, and succeeding treaties, recognized the incursions of the *bandeirantes* and formally included these areas in the colony of Brazil.

Brazil in the 18th century had grown into a predominantly rural and coastal society. Wealth was concentrated in the hands of a few landholding families. The principal products were sugar, tobacco and cattle, but coffee and cotton were becoming increasingly important.

Despite the Jesuit missions, the *bandeirantes* had managed to reduce drastically the Amerindian population through enslavement, disease and massacre. Meanwhile, the population of African slaves had increased sharply. Brazil traded only with Portugal and, other than the marches of the *bandeirantes*, had little contact with its neighbors. All of this, however, was about to change, thanks to the discovery of gold at the end of the 17th century.

Gold shifted the colony's center of wealth from the sugar-producing areas of the northeast to the southeast. In 1763 this led to Brazil's capital moving from Salvador to Rio de

decision by Portugal to increase the tax on gold. But the Inconfidência Mineira, as it was called, ended badly, with the arrest of its leaders. One of these, Joaquim José da Silva Xavier, a dentist better known as Tiradentes, or Tooth-Puller, was hanged and quartered.

Other movements would probably have followed but for developments in Europe. In 1807, Napoleon conquered Portugal, forcing the Portuguese royal family into exile. King João VI fled to Brazil, making the colony the seat of government for the mother country, the only instance of such a turnaround during the colonial period.

Janeiro. At the same time, the captaincies were taken over by the crown, four years after the last Jesuits were expelled from Brazil.

Liberal ideas

Brazil was isolated, but not entirely shut off from the outside world. By the second half of the 18th century, the liberal ideas popular in Europe began to enter Brazil's consciousness. In 1789, the country experienced its first independence movement, centered on the gold-rush boom town of Ouro Preto. The catalyst was a

LEFT: coffee plantation workers and a mounted overseer, *c.*1870.
ABOVE: *Independence or Death* by Pedro Americo.

GOLD SPAWNS NEW TOWNS

In the mountains of Brazil's central plateau, the *bandeirantes* finally found what they had been looking for – gold. In 1695, a gold rush brought thousands of settlers to what is today the state of Minas Gerais, the first mass settlement of Brazil's vast interior. Towns sprang up in the mountains, and by 1750 the city of Ouro Preto had a population of 80,000.

The gold found in Minas Gerais made Brazil the 18th century's largest producer of this precious metal. All the wealth, however, went straight to Portugal – a fact that did nothing to please the colonists who were already feeling more Brazilian than Portuguese, and was to lead to calls for independence.

The Golden Age of Pedro II

Pedro II reigned for 49 years, from 1840 to 1889, using his extraordinary talents to give Brazil its longest continuous period of political stability. Despite his royal birth, Pedro was a humble man who felt uncomfortable with the traditional trappings of an emperor, but he was blessed with enormous personal authority, and what we would now describe as charisma. During the American Civil War, Abraham Lincoln remarked that the only man he would trust to arbitrate between north and south was Pedro II of Brazil.

Born in Rio de Janeiro, Pedro was classically educated. He married Teresa Cristina Maria, daughter of Francis I of Sicily, and fathered four children, though his two sons died in childhood. Fascinating illustrations of Pedro's character and scholarly interests are preserved in the modest but elegant neoclassical summer palace he built in Petrópolis (*see page 167*).

Pedro was not only learned but also politically astute. He managed to keep regional rivalries in check and, through his own popularity, extend the control of central government. Against this backdrop, Brazil grew wealthy and economically stable, and considerable technological progress was made. Yet Pedro also steadfastly pursued a series of risky and controversial foreign policies. And whereas he was successful in restoring internal peace to the nation, such policies led Brazil into armed conflict with its neighbors to the south.

Pedro was determined to maintain regional parity in South America, which led him to interfere with political developments in Uruguay, Argentina and Paraguay. As a result, Brazil fought three wars between 1851 and 1870. First, in 1851, to ensure free navigation on the vital River Plate and its tributaries, Pedro sent troops into Uruguay, gaining a quick victory and a new Brazil-friendly government, with which he then allied in order to overthrow the Argentine dictator Juan Manuel Rosas. This war also had a successful outcome.

A second incursion against Uruguay in 1864, however, provoked war with Paraguay. Allied with the losing side in Uruguay, Paraguay's ruler Francisco Solano López struck back against both Brazil and Argentina. In 1865, the so-called triple alliance was formed, joining the apparently invincible forces of Brazil, Argentina and Uruguay against Paraguay. But after initial successes, the alliance suffered a series of surprising setbacks, and the war dragged on until 1870, in the process becoming the longest in South America in the 19th century.

The consequent elevation to prominence of Brazil's military leaders meant that Pedro needed their support to remain in power – and when he lost it, he quickly fell from grace in spite of his popularity with the masses. Ironically, the issue that led to his demise was slavery, whose abolition, from today's perspective, was perhaps his greatest and most admirable achievement.

In the latter half of the 19th century the Brazilian economy was still overwhelmingly agricultural, and slaves continued to play a major role, especially in the northeast. However, in the 1860s an abolitionist movement gathered pace, which eventually led to the end of slavery in 1888. Slavery was clearly doomed: bringing slaves into the country had been outlawed in 1853, so the existing slave population was in decline, and Brazil was increasingly isolated in maintaining the institution after other countries had banned it. Nevertheless, its abolition set the nation's landholders against Pedro.

By this time, the military, like the landholders, felt under-represented in government, and in November 1889, a military revolt led to a bloodless coup. Pedro II was deposed, and Brazil's most popular leader ever was forced into exile. He died in Paris, aged 66, where he was given a royal funeral. ❏

LEFT: Dom Pedro II, remembered as a wise ruler.

Brazil's changed status led to the crown opening up commerce with other nations, in particular England, Portugal's ally against Napoleon. When King João at last returned to Portugal in 1821, he named his son, Dom Pedro, as regent, making him head of government for Brazil. The Portuguese parliament, however, refused to recognize Brazil's new situation, and attempted to force a return to colonial dependence. Realizing that Brazilians would never accept this, on September 7, 1822 Pedro declared independence from Portugal, in the process creating the Brazilian Empire, the first monarchy in the Americas.

With Portugal still recovering from the Napoleonic wars, Brazil faced little opposition from the mother country. Helped by a British soldier of fortune, Lord Alexander Thomas Cochrane, Brazilian forces quickly expelled the remaining Portuguese garrisons. By the end of 1823 the Portuguese had left and the new nation's independence was secured. The following year, the United States became the first foreign nation to recognize Brazil, and in 1825 relations were re-established with Portugal.

Internal divisions

The ease with which independence was won, however, proved to be a false indication of the young nation's immediate future. During its first 18 years, Brazil struggled to overcome bitter internal divisions, which in some cases reached the point of open revolt. The first disappointment was the emperor himself, who insisted on maintaining the privileges and power of an absolute monarch. Pedro I eventually agreed to the creation of a parliament, but fought with it constantly. Already widely disliked, he plunged Brazil into a reckless and unpopular war with Argentina over what was then the southernmost state of Brazil, Cisplatina. Brazil lost the war and Cisplatina, which is now Uruguay.

Pedro I abdicated in 1831 in favor of his five-year-old son, and, from 1831 to 1840, Brazil was ruled by a triple regency of political leaders who ran the nation in the name of the young Pedro. The next nine years were the most violent in Brazil's history, with revolts and army rebellions in the northeast, the Amazon, Minas Gerais and the south. Brazil appeared to be on the verge of civil war as regional factions fighting for autonomy threatened to tear the nation apart. In particular, the *farrapos* war, in the south, lasted 10 years and almost led to the loss of what is today the state of Rio Grande do Sul.

In desperation, it was agreed in 1840 to declare Pedro II of age and hand over rule to a 15-year-old monarch. They were right to do so *(see page 36)*. It is ironic that Brazil's most successful emperor was also its last.

Debts of the military

The end of the monarchy in 1889 marked the arrival of what was to become Brazil's most powerful institution – the military. From 1889

to the present day, the armed forces have been at the center of almost every major political development in Brazil. The first two governments of the republic were headed by military men, both of whom proved better at spending than governing. By the time a civilian president took office (Prudente de Morais, 1894–8), the country was deep in debt. The problem was faced by the country's second civilian president, Manuel Ferraz de Campos Salles (1898–1902), who was the first to negotiate rescheduling the foreign debt, and is credited with saving Brazil from financial collapse.

Campos Salles and his successor, Francisco de Paula Rodrigues Alves (1902–6) put Brazil back on its feet and set an example that few

RIGHT: slaves building a new road in Rio, depicted by Jean Baptiste Debret.

presidents have matched since. Brazil went through a period of dramatic social change between 1900 and 1930, when large numbers of immigrants arrived from Europe. Economic and political power shifted to the southeast. While certain states, namely São Paulo and Minas Gerais, increased their power and influence, the federal government had very little of either, becoming a prisoner of regional and economic interests.

Economic woes lead to coup

After World War I, in which Brazil declared war on Germany but did not take an active role,

The political crisis reached its zenith following the 1930 election of the establishment candidate Júlio Prestes, despite a major effort to mobilize the urban masses in favor of the opposition candidate Getúlio Vargas, governor of the state of Rio Grande do Sul. The opposition dug their heels in and refused to accept the election result. With the support of participants and backers of the lieutenants' movement, a revolt broke out in Minas Gerais, Rio Grande do Sul and the northeast. Within just two weeks, the army had control of the country, overthrowing Prestes and installing Getúlio Vargas as the new president.

economic woes again beset the country. Spendthrift governments emptied the public coffers, while rumors of widespread corruption led to public unrest. Military movements also resurfaced, with an attempted coup in 1922 and an isolated revolt in São Paulo in 1924, put down with massive destruction by the federal government, whose troops bombarded the city of São Paulo at will. The dissatisfaction in the barracks was led by a group of junior officers who became known as the *tenentes* (lieutenants). These officers were closely identified with the emerging urban middle class, which was searching for political leadership to oppose the wealthy landholders of São Paulo state and Minas Gerais.

The Vargas era

The rapid ascension of President Vargas signaled the beginning of a new era in Brazilian politics. A man linked to the urban middle and lower classes, Vargas represented a complete break from political control in the hands of the rural elite. The coffee barons of São Paulo and the wealthy landholders of other states and regions, the political power brokers of the old Republic, were suddenly out. The focus of politics in Brazil was shifted to the common man in the fast-growing urban centers.

Ironically, this dramatic upheaval did not lead to increased democracy. Intent on retaining power, Vargas initiated a policy marked by populism and nationalism that kept him at the center of political life for 25 years. During this period, he set the model for Brazilian politics for the rest of the 20th century, which saw the country alternate between populist political leaders and military intervention.

Vargas's basic strategy was to win the support of the urban masses and concentrate power in his own hands. Taking advantage of growing industrialization, Vargas used labor legislation as his key weapon: laws were passed creating a minimum wage and social security system, paid vacations, maternity leave, and medical assistance. Vargas instituted reforms that legalized labor unions but also made them dependent on the federal government. He quickly became the most popular Brazilian leader since Dom Pedro II. In the new constitution, which was not drafted until 1934, and then only after an anti-Vargas revolt in São Paulo, Vargas further increased the powers of the central government.

With the constitution approved, Vargas's "interim" presidency ended and he was elected president by Congress in 1934. The constitution limited him to one four-year term, with elections scheduled for 1938, but Vargas refused to surrender power. In 1937, using the invented threat of a communist coup and supported by the military, Vargas closed Congress and threw out the 1934 constitution, replacing it with a new document giving him dictatorial powers. The second part of the Vargas reign, which he glorified under the title The New State, proved far more tumultuous than his first seven years.

Brazil at war

Growing political opposition to Vargas's repressive means threatened to topple him, but the president saved himself by joining the Allies in World War II, declaring war on Germany in 1942. He sent an expeditionary force of 25,000 soldiers to Europe, where they joined the Allied Fifth Army in Italy, making Brazil the only Latin American country to take an active part in the war. Brazilian losses were light (some 450 dead), and the war effort served to distract the public and lessened the pressure on Vargas.

With the war winding down, however, Vargas was under threat from the military that had put him in power, so he approved measures legalizing opposition political parties and calling for

a presidential election at the end of 1945. But while he bargained with the opposition to prevent a coup, Vargas also instigated his backers in the labor movement to join forces with the communists in a popular movement to keep him in office. Fearful that Vargas might succeed, the military ousted him from power on October 29, 1945, ending a 15-year reign.

In 1945 Vargas's former war minister, General Eurico Gaspar Dutra, was elected president, serving a five-year term during which a new, liberal constitution was approved. Then in 1950, Vargas returned to power, this time elected by the people.

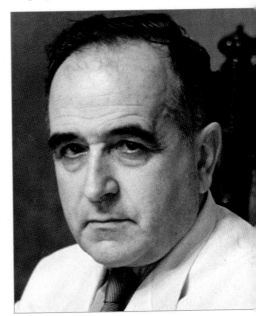

DEMISE OF A DICTATOR

During his final years in office following his 1950 election, Getúlio Vargas tried to safeguard his position by introducing nationalistic measures, such as the nationalization of oil production; nevertheless, he rapidly lost ground in the popularity stakes.

A political crisis sparked by an attempt on the life of one of his main political opponents, allegedly planned by a Vargas aide, finally brought the Vargas era to an end. When he was given an ultimatum by the military either to resign or be forced out of office, Vargas instead chose a third route – on August 24, 1954 he committed suicide in the presidential palace. His death was to have a profound effect on Brazil.

LEFT: inauguration of Avenida Paulista, São Paulo.
RIGHT: Getúlio Vargas in the news, 1938.

New faces

The eventual removal of Vargas from the political scene after his suicide in 1954 cleared the way for new faces. The first to emerge came again from the twin poles of Brazilian 20th-century politics, São Paulo and Minas Gerais. Juscelino Kubitschek from Minas and Jânio Quadros from São Paulo both used the same path to the presidency, first serving as mayors of their state capitals, and then as governors. Populism, nationalism and military connections, the three leading themes of modern Brazilian politics, all played a part in their careers. Two new factors were the increasing

incentives were used to build roads, steel mills and hydroelectric plants, creating the precedent of direct government involvement in infrastructure projects. But Kubitschek's biggest project was the building of Brasília.

The idea of a new federal capital in the heart of the country came to obsess Kubitschek. Upon taking office, he ordered the plans drawn up, insisting Brazil would have a new capital before his term ended, designed by Brazil's best architects *(see page 124)*. He wanted to develop the near-deserted central plain by moving thousands of civil servants from Rio. Nothing existed at the chosen site, so he faced enormous oppos-

linkage of economic growth with political developments and Brazil's growing economic and political ties with the outside world.

Kubitschek's vision

Kubitschek, an expansive and dynamic leader with a vision of Brazil as a world power, was elected president in 1955. He promised to give the country "Fifty years of progress in five." For the first time, Brazil had a leader whose primary concern was economic growth. Under Kubitschek, there was rapid industrialization: foreign auto manufacturers invited to Brazil provided the initial impetus for what was to become an explosion of growth in the city and state of São Paulo. Government funds and/or

ition from bureaucrats with no desire to leave the comforts and pleasures of Rio de Janeiro for an inland wilderness.

Between 1957 and 1960, construction of the new city continued at full speed, and on April 21, 1960, Kubitschek proudly inaugurated his capital. But while Brasília became a symbol of Kubitschek's dynamism, it also became an unceasing drain on the country's treasury. Brasília, and other grandiose public works projects, meant that the Kubitschek administration left office having produced not only rapid growth, but also a soaring public debt, high inflation and vast corruption.

The situation seemed ready-made for Jânio Quadros, a self-styled reformer who used a broom as his campaign symbol, promising to sweep the government clean of all corruption. Instead, he embarked on a short but memorable administration culminating in an institutional crisis that ultimately brought an end to Brazil's experiment with democracy. Quadros was impatient, unpredictable and autocratic. Insisting that everything be done exactly his way, he attempted to ignore Congress, sparking an open confrontation with the legislative branch, and surprised his followers by moving Brazil closer to the bloc of non-aligned nations. Finally, he resigned from the presidency without warning on August 25, 1961, seven months after taking office, citing the "terrible forces" which were aligned against him.

The resignation of Quadros created an immediate crisis, once more bringing the military to the center of political developments. Military officials threatened to prevent Quadros's leftist vice-president, João Goulart, from taking office, but Goulart had the support of army units in his home state of Rio Grande do Sul. Fearing a civil war, the military agreed to negotiate a solution to the impasse, permitting Goulart to assume the presidency but also instituting a parliamentary system of government with vastly reduced powers for the president.

Populist program

This compromise solution failed to work in practice, and in 1963 a national plebiscite voted to return to presidential rule. With his powers enhanced, Goulart launched a populist, nationalistic program that moved the country to the left. He announced sweeping land reforms, promised widespread social reforms, and threatened to nationalize foreign firms.

His economic policies, meanwhile, failed to stem inflation. The cost of living soared, contributing to a wave of strikes supported by Goulart's followers in the labor movement. Opposition grew, centered on the middle classes of São Paulo and Minas Gerais whose political leaders appealed to the military to intervene. Finally, on March 31, 1964, claiming that Goulart was preparing a communist takeover of the government, the military orchestrated a bloodless coup.

LEFT: President Juscelino Kubitschek at the ceremony inaugurating Brasília.
RIGHT: General Emilio Medici, president 1969–74.

While the 1964 coup was the fourth time since 1945 that the military had intervened in the government, this was to be the only instance where the generals remained in power. For the next 21 years, Brazil was governed by a military regime, which clamped down on civilian corruption (while indulging in much of their own). Five army generals occupied the presidency during this period. The first was Hum-

berto de Alencar Castelo Branco, who concentrated on resolving the delicate economic situation. He introduced austerity measures to attack inflation and reduced government spending sharply, thus restoring economic stability, and setting the stage for the strong growth years that were to follow. His administration also adopted measures to limit political freedom: existing political parties were suspended and replaced by a two-party system, one party (Arena) supporting the government, the other, the liberal Democratic Movement Party (MDB) representing the opposition; mayors and governors were appointed by the military and presidents were chosen in secret by the army.

THE BRAZILIAN MIRACLE

The dramatic economic upturn of the 1970s brought Brazil into the international spotlight and spurred the old dream of becoming a major world power.

Military repression

During the presidency of General Arthur da Costa e Silva, Castelo Branco's successor, the military introduced a new constitution making Congress subordinate to the executive branch. A wave of opposition to the military in 1968 led Costa e Silva to clamp down. The closing of Congress and severe restriction of individual rights marked the beginning of the most repres-

years were the most dramatic of the military regime not only because of severe suppression of human rights but also due to the economic growth that Brazil enjoyed. While in power, Medici and his successor, General Ernesto Geisel (1974–9), saw the economy surge ahead. These boom years brought unprecedented prosperity, providing full employment for the urban masses and high salaries for middle-class professionals and white-collar workers. As a result, some Brazilians were inclined to accept military rule and tolerate the lack of personal and political freedom. Brazil's increasing economic clout led the military to adopt a more indepen-

sive years of the military regime. The doctrine of national security gave the government the right to arrest and detain without habeas corpus. The military embarked on a war against "subversion," and launched a bid to erase the influence of the left, via imprisonment without trial, torture, and censorship. Editors who opposed the regime were obliged to bring out publications containing blank spaces. When the military banned this, they filled the spaces with cookery recipes and other outlandish items before many of them were forced into silence.

Ruthless military repression peaked during General Emílio Garrastazu Medici's government. He assumed the presidency after Costa e Silva suffered a fatal stroke in 1969. The Medici

dent foreign policy, breaking with traditional adherence to US-backed positions.

Liberalization

With the advent of the 1980s, the military regime fell on hard times. Economic growth slowed, then slumped. Following a debt moratorium by Mexico in 1982, the Latin American debt crisis exploded. New foreign loans dried up, and interest charges on previous loans outstripped the resources of the government.

General João Baptista Figueiredo – the last of the military presidents – took office in 1979, promising to return Brazil to democracy, and announced an amnesty for political prisoners and exiles. The government went ahead with other liberalizing steps: press censorship was lifted, new political parties founded, and elections for governors and Congress were held. But increasing political freedom did little to offset the gloom of recession from 1981 to 1983.

In January 1985, an electoral college chose Tancredo Neves as Brazil's first civilian president in 22 years. A moderate who had opposed the military regime, he was acceptable to both conservatives and liberals. Brazil's transition to democracy, however, was halted as Neves fell ill the night before he was to be sworn in and died a month later, plunging Brazil into another political crisis. The vice-president, José Sarney, instantly assumed the presidency, but he was a conservative who had little support among the liberals who were now returning to power.

Once in office, Sarney attempted populist measures such as an ill-fated land reform program to secure the support of the liberals who controlled Congress. But the country's economic difficulties worsened. Weighed down with foreign debt and lacking the resources for investments, the government was unable to provide effective leadership for the economy.

The Cruzado Plan, and after

By the start of 1986, with inflation running at an annual rate of 330 percent, Sarney was facing a slump in popularity and pressure from the left for a direct presidential election. His response was the Cruzado Plan, an unorthodox economic package that froze prices while letting wages continue to rise. After years of seeing their spending power eroded by inflation, Brazilians threw themselves into the ensuing consumer boom. The president's popularity rose sharply; claiming co-responsibility for the plan, the politicians of the MDB, who now supported Sarney, swept to victories in the congressional and state elections of November 1986.

However, the long-term success of the Cruzado Plan depended on cuts in government spending, which Sarney, keen to hold on to his newfound popularity, was reluctant to make. Inflation returned with a vengeance, and was to survive a sequence of increasingly ineffectual economic packages introduced throughout the remaining years of the Sarney administration.

The return of high inflation in 1987 coincided with the start of the National Constituent Assembly, charged with drafting a new democratic constitution. Announced in 1988, the Constitution's significant advances included the end of censorship, recognition of Amerindian land rights and increased worker benefits.

On the downside, powerful lobbies, and the formation of an informal conservative majority within the Assembly, blocked progress on controversial issues such as land reform. In addition, the upsurge in nationalism, which had contributed to Brazil's declaration of a moratorium on its debt with foreign banks in Febru-

ary 1987, led to the inclusion in the Constitution of measures directed against foreign capital.

By distributing political favors and government concessions, President Sarney won Congressional approval to extend his term in office until March 1990. But his support dwindled as inflation accelerated and discontent grew.

Humble origins

The course of Brazil's ship of state was altered with the arrival of Lula. Luiz Inácio Lula da Silva was born in 1945 in the town of Garanhuns in the drought-stricken northeast, to Aristides, an illiterate smallholder, and Eurídice, his illiterate wife. Lula was the seventh of the eight children who survived infancy. (Four

LEFT: an offshore oil rig. Oil is vital to the Brazilian economy.

RIGHT: President Fernando Collor de Mello.

more died prematurely.) "People got up in the morning and had no bread and no money to buy bread," he relates. "When it rained my brothers and sisters made a little dam of sand in the street to catch the water. The alternative was the pond where the animals relieved themselves... There was no education, no knowledge." Three months before his birth his father went off to São Paulo, the industrial capital, with another woman. Lula did not meet his father until years later, when his mother sold everything and took the family on a 13-day lorry journey down to São Paulo. Aristides was against the boys going to school, so Lula and

Chico cut wood in the mangrove swamps and fetched water for the slum-dwellers. "My friends say my neck is thick because I had to carry so much wood on my head," he says.

Nevertheless, he learned to read and write and eventually got a job in a factory, where a power press one day took off the index finger of his left hand, stamping him for life as a manual worker.

He blossomed in the industrial atmosphere, rising in the trade union ranks. In São Paulo, in 1980, along with other trade unionists, Christians, Social Democrats, Marxists and Trotskyists, he founded the Workers' Party, the Partido dos Trabalhadores (PT), which was free from associations with old-style politicians.

In 1986 Lula won a seat in the lower house of the Federal Congress with a vote of 650,000, the largest number then achieved.

Collor and Cardoso

In the municipal elections of November 1988, control of many state capitals (including Brazil's largest metropolis, São Paulo) was won by the new Workers' Party. When the long-awaited direct presidential elections were held in November 1989, Luiz Inácio Lula da Silva, the PT candidate, making his first presidential bid, emerged as a strong contender.

The traditional parties suffered overwhelming rejection, while two outsiders ended up going through to the final round of the elections a month later. One of them was Lula. His opponent was Fernando Collor de Mello, the 40-year-old former governor of the politically insignificant northeastern state of Alagoas, running on the ticket of the virtually unheard-of National Reconstruction Party.

Mixing an appeal to youth and modernity with a moralizing discourse that reminded many of Jânio Quadros, and including a hefty dose of preaching against Lula's "communism", Collor beat the PT candidate by a narrow margin. Taking office in March 1990, with the authority that came from being Brazil's first directly elected president in three decades, he immediately attacked inflation with a brutal fiscal squeeze that included an 18-month "compulsory loan" of 80 percent of the nation's savings.

Musical chairs

Although these measures forestalled the threat of hyperinflation in the short term, they did not address Brazil's underlying fiscal malaise, and inflation soon crept back. When it came to light that Collor's closest associates had been milking the state of millions of dollars through illegal scams, the middle classes rose against him, taking to the streets in their thousands, demanding his impeachment.

Collor was replaced by his deputy, Itamar Franco. Although in many ways a lacklustre president, Franco soon won respect for his integrity. However, in 1994, Fernando Henrique Cardoso was elected as president by a clear majority. Cardoso's popularity was based on the success of his Plano Real, the financial plan he introduced as finance minister in Franco's government. This linked Brazil's latest currency, the *real*, to the US dollar in a relationship that retained the flexibility needed to accommodate international financial shocks, while giving the currency an anchor to prevent it being dragged back into a tide of rising inflation.

Cardoso pursued with a vengeance the path of privatization, started by Collor. He opened up the Brazilian economy, attracting substantial investment from overseas. In October 1998, Cardoso was re-elected for a second four-year term. He faced a setback at the beginning of 1999 when the *real* halved its value against the US dollar, The first half of 2003 showed a contraction of the country's gross domestic

high on the list. The arrival of Lula meant that prejudice against state activity was removed. The state could expand again. Yet Lula, who had in his youth suffered the effects of rocketing prices on the poor, was not prepared to let inflation roar away, as many bankers, both local and foreign, had feared. Whereas in 2002, the last year of Cardoso's government, prices rose by 12.5 percent, towards the end of 2006 and the end of Lula's first four-year term, they were gradually inching down to half that figure.

The stock market prospered, not least because it tempted foreigners to bring their money into

product (GDP), while industrial output shrank by 3.7 percent, early indications of a possible recession *(for more on Cardoso's privatization policy, see page 52).*

Lula comes to power

In 2002, at his fourth attempt, Lula won the presidency, with over 60 percent of the vote. During the presidency of Cardoso, who was ideologically close to the British prime minister Tony Blair, the accent had been on a continued shrinking of the state, with privatization

Brazil in order to gamble on the share prices. At the end of November 2006 the index of the São Paulo exchange topped 42,000: in 2002 it had been languishing down at 11,268.

Lula was re-elected in October 2006, again with 60 percent of the vote, despite officials of the PT being implicated in several financial scandals during the previous year. He represents the hope not just of a nation, but of much of Latin America. He is the senior member of a new generation of leaders in the region, which include Néstor Kirchner in Argentina, Tabaré Vázquez in Uruguay, Michelle Bachelet in Chile, Hugo Chávez in Venezuela, Rafael Correa in Ecuador, and Daniel Ortega in Nicaragua. ❏

LEFT: the Banco Mercantile in São Paulo, the financial and commercial center of the country.
ABOVE: fellow presidents: Lula with Hugo Chávez.

COUNTRY OF THE FUTURE

Economic cycles of boom and bust plagued the country for decades. Recently they have been replaced by steady growth, and Brazil is beginning to make its presence felt on the international stage

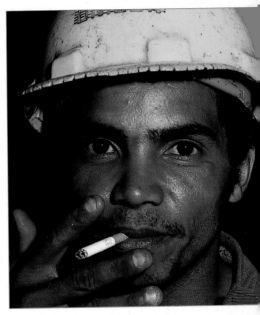

Brazil is the fifth-largest country in the world, with an area of 8.5 million sq. km (3.3 million sq. miles). Having expanded over the centuries from a narrow strip of land along the Atlantic Ocean to absorb most of Amazonia and the grassy plains to the south, it won the race with its neighbors to control the largest share of South America's landmass.

The population, 74 percent of which is Catholic, is pushing up towards 200 million people – according to the UN, in 2005 it stood at 182.8 million. From being a place of country-dwellers it is now 83 percent urbanized, even if many of the supposed urban dwellers live in very small towns.

Now Brazilian governments are beginning to make waves on the world stage, as well as in the rest of Latin America and its own society.

Progress has not been painless. Since colonial times, Brazil has gone through alternating cycles of boom and bust. Industrialization came late. From colonial days until midway through the 20th century, Brazil was primarily a rural society with a monocrop economy. First it was timber, then sugar, shifting in the 18th century to gold. After the rubber boom, coffee emerged as the economy's workhorse. As late as the 1950s, coffee still provided over half of Brazil's export revenue, 65 percent of the workforce was farm-based, and the main function of the banking system was to supply credit to farmers.

Modernization

World War II provided the first stimulus to Brazil's industry when the conflict cut off sup-

LEFT: oil lights up the skies: Petrobras oil rig.
RIGHT: an industrial worker takes a break.

plies of manufactured goods, forcing the development of local substitutes. To expand further, however, Brazil's infant industries needed a strong push, and this was provided by the government – more specifically President Juscelino Kubitschek, who took office in 1955.

Kubitschek made economic growth the primary goal throughout his administration, and this policy has been followed by all succeeding governments. He also established the development model that was copied with modifications by his successors: it involved government intervention in managing the economy, and an important role for foreign capital investment.

Kubitschek poured government money into infrastructure projects (highways and power plants) while inviting foreign auto makers to establish plants in São Paulo. Government loans also financed the private sector, with the result that for the period 1948–61, the Brazilian economy grew at an average annual rate of 7 percent.

At this point, two of the great evils of Brazil's 20th-century history – high inflation and political instability – ended the first spurt of economic growth. With the 1964 coup, the new military rulers turned to austerity measures to trim down inflation. By 1968 inflation was under control and the economy was poised for a historic take-off. Starting in 1970, Brazil enjoyed four straight years of double-digit eco-

percent of the population in the cities). By 2001, this figure had grown to 81 percent.

Nowhere was this more apparent than in the state of São Paulo. With São Paulo city receiving the bulk of new investments in the private sector, the state's industrial park exploded, emerging as the largest in Latin America and one of the most modern in the world. São Paulo's miracle has continued to the present day. Currently, the gross domestic product of São Paulo state is larger than that of any nation in Latin America except Mexico.

But the miracle years brought more than dramatic social and economic changes. They pro-

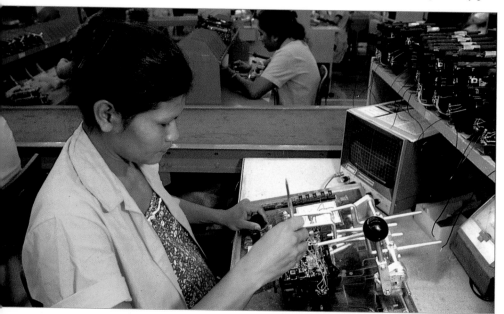

nomic growth that ended with a 14 percent expansion in 1973. The rate of growth then slowed, but it never fell below 4.6 percent, and averaged 8.9 percent a year from 1968 to 1980.

The Brazilian Miracle

These boom years became known as the period of the Brazilian Miracle, and they changed the face of Brazil for ever. Led by São Paulo, the country's major cities underwent rapid industrialization, and this attracted waves of peasant migrants fleeing their precarious existence in the nation's rural areas.

Between 1960 and 1980 Brazil changed from a rural nation (55 percent of the population in rural areas) into a majority urban nation (67

duced a profound effect on the national psyche. Accustomed to playing down the value and potential of their country, Brazilians in the 1970s saw this sleeping giant begin to stir.

Ecstatic with the success of their economic programs, the generals abandoned their initial goal of providing the framework for growth and embarked on a wildly ambitious scheme to turn Brazil into a world power. Moderation was abandoned and the military drew up massive development projects.

The problem, however, was finding a way to finance these dreams. The government, the private sector and the foreign companies did not have the resources required. Clearly another partner was needed. In 1974 that partner appeared. Following the 1973 oil shock, international banks, overflowing with petrodollars, sought investment opportunities in the developing world. And no other developing nation could match the growth record of Brazil, let alone its potential. Soon, pin-striped bankers were flying down to Rio, Brasília, and São Paulo from New York and London, followed shortly by colleagues from Frankfurt, Tokyo, Paris, Toronto, Geneva, Chicago, and Los Angeles. The rules of the game were disarmingly simple. The generals presented their blueprints for Brazilian superpowerdom and the bankers unloaded the dollars. There was no collateral.

communications (television, postal services and telecommunications), in some instances, it also poured into the pockets of generals and technocrats.

Then in 1979 the bubble burst. The second oil shock doubled the price of Brazil's imported petroleum, while at the same time interest rates shot up and the prices of commodities on international markets came crashing down. Brazil's trade balance recorded a deficit in 1979 that was nearly three times that of 1978.

At first, however, neither the generals nor the bankers were willing to admit that the party was over. The borrowing continued, only now

In 1974 Brazil borrowed more money than it had in the preceding 150 years combined. When the decade finally bowed out five years later, a total of US$40 billion had been transferred to Brazil. During these years, money poured into transportation (new highways, bridges, and railroads across the country, and subways for Rio and São Paulo), industry (steel mills, a petrochemical complex and consumer goods factories), the energy sector (power plants, nuclear reactors, and a program looking into alternative energy and oil exploration), and

the incoming dollars went to pay for imported oil and to cover previous loans now falling due.

Lengthy recession

In 1981 the situation worsened, with a recession in the United States that was felt immediately by Brazil. Three years of recession forced Brazil into a lengthy depression. Many small and medium-sized businesses failed, throwing thousands into unemployment. Large industries laid off workers, leaving the poorest increasingly desperate, reliant on woefully inadequate and underfunded welfare provisions.

The decision by Mexico in 1982 to impose a moratorium on international loan interest triggered the so-called Latin American debt crisis.

LEFT: assembling products at a factory owned by the Dutch company, Philips.
ABOVE: a robot at work in a Volkswagen car factory.

In response, international lending institutions cut off the flow of development loans.

The future looked grim. Twenty years of military government were drawing to a close, leaving the country with rampant inflation and a plethora of inefficient government-owned industries built on the largesse that the generals dispensed to appointees who presided over them. For 20 years the civil service had run amok, creating endless jobs of dubious worth, which nonetheless paid gold-plated salaries and bore a lifetime guarantee. By 1987, a staggering 60 percent of the economy was controlled by the government.

Brazil's manufacturing industries, built on import substitution policies pursued by successive governments after World War II, were soft-bellied and inefficient, often run by political appointees who were neither qualified nor experienced for the jobs they had been given.

Remarkably, Brazil rose to the challenge. Before the debt crisis, exports had been dominated by raw materials and agricultural products, which provided the income to pay for imports of oil and capital goods. But during the 1980s, the overweight industries that had developed in the protected environment of import substitution began to slim down and

THE ALCOHOL FUEL PROGRAM

Brazil was the first country to embrace a renewable energy source to power motor vehicles. The government-sponsored program to develop the use of sugar-cane alcohol as a substitute for imported petroleum was a great technical success and took Brazil to the forefront of ethanol fuel technology. The Pró-Álcool program began in 1975 as a means of reducing dependence on imported oil in the wake of the international petroleum crisis in 1973. A sustainable, renewable, low-pollution fuel was developed, and by 1989 more than 90 percent of it was used by ethanol-only cars.

Yet the transformation of thousands of hectares of land from mixed agricultural production to sugar cane

monoculture left thousands of rural workers landless, forcing them into low-paid, short-term seasonal jobs in the sugar industry. This created a social problem that contributed to crime and political unrest.

In 1990 the program collapsed, partly due to the declining price of oil, which made it less economically viable; but 2003 saw a dramatic increase in the production of ethanol, as the government began to revive the scheme. And in 2005, government-backed Petrobras signed a contract with a Japanese company for a joint-venture, based in Japan, that would import ethanol from Brazil. With widespread concern about global warming, it seems that ethanol is back on the agenda.

become more efficient. The need to export opened up new, larger markets, which encouraged the expansion of manufacturing capacity beyond what the domestic market could support. Brazilians often refer to the 1980s as the "lost decade", but, in truth, it was a period of positive foundation-building.

However, it was also a decade plagued by inflation, which held back the expansion of Brazil's industries. During these years, Brazil adapted to high inflation by index-linking virtually everything in the economy and, in the process, making market forces a hostage to government policies. All monetary contracts, from salaries and loans to savings and time deposits, were indexed to inflation, receiving adjustments every month.

Financial manipulation

The Brazilian middle class became adept at manipulating their money, timing purchases to their best advantage and using an array of financial mechanisms to maintain their purchasing power. A topic of conversation often heard over breakfast in a business district café was the performance of the "overnight" – a financial mechanism known to most money dealers the whole world over but not normally indulged in by the salaried middle class.

During this period the government controlled everything. Prices were indexed, then they were controlled. Then they were frozen and then controlled again in a constant back and forth that left corporate planners dizzy. Wages, too, were at times frozen, at times linked to a government index which routinely left wage earners with less purchasing power. Exchange rates fluctuated daily, and most transactions, from the purchase of a refrigerator to multi-million-dollar construction contracts, were priced in dollars.

Similar conditions prevailed at corporate level. A company's principal activity became secondary to its financial planning, its profit primarily dependent on how adept it was at financial manipulation. Planning for the medium term became very uncertain, and long-term objectives were little more than wishes.

The financial uncertainties of the decade acted as a powerful disincentive to multi-

LEFT: an ethanol distillery, processing sugar cane to produce fuel for Brazil's "flex-fuel" cars.
RIGHT: tending a sugar-cane field the hard way.

national firms who might otherwise have considered investing in Brazil. Curiously, those already well established, such as Volkswagen, continued to make healthy profits, but Brazil needed new investment from multinationals to get its industry up to speed, and that would not happen until inflation was under control.

Privatization program

Brazil's first directly elected president, Fernando Collor de Mello, although removed from office in 1992 after only three years, set in motion many of the reforms that have brought Brazil into the mainstream of world trade. He

instigated a program of privatization, selling off government-owned industries that were viable, and closing down those that were not. He tore down many of the protectionist import tariffs and restrictions. And he began the taming of the rampant civil service, trimming the excesses of over-employment.

But his attempt to do the same with the economy failed completely. His financial plan went the same way as the four other attempts between 1986 and 1995. Each was announced with a bold, macho fanfare, and a new currency, and each rapidly lost momentum as inflation returned with a vengeance, reaching a remarkable peak of more than 2,100 percent in 1993.

The Plano Real

There followed two years of continued financial mismanagement by provisional president, Itamar Franco, who had been Collor's deputy. Then, in July 1994, the Plano Real was introduced by the then little-known Finance Minister, Fernando Henrique Cardoso. He managed to link the new currency, the *real*, to the dollar in a way that left enough flexibility to enable it to withstand regional financial fluctuations without allowing inflation to get going again.

His election as president later the same year was in no small way a result of the effectiveness of the Plano Real. Throughout his first term, Cardoso and Finance Minister Pedro Malan exercised tight fiscal control, bringing inflation down to single figures.

The privatizations carried out during the Cardoso government brought protests from many who said that public property was being sold off at knock-down prices for the sake of pervasive economic orthodoxy, as set out by the international financial institutions. Government receipts from privatization, which in 1995 had come to a mere US$1.6 billion, totalled nearly US$30 billion in 1997 and the following year rose to US$37.5 billion.

Critics of Cardoso said that private individ-

MERCOSUL: SOUTH AMERICA'S TRADING BLOC

While North America has the North American Free Trade Area and Europe has the EU, South America has Mercosul – or Mercosur, as it is known in the Spanish-speaking countries. It grew out of a history of ineffectual trade negotiations and treaties stretching back to the 1930s. Progress was impeded by economic and political factors, not least the macho posturing of dictatorial governments in the 1960s and 1970s.

The Treaty of Asunción of 1991 established the mechanism and structure of Mercosul, covering Argentina, Brazil, Paraguay, and Uruguay, with aspirations to promote greater economic integrations than would be offered by a mere free trade area. Like the EU, it swept away customs posts, set standard external tariffs, and outlawed restrictions on trade,

ending the postwar years of protectionism and import substitution policies favored by the military regimes.

It has gone from strength to strength, with Venezuela joining as a full member in mid-2006, bringing the forceful ideas of President Chávez and a large pool of oil wealth. Chile was told that the special trade relationship it had chosen to forge with the US precluded it from full membership. At a meeting in Rio in January 2007 there were further talks about the full membership of Bolivia, whose leader, Evo Morales, called for concessions on membership given his country's weak economy. Progress was made on fashioning a new Bank of the South to finance major projects, including the projected natural gas pipeline to link Venezuela and Argentina.

uals and financial institutions were being enriched at the expense of the public good, citing the Companhia Vale do Rio Doce (CVRD), the world's biggest single source of iron ore. The government sold 42 percent of the company in 1997 for US$3.3 billion. By the end of 2005, as the world scrambled for iron ore, the worth of the shares had increased 15 times. In the first nine months of 2006 CVRD's net profits came to US$5 billion.

Brazilian public opinion would not permit even Cardoso to sell off the state company Petróleo Brasileiro (Petrobras), and it repaid the loyalty by making the country self-suffi-

new confidence. Its industry has survived the opening up of domestic markets to foreign competition, transforming itself into one of the most efficient in the world. Through Mercosul and other trade agreements, Brazil has become both a political and an economic leader in the region, avoiding the political and economic meltdown suffered by other South American countries.

Rich and poor

But the education system is signally failing to provide the majority of its young citizens with the skills they need to prosper in the 21st cen-

cient in oil in 2006, lending some to speculate that Brazil will join the Organization of Petroleum Exporting Countries (OPEC).

Brazil's manufacturing industry experienced steady growth during the second half of the 1990s, attracting a rush of foreign investment. The election in October 2002 of left-wing Luiz Inácio Lula da Silva, of the Workers' Party, made the international capital markets jittery, but the new president was – and continues to be – committed to good financial management.

Brazil in the 21st century has acquired a

LEFT: Carajás in Pará state, is one of the world's largest mining operations.
ABOVE: Petrobras' Urucu oil and natural gas plant.

tury. This will leave Brazil's vital and growing industries with a damaging shortage of employees of the quality they need to support their growth. Another major problem is the continuing disparity between rich and poor, which leaves Brazil with huge social and economic problems.

Brazil's predominantly young population (over 60 percent of the population is under 29) is at once one of its major assets and potentially one of its costliest burdens. Well educated and employed, today's young Brazilians will be the driving force behind the country's future prosperity. Badly educated and possibly condemned to a life of poverty, they will instead become a huge financial and social burden.

The right environment

Industrialization is a messy business, and Brazil is experiencing all the side-effects seen decades ago in Europe and the United States. Brazilians are well aware that they are getting plenty of criticism from abroad for the damage being done to the Amazon forest by mining companies, gold prospectors, ranchers, wood-pulp factories, and pig-iron mills. And the country is slowly beginning to wake up to its responsibility as a protector of a huge tract of the Earth's surface.

However, although shocking scenes of flaming trees and polluted rivers appear on tele-

exploitation in the Amazon, and try to improve the country's image abroad. To continue progressing Brazil will need aid, since priorities such as housing, health care and education have first claims on government resources. The environmental issue is helping to teach this young giant that, like it or not, Brazil cannot solve all its problems on its own. In addition, the world's new set of environmental priorities is giving the country a growing importance.

Future growth

Although in many ways a spectacular success, President Cardoso's government had difficulty

vision in Brazil as frequently as they do elsewhere in the world, Brazilians' view of the problem is somewhat different from that of citizens of wealthier countries. Many people feel that they are being criticized for the same crimes as were committed by the rich nations during earlier decades and centuries. They defend themselves against charges of environmental destruction and human rights abuses by pointing to the way the United States achieved world supremacy while slaughtering animals and Amerindians, building dirty steel mills, and strip-mining once beautiful mountains.

Fortunately, both the government and concerned citizens' groups have taken steps to fight pollution, restrain the worst aspects of

STUNNING STATISTICS

With a recent GDP of over US$620 billion, Brazil is the world's eighth-largest economy, almost double that of South Korea, its main rival for the title of most developed emerging economy. Brazil is one of the world's major steel producers, and the eighth-largest car manufacturer, the fifth-largest aircraft manufacturer and fifth-largest arms exporter. Its hydroelectric potential surpasses that of any other nation, and it has the world's largest hydroelectric plant. It is also the largest producer of iron ore, sixth-largest producer of aluminum, and fourth-largest producer of tin. On top of all that, it is the largest exporter of coffee, the largest producer of sugar and orange juice, and the second-largest producer of soybeans.

in driving through some critical reforms that were designed to rein in the civil service, and exert control over the vastly inefficient and extravagant social security system. This left Brazil with a large and intransigent public spending bill, which resulted in a persistent budget deficit.

Meanwhile, Brazil is experiencing unprecedented levels of imports following the removal of trade barriers. This is partly due to the release of pent-up consumer demand. But the majority of imports are capital equipment, helping Brazil's industry to modernize and increase productivity. This will strengthen manufactur-

IRON ORE IN SPADES

Brazil's iron ore production is the highest in the world, with enough reserves in the Carajás region alone to satisfy the entire global demand for the next 500 years.

of major mining powers. Brazil is a world leader in production of gold and iron ore, as well as "high-tech" minerals such as titanium, vanadium, zirconium, beryllium, niobium and quartz, which are now in great demand.

The years of rampant inflation filled the coffers of the banks, giving them the resources to develop their expertise and services. The bank-

ing output and allow the rapid growth in export sales to continue. The election in 2002 of President Luiz Inácio Lula da Silva signaled a new era for Brazil's presence in international trade. Re-elected to a second term of office in October 2006, he is committed to closer ties with the other members of Mercosul, and greater negotiations with other Latin American countries and the United States on the establishment of new trade agreements.

Minerals will continue to play a key role, having already placed Brazil in the select company

ing system is well developed and stands to benefit enormously from the closer trading and financial links being established with other South American countries.

As already mentioned (see page 45), the stock market has prospered immensely, not least because it has tempted foreign investors and speculators. Some Brazilians, including, most notably, the bankers, got very rich indeed in Lula's first four-year term as president, and are looking forward to continued prosperity in his second.

When the people of Brazil elected Lula they voted for change. His challenge, in his second term, is to meet the high expectations of all the Brazilian people. ❏

LEFT: Brazil's fast-growing population is reflected in overcrowding on São Paulo's subway rail system.
ABOVE: traders in the Mercantile & Futures Exchange.

THE PEOPLE OF BRAZIL

Brazil is sometimes referred to as a melting pot, but this implies that people from many different backgrounds have blended together. They are, in fact, proudly different, but also proud to be Brazilians

Brazil is a diverse nation. Its people share only a common language and a vague notion of Brazil's cultural shape. They worship a dozen gods, and their ancestors came from all over the globe. This is a legacy of Brazil's colonial past. Among the countries of the New World, it is unique. Where the Spanish-American colonies were ruled by rigid bureaucracies and the future United States by a negligent Britain, Brazil's colonial society followed a flexible middle course. The Portuguese colonists were not outcasts from their native land like the Puritans of New England. Nor were they like the grasping Spanish courtiers fulfilling a brief colonial service before returning home. They were men – and for decades, *only* men – who retained an allegiance to the old country but quickly identified with their new home.

In his classic work on Brazil's origins *Raizes do Brasil*, historian Sergio Buarque de Holanda (father of songwriter Chico Buarque) writes: "He [the Brazilian male] is free to take on entire repertoires of new ideas, outlooks and forms, assimilating them without difficulty."

Racial mixing

The Spanish grandees hated the New World, the Puritans were stuck with it, but the Portuguese *liked* Brazil – particularly its native women – and the colonizers' desire married with the beauty of the indigenous females to begin a new race. The first members of that race – the first Brazilians – were *mamelucos*, the progeny of Portuguese white men and native Amerindian women. Later, other races emerged – the *cafu-*

sos, of Amerindian and African blood, and the *mulatos*, of Africans and Europeans.

Octavio Paz, in his essay on the Mexican character, *The Labyrinth of Solitude*, notes his compatriots' ambivalence about race. There is not, in the whole of Mexico, a single monument to the conquistadors, he observes, and yet most *mestiços* (of European and Amerindian parentage) anticipate the time when their blood will be "purified" through miscegenation, and their descendants will be able to pass legitimately as white.

In Brazil, the fusion of race is more complete. Pedro Álvares Cabral is honored by all Brazilians as the country's "discoverer," yet the Amerindian past is not disdained. Diplomat

---

LEFT: bright-eyed Afro-Brazilian girl.
RIGHT: European influences are strong in the south.

William Schurz, in his 1961 book *Brazil,* notes that numerous Amerindian family names have been preserved. He lists Ypiranga, Araripe, Peryassu and many others, some of which belong to distinguished families in Pernambuco and Bahia.

But in contemporary Brazil, Schurz might have pointed out, the Amerindian is only a shadow of the other races. Historians believe as many as 5 million Amerindians lived in the area at the time of the European discovery in 1500. According to Amerindian leader Ailton Krenak, approximately 700 tribes have disappeared from Brazilian soil since that time, hav-

ing fallen victim to disease, extermination, or gradual absorption through miscegenation. About 180 tribes have survived, as have a similar number of languages or dialects. They comprise about 700,000 people, mostly living on government reservations in Mato Grosso and Goiás or in villages deep in the Amazon.

Brazil's *mestiço* population, meanwhile, has tended to melt into the white category. Only about 2–3 percent of Brazilians, mostly in the Amazon or its borders, consider themselves *mestiços*, but in reality, throughout the north and northeast, many nominal Caucasians are in fact *mestiços*.

INDIGENOUS LANGUAGES

There are around 180 languages used in Brazil, and about 130 of them are considered endangered because they are spoken by groups with populations of fewer than 600. Many are on the verge of extinction, spoken only by a handful of people, mostly elderly, which means the languages are unlikely to outlast this generation. Most speakers of indigenous languages today are bilingual (in Portuguese and their own tongue), but there are parts of Amazonas and Pará where most of the women and children speak only their own language – Mundurukú – although men tend to speak some Portuguese. Kayapó is another indigenous language that is flourishing orally, although only a fairly small proportion of the estimated 4,000 speakers are literate in it.

African culture

The history of African and the associated mixed-race people in Brazil has been complex. Despite now having the largest black population outside of Africa, Brazilians are known for being ambivalent about their black heritage. In the past, racism existed but was simply denied. In recent years, however, there has emerged an awareness of both Brazilian racism and the rich legacy that Africans have introduced to Brazil.

Gilberto Freyre, the Pernambucan sociologist, brings scholarly eloquence to the subject. In his epoch-making 1936 volume *Casa Grande e Senzala,* Freyre says: "Every Brazilian, even the light-skinned and fair-haired one, carries about with him in his soul, when not in soul and body alike, the shadow, or even the birthmark, of the aborigine or the negro. The influence of the African, either direct or remote, is everything that is a sincere reflection of our lives. We, almost all of us, bear the mark of that influence."

Starting in colonial days, entire portions of African culture were incorporated wholesale into Brazilian life. Today, they are reflected in the rhythmic music of samba, the varied and spicy cuisine of Bahia and the growth of African-origin spiritist religions, even in urban centers. And the mark of that influence, as Freyre said, goes far beyond mere religious and culinary conventions.

Change in racial views

Recent years have seen the rediscovery and redefinition of Brazil's African past, including the revision of racist views of history. Brazilian history books at the turn of the century often contained racist passages. One text portrayed Brazil's earliest African slaves as "accepting the most grotesque of fetishes". Another noted that "negroes of the worst quality, generally those from the Congo, were sent to the fields and the mines." The preamble of an early 20th-century immigration law said, "It is necessary to preserve and develop the ethnic composition of our population by giving preference to its most desirable European elements."

Modern social scientists, starting with Freyre, have catalogued the real achievements of Brazil's earliest black residents. For example, the Africans often possessed highly developed manual skills in carpentry, masonry and mining. Much of the best baroque carving that still graces the colonial churches of Bahia was done by Africans.

In Minas Gerais, the illegitimate son of a Portuguese builder and a black slave woman led Brazilian sculpture and architecture into the high baroque. Antônio Francisco Lisboa, called Aleijadinho ("The Little Cripple", because of a deforming disease that some have attributed to arthritis, others to leprosy), started late in the 18th century with his elegant São Francisco church in Ouro Preto and the larger, more elaborate, São Francisco in São João del Rei. He also created 78 sinuous and lifelike soapstone and cedar carvings at the Basílica do Senhor Bom Jesus de Matosinhos in Congonhas do Campo.

Aleijadinho's miracle is that he created an informed yet innovative artistic idiom at the edge of Western civilization. During his remarkable 80-year lifetime he never studied art and never saw the ocean. Yet his Congonhas statues are numbered among the greatest collections of baroque art anywhere in the world *(see page 212)*.

In addition to their artistic attributes and manual skills, many Africans, especially the Yorubás of West Africa who dominated in Bahia, brought sophisticated political and reli-

gious practices to Brazil. Historians noted that they practiced the Islamic religion and were literate in Arabic. Their culture was rich in music, dance, art and unwritten but majestic literature. Writes Freyre, "In Bahia, many… were, in every respect but political and social status, the equal or superior of their masters."

Rebellion against slavery

These proud Africans did not simply accept their bondage. Brazil's previous view of its African slavery as "less rigorous than that practiced by the French, English or North Americans" has been revised by historians, who note that nine violent slave rebellions rocked the province of Bahia between 1807 and 1835.

LEFT: children sometimes earn money for the family as street vendors.
RIGHT: a market trader in Rio.

A German visitor to a Bahian plantation in the 19th century, Prince Adalbert of Prussia, reported that "The loaded guns and pistols hanging up in the plantation owner's bedroom showed that he had no confidence in his slaves and had more than once been obliged to face them with his loaded gun."

The story of Brazilian slavery is inevitably harrowing. Historians believe 12 million Africans were captured and shipped to Brazil between 1549 and the outlawing of the Brazilian slave trade in 1853. Of that number, about 2 million people died on the slave boats before reaching Brazilian shores.

council, community and private property, a tribal army, and a priestly class.

In some respects, however, Brazilian slavery was more liberal than its equivalents elsewhere. Owners were prohibited by law from separating slave families, and were required to grant slaves their freedom if they could pay a fair market price. A surprising number of slaves were able to achieve manumission. Freed slaves often went on to form religious brotherhoods, with the support of the Catholic Church, particularly Jesuit missionaries. The brotherhoods raised money to buy the freedom of more slaves, and some of them became quite wealthy.

Once in Brazil, white masters treated their slaves as a cheap investment. An African youth enslaved by the owner of a sugar plantation or gold mine could expect to live eight years. It was cheaper to buy new slaves than preserve the health of existing ones.

Enslaved Africans in the northeast were often in flight. Historians know of at least 10 large-scale *quilombos,* or slave retreats, formed during colonial days in the interior of the northeast. The largest of these, Palmares, had a population of 30,000 at its peak, and flourished for 67 years before being crushed in 1694. Palmares, like the other great *quilombos* of the 17th and 18th centuries, was run along the lines of an African tribal monarchy, with a king, a royal

In Ouro Preto, one such brotherhood built the magnificent baroque jewel, the Igreja da Nossa Senhora do Rosário dos Pretos, one of the most beautiful colonial churches in Brazil. In a backlash against slavery and racism, Rosário dos Pretos discriminated against whites.

Brazilian slavery finally came to an end in 1888, when Princess Regent Isabel de Orleans e Bragança signed the Lei Áurea (Golden Law) abolishing the institution. This law immediately freed an estimated 800,000 slaves.

Socio-economic development

Brazil's history of racism and slavery left its non-white population unprepared for the 21st century. Today, Afro-Brazilians lag behind in socioeconomic terms, creating a vicious circle that has resulted in persistent discrimination.

According to São Paulo human rights attorney Dalmo Dallari, "We have, in our Constitution and laws, the explicit prohibition of racial discrimination. But, it is equally clear that such laws are merely an expression of intentions with little practical effect." Dallari and others point to persistent and widespread discrimination. Blacks barred at the doors of restaurants and told to "go to the service entrance" by doormen at apartment buildings are among many examples.

There is also a more subtle face to Brazilian racial discrimination. São Paulo's ex-State Government Afro-Brazilian Affairs Coordinator, Percy da Silva, said: "While it may be true that blacks are no longer slaves, it is also a fact blacks do not have the same opportunities as whites. We are, to a great extent, stigmatized, seen as inferior. We must show a double capacity, both intellectual and personal, to be accepted in many places, especially the workplace."

Thankfully, this began to change with the appointment by President Lula in 2002 of the first black cabinet officals, though there still remain very few black diplomats, corporate leaders, or legislators.

Statistically, the economic condition of Afro-Brazilians was amply documented in a 2004 report published by the Brazilian Census Bureau (IBGE). The report showed that, while whites formed 51.4 percent of the total population, 84.2 percent of the richest 1 percent of Brazilians were white. Nearly half of whites in the 18–24 age bracket – 46.6 percent – attended college. On the other hand, when it came to the 48 percent of Brazil's population categorized as Afro-Brazilian or mixed-race, only 16.5 percent in the same age bracket attended college. Of Brazil's richest 1 percent, only 15.8 percent were black or brown, but of the poorest 10 percent, exactly two-thirds were black or brown. The average income for an adult white Brazilian in 2004 (the latest available figures) was US$380 a month, while for black and brown adults it was only US$200 per month, just over half.

In 2004 the richest 10 percent of Brazilian society still controlled 45 percent of the nation's wealth, while the poorest 50 percent had to divide a mere 14 percent of the nation's riches. Fully one quarter of Brazil's population lived below what officials stunningly dubbed "the misery line," defined as personal income of about US$50 per month or less.

But social inequalities are an old story in Brazil. In his classic study contrasting US and Brazilian development, *Bandeirantes e Pioneiros*, author Vianna Moog writes, "Right from the start, there was a fundamental difference of motivation between the colonization of North America and that of Brazil. In the former case, the initial sentiments were spiritual, organic and constructive, while in the latter, they were

predatory and selfish, with religious influences only secondary." The foundations were laid for a lasting pattern of social inequalities.

Women's role

Historically, the treatment afforded women in Brazil has not been much better than that extended to blacks or the poor. Mrs Elizabeth Cabot Agassiz, wife of the famed Swiss-born naturalist, Louis Agassiz, noted that, during their 1865 visit to Brazil, special permission was needed from Emperor Dom Pedro II for her to attend one of her husband's lectures. "Ordinarily, no women were allowed," she wrote later. "Having one on hand was evidently too great an innovation of national habits."

LEFT: many families live in cramped conditions in the city *favelas*.
RIGHT: vital discussion in a city street.

But fast forward to the early 1990s and look at the front page of a leading Brazilian newspaper, featuring photos of the Finance Minister meeting with the mayors of São Paulo and Santos, Brazil's largest port city. All three officials were women. And in 2002, Rosângela Matheus became the first female governor of Rio.

But while welcome progress has been made, women still lag behind in terms of most economic indicators. According to the IBGE, as of 2004 women members of the workforce were disproportionately represented in the lowest income brackets, with 71 percent of women earning US$200 a month or less, against only 55 percent of men. Perhaps even more stunning is the fact that, even among Brazilians with 11 years of education or more, women's earnings were only 57 percent of men's. A 2006 study by the Brazilian Development Bank (BNDES) was even more piquant, finding that among professionals and managers, women with the same qualifications and experience as men earned only 91 percent of what their male colleagues earned. While noting that women had scored some gains in the previous decade, the study concluded, "At the present rate, professional women will catch up with men in 75 years."

A nation of immigrants

Like the United States, Brazil is a nation of immigrants, and not just from Portugal, the original colonizing country. Rodrigues, Fernandes, de Souza and other Latin names dominate the phone book in some Brazilian cities. But, in others, names like Alaby or Geisel, Tolentino or Kobayashi, appear more than once.

The presence of many ethnic groups in Brazil dates from the 1850s, when the imperial government encouraged European immigration to help rebuild the labor force as the slave trade declined. The first incomers were German and Swiss farmers who settled mainly in the three southern states of Rio Grande do Sul, Santa Catarina and Paraná, where the soil and climate were most similar to those in Europe.

For decades, some communities, such as Novo Hamburgo in Rio Grande do Sul and Blumenau in Santa Catarina, were more German than Brazilian. Protestant religious services were as common as Roman Catholic ones, and

THE ITALIAN INFLUENCE

Starting in the 1870s, nearly a million Italian immigrants, fleeing poverty and hardship in Europe, flooded into São Paulo state. Many worked on coffee plantations in the interior, while others entered the growing urban workforce in São Paulo and neighboring cities. Within one generation, the Italians were established in the trades and professions; within two they were a new elite, with nouveau riche millionaire families such as the Martinellis and the Matarazzos. One of Brazil's first skyscrapers was the 30-story Martinelli Building, built in São Paulo in 1929. A few decades later, the 46-story Itália Building went up on Ipiranga Avenue – the tallest building in South America when it was completed in 1965.

Another half a million Italians arrived in Brazil during the late 19th century. Used to working on the land, they had little taste for city life, and instead of staying in São Paulo most of them headed south and settled in a temperate, hilly region of the southern state of Rio Grande do Sul. They brought the secrets of viniculture to a country where wine production was negligible. Today, the industry, although relatively small, is flourishing, and Brazil's best wines are produced in the region around Caxias do Sul *(see page 330 for more detail)*. In 1931 Caxias inaugurated its signature event, the annual Festival of the Grape, held in February to March, the kind of festival that the forebears of the Italian immigrants knew how to organize and celebrate.

German rather than Portuguese was the first language of most residents. Such towns still bear the distinctive mark of their Teutonic heritage, with Alpine-style architecture dominating the landscape and restaurant menus offering more *knackwurst* and *eisbein* than *feijoada*.

By the turn of the century, Brazil was hosting immigrants from around the globe. According to records held by the foreign ministry, a total of 5 million immigrants arrived on Brazilian shores between 1884 and 1973, when restrictive legislation was adopted. Italians sent the greatest number, 1.4 million; Portugal sent 1.2 million people, Spain sent 580,000, Germany

mostly from today's Syria and Lebanon, during the early 20th century. Sprawling commercial districts in two cities – around Rua do Ouvidor in Rio and Rua 25 de Março in São Paulo – feature hundreds of shops owned by people of Middle Eastern origin.

Despite the impact of mass communications and the trend toward political centralization, the process of molding diverse populations into one is far from complete. One reason is the strength of regionalism: when this comes to the fore, all shades of the racial and religious spectrum blend together, and regional solidarity becomes the defining factor. ❑

200,000 and Russia 110,000, including many Jews who settled in São Paulo and Rio.

The call for immigrants reached far beyond the borders of Europe. Starting in 1908, with the arrival in Santos harbor of the *Kasato Maru*, 250,000 Japanese left their homeland to live permanently in Brazil. The descendants of these people, who were fleeing crop failures and earthquakes in their native islands, still live in metropolitan São Paulo, most visibly in the Japanese Liberdade district *(see page 190)*.

The Middle East sent 700,000 immigrants,

LEFT: Rosângela Matheus became the first woman governor of Rio in 2002.
ABOVE: old meets new: a *gaucho* with his laptop.

SOCIAL ISSUES

Divorce and abortion are two areas in which Brazilian laws have lagged behind those in many Western countries. Until 1977, in Brazil divorce was unlawful, but there was a provision for legal separation, known as a *desquite*. This guaranteed that a woman could claim alimony, but did not mean that a marriage was legally terminated, so neither party could remarry. Changes to the law have rationalized the situation, and it is now possible to convert a *desquite* into a divorce after three years' separation. Abortion is more problematic. In September 2005, a bill to legalize abortion was presented to Congress, but the power of the Catholic Church and the pro-life movement prevented its approval.

THE AMERINDIANS

The survival of Brazil's indigenous people, with their many different languages, hangs in the balance. In recent years, some of their expropriated land has been returned to them, but there is still a long way to go

The first contact Brazilian Amerindians had with European civilization was in 1500, when the Portuguese explorer, Pedro Álvarez Cabral, blown off course on a voyage to India, reached the shores of their country. For many years Brazilian historians estimated that there were about 4 million Amerindians in Brazil at that time, but more recently some anthropologists have begun to believe there may have been far more, possibly as many as 30 million. This new way of thinking came about because many old Amerindian settlements are still being uncovered as new areas of Amazon rainforest are cut down.

Until recently, anthropologists also agreed that the ancestors of all Amerindians had migrated from Central Asia across the Bering Strait and down through the Americas about 10,000 years ago. However, ancient pottery finds in the Amazon and the wide variety of indigenous cultures have led some experts to believe that Amerindians have lived in Brazil much longer, and may have come across the Pacific.

Tropical forest provides abundant timber, but it is a poor source of stone, and the Amerindians' shifting lifestyle left few of the lasting monuments considered the mark of advanced civilizations. Yet any assumption that Stone Age Amerindian culture was primitive has been challenged by recent archeological discoveries, which suggest that substantial, permanent, and highly organized cities existed in pre-Columbian Amazonia. Once again, the accepted view of Amerindian history is under new scrutiny.

Mixed messages

Early Portuguese explorers were greatly impressed by the Amerindians' innocence and generosity. They were regarded as "noble savages," and some were shipped to Europe to be paraded before royalty. Thus, in the early post-contact years, the Amerindians were relatively well treated, but soon the colonizers' greed and the serious shortage of labor on their sugar plantations led them to overcome any moral scruples. Raiders – known as *bandeirantes* – traveled up from São Paulo to bring back Amerindians as slaves. Their brutality was legendary, and appalled Jesuit missionaries who opposed enslaving the indigenous people. The Jesuits tried to protect and convert the Amerindians by forcing forest-dwelling tribes to live in *aldeias* (settlements). The missions replaced native culture with Christianity and hard labor, but encouraged the people to resist enslavement. There is still debate over whether the Jesuits defended or helped crush the Amerindians. Whatever their motives, both missionaries and *bandeirantes* introduced Western diseases such as measles and influenza, and hundreds of thousands of Amerindians died as a result.

Slavery and violence

In 1755 Portugal freed all Amerindians from slavery, but the effects were negligible. The Jesuits were soon after expelled, and their missions were put under the control of lay directors who could make profits from the indigenous

the Portuguese royal family fled to Brazil in 1807, whites outnumbered Amerindians. A new edict was issued, permitting enslavement of Amerindians in the south. In 1845, the indigenous people were restored to mission life, just in time for their labor to be exploited for extracting rubber from the rainforest.

As the need for labor declined, extreme racial "solutions" came to the fore. In 1908 Hermann von Ihering, director of São Paulo Museum, defended the extermination of all remaining Amerindians in Santa Catarina and Paraná who threatened German and Italian immigrants. In the early 1900s, *bugreiros*, hunters hired by the

people's forced labor. Under the Jesuits, the seven Guaraní missions held 30,000 Amerindians. By 1821, unable to adapt to life in crowded settlements, forced to labor as debt slaves, and at the mercy of alien diseases, only 3,000 had survived. Furthermore, the introduction of alcohol had corrupted Amerindian culture, and whites consequently regarded them as lazy, shiftless, and incapable of integration.

The advance of cattle ranchers across the northeastern plains, and of gold miners in the south, resulted in bloody conflicts. By the time

LEFT: a young girl wearing vegetable-dye body paint.
ABOVE: Cayapó Indian dressed as a chieftain, *c.*1870.
RIGHT: looking to an uncertain future.

FAIR-WEATHER FRIENDS

Despite the relatively fair treatment accorded them by the Europeans in the early years of colonization, some of the indigenous people were rightly suspicious, realizing that attitudes could change to suit circumstances. "Do not trust the whites. They are the men who control the lightning, who live without a homeland, who wander to satisfy their thirst for gold. They are kind to us when they need us, for the land they tread and the rivers they assault are ours. Once they have achieved their goals, they are false and treacherous." So wrote Rosa, a Borôro Amerindian, many years later, and she was right: the men "without a homeland" had little respect for the lands of those they conquered.

colonists, prided themselves on poisoning, shooting or raping Kaingáng people who tried to stop the construction of a railroad line.

Fewer than a million Amerindians survived, but public opinion began to turn. In 1910, the explorer and humanist soldier, Cândido Mariano da Silva Rondon – who instructed his troops: "Die if you have to, but never shoot!" – formed the Fundação Nacional do Indio. It was nevertheless too late to stop the widespread destruction of indigenous cultures. In 1960, anthropologists found that one-third of the 230 tribes known to exist in 1900 had vanished. As the agricultural frontier moved west, then north,

one group of Amerindians after another became extinct, and the population dropped to 200,000. When, in the 1960s and 1970s the government built a huge network of roads across the Amazon jungle and encouraged white settlers to move in, it seemed that the few remaining Amerindians would soon be exterminated. But since then they have staged a remarkably successful comeback.

The Panara

At the end of the 1960s, the Panara (or Krenakorore, as they were known at the time) were rumored to be a fierce and elusive people. They were seen as an obstacle in the drive to open up the interior of Brazil to economic development through the construction of the

> ### FOLK MEMORIES
> Modern Brazilians are reminded of their country's indigenous roots daily, through place names, foods, and the rituals of *umbanda* – and even the national passion for cleanliness.

Cuiabá–Santarém highway across the hitherto isolated Amazon basin. The Panara were contacted by anthropologists just days before the highway construction teams reached their land.

Once contacted, they were devastated by disease and reduced to begging in order to survive. In 1975, 79 demoralized survivors were taken by plane to the Xingú Amerindian reserve over 1,000 km (620 miles) away, an action that caused outrage at home and abroad. With the help of a group of anthropologists, the Panara waged a campaign to regain their land. The political climate, in Brazil and internationally, changed and their demands began to receive a more sympathetic hearing.

Some 20 years after their expulsion the wheel turned full circle. In October 1995, a small group of Panara people was taken back to their traditional lands in northern Mato Grosso and southern Pará in the Amazon basin. They found much of the land devastated by gold mining, cattle ranching, and logging. Even so, the Panara are slowly reconstructing their old life, with its myths, rituals, songs, dances, and rhythms of work; and an area comprising more than 490,000 hectares (1.2 million acres) of unoccupied forest was finally recognized in the Brazilian courts as their reserve in 1996.

The attitude of the establishment has evolved since the creation of the Xingú Park reserve, where several different tribes coexist. Though flawed, the reserve can be considered a success. The Xingú retain their tribal organization because contact with "civilization" is limited, but many have developed business activities and been elected as government officials.

Amerindian affairs are now under the jurisdiction of FUNAI (Fundação Nacional do Indio), Rondon's agency, which was rehabilitated in 1967, but is considered to be inefficient and has been found guilty of corruption. FUNAI is responsible for demarcating Amerindian tribal

LEFT: a young Yanomami mother and baby.
RIGHT: a Kayapo man wearing a brilliantly colored feathered headdress.

land as protection against ranchers, miners, and loggers. Claims have been weakened, however, by a 1996 decree that allows these groups to challenge the demarcation process.

Staging a recovery

The Panara's return to their ancestral land is symbolic of a revival in the fortunes of Amerindians. The 2000 census showed numbers had increased by 138 percent since 1990; there are now 700,000 Amerindians in the country. Once the demarcation process is complete, their territories will cover about 10 percent of Brazil's total landmass. In 2005 the Minister of Justice said that all indigenous lands would be demarcated by the end of 2006, but at the time of writing the process has not yet been completed.

Gold-panners frequently invade the large reserve allocated to the 27,000-strong Yanomami who live near the border with Venezuela. These illegal prospectors, known as *garimpeiros* – whom the government is either unable or unwilling to police – have brought with them violence, pollution, and disease epidemics.

Other Amerindian groups find it difficult to deal with the strains imposed by the modern world. There are about 25,000 Guarani-Kaiowa Amerindians in some 22 villages scattered over largely deforested scrubland in Mato Grosso do Sul in central Brazil. Without adequate provision of reserves to sustain them, many are forced to work as farm laborers. A large proportion of them are unable to cope with the traumatic change this brings to their lifestyle, and there has been an alarmingly high rate of suicides. Government health agency FUNASA reported that 199 Guarani committed suicide between 2000 and 2003, the majority of them in their teens or early twenties.

The Guarani-Kaiowa Amerindians have started to fight back, though. They have carried out a series of *retomadas* – retaking the lands from which they had been expelled. *Retomadas* are often violent, as the new occupants, predominantly cattle-rearers, struggle to retain their hold on the land. But the Amerindians are determined: in 2000, indigenous groups throughout Brazil staged a well-publicized demonstration at the country's 500th "birthday" celebrations. ❑

THE STRUGGLE FOR SURVIVAL

The unhappy history of Amerindian contact with whites means that today casual visitors are not welcome in reserves administered by FUNAI. Even bona fide researchers must be willing to apply in advance and wait months.

Amerindians throughout Brazil are still in crisis, and some are taking desperate measures. In March 2003, the Cauruaia in the south west of Pará seized hostages in protest at miners on their reserve poisoning the rivers and wildlife with mercury in order to extract gold.

Although indigenous groups initially welcomed the election of President Lula da Silva in 2002, the following year saw a disturbing escalation of murders and attacks throughout the country. President Lula's ratification, in April 2005, of the Raposa Serra do Sol territory in the northern state of Roraima, a 16,800-sq. km (6,500-sq. mile) area that is the traditional home of some 15,000 Macuxi, Wapichana, Ingarikã, Patamona and Taurepang people, represented a victory for Amerindians in the region, who have struggled for more than 30 years for recognition of their land rights. However, progress has been slow: many of the settlers remain on the land they have been ordered to leave, and tension is high. More than 20 indigenous people have died in disputes over the territory, while hundreds more have lost homes and livestock, according to a report by Amnesty International. The indigenous people still await a happy outcome.

SAINTS AND IDOLS

The beliefs of the Brazilian people are derived from a blend of Amerindian, African, and European traditions, which feeds inherent mystical tendencies and embraces faiths – and superstitions – of all kinds

Se Deus quiser… (God willing…) is one of the expressions you are most likely to come across throughout Brazil, a country where world religions, millenarian cults and *ayahuasca*-induced sects coexist peacefully, setting an example to an intolerant world. Some attribute the force of religion to the people's deeply felt mysticism. Others credit it to the frequent absence of the state, which means that people, especially migrants, turn to religion to fill the gap. Either way, even though "modernity" and Westernization appear to have made more people less religious (or more hesitant to proclaim their faith publicly), religion permeates all levels of Brazilian life.

In the northeastern city of Juazeiro do Norte, women wear black every Friday, and on the 20th day of every month. They are in mourning for the death of Padre Cícero, who according to legend did not really die, but was transported to heaven. It is widely believed that Padre Cícero's fingernail clippings possess therapeutic properties (*see page 75*).

Also in the northeast, farmers draw magic circles around their sick cows and pray to Santa Barbara (or her Afro-Brazilian equivalent, Iansã) that their cows will not die. The same farmers place six lumps of salt outside their homes on the night of Santa Lucia, December 12. If the dew dissolves the first lump, it will rain in December; if it dissolves the second lump, rain will come in January; and so on. If no dew dissolves the salt, drought will plague the *sertão*, the backlands of the northeastern region.

LEFT: robed worshipers in the Valley of the Dawn.
RIGHT: a Catholic priest in a pensive mood.

Religion and politics

Religion and state are officially separate entities in Brazil, but in practice the various Churches have always sought to influence events. Up until the end of the 20th century the vast majority of Brazilians were baptized into the Roman Catholic faith, so a close relationship between the Catholic Church and the state was accepted as the norm.

With the recent growth of new players on the scene, the Evangelical Churches (particularly the more radical Pentecostal sects, *see page 71*), their acquisition of radio stations and television channels to get their message across, and their success in political elections, the crossover between politics and religion has continued.

Brazil is the world's largest Catholic country, where the progressive ideas of liberation theology flourished in the 1970s and 1980s, when many bishops, priests and nuns decided to fight for the poor and oppose military rule, following, they claimed, the example of Jesus Christ. Instead, they were accused by both the military and the Vatican of being Marxists, and many priests, nuns and lay-workers were imprisoned and tortured. In 1984, Leonardo Boff, a leading liberation theologian, was summoned to the Vatican to be cross-examined by Cardinal Ratzinger, now Pope Benedict XVI. Boff asked for the date to be changed, because

Davi Kopenawa Yanomami, a shaman from the northwestern Amazon, says that since the arrival of the whites, many of the spirits' houses have been burned and emptied. Today, he claims, "The words of the whites have created an obstacle to the voice of the ancients." Shamans and other indigenous leaders like Davi fight to preserve their cultural heritage as well as their environment. André Baniwa, also from the Amazon region, says that missionaries demonized indigenous faiths, and that nowadays it is necessary for schools to pass on traditional knowledge and mythology to children, as oral transmission has lost some of its effectiveness.

it clashed with the date of the National Assembly of Prostitutes, to whom he was an advisor. After all, he explained, prostitutes are the first in the Kingdom of God.

Ancient voices

The nation's Amerindian heritage is partly responsible for Brazilians' deep-rooted mystic beliefs. At present the indigenous population of Brazil is composed of around 225 ethnicities, speaking 180 languages, so there are many different ways of life and perceptions of the afterlife. One common strand is an inextricable link with nature and ancestral lands. In the past 500 years, the Indian population has been reduced to the 2006 level of around 600,000.

Cults of African origin

African beliefs are the second major influence in Brazil's religious culture. Visitors to Brazilian beaches in December, January, and February often find flowers, perfume bottles and cakes of soap still in their wrappers, tossed on a shore that is strewn with burned-out candles. Followers of *candomblé* and *umbanda* will have offered these to the West African sea goddess Iemanjá, who is sometimes characterized as the Virgin Mary, sometimes as a sea goddess or a mermaid. If the offerings sink beneath the waves or are carried out to sea, Iemanjá is said to accept them. If they return to shore, however, she has rejected them.

The famous New Year event, when up to 2

million people pack Rio's beaches, began with these ceremonies in the 1970s. By 1992 the city mayor saw it as a chance to attract more tourists. The massive crowds and noise have since caused *candomblé* and *umbanda* groups to move their celebrations to the days leading up to December 31. In Salvador, on the Rio Vermelho beach, there is a huge party to celebrate Iemanjá at the beginning of February.

Although the census of 2000 would have one believe that *candomblé* is numerically unimportant, the National Federation of Afro-Brazilian Tradition and Culture (FENATRAB) has estimated that around 70 million Brazil-

ians are in some way linked to the *terreiros* (sacred land where ceremonies are performed). Until recently *candomblé* was looked down on as an inferior religion, and those who practiced it would often declare themselves to be followers of other faiths, particularly Catholicism; many people do follow more than one religion.

African slaves brought *candomblé* to Brazil. It was only officially recognized as a religion in Bahia, its stronghold, in 1976. It survived so long, even when outlawed, by adopting the identities of Catholic saints for its deities, the

LEFT: gaily dressed *baianas* set off in procession to pay homage to Iemanjá.

ABOVE: a *macumba* dancer taking part in Carnival.

orixás, so when a slave appeared to be worshiping St George, he was really paying homage to Xangô, the god of thunder. This element has been incorporated into the religion.

During a *candomblé* ritual, when priestesses are ordained, they have their heads ceremonially shaved and the blood of a hen or goat is smeared on their foreheads, along with chicken feathers. The ceremony is accompanied by *atabaque* drums, chants in various African languages, and frenetic dancing that is kept up until the initiates fall into a trance.

Voodoo cults, similar to those still practiced in Haiti and elsewehere in the Caribbean, have developed roots in a few parts of Brazil. In Maranhão, situated in northeastern Brazil, and on the northern national border with the Guianas, the descendants of those slaves who managed to escape to freedom cultivated African sociopolitical structures and cults far removed from the domination of the white man. These practices continued until early in the 20th century.

Evangelical explosion

It came as something of a surprise when the 2000 census revealed that the Evangelical population had doubled in the space of nine years to some 26 million people. While the numbers of clergy and laymen in the Catholic Church stayed the same, Evangelical churches multiplied. In Brazil people tend to look at Evangelicals (often called *crentes*) with a mixture of suspicion and respect. Scandalous images of some well-known Pentecostal priests enjoying the good life have been widely shown on national television. The biggest concentrations

TRACING ANCESTORS

One by-product of Brazil's thriving African religious cults has been the maintenance of an oral history among the Afro-Brazilian community. The leading priestesses of *candomblé*, such as the late Olga de Alaketu and Mãe Menininha do Gantois, could recite the names of their African ancestors and the ancestors of members of their community, going right back to generations still in their African homeland.

They described in detail how their ancestors were captured, bound and transported on slave ships to Brazil. The priestesses passed this knowledge on to the new spiritual leaders of the community, who memorized the vast genealogy.

of Evangelicals, especially the Pentecostal Churches, are found on the peripheries of large cities and in agricultural frontier zones. The common thread between these zones is that both have a great number of uprooted migrants in search of a better life in places where the state presence is tenuous. This encourages people to turn to religious networks for support, education, and a sense of belonging.

Salaam Aleikum

Islam appears to have arrived in Brazil with slaves brought from West Africa. An attempt at revolution in 1830s Salvador was planned by

Virgin Mary, and Xango, the god of thunder, is transposed into St George the dragonslayer. Syncretist cults such as *umbanda* may also include the god of war, Ogun, god-like figures called *orixás*, and demon-like forces, *exus*, which are part of African rituals.

Umbanda belongs to a mystic movement called "spiritism", which includes African-inspired figures as well as Brazilian mediums and semi-deities such as Pai João, Caboclo and Pomba Gira, plus the mystical theological concepts of Allan Kardec, a European. Some of the most popular images on *umbanda* and spiritist altars are St Cosme and St Damyan, St George

Muslim freedmen and slaves (*malês*), but the revolt was foiled just before it was about to begin, and the state's response was drastic repression. In the 20th century, Muslim immigrants from the Middle East came to Brazil, and have since built some impressive mosques in many different regions around the country, especially in and around São Paulo.

Religious blending

The mixture of Amerindian, African and European cults results in a unique form of syncretism – blending of religions – in Brazil, where Catholic Santa Barbara is Iansã of the Afro-Brazilian cults, where Iemanjá, the goddess of the sea, often assumes the form of the

slaying the dragon, Iemanjá in a white flowing dress, or the cigar-smoking figure of Pai João.

Santo Daime, one of the world's fastest-growing cults, was created by Raimundo Irineu Serra, who migrated to the Amazon forest from the northeast. He Christianized shamanic traditions at the start of the 20th century.

During 12-hour rituals accompanied by music, followers ingest a potent drink made from *ayahuasca* (derived from an Amazon vine) in order to gain self-understanding and experience God or the Internal Superior Self. *Ayahuasca* was renamed Daime because of the invocations the faithful make while consuming the drink: *Dai-me amor, dai-me luz* (Give me love, give me light).

Brasília's millennium sect

Thought by believers to be the center of a magnetic field giving off cosmic energy, the city of Brasília has attracted various modern religious cults. The best known is the Vale do Amanhecer (Valley of the Dawn) movement, based in a nearby valley of the same name. Believers have built an enormous temple filled with new deities and religious figures that include Aluxá, Jaruá, White Arrow – an Amerindian deity – and the medium Aunt Neiva, the founder of the movement. Situated about 60 km (35 miles) from Brasília, the Valley of the Dawn occupies 9 hectares (22 acres) of land and is currently the largest such center in Brazil *(see page 307)*.

Aunt Neiva founded the movement in 1959, and moved to the town of Planaltina 10 years later. Today the Valley has more than 30,000 inhabitants, and the movement has also spread to other countries.

On arriving at the Valley of the Dawn, visitors see dozens of women in long robes decorated with silver-sequined stars and quarter-moons. The men wear brown trousers, black shirts and ribbons that cross their chests, and they carry a leather shield. These are the mediums who lead thousands of the sect.

Aunt Neiva believed that there were about 100,000 Brazilians with the powers of a medium, and she herself registered 80,000, according to her follower Mario Sassi. "Two-thirds of humanity will disappear at the end of the millennium, but we, here in the Valley of the Dawn, will be saved," Aunt Neiva preached. The millennium has passed and they are still there. They believe that the third millennium started many years ago, and we are now in a period of improvement and transition. However, with more and more people, apparently unconnected to the movement, moving to the valley, a high number of criminal incidents have been registered.

Patron saint

The patron saint of Brazil is Nossa Senhora Aparecida, the Virgin of the Conception. Three centuries ago, a broken terracotta image "appeared" in a fisherman's net in the Paraíba River between Rio and São Paulo. Today, the Basilica of Aparecida, on the highway between the two cities, houses the terracotta image and receives more than 7 million pilgrims a year *(see page 91)*. A number of legends, stories, superstitions, and presumed miracles have been woven around the image. In 1999, a religious theme park linked to the shrine was constructed at a cost of US$70 million.

Another popular representation of the Virgin Mary is Our Lady of the "O", a euphemism for the pregnant Virgin. The upper clergy tried to suppress the cult of this figure in favor of Our Lady of the Conception (without a

In the late 19th century, a preacher called Antônio Conselheiro founded the autonomous community of Canudos in Bahia, where land was shared collectively, and there were no police or taxes, landlords or servants. Liberated slaves had equal access to land. This soon became a well-populated town – in four years it was the largest in Bahia, after Salvador. The draining of labor from the surrounding farms and Conselheiro's anti-republican position meant it was only a matter of of time before the state and landed interests struck back. Conselheiro's men repelled four heavily armed military incursions, but in 1897 the army got the upper hand and slaughtered thousands of his followers.

FAR LEFT: religious procession in Salvador. **LEFT:** the trappings of Christianity and an Afro-Brazilian cult. **RIGHT:** a statue of the revered Padre Cicero.

distended belly). Some Brazilians call this figure "Our Lady of March 25," to mark Christ's conception nine months before Christmas. Due to the perils of childbirth, Our Lady of the "O" is worshiped by pregnant women.

Curative properties of saints

Other saints are believed to have therapeutic or healing properties. Santa Lucia is supposed to cure bad eyesight and blindness. Santa Barbara protects worshipers against lightning. São Brás, the Bishop, protects believers against sore throats and choking on fish bones. Another popular saint, carved in wood or

molded in plaster of Paris, is St Jude, who always wears tall boots. This is the saint who is known in Europe as the patron of lost causes.

Many images that once bore a religious connotation have survived without their former mystical aura. One example is *carrancas*, which were wooden figureheads attached to the prows of paddle-wheel steamers and other vessels sailing the São Francisco River from 1850 to about 1950. Today, on the beach in Nazare, Portugal, fishermen paint eyes on the prows of ships to "see" the dangers underwater. Similar prow figures served the same purpose in Guiné and other parts of Africa. The Brazilian *carrancas* were carved in the form of monsters, originally to frighten off the

spirits of the waters that were a menace to shipping. The *carranca* gazed downward, and the crew aboard ship saw only the elaborate mane, so as not to be frightened by its terrible features. The São Francisco River is rich with legends of water spirits, such as the *caboclo da agua* (the backwoodsman of the water), who send ships down to a watery grave.

Religious art

A popular subject for Brazilian artists through the centuries has been the crooked angel. Some of the carved and gilded angels in Salvador's São Francisco church and other churches in Bahia have malicious features – they are often depicted as wall-eyed or cross-eyed.

As well as angels, the arts and crafts fairs of Brazil are full of sculptures of them the saints. Among the most original of them re the no-neck images of Santa Ana made by woodcarvers from the northeastern state of Ceará. In *umbanda* shops you can find beautiful and elaborate religious artifacts, as well as potions and concoctions to grant wishes or cure maladies. And you will often find Indians selling artifacts on the street that mimic objects with spiritual meaning.

The state of Minas Gerais is home to hundreds of baroque churches that bear testimony to that institution's wealth and power. In Ouro Preto, Mariana, and Diamantina you will see altars covered in gold leaf and sculptures by the famous Aleijadinho who, even when crippled by disease, tied chisels to his hands and went on carving eloquent soapstone statues of saints and prophets (*see page 57*).

VOTIVE OFFERINGS

The church in Juazeiro do Norteis filled with ex-votos (votive offerings) carved in wood in the shape of injured limbs or parts of human bodies. When someone is cured of an illness they carve an image of the wounded part of their body and, after making a pilgrimage to Juazeiro, hang the carving in the ex voto chamber of the church as a token of gratitude.

Churches in Caninde and Salvador are filled with ex-votos, too, the more recent ones made of wax at the encouragement of the priests, who melt them down and sell them as candles. There are delicately carved femurs, tibias, hands, elbows, pock-marked heads, eyes, perforated abdomens, and so on.

The cult of Padre Cícero

Some of Padre Cícero's followers honor him by wearing black on the day of his death (June 20). Cícero was considered a messiah who would turn the dry backlands into a green garden of paradise, where hunger and poverty would cease. A verdant valley was named the *Horto* or Garden of Gethsemane, and the city of Juazeiro do Norte was called the New Jerusalem. Some of his followers even collected his nail clippings, believing they had magical properties.

Padre Cícero first gained fame when an elderly woman, Maria Araujo, received the

SLAVES CHURCH

The Igreja do Rosário dos Pretos in Salvador was built by slaves and freedmen in the 18th century as they were barred from attending "white" churches. Mass is still said in the Yoruba language, brought from Nigeria.

of plaster of Paris images of him have been sold throughout the country.

Through woodcarvings, songs and poems published in chapbook form, the Padre Cícero legend has been carried forward. A statue of the priest was built in Horto in the 1960s, and his church has become a popular shrine that annually manages to attract thousands of followers.

host from his hands at Mass in the church in Juazeiro do Norte, then fell to the floor in convulsions. Blood in the form of the "sacred heart" was said to appear on the host. Balladeers wandered throughout the *sertão* singing the praises of the miraculous priest and the "miracle of the Sacred Heart," More skeptical observers suggested that Maria Araujo suffered from tuberculosis and had coughed up blood, or suffered from bleeding gums.

Hundreds of woodcarvers have sculpted images of Padre Cícero, and literally millions

Since the death of Padre Cícero, numerous messianic cults have appeared, of which the most famous is found in the northeast, centered around Frei Damião, a Calabrian priest who arrived in Brazil in his youth and who preaches with the same fire-and-brimstone images used by other prophetic figures over the past three centuries.

Religious dates

If you intend to travel during a national holiday, which is usually a religious date, you should book hotels and flights well in advance. This applies especially to Semana Santa – Holy Week – which precedes Easter and is celebrated 40 days after Ash Wednesday. ❑

LEFT: a dazzling gilt altar in the Igreja da Ordem Terceira de São Francisco in Salvador.
ABOVE: paying tribute at Bom Jesus da Lapa, Bahia.

THE BODY BEAUTIFUL

Brazil is perceived as a land of beautiful people, but the constant search for a beautiful face and body – which can revolve around healthy exercise and clean living – increasingly involves expensive, invasive surgical procedures, as aging becomes the biggest taboo

Brazil was known as the land of beautiful people long before supermodel Gisele Bundchen strode onto the international catwalks in 1994. Images of gorgeous half-naked women in glitter and feathers, gyrating to samba, captured the global imagination long ago. And then there are those world-famous Brazilian bikini bottoms – two tiny triangles held together with string, giving them the nickname "dental floss."

There are, however, signs that *cariocas* are tired of this image. In 2005 Rio de Janeiro's legislative assembly approved a ban on post-cards displaying images of women in these tiny, revealing bikinis. And, while beachwear may be minimal, topless bathing has never caught on in Brazil, even in the most liberal of settings, and local people can be disapproving of foreign visitors stripping off.

Work that body

The cult of the beautiful people is rooted in the country's everyday life, and particularly in Rio de Janeiro. It is dubbed the "marvelous city," and it seems as if its inhabitants aspire to be as physically perfect as the city's stunning geo-graphical features. Every morning, as soon as the sun rises, image-hungry creatures appear on Ipanema beach, the epicenter of chic.

Trim, tanned octogenarians in tiny trunks salute the sun in a series of yoga stretches. Hulking teenagers hang from iron bars and heave themselves on and off gym equipment on the beach, where you will also find groups doing aerobics, t'ai chi, Pilates or just a simple

stretch class. In Brazil, the obsession with the perfect body is a democratic one, where age or poverty are no barriers in the quest for beauty. The philosophy is that if you want a good body, you have to work at it. And work they do, squeezed into skintight suits, attached to pedometers, weight belts, or heart-rate moni-tors as they strive for physical fitness.

Cities in the south of Brazil rival those in the United States in obsessing about health. Health food shops are found throughout the country, and "natural" restaurants are the latest craze. Wheatgrass (known as *clorofila*) is widely available as a supplement in fresh juices, and is said to eliminate toxins and generally cleanse the body.

LEFT: beauty on the beach.
RIGHT: keeping fit can be hard work.

Plastic people

Body fascism is the flip side of this phenomenon, in which individuals try to live up to an ideal. It is virtually impossible to be a model, or even an actor, without plastic surgery.

Juliana Borges, who became Miss Brazil in 2001, and competed in the Miss Universe competition the following year, made no secret of the fact that she had undergone 19 surgical procedures – and she was only 22 years old. "Plastic surgery made me more beautiful and gave me confidence in myself and the perfect measurements that won me this title," she said afterwards. She is not alone – more and more beauty competition contenders are resorting to cosmetic surgery of various kinds.

Brazil is the cosmetic surgery capital of the world, and the world's foremost plastic surgeon is Brazilian Ivo Pitanguy, who has a state-of-the-art clinic in the Botafogo area of Rio de Janeiro, which he founded in 1963.

Daily, Rio's clinics – not all anything like as reputable as Dr Pitanguy's – do battle against wrinkles, blemishes, fatty deposits, cellulite, sagging bottoms, imperfect noses, and breasts that are never quite the right size. The struggle to rejuvenate *carioca* matrons or to give the young the perfect body involves all the tech-

DETOX IN COMFORT

Spa resorts are a relatively new concept in Brazil, but the focus on beautiful – and healthy – bodies means that they are now much in demand, and the incredibly scenic landscape and seemingly endless coastline make an obvious setting for this kind of holiday. Ilha Grande on the Costa Verde and Guarujá, some 70 km (40 miles) from São Paulo, are two places where luxury spas are taking off, offering all kinds of treatments. Programs include massage, spa treatments, yoga sessions, hiking in the rainforest, and sea kayaking, all in beautiful surroundings, with diets specially geared towards detoxification. Some are designed to push you to extremes, others just allow you to indulge.

niques of the profession, and everyone talks quite openly about it.

Going under the knife is not perceived as an act of vanity or a betrayal of self, but as a human right. Top plastic surgeons provide free operations one day a week to the poor in Rio. Maids, and others in very poorly paid service industry jobs, pay for surgery by hire purchase, as those in Europe or the United States would pay for a car. And it's not just women: men between the ages of 35 and 45 – mainly lawyers, economists, and financial executives – have become the new patrons.

In the run-up to Carnival, people practically line up for operations, and surgeons work around the clock. Brazil sometimes runs out of silicone in the period before Carnival when demand for breast and buttock implants reaches record levels. Possible side effects seem to deter no one.

A pale image of beauty

One of the disturbing aspects of Brazil's emphasis on beauty – or the portrayal of it by the media and the advertising industry – is its endemic racism. Huge advertising hoardings are dominated by images of fair-skinned, blonde women. Flick through the pages of any national magazine, turn on the television, and you will notice the same thing. Gisele Bund-

from skin diseases. Vast quantities of Botox are injected daily into the faces of dissatisfied Brazilians. Botox is derived from botulinum toxin, and works by temporarily paralysing muscles. Expression lines on the forehead and around the eyes disappear and lips regain their youthful fullness – at least for a few months, before the procedure has to be repeated.

The advantages of this treatment, as opposed to surgery, are manifold: it is less expensive, less invasive, and much less painful, and has a much shorter recovery time. But it is not just the middle-aged who are undergoing treatment: the young are doing it too, starting in their

chen comes from the south of the country, where a large number of people are descendants of German, Italian, and Polish immigrants, and she is just the most prominent example of the essentially Caucasian idea of beauty that holds sway in Brazil.

Botox bonanza

Non-surgical treatments are acquiring more devotees every day. Many dermatologists claim to be seeing a higher percentage of people seeking aesthetic treatments than patients suffering

twenties, obviously believing that prevention is better than cure.

Setting a trend

In the United States, the UK, and many parts of Europe in recent years, plastic surgery and chemical implants for purely cosmetic reasons have ceased to be the province of the rich and famous, and become increasingly prevalent, and openly discussed. Television programs such as *Extreme Makeover* have no shortage of candidates who will undergo surgery and other procedures on camera, in order to get the work done for free. But for better or for worse, beautification is one field in which Brazil can claim to have led the way. ❑

LEFT: getting a sun tan is a serious matter.
ABOVE: model Gisèle Bundchen typifies the idea that blonde is beautiful.

CARNIVAL

Carnival in Brazil has a long and fascinating history.
While Rio's festivities are the best-known, other
cities, particularly Salvador, have equally loud,
colorful, and riotous celebrations of their own

Brazilians are some of the most musical, and most fun-loving, people in the world, and Carnival, "The Biggest Party on Earth," is deeply rooted in the nation's ethnic and racial heritage.

Carnival's roots are European, although experts disagree over the origin of the name. According to one school of thought, the word *carnival* comes from the Latin *carrum novalis,* a Roman festival float. A more probable explanation is that it stems from the Latin *carnem levare*, "putting away meat," since Carnival marks the last days before Lenten abstinence.

The Romans had more than 100 festivals during their year, of which the most famous was the December Saturnalia, marked by the temporary disappearance of class distinctions. Slaves and masters dined at the same table, drank the same wine and slept with the same women. Elements of Saturnalia were incorporated into Christmas and Carnival.

Pranksters and Carnival balls

In Brazil, pre-Lenten observances have existed since colonial days. However, until the 20th century they were a time for the prankster rather than for good-natured celebration. This aspect of Carnival was called *entrudo* and featured stink bombs and water balloons. *Entrudo* was so bad, decent citizens spent Carnival locked in their homes. One of those who didn't was architect Grandjean de Montigny, who died of pneumonia in 1850 after being doused with water during Carnival. It wasn't until the early

---

PRECEDING PAGES: having a ball at Carnival. **LEFT:** Carnival glitz and glitter. **RIGHT:** you can look as silly as you like at Carnival time.

1900s that a stop was finally put to *entrudo*. The indiscriminate tossing of confetti and streamers is all that remains of the bad old days.

The fancy-dress ball was part of European Carnival as early as the 18th century. Paris and Venice had the best masked Carnival balls. This custom hit Rio in 1840 with a chic event at the Hotel Itália on Praça Tiradentes, but it lost money, and it wasn't until 1846 that another one was held, this time in São Cristóvão. The first modern Carnival ball was the High Life, at a Copacabana hotel in 1908. The formal City Ball was inaugurated in 1932 at the Teatro Municipal. By then there were no fewer than 100 fancy-dress balls in Rio de Janeiro at Carnival time.

For Rio's working class, music, dance, and drink were, and still are, the main Carnival diversions. A Portuguese immigrant, José Nogueira Paredes (nicknamed Zé Pereira), is credited with originating the first Carnival club. One of his ideas was to get everybody in the club to play the same kind of drum, creating a powerful, unified sound. This technique became the basis for the modern samba school *bateria* or percussion section.

The working- and middle-class clubs, called *blocos*, *ranchos* or *cordões*, played European-origin ballads known as *choros*. In the 19th century they often had charitable or political

from French history and *Don Quixote* were featured. By 1900 the annual downtown parade of such groups, called *Grandes Sociedades*, had become the highlight of Carnival.

Black Brazilians first became involved in Carnival in the late 19th century, partly due to the severe drought in the northeast in 1877, which brought many freed slaves, along with their music and dance traditions, to Rio.

Today's celebration of Carnival in Rio has three main features: frenzied street events, traditional club balls, and the samba parade.

Street Carnival draws thousands of revelers, many dressed as clowns, television personali-

aims, and were also active off-season. Many of these predominantly white clubs still exist, including the Clube dos Democráticos, which annually kicks off the downtown street Carnival.

Carnival parade

One of the main contributions of the clubs to modern Carnival was the parade, complete with elaborate costumes, wheeled floats, and appropriate musical accompaniment. Parade themes stressed Bible stories, mythology, and literature.

The first parade was organized in 1855 by a group grandly named *O Congresso das Sumidades Carnavalescas*, which marched before an elite audience, including the emperor. Over-dressed Cossacks and tableaux depicting scenes

ties or animals. The most common sight is men dressed as women: for example, the Bloco das Piranhas is a group of men who always turn up kitted out as prostitutes. Another element that has become an integral part of the Rio Carnival scene is the welcome extended to the international gay community, which has served to enrich the social diversity of the event.

Carnival nights belong to the club balls. Among events attracting both *cariocas* and tourists are nightly bashes at the Sírio-Libanês, Flamengo, Fluminense, Scala and Monte-Líbano clubs. The contest for best costume is held at several balls and features outrageous get-ups which depict everything from medieval troubadours to Roman Catholic archbishops.

The samba centerpiece

But the undisputed centerpiece of any Rio de Janeiro Carnival is the main samba school parade. The samba parade is the most African of the Carnival events, due mainly to the popularity of the dance, which is a mix of European folk influences and African techniques. The parade was taken off the streets in 1984 when the Sambódromo, designed by Oscar Niemeyer, with a capacity for 58,825 people, was completed in a record nine months.

Modern samba music dates from the 19th century, when the tones of the former slaves met the stylized European sound of Rio. The recount or develop the theme, and the huge floats must detail it through the media of papier-mâché figures and paintings.

Each school's presentation includes the "opening wing," the *Abre-Alas*, consisting of a group of colorfully costumed *sambistas* marching next to a large float. The float depicts an open book or scroll and is, in effect, the title page of the school's theme. Behind the *Abre-Alas* is a line of formally dressed men, the *Comissão de Frente*, or Board of Directors, who are chosen for their dignified air.

The real event begins with the appearance of the *Porta Bandeira* (Flag Bearer) and the

word "samba" is believed to derive from the Angolan word *semba*, originating in a ceremony in which men were allowed to select female partners from a circle of dancers.

Today the samba schools that parade in the Sambódromo are judged by a government-appointed jury. Each school's presentation must have a central theme, such as a historical event or personality, or an Amerindian legend. The theme embraces every aspect of the school's presentation. Costumes must accord with historical time and place. The samba song must

LEFT: a sea of dancers and Brazilian flags in a Rio street parade.
ABOVE: strutting their stuff in the Sambódromo.

SAMBA SCHOOLS

The first samba school was called *Deixa Falar* (Let Them Talk), founded by black residents of Rio's Estácio district in 1928. Participants followed no fixed route and were poorly organized, but the size of their clever routines made them different. It wasn't long before other black districts set up rival organizations. By 1930, there were five groups and so many spectators that police had to clear an area around Praça Onze for their parade. These early groups practiced on school playgrounds, hence the name samba "schools," There are now 58 registered samba schools. When the state government decided in the 1980s on a special stadium for the annual parade, they built it in Estácio to honor the samba pioneers.

Mestre Sala (Dance Master), dressed in lavish 18th-century formal wear. The *Porta Bandeira* is a female dancer who holds the school flag during an elaborate dance routine with her consort. The bulk of the samba school follows on behind, including the small army of percussion enthusiasts known as the *bateria*. Their role is to maintain a constant rhythm to help other members of the school keep up with the tempo.

Behind the *bateria* are the major samba school *alas*. These groups of *sambistas* illustrate aspects of the school's theme through their costumes. If the theme is an Amazon myth, one of its main *alas* might be *sambistas* dressed as Indians; another could have members dressed as Amazonian animals. The compulsory *ala das Baianas* group consists of dozens of elderly women dressed in the flowing attire of Bahia. They honor the early history of samba, although in the 1930s they were all men, who, acting as security guards for the schools, used the billowing dresses to conceal knives and razors.

In between the major *alas* are lavishly costumed individuals depicting the main characters of the school's theme. These are *Figuras de Destaque* (Prominent Figures), often played by local celebrities. The preferred personalities for these roles are voluptuous actresses. There will

THE ALTERNATIVE CARNIVAL

Followers of African-origin religions bring a more mysterious element to Carnival in the northeast. In Salvador, performers of the *afoxé* conduct subdued, reverent processions during Carnival. They dress in flowing satin robes and carry banners and canopies. Monotonous music, often sung in African languages, provides an eerie accompaniment. In Recife, too, Afro-Brazilians maintain a parallel tradition. Maracatu, like *afoxé*, is a procession that mixes theatrical and musical elements. The central figure is a queen, surrounded by elaborately costumed consorts. Each group is called a nation. The larger the nation, the more consorts, counselors, and ambassadors surround its queen.

also be groups of dancers known as *passistas* – agile young people who often stop to perform complicated dance routines.

Visual extravaganza

Finally, there are the giant Carnival floats, *Carros Alegóricos*, created from papier-mâché and styrofoam, which present the major motifs of a school's theme. The impact of the floats is primarily visual, and critics argue that they detract from the music which, they insist, should be the mainstay of the parade (*see box opposite*).

ABOVE: Filhos de Gandhi, an *afoxé* group take part in Salvador's Carnival.
RIGHT: pounding out the samba rhythm.

Carnival in the northeast

Rio is not the only Brazilian city with a tradition of fervent Carnival revelry. Many experienced travelers prefer Carnival in the northeast's coastal cities of Salvador and Recife, where non-stop street action is the highlight.

The centerpiece of Carnival in Salvador (capital of Bahia state) is a glittering music festival on wheels called *Trio Elétrico*. It began in 1950 when a hillbilly singing act called *Dodô and Osmar* drove a beat-up convertible through the city during Carnival week playing pop and folk tunes. Instead of convertibles, Bahian musicians started using flat-bed trucks with flashing lights, streamers and elaborate sound systems – and added a third performer.

Today, there are dozens of *Trio Elétrico* groups. Praça Castro Alves was the traditional headquarters of Bahian Carnival, but increasingly the Barra-Ondina stretch is becoming the focus. The *Trio Elétrico* repertoire is dominated by samba; by a hopped-up northeast dance music called *frevo*; by a new style called *deboche*, which blends traditional Carnival sounds with rock and roll; and by *axé*, a highly erotic, rhythmic dance music.

The pre-eminent Carnival music of Recife (capital of Pernambuco state) is *frevo*. While Carnival in Bahia moves horizontally, as fans follow musicians through the streets, in Pernambuco the movement is vertical – dancers seem to leap up and down like ballerinas in double time. *Frevo* is a corruption of the Portuguese word for boiling – *fervura* – because it ignites the passions of its listeners. It may have evolved as a musical accompaniment to capoeira *(see page 106)*, the northeastern dance and martial art. But modern *frevo* has been simplified musically, and its listeners freed to invent their own dance routines. The best venue for *frevo* is the Recife suburb of Olinda. Olinda residents are Carnival purists who still dance only to acoustic instruments. Three-meter (10-ft) wood-and-cloth Carnival figures are another feature of Olinda's celebrations.

Skilled *frevo* dancers, called *passistas*, wear knee britches and carry colorful umbrellas. The attire is a throwback to colonial days and the umbrellas may derive from the ornate canopies used by African kings. ❏

HOW SAMBA BECAME BIG BUSINESS

The man who practically invented the form of the contemporary samba parade, Joãozinho Trinta, attacked the view that Carnival has become too dependent on visual extravaganza saying, "Only the rich enjoy poverty. The poor want luxury." He also pointed out that strong visual elements were needed to make the parade appeal to foreign tourists and, especially, local television viewers.

Now residents and tourists alike can learn about, and appreciate, samba all year round. Rio's city government has inaugurated the US$40-million Cidade do Samba (City of Samba), where visitors can see how samba school artists put together costumes and parade floats. Top samba musicians and dancers perform frequently. The site is a cross between a theme-park attraction and a Hollywood backlot. Rio's Samba School League is still looking for sponsors to help build a proposed Samba Museum for the same venue in the Gamboa neighborhood, near Rio de Janeiro's docks.

In recent years, the parade has become big business. Companies including Nestlé and Petrobras, Brazil's state oil company, swap sponsorship dollars for community good will. In 2006, parade-winner Vila Isabel obtained a US$1 million grant from Venezuelan state oil corporation PDVSA. The samba school's theme was Latin American unity and prominently featured Venezuelan national hero Simon Bolívar.

FESTIVALS

Brazil is a year-round festival packed with celebrations involving music, dance, and, quite often, fireworks. Many of the festivals are based on Catholic saints' days, but even for the pious these usually involve a lot of fun alongside the religious observances

Festivals and celebrations in Brazil, as in most Catholic countries, tend to follow the liturgical calendar. After Carnival, the next big event on that calendar is the colorful *Festa do Divino*, held just before Pentecost Sunday (late May or early June). Two of Brazil's most strikingly beautiful colonial-era towns – Alcântara in the northeast state of Maranhão and Paraty, 250 km (150 miles) south of Rio on the coast – feature some classic *Festa do Divino* celebrations.

Townspeople dress in colonial attire, many of them taking the roles of prominent figures from Brazilian history. The climax is a visit from the "emperor," who attends a procession and Mass in the church square. In a gesture of royal magnanimity, he frees prisoners from the town jail. Strolling musicians, called *Folias do Divino*, serenade the townsfolk day and night. Banners are emblazoned with a white dove against a red background, symbolizing the coming of the Holy Spirit to the Apostles amid tongues of fire.

The June festivals

Soon after Pentecost begins one of Brazil's most interesting celebration cycles, the June festivals. Brought to Brazil by the Portuguese, they were originally summer solstice fertility rites, attached to convenient Christian saints' days. The feasts of saints John, Anthony and Peter all fall in June – a good excuse for an entire month of festivities.

The feast of St Anthony, patron of lost possessions and women in search of husbands,

begins on June 12. Strictly religious observances dominate this saint's day, but the feast days for John and Peter are festive and far more secular. St John's days, June 23 and 24, are characterized by brightly illuminated balloons filling the skies and bonfires blazing through the night – though in recent years the authorities have discouraged kerosene-powered balloons, on the grounds that they are fire hazards.

St Peter's feast days are 28 and 29 June. Fireworks, ample food, and drink and folk music, usually played on an accordion, are the main elements for celebrating this occasion. St Peter is especially honored by widows, who place lighted candles on their doorsteps during the two-day festival.

LEFT: Boi-Bumba dancers at Parintins Folk Festival.
RIGHT: celebrating São Sebastião, patron saint of Rio.

Most June festivities take place outdoors. Participants dress up like old-fashioned country people, or *caipiras*. Country music, square dancing and mock wedding ceremonies (at which the bride may appear pregnant) feature at the most authentic June festival parties.

In the São Paulo suburb of Osasco, Brazil's largest bonfire, measuring some 20 meters (70 ft) high, is lit during the last week of June. Consisting entirely of long-burning eucalyptus logs, the fire takes a week to burn itself out.

Brazilian president Lula da Silva is a June festival devotee. He has held one in the Presidential Palace every year since 2003.

October celebrations

October in Brazil is also a month-long cycle of religiously inspired celebrations, including three of Brazil's most characteristic festivals. One of these events, Nossa Senhora de Aparecida, on October 12, is also a national holiday.

In October 1717, "the miracle of Aparecida" occurred in Guaratingueta, situated about halfway between Rio and São Paulo. The colonial governor of São Paulo was passing through the town at lunchtime when he stopped at a fisherman's cottage demanding a meal for his party. The fisherman and two friends hurried to their boats on the Paraíba River but failed to

FESTIVALS IN SALVADOR

At New Year, while the rest of Brazil is honoring Iemanjá, Salvador (Brazil's former capital) celebrates the colorful festival of *Bom Jesus dos Navegantes*. A procession of small craft burdened with streamers and flags carries a statue of the Lord Jesus of Seafarers from the harbor to the Boa Viagem Church. Thousands line the beaches to watch. Legend has it that sailors participating in the event will never die by drowning. (A similar procession takes place on the same day in Angra dos Reis, 150 km/90 miles south of Rio.) The tradition dates from the mid-18th century.

In mid-January, Salvador prepares for another spectacle unique to this city that so loves pageantry – the *Festa do Bonfim*. Central to the event, which takes place in a

Salvador suburb, is the Washing of the Steps at the Bonfim Church. Scores of Bahian women, dressed in traditional flowing garments, scour the stairs of the church until they are sparkling white. Crowds throng the tree-shaded church square to witness the women's labor.

Visitors may take part in a Bahian tradition by buying colorful Bonfim ribbons from hawkers in the square. Tie the ribbon around your wrist with several knots, each knot being a wish. When the ribbon accidentally breaks, your wishes will be granted – but only if the ribbons were a gift, so the trick is to buy and then exchange them.

Iemanjá, the festival of the Queen of the Seas, is celebrated in Salvador on February 2.

catch any fish. So they prayed. When they cast their nets again, they pulled a small black statue of the Blessed Virgin Mary out of the river. With the image aboard their craft, they landed a catch that nearly burst their nets.

This story quickly spread to the surrounding countryside, and in 1745 a rustic chapel was built to house the statue. Mainly because of the shrine's strategic location on the Rio–São Paulo highway, the cult of Our Lady of Aparecida grew and, in the mid-19th century, a church more grand than the first was built.

The coronation of the original statue in 1931, as the Vatican-anointed patron saint of Brazil,

In comparison, the pretty Igreja de Nossa Senhora da Penha in Rio is hardly imposing, but it has an unusual history. Located atop a 92-meter (300-ft) cone-shaped hill, Penha represents one of Brazil's oldest lay religious organizations. Penitents can be seen climbing its 382 steps on their knees. The order of Penha was founded in the 17th century by a Portuguese landowner called Baltazar Cardoso, who believed he had been saved from death in a hunting accident by divine intervention. The incident took place in Portugal, near a mountain called Penha. Later in the century, the lay order that Cardoso founded as a result of his experience transferred its activities

made Aparecida the country's chief religious shrine. This increased the desire to build a bigger church, and by 1978, the main outlines of the cathedral were completed. The second church, the world's largest after St Peter's in Rome, still stands on a hill overlooking the newer one.

The latter basilica is a massive structure quite out of proportion with its surroundings, but this cathedral, with its enormous nave and network of chapels and galleries, is visited every year by about 7 million pilgrims. About 1 million visit Aparecida in October alone.

LEFT: the ritual of washing the steps during the Festa do Bonfim in Salvador.
ABOVE: fervent devotees of Círio de Nazaré.

to Brazil, and it found a rocky cone in Rio that was a small-scale copy of Penha in Portugal. The first church was built on the rock in 1635, and two more later went up on the same site. The third, built in 1871, now plays host every year to the Penha October festivities. Not only do worshipers participate in religious ceremonies every Sunday in October, they also enjoy a festival at the base of the hill, renowned for its good food, abundant beer and live music.

Festival in the Amazon

October also marks the chief religious observance in the Brazilian Amazon – the festival of Círio de Nazaré in the city of Belém, at the mouth of the Amazon. Belém annually attracts tens of thousands of penitents and tourists for the remarkable procession, a four-hour cortége along 5 km (3 miles) of streets on the second Sunday of October. A thick rope, 400 meters (1,300 ft) long, is used to drag a colorfully decorated carriage bearing the image of Our Lady of Nazareth. Pilgrims who succeed in grabbing hold of the rope believe they are granted favors. When the image reaches the basilica, a 15-day festival, similar to the Penha festivities, begins.

The Círio de Nazaré story tells of a mulatto hunter named José de Sousa, who found an image of the Virgin in the forest. It was later placed in a chapel where it was said to effect

Santa Claus. Another aspect of Christmas that hasn't changed is the Christmas Eve supper. Turkey, *rabanada* (a kind of French toast) and ham still adorn many dinner tables.

New Year's wishes

New Year's Eve in Brazil rivals Carnival for fun, music, and color. In recent years, Salvador (Bahia) and the São Paulo resort of Guarujá have vied with each other for New Year's Eve spectacle, fireworks and tourist dollars, but the most popular New Year's Eve celebration takes place in Rio de Janeiro, where crowded club balls are a rehearsal for Carnival. An elaborate

miraculous cures. The first procession displaying the image took place in 1763. The rope was added only in the 19th century.

Christmas

Christmas is the chief religious and family observance. Brazilian children believe that Santa Claus (Papai Noel) distributes gifts to families around the world on Christmas Eve. He enters through an open window, and leaves presents in shoes that have been left for this purpose on the floor or the window sill.

The contemporary celebration of Christmas in Brazil had its origin in the turn-of-the-century influence of German immigrants, who introduced the Christmas tree, gift-giving and

firework display splashes brilliant, many-colored hues across the velvet sky at midnight.

The best place to observe New Year's celebrations is on one of Rio's beaches, especially Copacabana. Hundreds of *Filhas de Santo*, white-robed priestesses of the Afro-Brazilian religions, launch wooden vessels on the waters. The tiny boats are filled with flowers and gifts for Iemanjá, the Queen of the Seas. When the tide carries one of the boats to sea it means Iemanjá will grant the gift-giver's wish. Very often, the wish is simple: to spend another New Year's Eve on the beach at Copacabana. ❑

LEFT: New Year's Eve fireworks at Copacabana.
ABOVE: lighting a candle for Iemanjá.

Boi-Bumba

The Amazon city of Parintins, 400 km (250 miles) east of Manaus, has found a way to make a centuries-old cowboy tale into an annual festival of music, color, and imagination that rivals Carnival. The last three days of June mark the Parintins Folk Festival, organized annually since 1913 and centered around a recounting of the *Boi-Bumba* fable. Two rival groups – Caprichoso and Garantido – vie with each other for popular acclaim as they fill the town with banners and balloons in their respective colors, blue-and-white for Caprichoso and red-and-white for Garantido. Each group, composed of up to 3,000 marchers and 500 musicians, parades through the streets for its annual staging of the *Boi-Bumba* legend. The best show, based on costumes, music, and adherence to Amazon folklore, is proclaimed the winner.

The story itself reads like a folk opera. *Boi-Bumba* recounts the tale of a black ranch hand named Francisco whose pregnant wife, Catirina, pleads for a "special meal" of succulent bull's tongue. Francisco obliges by slaughtering the ranch owner's favorite bull. But his action turns him into a fugitive. In the trackless jungle, Francisco meets a native shaman and his luck changes. Together they conjure up the Amazon spirits, who bring the favored bull back to life. Now, it's the ranch owner's turn to slaughter a bull as he welcomes back the prodigal cowpoke.

The *Boi-Bumba* legend offers broad scope for depicting Amazon jungle animals and colorful characters from regional folklore. Costumes, especially the headdress representing the bull, have become more elaborate with each retelling. The story is acted out through intricate dance routines to the beat of the *toada*, an hypnotic rhythm based not on African traditions like samba but on Amazon Indian music. Each presentation can last up to three hours.

As with Carnival, the Parintins Folk Festival has become somewhat commercialized in recent years. Laser shows and fireworks have been added. Big beer companies have emerged as sponsors. Some of the better-known *toada* singers have released albums and turned professional. As many as 50,000 spectators turn up every year for the three days of shows, parades, and regional cuisine, arriving by boat and plane, since Parintins has no road links to the outside world. Meanwhile, in 2006 Parintins become the first Brazilian municipality with city-wide WIMAX Internet access, making it totally plugged in while still geographically remote.

Originally called *Bumba-Meu-Boi*, the story and folk dance behind the festivities are thought to have originated in the coastal state of Maranhão in the 18th century. They were based on European models but modified by the region's black slaves. In some retellings, ranch hand Francisco becomes Father Francisco, or Chico, a black slave. The hand of the Portuguese Jesuits can be seen in the themes of death and resurrection, flight and redemption. As in the Old Testament, the prodigal is always received "with great rejoicing," in this case a good excuse for explosive music and dance.

Folkloric groups in Maranhão still make *Bumba-Meu-Boi* presentations in June. The tradition is also kept alive in Manaus and other Amazon basin cities, and in other Brazilian states, but there is no rival for Parintins when it comes to fervor and spectacle. In the southern states, it is called *Boi-de-Mamao* or *Boizinho*. In some parts of the northeast, it is *Boi-de-Reis*. The phrase *Bumba-Meu-Boi* is akin to the American cowboy chant "Get along, little doggies."

The Great Drought of 1877 sent thousands of farm workers from Maranhão to the Amazon in search of work as rubber-tappers. The *Bumba-Meu-Boi* tradition they brought with them was gradually enriched by Amazon music and folklore, making it one of the most complete mixtures of Amerindian, European, and African cultural elements in Brazil. ❑

RIGHT: animal figures loom large.

FOOD

The seafood and river fish are fresh from the water, the beef melts in your mouth, and the tropical fruits are delicious. Ice-cold beer, and the national drink, *caipirinha*, are good accompaniments, and, of course, there's an awful lot of coffee

From giant Amazonian river fish to succulent steaks, and with an abundance of tropical fruits and vegetables, Brazilian food offers something for all tastes and appetites. The most traditional dishes are variations on Portuguese or African foods, but there is a wonderful variety of foods, reflecting Brazil's size and the influence of its many immigrant groups. Seafood, sushi, barbecued meat, Italian dishes, and delicious salads are widely available. However, the staple diet for many Brazilians still consists of rice, beans and *farinha* – dried, ground manioc.

A favorite throughout the country is the *churrasco,* or barbecue, which originated when the southern gauchos roasted meat over open fires. Most *churrascarias* offer a *rodizio* option: for a set price, you eat all you wish from a variety of tender meats selected from the spit.

Brazilians enjoy hot pepper *(pimenta)* and local *malagueta* chilies, but peppery sauce is served separately, to allow for personal choice. Many restaurants prepare their own sauce, sometimes jealously guarding the recipe.

In many restaurants a portion is large enough for two people, and it is perfectly acceptable (except in the smartest places) to ask for a dish to share. *Comida a kilo* restaurants (literally meaning food by weight) are great places where you can get a wide choice of cheap, usually good-quality dishes. Because you help yourself you can sample unfamiliar foods, and you are not limited by a poor knowledge of Portuguese.

Bahian cooking

The spiciest Brazilian food is found in Bahia, where an African influence can be tasted in the *dendé* palm oil and coconut milk *(see page 229*

for more on Bahian cooking). One of the great Brazilian dishes, *feijoada*, originated in Bahia. It consists of black beans simmered with a variety of dried, salted, and smoked meats (and often the tail, ears, and feet of a pig). It was developed as food for slaves, whose masters ate all the better cuts of meat, but is now considered Brazil's national dish (although it is not found everywhere). *Feijoada* for Saturday lunch is an institution in Rio de Janeiro. Hotels vie with each other to serve the best *feijoada.* The meats are served in separate bowls, so you know what you are eating, and it is accompanied by white rice, finely shredded kale *(couve)*, *farofa* (toasted manioc root meal), and sliced oranges. Oranges may seem a strange accompaniment, but they provide a perfect tangy foil for the richness of the dish.

Portuguese cooking

One of the Portuguese imports that is popular in Brazil is *bacalhau* (dried, salted cod). On sale in shops and markets it looks like sheets of stiff, gray cardboard, but when soaked and cooked it is transformed. It is most often served in rissole-like balls – *bolinhos de bacalhau* – which are meltingly rich. Another Portuguese dish is *cozido*, consisting of stewed meats and vegetables (usually several root vegetables, squash, cabbage and/or kale) served with broth.

In the Amazon, a few exotic dishes can be found, including those prepared with *tucupi* (manioc leaves, which numb the tongue). The rivers produce a great range of fish, including piranha and the giant pirarucu. In some parts of the south, the cuisine reflects a German influence, and Italian and Japanese immigrants brought their culinary skills to São Paulo, where there are some excellent restaurants.

Snacks

Salgadinhos are Brazilian savory snacks, often served as appetizers with a beer, or as a quick snack at lunch counters – *lanchonetes* – a Brazil-

Regional specialties

Specialties include seafood dishes in the northeast and along the coast. Try *peixe a Brasileiro*, a delicious fish stew served with *pirão* (manioc root meal cooked with broth from the stew until it attains the consistency of porridge). In the inland areas of the northeast, tasty dishes include *carne seca* or *carne de sol* (dried salted beef, often served with squash) and roast kid. Minas Gerais has a hearty pork-and-bean cuisine – the tasty pork sausage is called *linguiça* – and *queijo minas* cheese is good.

LEFT: *acarajé* is a typical Bahian dish.
ABOVE: a tempting array of regional specialties, served in traditional earthenware pots.

GUARANÁ

A fruit that is rarely seen but widely consumed is *guaraná*. The reddish, seed-filled fruit is borne, in the Amazonian wild, on woody vines that seek the sun in the rainforest by climbing up other trees. The seeds are highly prized and have been used by the indigenous population for centuries. *Guaraná* was rediscovered in the 20th century; it can be found in capsules, powder or paste form. Its chemical composition is akin to that of ginseng, high in caffeine and other, reputedly aphrodisiac, substances. Visitors and residents are most likely to encounter the product in its canned form, in the refreshing, sparkling soft drink Guaraná, whose sales rival those of the cola producers.

ian alternative to the US-style fast-food outlets that are also evident throughout the country. *Salgadinhos* are unusually small pastries stuffed with cheese, chicken, palm heart, and so on. Other tasty snack foods include *pão de queijo* (a cheesy bread) and *pastel* (two layers of a thinly rolled, deep-fried, pasta-like dough with a filling sealed inside). Instead of french fries, try *aipim frito* (deep-fried manioc root).

Desserts and *docinhos*

Most desserts are very sweet, and are made from fruit, coconut, egg yolk, or milk. Portuguese-style egg yolk desserts are delicious, especially *quindim* (a rich, sweet egg yolk and coconut custard). The custard makes another appearance in *olhos de sogra* (mother-in-law's eyes), in which it is used to stuff prunes. Condensed milk, boiled up into super-sweet *doce de leite*, is a perennial favorite. *Docinhos* – little sweets – consumed at all times of the day, are just miniature versions of these desserts.

Fruits and juices

Watermelon, papaya, pineapple, and bananas are among the vast array of fruits on offer. There may also be some with which you are unfamiliar, such as the pink, pellet-like *acerola*. It is used mainly for juice, and is said to contain the highest concentration of Vitamin C of any fruit in the world. Guava fruit, yellow on the outside and a surprising pink inside, is extremely perishable, and so is frequently made into preserves. Sticky guava paste, *goiabada*, contrasts with sharp white cheese in a favorite Brazilian dessert, known as *Romeu e Julieta*.

Rio's juice bars are great places in which to familiarize yourself with the local fruits. There's a vast choice – *açaí, acerola, graviola,* as well as fruits that will be more familiar. Or you can opt for a *vitamina*, a thick, creamy shake that will include banana with one or two other types of fruit, and sometimes oat flakes or wheat germ, and is very similar to what is now marketed abroad as a "smoothie." If you are watching calories, you should ask for *sem açúcar* (without sugar). ❑

RIGHT: Regular local markets, selling an extensive selection of fresh fruit and vegetables, are perfect examples of the country's agricultural abundance.

ABOVE: Although cayenne pepper is readily available, it is only in Bahia state that food is spicy hot – or served with an optional hot sauce. In the rest of the country cooks use just a pinch, to give food a piquant flavor.

LEFT: Seafood is plentiful all along Brazil's coast, but the northeast region has a particular reputation for its fish, shrimp, crabs, and lobster. One of the tastiest varieties of fish is *badejo*, a sea bass with firm white meat.

BELOW: One of Brazil's finest features is the wonderful range of fruit, such as fresh guavas. There's always something exotic in season, and most make great juice.

Brazil and coffee *(café)* are synonymous with each other. Money earned from coffee sales boosted the country's economy in the early 20th century, and it is still one of Brazil's most successful exports.

Brazilian coffee is roasted dark, ground fine, prepared strong, and drunk with plenty of sugar. Coffee with hot milk *(café com leite)* is the traditional breakfast beverage. Once breakfast is over, it is served black in tiny demitasse cups. These *cafezinhos* (little coffees), offered to visitors to any home or office, are served piping-hot at all *botequins* – male-dominated stand-up bars. There are even *botequins* that serve only *cafezinho*. However you like it, Brazilian coffee makes the perfect ending to a good meal. Decaffeinated coffee is now available in supermarkets, but as Brazilians do not favor the concept, finding it in restaurants may still be difficult.

LEFT: *Feijoada* is regarded as Brazil's national dish. It consists of black beans, and a variety of dried, salted meats. It was originally made out of leftovers to feed slaves.

ABOVE: Cashew nuts grow in abundance in Brazil and are particularly prevalent in Bahian dishes. They also make popular snacks.

BELOW RIGHT: Chunks of sugarcane *(cana)* are sold on sticks as a snack, and are particularly popular with children.

LEFT: Green tea *(chimarrão)*, sipped through a silver straw fitted with a strainer, is a *gaucho* tradition still favored in southern Brazil.

A PASSION FOR SOCCER

In a game played with passion all over the world, Brazil – the only five-times winner of the World Cup – is pre-eminent. The "beautiful game" is also a great leveler, arousing equal enthusiasm in people right across the social spectrum

Brazilians did not invent soccer, they just perfected it. Today Brazil is probably as well known around the world for its unique style of soccer as it is for its coffee or Carnival.

The game arrived in the country just before the turn of the 20th century, brought to São Paulo by a young Brazilian-born Englishman named Charles Miller. Upon Miller's return to Brazil as a young adult, he began to teach soccer to his acquaintances at the São Paulo Athletic Club (SPAC), a British community club. In 1901, a citywide soccer league was formed, of which SPAC were champions in 1902, 1903, and 1904.

But 1904 was the last time a major soccer trophy in Brazil was won by British descendants. Brazilians themselves were quick to learn the game and soon were beating the British at their own sport.

Passion of millions

Today, soccer is an all-consuming passion for millions of Brazilian fans, reaching a peak every four years when soccer's World Cup is organized somewhere in the world. Factory managers and shopkeepers install television sets in the workplace in a mostly futile effort to keep absenteeism to a minimum on the days when the Brazilian squad is playing. In fact, most businesses simply shut down at game time and let their employees watch the matches – and then join the frenzied celebrations when the team wins, which is most of the time.

Known as *futebol* in Brazil, soccer is so hugely popular that some of the world's largest

stadia have been erected around the nation. Rio de Janeiro's giant oval Maracanã Stadium was able to cram in nearly 200,000 people when first built in 1950 (its official record of 183,341 spectators was set on August 8, 1969 when Brazil played Paraguay for a World Cup slot). After a recent refurbishment, the capacity was reduced to today's 103,000 spectators, while comfort and safety were improved: bleachers were divided into five sectors, individual seats were augmented, and boxes were added. Morumbi in São Paulo can hold some 70,000 onlookers, and five other Brazilian facilities can handle 80,000–100,000 fans each.

One of the reasons for soccer's popularity in Brazil is that it is a sport that is readily

LEFT: Ronaldo is fêted after scoring in the 2002 World Cup. **RIGHT:** an enthusiastic supporter.

accessible to all, as no expensive equipment is required, and makeshift pitches can be set up anywhere. The game has attracted many players from Brazil's slums, who see soccer as a ticket out of poverty. Indeed, there are many rags-to-riches tales of shantytown kids who have excelled at the game.

Soccer's greatest players

The richest and most famous of these is Edson Arantes do Nascimento, known to the world by his nickname, Pelé. Legend has it that Pelé, a frail boy from a small city slum in Minas Gerais, had never even owned a pair of shoes

when he was contracted at the age of 15 to play for the Santos Soccer Club. One year later, he helped the national team to Brazil's first World Cup win. And four years later, together with another national soccer legend, bandy-legged dribbling genius Garrincha (Manoel Francisco dos Santos), whom many in Brazil affirm was even better than Pelé, he was instrumental in propelling Brazil to its second consecutive win of the world's most prestigious soccer trophy. Pelé was injured during the 1966 World Cup finals, staged that year in England, as a result of foul play, but in 1970 he was back, and Brazil won the World Cup title for a record third time. By the time he retired in 1977, Pelé had scored an extraordinary 1,300 goals. To date, no other player has even reached 1,000.

Many distinguished commentators consider the 1970 Brazilian squad to be the best ever. The fluid attacking, flexible ball play and clever playmaking, known as *gingado*, the hallmark of Brazilian soccer, enthralled fans around the world. The names of the many great players in that squad – including Pelé, Tostão, Gerson, Jairzinho and Carlos Alberto – are still invoked nostalgically today.

The dream of millions of today's Brazilian youths is to follow Pelé's and Garrincha's examples and play for one of the large metropolitan clubs. And the ultimate honor is to be picked for the national squad.

Unmissable attraction

One thing that really shouldn't be missed while in Brazil is a visit to one of the country's soccer league matches, such as the classic Flamengo

WORLD CUP VICTORIES

Brazil have won the World Cup five times – twice more than any other country.

Sweden 1958: Brazil had its first taste of raising the winner's cup in 1958 when they defeated the host country, Sweden, in the finals (5-2), and the world got a glimpse of the player who would go on to be considered the greatest footballer of all time: 17-year-old Edson Arantes do Nascimento, or Pelé.

Chile 1962: The Brazilian squad won its second World Cup title, beating Czechoslovakia 3-1 during the final match. Garrincha was the top name in a championship marked by violent play throughout the first phase of the tournament.

Mexico 1970: The Brazilian squad, with a host of top play-

ers, was irresistible in 1970, beating Italy 4-1 in the final and winning a coveted third world title. However, it was to be 24 years before Brazil would win another World Cup.

Italy 1994: Led by top goalscorer Romário, Brazil defeated Italy in an emotion-laden final that ended in a 0-0 draw, forcing a penalty shootout, the first time in World Cup history. Coach Carlos Alberto Parreira adopted a more defensive posture, which proved successful.

Japan/South Korea 2002: Brazil overcame a highly regarded German squad 2-0, with two goals by leading scorer, Ronaldo. The country went wild, with millions chanting "*Penta Campeão*" (five-times champion) in the streets in all the cities and towns of the nation.

versus Vasco da Gama or Fluminense (the "Fla-Flu") in the giant Maracanã Stadium. Even if the game itself is dull, the spectacle of the fans is worth the price of admission: at a big match, the fans are as much a part of the action as are the players.

National tournaments

There are two important national soccer tournaments played in Brazil each year. The Brazilian Championship (Brasileirão) is disputed by 20 clubs between March and November. The three top finishers go on to battle other South American squads for the Copa Libertadores,

The other important event is the Brazil Cup (Copa do Brasil) championship, held during the first half of the year, with the top, traditional clubs plus representatives chosen by each state.

Five-times victorious

Brazil has won an unprecedented five World Cup titles *(see box opposite)*, a clear demonstration of the effectiveness of the unique style that has developed in the country and the constant emergence of talented players. Brazil is the only nation that has qualified to play in every World Cup tournament since the event was created in 1930.

and the winner plays the European champion in a final each year in Tokyo. The top seven finishers enter the continent-wide South American Cup tournament.

The day of the final game is effectively a national holiday: if you are visiting the hometown of the national champion on the evening the title is won, brace yourself for an unforgettable experience. Hundreds of thousands of fans will emerge into the streets for a night of carousing that rivals Carnival.

The entire mood of the country can be altered by the success or failure of the national team during the World Cup. In 1970, the third World Cup title win in Mexico gave a tremendous boost to the previously unpopular, dictatorial military government headed by General Emílio Garrastazu Medici.

Future hopes

The 2014 World Cup is scheduled to take place in South America, and Brazil is actively seeking to host the event. The South American Football Federation (CSF) voted to back the country as its candidate, making Brazil the odds-on favorite. ❏

LEFT: you don't need a lot of expensive gear to play football – some even do it with bare feet.
ABOVE: football fans go wild with excitement.

SONG AND DANCE

The vast variety of music in Brazil is matched only by its quality. Whatever your musical taste, you should be happy here, where music takes to the streets as well as to the clubs, bars, and concert halls

O n a Saturday night in any sizeable Brazilian town, a vast musical choice presents itself. Will you tap cutlery to a samba *pagode* in a tile-floored bar, or dance hip-to-hip to the simple rhythm of the *forró*? Try the tango-like ballroom virtuosity of the *gafieira*, or converse over the twinkling swirls of *choro* played on mandolins and violas? Alternatively, you could smooch to sensuous bossa novas in the bars of Ipanema once haunted by The Girl. Or queue to see ear-bleeding techno-rock bands or hear exhilarating drum-and-bass hip-hop and electronica DJs perform in small city clubs and bars, or hangar-like *favela* venues from where baile-funk spins through cyberspace to Europe's hippest nightspots. Even the Amazon no longer echoes to a soundtrack of howler monkeys and parakeets, as raves lure thousands of dancers via the internet, to jungle clearings, and, on a daily basis, the indigenous people hook into the world's soundtracks through cyberspace.

In nightclubs, jazz takes turns with the melancholy of Portuguese *fado*, Brazilian torch singers, and the legends of MPB (Musica Popular Brasileira) like Roberto Carlos and Rita Lee, and younger favorites, such as Marisa Monte and Daniela Mercury, perform poetic anthems. Leading lights of the 1970s Tropicalia movement continue to draw young audiences: Gilberto Gil and his collaborator Caetano Veloso still woo with sensual, laid-back singing and eclectic music; Veloso also joins his son Moreno's neo-Tropicalia experimentations, while Tropicalia divas Gal Costa and Maria Bethania still cast spells. The ageless Jorge Ben Jor, Brazil's James Brown, is seeing his back catalogue of funk-samba cannibalized by a new generation of producers around the world.

Heterogeneous nation

Whatever your taste, Brazil's choices are dazzling. The reason for such variety is the country's vast size. It states are nations, each with its own traditions and customs, its superstars, dances, and musical styles. Music changes with geography, and follows migration paths, but regional folk music remains very much alive: The gauchos of Rio Grande do Sul sing to accordions like their 19th-century German forebears; the *boleros* of Mato Grosso do Sul possess the drama of the Spanish culture in neighboring Paraguay; and northeastern rhythms – the *baião* and *maracatu* in the interior, and the faster *frevo* on the coast around Recife – dominate wherever *nordestinos* have moved. *Forró*, the mainstay of the *nordestino*, is now universally popular.

Salvador, in Bahia, the original Brazilian capital and a significant slaving port, remains heavily African in cuisine, colloquialisms, religion, and music. Its Carnival is less commercialized than Rio's, and the strong African elements in its music have inspired many national trends.

The extraordinary diversity of Brazil explains why so many musical genres coexist with equal vigor. Successive waves of immigration have left their imprint: the Portuguese colonists and Jesuit missionaries, the Africans who came as slaves, and the economic and political refugees

Rhythm-makers

Brazilian culture has always been open to a blending and fusion of genres. The 16th-century European missionaries saw Catholic liturgy adapted by the slaves and indigenous people to their ritual songs and choreography; in the northwest of Amazonas state, Tucano Amerindians still sing Gregorian *glorias* and *credos*. Otherwise, the music of indigenous Brazil focuses on rhythm over melody, its principal instruments being maracas and rattles, and sometimes simple flutes and pan pipes.

For four centuries, the Portuguese colonizers held the dominant influence, defined Brazilian

from 19th- and 20th-century Europe and Asia. Culturally mixed and socially hierarchical, Brazil has one foot in the computer age, the other in the 17th century. It is more than 80 percent urban, yet so recently urbanized that large sectors of the city population retain the cultural habits of the *sertão*. Still predominantly an oral culture, it is nonetheless exposed to the rest of the world through radio, television and the internet, and the latest international hits reach the remotest corners of the country, where folk music is still solidly alive.

LEFT: sometimes people just can't help dancing.
RIGHT: small groups of samba musicians in the *favelas* sometimes play together for life.

harmonic structures, and established the four-beat bar and syncopation that later blended so well with African rhythms. The Portuguese basis of Brazilian folk dance includes "dramatized dances" linked to the Catholic calendar. The liveliest and most profane is *Bumba-Meu-Boi*, a comic representation of the *tourinhos* (Portuguese bullfights), and a colorful, rhythmic, essentially African affair, popular in the states of Pernambuco, Maranhão and Bahia.

Although the Portuguese introduced the *cavaquinho* (similar to the ukulele, but usually steel-stringed), *bandolim* (mandolin), *violão* (Portuguese guitar, resembling a large mandolin, Indian sitar or Greek bazouki, with five pairs of strings), the Portuguese bagpipes, piano, viola and harp, it was the Spanish guitar that became the backbone of Brazil's popular music (although the German accordion is still heard at country parties in many regions).

The Portuguese provided the lyrical-poetic framework and range of themes and emotions now central to popular music, but from Africa came *axé* (a Yoruba word meaning joy and strength). The majority of Brazil's slaves came from Angola, Congo, and Sudan, but Brazil's plantation owners, unlike those in the US, broadly tolerated their rhythmic dances and trance rituals. Once freed, and organizing their own religions, they were repressed by the

The word samba derives from the Angolan *semba*, a synonym for *umbigada* – literally, a navel thrust. It was danced originally in a circle, with a soloist in the middle who clapped and danced, then stopped in front of one person, and, with a cheeky *umbigada*, swapped places. Variations of *umbigadas* – *samba de roda*, *jongo*, *tambor-de-crioulo*, *batuque*, and *caxambu* – survive virtually unchanged today in Afro-Brazilian communities all over Brazil.

The Afro-Brazilian rhythms made their first, tentative foray into the salons of white urban society in the late 18th century in the form of the *lundu*, a toned-down couple dance accompanied

authorities, and resorted to disguising their animist gods as Catholic saints – the process known as syncretism that is found throughout the former Spanish and Portuguese colonies.

Origins of samba

For the Afro-Brazilian, music is traditionally both social and religious. The instruments used with varying rhythms in religious ceremonies such as *candomblé*, and at parties, clubs and concerts, include the *atabaque* drums, *ganza* metal rattles, the *cuíca* drum, whose skin is pulled to make a hoarse rasping voice, and conical *agogo* bells, beaten with a stick or metal rod. With the *violão* or *cavaquinho*, these form the basis of Brazil's national music: the samba.

THE CRYING GAME

Choro (meaning crying or sobbing) is a guitar-based song style accompanied by emotional singing to sensual Afro-Brazilian rhythms. It lacks the brash percussive exhilaration of samba. The early 20th-century composer Heitor Villa-Lobos spent his spare time playing *choro* in Rio's bars and cafés, whilst professionally weaving together Bach and folk music in his magnificent *Bahianas Brasileiras*.

Choro thrives in many Brazilian cities, in delightfully old-fashioned bars and clubs, spurred on by the devoted *choro* fan, samba icon, guitarist, and composer Paulinho da Viola. He also inspired the popular young neo-*choro* ensemble Os Ingenuos from Salvador.

by viola and sitar. In the second half of the 19th century, slave bands performing on country plantations and in city ballrooms were obliged to copy fashionable European dance rhythms like the polka and the mazurka. But playing for themselves, they injected their own sensuous thrusts and swings, and from those sessions emerged the *maxixe*, an extravagant, rhythmic form of tango. Fred Astaire's version in the 1933 Hollywood film *Flying down to Rio* coincided with the *maxixe*'s decline in Rio in the face of samba's increasing popularity in Carnival parades. In today's *gafieiras* (dance halls), couples still mix *maxixes, habaneras, choros* (samba's precursor, *see panel opposite*), and sambas with extravagant virtuosity.

The rise of samba

Samba's official history began in 1916, with *Pelo Telefone*, the first samba on record and an instant hit at Carnival that year. The first samba school, composed of scores of percussionists whose rhythms drive the revelers, was founded in the 1930s, and today every Brazilian town and city has its own. The oldest school, Mangueira, is acknowledged in scores of songs, and the 70-something singer, Elza Soares, whose voice is as huskily sexy as in her 1960s heyday, today mixes sambas and Mangueira tributes with hip-hop fusions.

The best-known samba form is *samba enredo* (story-samba), sung by an amplified voice accompanied by a guitar and *cavaquinho*, to a responding chorus of the thousands of voices in the *desfile* (procession) who "converse" with the drummers sashaying in their finery. Other sub-genres include *samba do morro*, played on percussion instruments only, *samba do breque* (break), which pauses abruptly to allow a wry interjection, then starts again, and the perennial ballad version, *samba-canção*, the "Frank Sinatra of sambas", popular in clubs and bars.

With musical frontiers blown wide open today, and fashions flashing by, samba fusions are virtually limitless. But samba-rock, samba-funk, samba-reggae, and samba-rap must bow to the domination of *samba-pagode*, the sound of Rio's *favelas* since the 1980s. Performed typically at informal neighbourhood get-togethers, it involves all ages. *Cavaquinhos* and banjos sing out the melodies, and the dancers are driven by *pandeiro* (frame drum) and *tamborim* beats. In the late 1980s, David Byrne (ex-Talking Heads) released a significant set of tasters on his Luaka Bop compilation *O Samba*. The compelling collection of classic samba singers it introduced included Zeca Pagodinha, today's *pagode* idol.

Pagodinha (Little Pagode Singer) was a *sambista* from birth. He packs his infectious songs with slang and performs them as casually as a storyteller in a bar. Superstar Seu Jorge *(see page 108)*, who emerged from a generation raised on hip-hop, pays homage to Pagodhina,

but his favorite is *samba partido-alto* (high party), with its addictive percussion and sharp beats created with palm-slaps on a *pandeiro*.

Samba, like most great musical genres, is wide open to adaptation, and many samba singers now also include bossa novas in their repertoires. Jazz samba is today an international fusion style, and Tania Maria one of its most popular exponents outside Brazil. The veteran 1960s samba-jazz group Os Ipanemas enjoyed a recent Buena Vista-style comeback with their album *Samba is a Gift*, which drops trombone and saxophone into the samba mould. In 2006, the sanitized *pagode*-pop of Só Para Contrariar broke the records with a debut album that sold 3 million copies.

LEFT: samba has the kind of infectious rhythm that gets everyone up on the dance floor.

RIGHT: Bebel Gilberto – following in father's footsteps.

While Rio holds the world records for Carnival visitors, numbers of samba schools and gyrating feather-clad dancers, Salvador in Bahia offers a more interactive experience in the colonial streets, which echo to the sound of *blocos* (formation drummers). But a new rival to Salvador is Olinda, the colonial town attached to Recife, whose local *frevo* rhythm outranks even Rio's sambas in intensity.

Bossa nova

Samba is traditionally the voice of black Brazilians and forever associated with Carnival. But bossa nova (new wave) is also synonymous

with Brazil, and its birthplace – Rio. Bossa nova exploded onto the worldscene in 1964, when the classically trained pianist and composer Antonio Carlos "Tom" Jobim, the shy young guitarist João Gilberto, and his sultry-voiced wife Astrud, held New York's Carnegie Hall in thrall to *Garota de Ipanema* (The Girl from Ipanema), *Desafinado* (Out of Tune), and *Samba de uma nota só* (One Note Samba). Bossa nova had taken shape several years earlier in Rio, the outcome of a quest by Jobim and other young *carioca* intellectuals for a calmer samba, in response to America's West Coast cool jazz scene led by Stan Getz and Charlie Byrd. Bossa nova would bewitch the world, and inspired scores of schmaltzy covers.

The construction of bossa nova relied on João Gilberto's wholly original approach to the guitar, mixing jazz harmonies with a chunky, persistent, offbeat rhythm extracted from the guitar itself. It requires considerable skill to play bossa nova: one musician described it as "like talking in a long sentence, but one in which you switch language every two words". The most significant lyricist was the poet and former diplomat, Vinicius de Moraes, whose legacy remains in such exquisite songs as *Eu sei que vou te amar* (I know that I will love you). Jobim was a magnificent pianist and a charismatic frontman. Working in their apartments and the local bars of Rio's chic Zona Sul neighbourhood, the three men and their collaborators perfected songs that remain in the international repertoire half a century later.

The musicians in *favelas* overlooking Zona Sul had little interest in this middle-class style,

CAPOEIRA

One of the many attractions on the beaches of Rio is the sight of two young acrobatic men caterpillar-looping, doing backflips and highkicks in the ancient art of *capoeira*. *Capoeira* is Brazil's national sport, brought by slaves from Angola more than 500 years ago. It landed in Salvador and was adopted by all African slaves as a mark of identity. After abolition in 1888, *capoeira* was outlawed, but it remained popular among criminal gangs of freed men, performing in secret. Legalization followed the opening of the first Academia, in 1937 in Salvador, by Mestre (Master) Bimba, whose style was fast and modern. Five years later, Mestra Pastrinha's Academy promoted the slower, traditional version, *Capoeira Angola*, which remains popular

today. *Capoeira* is a sport and martial art, often incorporated into modern dance and break-dancing. The crucial "voice" of *capoeira* is a twangy African bow *(berimbau)*, a single steel-stringed instrument, hit with a stick, accompanied by a *pandeiro* (tambourine), metal *agogo* bells, and conga-like *atabaque*. The audience traditionally sits or stands in a circle, cheering and clapping. In Brazil's *favelas*, *capoeira* schools offer underprivileged youth self-expression, discipline and respect, as well as a connection with their African roots.

For observers, it is hypnotic, intense, and often amusing, as the two performers outwit each other with fake moves and false dramas.

but in today's era of fusion, the classics are now intergrated into the mosaic of styles cannibalized by every Brazilian DJ and musician. João Gilberto's daughter Bebel has built a successful reputation in Europe based on such a repertoire.

Tropicalia

In reaction to the cool of bossa nova, the late 1960s saw a very different revolution, born under increasing political turmoil and the impact of Beatles songs and West Coast American rock. "Tropicalia" was seeded in Salvador, where a group of students besotted with local folk music and Beatles songs included guitarists and songwriters Gilberto Gil and Caetano Veloso, the avant-garde composer Tom Zé, and ex-bossa nova singer Gal Costa. The clan migrated to São Paulo, then the hub of an explosive new arts scene, and Gil's collaborations with the whacky, musically brilliant trio Os Mutantes (The Mutants) led to their anthemic psychedelic song, *Domingo no Parque* (Sunday in the Park). With Veloso's *Alegria, Alegria* (Joy, Joy), they launched an era with loud, irreverent songs and Dadaist performances on live TV Globo, shocking the traditionalists but delighting young hippy fans. The song lyrics strikingly juxtaposed concrete poetry with images from pop culture, but pushed the buttons of the establishment, until the military government in 1969 arrested and imprisoned Veloso and Gil, and forced them into exile. They chose to live in London. By the time of their return in 1972, Tropicalia had unified the young generation, and every group was electric – and Tropicalist.

More than 30 years on, the Tropicalia pioneers still carry musical clout: Caetano Veloso, with his sinuous melodies and poetic wit; Gil, now Minister of Culture, still playful, rhythmic and mesmerizing, and carrying the torch for Bob Marley's songs. The third significant musician of that generation, Chico Buarque, was never a Tropicalia member but a politically active poet, writer and singer. Today he is still adored, but retired from performing to write intense novels. Milton Nascimento, a brilliant songwriter, has a background in church choral music, but also has Afro-Brazilian ancestry.

LEFT: Caetano Veloso, who has been writing and performing since the 1960s.
RIGHT: Milton Nascimento is still immensely popular.

The queen of Brazilian rock today is former Tropicalia star and Os Mutantes singer Rita Lee. Many of these artists still produce significant, relevant work more than 30 years after their Tropicalia heyday, and in interesting collaborations with the young "*novo tropicalismo*", electronica generation.

Moving on

Musical changes still reflect regional differences but, increasingly, in the age of the internet, São Paulo has returned as the hub of a musical revolution, through the proliferation of hip-hop and electronic music there. But most

challenging to its status is the state of Pernambuco and its capital city, Recife, where Chico Science's Nacao Zumbi, the singer Otto, and DJ Dolores are based.

Occupying a space outside both the electronic dance scene and the post-Tropicalia clan are the Brazilian rockers, who always possessed a certain sweetness: from the teenaged, miniskirted girls in the mid-1960s; to the innovative 1980s rockers, whose direct, urban and often mocking or humorous songs were a far cry from traditional romanticism; to 1990s rappers, who continue in this vein by tingeing their diatribes with humour. The current craze for the mostly girl group, Cansei de Ser Sexy (Tired of Being Sexy, a Beyoncé quote), marks

Seu Jorge

The shockingly realistic film *Cidade de Deus* (City of God), released in 2003 and nominated for four Oscars, was set in one of Rio's most violent *favelas* (shantytowns), many of which are just yards from the most famous beaches in the world. The film launched one of Brazil's most talented and now best-known young singers, Seu (Sir) Jorge, who played Knockout Ned. The role was conceived for the lanky young singer/songwriter by the co-director, Fernando Meirelles.

Jorge had grown up in a *favela* like the one in

the film, but escaped its poverty and the usual short life-span through music and community theater after spending several tough teenage years on the streets, busking and involved in risky street life.

Seu Jorge was already a key player on Rio's exploding new music scene by the time he was cast for the film. Meirelles knew his first group, Farofa Carioca, which played electronic versions of the catchy funk-sambas created in the late 1960s hits by Jorge Ben Jor, who – like Jorge – is a passionate *carioca* (Rio resident), with samba in his blood.

Jorge went solo with his album *Samba esporte fino* (released in the UK as *Carolina*), a collaboration with Beastie Boys producer Mario Caldato. The title song was an international club hit and

appeared on several compilations released in Europe, which contributed to the explosive interest in the new generation of Brazilian artists, and this bewitching young performer in particular.

Through Meirelles, Jorge was invited by Wes Anderson to appear in his 2004 film *The Life Aquatic with Steve Zissou*, alongside Bill Murray, Anjelica Houston and Willem Dafoe. Every reviewer mentioned the elusive black guy in the red beanie hat who sang bizarre Portuguese versions of the David Bowie hits *Rebel, Rebel, Rock'n'Roll Suicide, Life on Mars,* and *Starman*. During filming, Jorge recorded his second solo album, *Cru*, in Paris, produced by Gringo de Parada of the Favela Chic club. A stunning collection of guitar-backed songs, it opens with a small samba guitar *(cavaquinho),* light and jangly against the jumpy samba rhythm that threads through the whole album. Squeaky *cuíca* drums converse with the voice, and earth-shaking beats of a *surdo* (big Carnival bass drum) drive you to dance. Jorge's erotically slow, bossa nova-paced version of Elvis's *Don't*, his nervy remake of Serge Gainsbourg's suicidal chant, *Chatterton*, and the gorgeously romantic *Fiore de la Città* by veteran song-writer Robertinho Brandt, all contributed to make it an award-winning album. The backing is deliberately simple to showcase the singer's extraordinary soulful flights from falsettos to gravelly, smokey depths.

While leaning towards acoustic/melodic music, Jorge also acknowledges the wave. His passion is for "live" guitars (by João Gilberto, Gilberto Gil, and Jorge Ben Jor who Brazilianized the instrument), and for Zeca Pagozhino, "the greatest samba singer and a chronicler of people".

Although part of the electronic generation, and recognizing its significance, he mostly operates apart from the pioneering DJ/producers, laptop manipulators, and sound collagists like Bid, DJ Dolores, MarceloD2, the Instituto Collective, Tejo, Black Alien & Speed (whose hard-core 2001 Nissan 4x4 ad campaign took Europe by storm), and electro-acoustician Fernanda Porto.

Jorge is an old-fashioned singer/songwriter with an ear for a tune and a way with poetic lyrics; he's also an ambassador for the new wave. An icon in Rio, he is committed to transforming life in the *favelas*. *Cru* closes with the song *Eu Sou Favela* (I am Favela), fittingly spare and tense. "A *favela* is a social problem. People in the *favelas* are dignified and proud, and they can also be chic," he says. ❑

LEFT: the man with his guitar.

a nostalgic return to 1970s post-punk LA girl groups who reject the clichés of girls in rock, and add copious measures of kitsch that Carmen Miranda would surely envy.

Re-Africanization

The late 20th-century shift away from Rio and São Paulo to Salvador and Recife as focuses of Brazil's music scene was triggered by the 1970s move for "re-Africanization" in Bahia. Groups of beautifully elegant women dancers, dressed in the white crinolines and headwraps associated with the Afro-Brazilian *candomblé* religion, began to make their presence felt during Carnival. Parading through the streets, they danced not to the frenetic *trio elétrico* or samba of Rio but to African rhythms – *afoxés* - beaten out on *agogo* bells. These stately descendants of slaves became the nerve centres of a growing black consciousness movement.

Around the same time, Bob Marley records were arriving in Bahia, and the Baianos immediately identified with reggae. Gilberto Gil adopted rasta colours, recorded in Jamaica, and inspired a generation. His spine-tingling concert with Jimmy Cliff was a landmark recognition of reggae's connection with black Brazil. Reggae became particularly associated with the port cities, whose slave descendants lend them a strong African character. In August, the Reggae Festival in the northern port of São Luís sees thousands of reggae fans in rasta threads flock to see Gil and other Brazilian musicians performing alongside the Jamaican idols.

Inspiring Paul Simon

Salvador's post-reggae Carnival generated new dances and new singing stars, led by Margareth Menezes, Daniela Mercury, the *candomblé*-gospel diva Virginia Rodrigues, and the musician, composer and producer Carlinhos Brown. Their international popularity helped put Salvador on the world music map. The early 1980s saw the formation of the first community drumming groups *(blocos afros)*, Olodum, who stirred up Carnival with their massive parades of drummers beating out Afro-Brazilian rhythms. Olodum caught the ear of Paul Simon in the 1990s, and provided the rhythmic framework for his *The Rhythm of the Saints* album. Olo-

RIGHT: Olodum shot to fame in collaboration with US songwriter Paul Simon in the 1990s.

dum also performed on an album and video by Michael Jackson.

Many of Olodum's 300 or so permanent members were street kids who discovered identity and pride through their involvement. The group offered free classes in Yoruba and Portuguese, literacy, computing, and music at the Olodum centre, and added metalwork and carpentry workshops.

Carlinhos Brown was key to establishing self-supporting, community-based education centers operating through music and culture. "In Bahia, the drum has become the synonym of employment, education, social ascension,

and, of course, polemic," decreed the leading news magazine *Veja* in June, 1998. Brown described his third solo album, *Bahia do Mundo*, in 2001, as a tribute to the country's black musical traditions, and asserted: "Drum-and-bass, house, and even funk exist because of samba schools, and trance only exists because of Brazilian Carnival."

With funds from UNICEF, Brown built a school for music, literacy, and maths, and recording studios to nurture musical talent. For a decade, he directed the percussion band Timbalada, which toured the world, and his 2002 album, *Tribalistas*, recorded with Bahia's singer-producer and superstar, Marisa Monte, and Arnaldo Antunes, received five Grammy nominations for a surprisingly low-key, mostly acoustic collection of rock, soul, and samba-influenced songs led by Monte's luminous voice and Antunes' gritty baritone, and a guest appearance by the sultry Salvador vocalist, Margareth Menezes.

AfroReggae

In Rio, a similar development to the Olodum phenomenon led to the now internationally renowned community NGO, AfroReggae, which also began life as a drumming troupe. Founded by a young activist, José Jr, it developed through his newsheet *AfroReggae News* in

Rio's most violent *favela*, Vigário Legal. Centro Cultural AfroReggae was established as a landmark offering hope to the youth in a community fighting for survival among raging gang warfare. Financial, moral, and practical supporters included Caetano Veloso, and the Centro's classes eventually included *capoeira*, literacy and counselling.

The 1992 Funk Festival (whose anti-gangsta publicity featured children holding AK47s) led to the massively popular *funk-bailes* (balls) where few outsiders dared go. Young musicians and DJs in this hermetically sealed world produced soundtracks matching their violent lives, and reproduced in the hit movie, *Cidade de Deus* (City of God). Community projects began

to mushroom: at Rio's largest *favela*, Rocinha, a *casa* (community house) offered classes and workshops beyond those geared to Carnival, including sophisticated theater projects, photography and film production in the Audio-Visual Center, and music.

Music was the initial draw, and through their performances, AfroReggae became super-heroes. José Jr and his team exploited their popularity through music, creating fusions of reggae, hip-hop, funk, and samba. Today, there are AfroReggae centers in several Brazilian *favelas*, and the leaders have conducted workshops in deprived areas of Paris and London.

AfroReggae News now occupies a portfolio including AfroReggae Radio and their internet sites. The gritty 2005 documentary, *Favela Rising*, followed the story of José Jr and his partner, Anderson Sa (a former trafficker); and *Culture is Our Weapon: AfroReggae in the Favelas of Rio* (by Patrick Neate and Damian Platt, Latin American Bureau) is a warts-and-all document of the violence, police corruption, tragedies, and triumphs, and the heroism of this radical NGO, which operates with little government support.

The electronic century

Recently, the cutting edge of Brazilian music has shifted along the coast from Rio (now a thoroughly 20th-century center) through Salvador, to Recife, capital of Pernambuco. The "Pernambuco Sound" is built around a dynamic and diverse music scene that competes with São Paulo's electronica and hip-hop movement for international success. and in transforming the soundtrack to Brazil.

In the early 1990s, Nação Zumbi (Zumbi Nation, named after a legendary slave leader called Zumbi) were the first to fuse hip-hop, reggae, funk, and rock with local *maracatu* and coco rhythms using electric guitars, samplers with electronic effects, and an overlay of torrential drums.

Mundo Livre (Free World) draw on both samba and punk, led by devout Clash fan, Fred 04, a poet and *cavaquinho* player whose manifesto "Crabs with Brains" refers to the inhabitants of the mangrove swamps on which

LEFT: Marisa Monte is a megstar.
RIGHT: Carlinhos Brown on stage.
FAR RIGHT: Gilberto Gil, musician and politician.

Recife is built. Together Mundo Livre and Nação Zumbi, led by charismatic Chico Science, founded the Mangue Beat Movement – one of the most influential, revolutionary sounds since Tropicalia.

Another leading figure is DJ Dolores – confusingly, neither a DJ nor a woman, but Helder Aragão, whose group includes a dreadlocked female singer called Isaar, and performs brilliantly anarchic stage shows. Their smooth, hypnotic rhythms, meandering trombone solos, sampled insect calls and crunching electric guitars, have spawned imitators around Brazil and in Europe.

Exploring ancient traditions

Mestre Ambrosia and Siba explore and exploit the ancient musical traditions of the vast Brazilian interior, where dry, dusty landscapes spawn singers with predictably nasal, gritty voices. Otto, the best-known soloist in this new wave, is wildly unpredictable: his gravelly voice glides through songs concerned with environmental and social issues and punctuated with philosophical musings. Otto's third solo album (and the first to get a UK release), the award-winning *Sem Gravidade* (Without Gravity), released in 2003, confirmed his place in the international market, and that of his city, Recife. ❑

THE TRUTH ABOUT THE GIRL FROM IPANEMA

An intriguing legal action in 2005 sought to prevent an Ipanema woman from calling her boutique The Girl from Ipanema. It was brought by the copyright holders of Brazil's most famous song, the sons of the late composers, Antonio Carlos Jobim and Vinicius de Moraes. And the woman was Heloisa Pinheiro, said to have been the attractive 18-year-old who inspired the song in 1962 as she strolled past the bar patronized by the composers.

The song, the ultimate in easy listening, shot to fame in 1963 in a version by Stan Getz and Astrud Gilberto, and was recorded by dozens of singers, from Ella Fitzgerald to Frank Sinatra. In fact, the music was originally composed by De Moraes, a prolific poet and lyricist, for a musical comedy, *Dirigível*, and the words of this version, *Menina que Passa* (The Girl Who Passes By), were markedly different from the final English lyrics, written by the Oscar-winning American lyricist Norman Gimbel. Jobim and De Moraes did admit to having seen the alluring Heloisa stroll by as they sat at the Veloso bar-café – "a golden-tanned girl, a mixture of flower and mermaid, full of brightness and grace, but with a touch of sadness", as De Moraes wrote later. But the legend that they casually composed the song while sitting in the bar belied the hard graft that songwriting often entails.

Today the bar is known as A Garota de Ipanema (The Girl from Ipanema), located in Vinicius de Moraes Street.

CINEMA

Brazil's cinema industry is vibrant, and its actors and directors pick up prizes at international festivals with films that are hard-hitting and entertaining. The country has its own film festivals, as well as a landscape that attracts foreign movie-makers

Given the diversity and extremes of the Brazilian landscape it is not surprising that filmmakers – both Brazilian and international – have used Brazil as the backdrop and as a character in their movies.

The nascent Brazilian film industry had its ups and downs in the early days, reaching its first peak in the 1940s when the Atlântida Studio opened in Rio de Janeiro. For the next 25 years it turned out popular films targeting the masses, many of whom could not read the subtitles on the silent films. Only free delivery into thousands of homes of a similar style of entertainment via television was to burst its bubble (*see page 115*).

International recognition

The popularity of television did not stifle artistic endeavors on the big screen, however. In 1962 Anselmo Duarte's *O Pagador de Promessas* won the coveted Palme d'Or at Cannes, and it was at the same festival in 1964 that the world started to take notice of Brazil's Cinema Novo. Both Glauber Rocha's *Deus e O Diabo na Terra do Sol* and Nelson Pereira dos Santos's *Vidas Secas* were in competition, while Caca Diegues's *Ganga Zumba, Rei dos Palmares* was the closing film in Critics' Week.

In 1985 it was Hector Babenco's *O Beijo da Mulher Aranha* (Kiss Of the Spider Woman) that made its mark. William Hurt won the best actor prize in Cannes for his performance and also picked up the best actor Oscar at the 1986 Academy Awards. The film was also nominated for best picture, director, and screenplay.

If Cannes was good for Brazilian cinema, the Berlin Film Festival was even better, with Brazilian films picking up a string of prizes and critical acclaim throughout the 1970s, 1980s, and late 1990s. "Of all the European festivals, Berlin has always been the most curious about our filmmaking," says Walter Lima Jr, who won a Silver Bear in 1969 for *Brasil Ano 2000*.

When government production subsidies were pulled in the 1990s, Brazilian filmmaking virtually came to a halt, but some filmmakers never gave up, most significantly Brazil's most successful and prodigious producer, Luiz Carlos Barreto, responsible in 1976 for *Dona Flor e Seus Dois Maridos* (Dona Flor and Her Two Husbands). Directed by his son, Bruno, it remains the most successful Brazilian movie of all time, selling more than 12 million tickets and being nominated for a Golden Globe.

Academy Award nominations in consecutive years for producer Barreto put the Brazilian film industry back on track and bolstered its confidence in competing critically and commercially. In 1996 and 1997 Brazil received nominations for best foreign-language film, first for Fabio Barreto's *O Quatrilho*, a gentle story of pioneering Italian immigrants in southern Brazil; and then for *O Que é Isso Companheiro?* Bruno's movie (given the English title *Four Days in September*), was based on the true story of the kidnapping of the American ambassador to Brazil by a left-wing group in 1969.

Barreto's next project, and arguably his most ambitious to date, is a movie about the life of the current Brazilian president, Luiz Inácio Lula da Silva, based on Denise Paraná's book, *Lula: O Filho do Brasil* (Lula: Son of Brazil).

Glittering prizes

In 1998, Walter Salles Jr's *Central do Brasil* premiered at the Berlin Film Festival. The reception was rapturous. It won the Golden Bear for best film, while its leading lady, Fernanda Montenegro, won the best actress Silver Bear. Over a year later, *Central do Brasil*'s bandwagon rolled into Hollywood, with a nomination for best foreign-language film, Brazil's third nomination in three years. Montenegro was nominated for best actress, a first for a Brazilian performer. The global success of the film, both critically and commercially, turned the spotlight on Brazilian cinema and Salles, and neither has disappointed.

Salles has gone on to direct the highly acclaimed *Diarios de Motocicleta* (The Motorcycle Diaries), the story of the young Che Guevara's journey through South America; the English-language thriller, *Dark Water;* and most recently the football-based Portuguese-language drama, *Linha de Passe*.

But Salles does not have to stand alone on the international stage. In 2003 Fernando Meirelles served up the stunning *Cidade de Deus* (City of God), a movie about life in Rio's *favelas* that was considered by many critics, and the public, to be not only the most innovative and fresh movie of 2003, but quite simply the best. The movie won more than 50 international awards, and was nominated for four Academy Awards. Going full circle, Meirelles has since produced and part-directed a series for TV Globo, *Cidade dos Homens*, which is based on his film; but he returned to the big screen in 2005 to direct the highly acclaimed English-language adaptation of John Le Carré's novel *The Constant Gardener*, a film that won an Academy Award for Rachel Weisz as best supporting actress and received nominations for writing, editing, and music.

Meirelles has a three-year deal with Universal Pictures and Focus Features to bring Brazilian-made films, in English or Portuguese, to the stu-

LEFT: *The Kiss of the Spider Woman* won prizes when it appeared in the mid-1980s.
RIGHT: a scene from *Central do Brasil*.

dio. His next project is *Blindness*, a movie based on the 1995 novel *Ensaio Sobre a Cegueira* by Portugal's Nobel Prizewinning author José Saramago.

Brazilian film festivals

Despite promises by President Lula to support the arts, it is still not easy for Brazilian filmmakers to find the funding to make new films without the support of the local offices of the Hollywood majors or TV Globo *(see opposite)*. Yet the industry survives, especially in Rio, and trusts its existence and heart to the city where Latin America's premier film festival, Festival

do Rio, takes place in September and October.

In 2005, the festival jury voted Sergio Machado's *Cidade Baixa* (Lower City) the best home-grown movie, and its star, Alice Braga, who also appeared in *City of God*, the best actress. In 2006, Festival do Rio gave its top prize to Karim Ainouz's *O Ceu de Suely* (Suely in the Sky), which also screened at the Venice and Toronto festivals, with investment from France, Germany, and Portugal, as well as Brazilian funding. Produced by Walter Salles, it also picked up awards at the Rio Festival for director and for best actress, Hermilla Guedes.

Other major film festivals in Brazil include the São Paulo International Film Festival, that celebrated its 30th anniversary in October

LOVE STORY

Breno Silveira will follow *2 Filhos de Francisco (see box on page 113)* with *Era Uma Vez no Rio (Once upon a Time in Rio)*, a love story about a boy and girl from different social classes, due for release in early 2008.

2006; and the Gramado Film Festival, which will celebrate its 35th anniversary in August 2007. Gramado, once the premier festival for Brazilian productions, now awards prizes not only to Brazilian films but to the best movies that the rest of Latin America has to offer.

Brazil as backdrop

No consideration of filmmaking in Brazil would be complete without mentioning the number of foreign films, TV series, pop videos, and advertisement that have used beautiful Rio and the rest of Brazil as part of their backdrop.

One of the first to use Rio is still arguably the most famous – *Flying down to Rio* in 1933 – Thornton Freeland's musical that for the first time paired Fred Astaire and Ginger Rogers. Other notable early films to use Rio as a backdrop include Alfred Hitchcock's 1946 Word War II thriller *Notorious*, which starred Cary Grant, Ingrid Bergman and Claude Rains, and French director Marcel Camus's *Orfeu Negro* (Black Orpheus).

Premiering at the 1959 Cannes Film Festival, Camus's film, shot largely in the *favelas* of Rio and during Carnival, won the Palme d'Or and followed that by winning both the Academy Award and Golden Globe for best foreign-language film.

More recently, Brazil was used for the production of the James Bond blockbuster *Moonraker*; Roland Joffé's *The Mission*; John Boorman's *The Emerald Forest*; *Anaconda*, with Jon Voight and Jennifer López; and the comedies, *Moon over Parador, Woman on Top*, and *Mike Bassett: England Manager*. Rio was also famously the backdrop for Stanley Donen's rom-com *Blame it on Rio* that starred Michael Caine and Demi Moore, playing his daughter, in one of her first film roles. More recently, Brazil was also used for scenes in Michael Mann's *Miami Vice* (2006), while in the same year it was the turn of Bollywood to discover Brazil with Sanjay Gadhavi's hit action thriller *Dhoom 2*, set in Rio de Janeiro. ❏

LEFT: *City of God* captured the violence of *favela* life.

TV Globo

President Lula declared three days of mourning in August 2003 to mark the death of Roberto Marinho – not a previous president, or even a politician, but a media mogul. Dubbed the Brazilian Citizen Kane, the tycoon, one of Latin America's richest men, died aged 98, after a career spanning almost eight decades, during which his network reached 99.9 percent of Brazilian homes. Marinho was the head of the nationwide Globo television network, whose soap operas attract a huge following in Brazil and sell in large numbers around the world. The company is the fourth most prolific producer of TV programs in the world and the biggest network in territorial extent. Its audience comprises around 5 percent of the total worldwide network television audience. Globo's stranglehold on the market has been seen as a threat to the nation's democracy, and in the past Globo and the other Brazilian networks have been accused of a lack of political objectivity.

Television had started in a small way in Brazil in 1950, with TV Tupi making the first transmission in South America, but only truly began to affect the population with the launch of TV Excelsior's daily soaps in 1960. Marinho had taken over *O Globo*, one of Rio de Janeiro's principal newspapers, from his father in the 1920s. Some two decades later, he launched Radio Globo, the country's first truly national radio network; and 20 years after that, in April 1965, he did the same with TV Globo.

Marinho's timing was near perfect. It was the advent of video, satellite transmission, and other advancements, including the introduction of color television to Brazil in 1972. Sales of TV sets were boosted by events such as the moon landing and the World Cup – even the Carnival parades in Rio.

Marinho understood that the way to communicate with the Brazilian population – and deliver the audience sought by advertisers – was through television and radio. Due to poor educational standards, print would always be for the elite. Marinho also made sure that TV Globo's channel was delivered free and had something of interest each night for the entire population.

Anyone who had access to a television set had access to TV Globo, and many sets were never switched to the other channels, which include SBT, Banderiantes, Record and Cultura. Today, over 90 percent of homes have TV, and it is the major source of information and entertainment for many.

Pride of place on the small screen goes to the legendary short-run soap operas known as *novelas*. The most successful can hold the nation spellbound, from smart lawyers in the rich suburbs of São Paulo to penniless *favelados* in remote Manaus. Between June 1985 and February 1986 *Roque Santeiro*, a parody of the Brazilian government and politicians set in a small town in the interior, held an official audience share of 98 percent.

Globo's first true novela, *Véu de Noiva*, aired in 1969. Today Globo produces nearly 4,500 hours of new programming a year for its single channel, with

three daily *novelas* filling the 6pm to 9.30pm slot, along with the national news, *Jornal Nacional*. Advertising, attracting the attention of an audience in excess of 40 million, generates around 60 percent of the network's total billings.

If Marinho had a magic formula it was for Globo to have its finger firmly on the pulse of the Brazilian public, its tastes and aspirations. Critics may say that it is TV Globo that molds the tastes and opinions of the Brazilian public, yet no other TV network in Brazil (or the international satellite and cable channels) has come close to matching Globo's record of success and audience share.

For all those, from all sections of society, who attended Marinho's funeral in 2003, it was the end of an era, but not the end of his empire. ❑

RIGHT: Marinho with President Cardoso in 1999.

ART AND ARTISTS

Replenished by artists who began life as the children of poor immigrants, art in Brazil has blossomed since the 1920s, from the abstract work of the mid-20th century to today's vibrant mix of the traditional and the avant-garde

Contemporary Brazilian art is wonderfully hard to categorize. At first glance, it appears resolutely international and less identifiably Brazilian in character than, for example, Mexican art is identifiable as Mexican. Yet it does have a Brazilian flavor, albeit surprisingly subtle. Brazilian scholar Ivo Mesquita appoints a certain lightness of touch as the defining feature: "The ability to parody others as well as ourselves separates us from the tragic sensibility of our Hispanic neighbors." And, he could add, a playful delight in the new.

Brazilian artists are among the liveliest participants at the big international shows (the Venice and Sydney Bienals, and the Kassel Documenta). And there is much *intercâmbio* by Brazilian artists who do stints abroad, and foreign ones who settle in Brazil.

"The richest, liveliest and most varied range of conceptual and site-specific art has been produced in Brazil," writes art historian Edward Lucie Smith, comparing Brazilian avant-garde with that of the rest of Latin America. "Site-specific art" – usually large sculptures or installations – might include the cascading plastic curtains of Leda Catunda (b. 1962); the giant hair plaits of Tunga (b. 1952); the eery silhouettes of Regina Silveira (b. 1937); and the large but restrained sculptures of José Resende (b. 1945), their elegance made physical by arresting surface textures, such as rust on a steel curve.

In painting, there are the thick, vibrant abstract-expressionist brush strokes of Jorge Guinle (1947–87) and José Roberto Aguillar

(b. 1941), and the atmospheric city streets of Gregorio Gruber (b. 1951). In 1996, Ana Maria Pacheco (b. 1943) became the first non-European to be appointed Artist in Residence at Britain's National Gallery. Her brief involved developing art that makes reference to works in the national collection (*see page 122* for a gripping example of her work).

The birth of Modernism

Given the élan and confidence of Brazilian artists today, it might seem surprising that, before the early 20th century, the fine arts in Brazil were in the grip of an antiquated European academicism, as dictated by Rio's Academia Imperial de Belas Artes, founded in 1826.

LEFT: naïve painting by Ivonaldo.
RIGHT: *Praia do Barbosa*, by Dila.

The rebellion took place in São Paulo, a city that in the early 20th century was growing vertiginously, fuelled by the wealth of the so-called coffee barons. Unfettered by tradition, these nouveaux riches sunk their money into industry, monuments, and mansions, and put São Paulo at the cutting edge of new cultural trends.

The "Week of Modern Art", held in São Paulo in 1922, was the watershed. By today's standards, the event was relatively modest – an art exhibition in the lobby of the Municipal Theater and three days of poetry readings and lectures. But art in Brazil was never to be the same again. The exhibition was the gateway into the "isms" of the age: the angles and refractions of cubism, art deco stylism, Italian Futurism and the metaphors of Symbolism and Surrealism.

Six years later, the poet Oswald de Andrade coined the term *antropofagia* (cannibalism) to describe how Brazilian art had begun to relate to international trends. The word referred to the belief of some Brazilian Amerindian tribes that cooking and eating the bodies of enemies they had killed in battle would endow them with the strength and bravery of the vanquished. Applied to art, this idea was extremely liberating. Brazilian artists dipped into the art world's "isms" without becoming dominated by them.

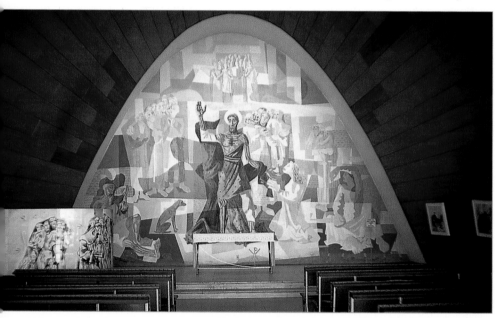

JAPANESE-BRAZILIAN ARTISTS

The post-World War II period saw the emergence of a school of Japanese-Brazilian artists, led by Manabu Mabe (1924–97). At first contracted to work as a field hand, Mabe moved to São Paulo city, where his reputation grew steadily, and his work became gradually more abstract. His stunning colors and forms mingle oriental harmony with bold Brazilian chromatic tones and light. Every painting of Mabe's is a sheer visual delight, with brush strokes of white daringly exploding in a field of stark reds, blues, and greens.

Far more cerebral and geometrical, using only two or three colors, is the work of Tomie Ohtake, who was born in Kyoto in 1913. Ohtake began painting professionally rela-tively late, after her family, also indentured farm workers (like Mabe and Portinari), moved to São Paulo. Her stage designs for *Madame Butterfly* at Rio de Janeiro's Municipal Theater are a landmark in Latin American scenography.

Mabe's son, Hugo, began his career painting landscapes with an Expressionist vigor, and over the years has gradually reduced them to abstracted form and color. A similar artist is Taro Kaneko, born in a rural region of São Paulo state, whose mountains and bays of Rio, and São Paulo's Jaragua Peak, are barely perceptible in his intense, thickly massed oils with explosive, unexpected colors. Kaneko's seas are gold or red, his skies green or orange, and his mountains are yellow or black.

Two women played key roles in the modernization of Brazilian art. Anita Malfatti (1889–1964) had studied at the Berlin Academy under Lovis Corinth, and in New York, before returning to Brazil and holding a groundbreaking exhibition in 1917, showing canvases that sung with Cézannesque colors and boldness. The younger generation loved her work, but Malfatti was crushed by a damning newspaper review written by Monteiro Lobato, a well-known novelist, from which she never fully recovered.

Tarsila do Amaral (1886–1973) wrote to her parents in 1923 from Paris, where she was studying under Fernand Léger: "I want, in art,

ing to Brazil, he spent the next 50 years affectionately portraying the mixed-race *mulata* woman in a variety of styles, most notably a decorative form of cubism.

Europe's art deco movement directly influenced two other distinctive stylists: Italian-born sculptor Vitor Brecheret (1891–1957) and Vicente do Rego Monteiro (1899–1970). Brecheret's impressive *Monument to the Bandeirantes* (Pioneers) in São Paulo's Ibirapuera Park dwarfs even the Mussolini school in monumentalism. Monteiro's paintings, often of biblical or indigenous scenes, have the feel of Egyptian bas-reliefs.

to be the little country girl from São Bernardo, playing with straw dolls." She achieved her aim by means of a uniquely sophisticated yet simple style that owed much to the uncorrupted eye of the child. A major restrospective in São Paulo in 1998 put her in the front rank of Brazil's 20th-century painters.

Emiliano di Cavalcanti (1897–1976), a prolific painter and vigorous draftsman, also did a stint in Paris as correspondent for a Brazilian newspaper, where he mixed with the great Cubists, Picasso, Léger, and Braque. Return-

José Pancetti (1904–58), perhaps Brazil's best-loved Impressionist, was a tubercular ex-sailor whose moody landscapes and seascapes reflected the state of his mind more than the bright scenery about him.

Candido Portinari

Candido Portinari (1903–62) is Brazil's Diego Rivera. His *War and Peace* fresco adorns the United Nations Building in New York, and his *Discovery and Colonization* painting is hung in the Library of Congress in Washington. Unlike Rivera, however, he never became a fashionable ambassador for his country. Indeed, he painted so intensively that he contracted cancer from his highly toxic paints and died young.

LEFT: a Portinari fresco in the Capela de São Francisco, Pampulha.

ABOVE: Portinari's works often depicted rural workers.

Born into a family of poor Italian immigrants who worked in the coffee plantations of São Paulo state, Portinari had a deep empathy with uneducated Brazilian laborers. He intentionally exaggerated the size of their hands and feet as if to say, "These are my only assets. When these are used up, I, too, am tossed aside." In his youth, Portinari joined the Brazilian Communist Party. In maturity, he painted a searing series on the *retirantes* – peasant farmers driven from their land by drought and debt.

Portinari's influence on other artists was such that his style of social realism became known as "Portinarism." His followers include Orlando

MANET'S INSPIRATION

Brazilian legend has it that the sparkling quality of the light reflected in Rio's Guanabara Bay provided the inspiration behind Impressionism. This belief is based on the occasion when a French frigate carrying 16-year-old Edouard Manet, the "father of Impressionism", docked in Rio de Janeiro harbor for three months in 1849. And there is some justificiation for it. Manet, whose art was characterized by lively scenes and bright colors, later wrote: "I learned a lot in Brazil. I spent endless nights looking at the play of light and shade in the ship's wake. And in the daytime, from the upper deck, I would keep my eyes on the horizon. That's how I learned how to capture a sky."

Teruz (1902–84), Thomaz Santa Rosa (1909–56), Enrico Bianco (b. 1918) and Proença Sigaud (1899–1979). Carlos Scliar painted in the "Portinarist" fashion for some time, reflecting the conditions of rural workers in Rio Grande do Sul. Gradually, however, he eliminated social elements and concentrated on landscapes with geometrical forms and planes. His best-known work is a pastel-toned teapot, with minimal use of light and shade.

By contrast, Orlando Terluz's (1902–84) countryside is a rich loamy brown, and the rural inhabitants of his paintings are full of a beatific innocence. Fulvio Pennacchi also concentrated on country pleasures, such as church fairs and parties. His migrants look like happy families on a pilgrimage, and his villages sometimes reflect the style of those in his native Tuscany.

Another Tuscan émigré, Alfredo Volpi (1896–1988), began his career with paintings of country scenes such as religious *festas*. But by the late 1950s he had reduced his pictures to just one element: the strings of colorful bunting that festoon rural church fairs. Volpi was known as the "flag painter," and his work was widely reproduced as silk-screen prints. The artist himself always claimed that his overriding interest was color.

The birth of abstract art

At the end of World War II, Brazil was enjoying increased prosperity. The São Paulo Museum of Modern Art (MASP) was built in 1948, Rio's Museum of Modern Art (MAM) opened in 1949, and, in the midst of São Paulo's Ibirapuera Park, the vast, custom-built Bienal Pavilion, designed by Oscar Niemeyer, went up, and hosted the first Bienal in 1951.

The Bienal is held on odd years and lasts three months, from September to December. It involves thousands of exhibits and hundreds of events. In the early days, it seemed that the greatest impact was caused by works brought in from abroad, which included Picasso's *Guernica*, Francis Bacon's triptychs and the vast canvases of the US abstract Expressionists. These days, there is a far more equal exchange.

The birth of the Bienal ushered in a phase of abstraction. The rivalry between São Paulo and Rio raged hotly, with artists in the former favoring art that was strictly about color and shape, and the Rio group, who dubbed themselves the "neo-concretists", permitting some symbolic associations with reality.

Ligia Clarke (1920–88) and Helio Oiticica (1937–80) were among the most influential abstract sculptors of their generation. Clarke created a series of tactile *borrachas* (rubber grubs), and another of feisty, hard-metal *bichos* (animals). Oiticica's work often had the throwaway feel of Carnival props. Bahian-born Rubem Valentim (1922–92) used symbols from Afro-Brazilian *candomblé* ritual to create exuberant, geometrically patterned canvases.

The regions

While São Paulo and Rio monopolize the art trade and are the main centers for international

rino Araujo has been compared to the nation's greatest sculptor, the 18th-century Aleijadinho. He specializes in myopic, crook, and one-eyed angels, archangels, cherubim, and seraphim. From the same region came Geraldo Teles de Oliveira (often known as GTO, 1913–90), whose mandala-like woodcarvings exemplify the best in folk art sculpture.

In Goiás, near Brasília, Siron Franco portrays wild animals with magical energy and blazing color. Snakes and the *capivara*, a native rodent with a round snout, are among his favorites. His human and animal faces have bold white, yellow, or fluorescent lines about the eyes.

exhibitions and ideas, many artists are rooted in their native regions. Indeed, though they are becoming fewer in number, Brazil still has a class of uneducated rural artisans from which, every now and again, an artistic genius emerges. It is this that makes the Bienals so exciting, bringing together the internationally focused, Internet and video-art set with simple rural artists, and indigenous artists working in feather, bone, and wood.

Minas Gerais has a tradition of breeding imaginative woodcarvers and potters. Carver Mau-

LEFT: *Equador No. 2*, a 1973 painting by the abstract artist Manabu Mabe.
ABOVE: *Tabôa na lagoa*, by Ana Maria Dias.

(Siron's father, a sharecropper, was so distraught when he lost his land, that he lay down and stared into the sun until he went blind.)

At the end of the 1980s, a bizarre and tragic accident occurred in Goiás. An illiterate man stole a discarded piece of hospital equipment containing a capsule of radioactive material. Fascinated by the blue glow emitted by the Cesium 137, he took it home and passed it around his family, most of whom susequently died in protracted agonies of radioactive poisoning. Franco produced a stunning series of paintings based on the incident that briefly turned his quiet town into a hive of international reporters and scientists.

In the 1960s and 1970s, the new city of Brasília attracted artists from all over Brazil to complete the decoration of Oscar Niemeyer's superb architecture. Bruno Giorgi's meteors adorn the lake before the Itamarati Palace. Ceschiatti's bronze sculpture of two seated females combing their hair sits in the pool of the President's Palace, while his mobile of streamlined angels floats permanently beneath the soaring ceiling of Brasília Cathedral, framed by Niemeyer's boomerang-shaped columns.

Recife is solidly represented by João Camara, who first caught the public's attention with his figures with tortured, non-anatomical limbs in *A Confession*, a protest against the repression of the military government in the early 1970s.

In the neighboring town of Olinda, Gilvan Samico draws on the *literatura de cordel* (chapbook) tradition of woodcut engraving. He has illustrated the ballads of Charlemagne and local legends such as those of the charismatic Padre Cícero and the bandit heroes Lampião and Maria Bonita. Samico's engravings are highly prized by museums, being several grades above the folk art of the northeastern wood engravers.

Aldemir Martins, who was born in Ceará, paints the flora and fauna of his native northeast. His subjects include exotic fruits such as *jenipapo*, jackfruit, *jabuticaba*, cashew, and the wrinkled *maracujá* (passion fruit).

The best of Bahian art can be found in the sculptures of Mario Cravo Junior, who experiments in wood and pigmented polyester resin for such creations as *Germination I, II,* and *III.* His son, Mario Cravo Neto, creates wrinkled, untitled forms from materials such as polyester resin and fiberglass.

Rio Grande do Sul is noted for its sculptors, particularly Vasco Prado, who is fascinated by pregnant mares. Francisco Stockinger's warriors of bronze and other metals have an ominous air, with limbs and faces merely suggested.

Tapestries

The Tangiers-born Madeleine Colaço (1907–2001) invented a form of tapestry stitch registered at the international Tapestry Museum in Lausanne as the "Brazilian Stitch." She and her daughter, Concessa, use flora and fauna motifs. The French-born Jacques Douchez and São Paulo's Norberto Nicola, on the other hand, have modernized Brazilian tapestry with their abstract designs and novel use of non-embroidered elements, including native plant fibers.

The sophisticated *naif*

For decades, Brazil's art critics have been arguing about whether "primitive" or *naif* (naïve) art can rank as art at all. Sooner or later, one feels, they will be forced to admit that not only is it art but it is currently enjoying a glorious heyday. Indeed, in its range of subject matter, styles and techniques, Brazilian *naif* has become supremely sophisticated.

Rodolfo Tamanini (b. 1951), whose paintings are hung in São Paulo's stock exchange, brings *naif* technique to contemporary reality. His subjects range from city scenes, such as a block of flats with incidents on every balcony, to luminous coastal vistas of virgin forest, sea, and sky. In direct contrast, Ernani Pavanelli (b. 1942), a former systems analyst, specializes in nostalgic snatches of daily life from a bygone era, his formally attired couples and family groups painted in Seurat-style pointillism.

Ivonaldo (b. 1943) uses strong colors and wry humor – his country people (and animals) all have vividly expressive eyes, whether they be bikini-clad sunbathers, weary cane-cutters or shy lovers.

Dila (b. 1939), from the interior of Maranhão, paints detailed portraits of backland life, particularly open-air markets, with much haggling and mountainous piles of fruit.

Isabel de Jesus (b. 1938), a former nun, is internationally recognized for her dreamlike fantasies in delicate gouaches. Her palette of turquoises, purples, yellows, and crimsons blends over delicate line drawings of cats, dogs, fish, horses, children, stars, wolves, and so on.

Several of the *naif* artists concentrate more on vegetation than people. Francisco Severino paints landscapes from his native Minas Gerais with botanical accuracy. Ferreira, a fisherman, and Edivaldo Barbosa de Souza, a former commercial artist, create luxuriant seascapes and riverscapes in which people are dwarfed by their environment.

Mittarakis, entitled *Rio de Janeiro, I Like You, I Like Your Happy People*, a quotation from one of the city's favorite old-time waltzes. Another quotation catches the eye, this one by Einstein: "Imagination is more important than knowledge," a statement that perfectly sums up the whole concept of naïve art.

One unmissable work is Aparecida Azedo's *Five Centuries of Brazil*. Viewed from a mezzanine level, it measures 1.40 meters x 24 meters (4½ ft x 78½ ft). Key events in Brazilian development are shown with bold simplicity, and explanations of the historical scenes depicted are given on the mezzanine's railings. ❏

The Museum of Naïve Art

The best collection of *naif* art in Brazil – and possibly the world – is in the Museu Internacional do Brasil in Rio de Janeiro, close to the Corcovado train station.

The museum is caretaker to what is estimated to be the world's largest collection of naïve art, with 8,000 works from around Brazil and many other countries. As you walk in, you are immediately hit by the impact of a vast canvas, measuring 4 meters x 7 meters (13 ft x 23 ft), by Lia

LEFT: an arresting image by Ana Maria Pacheco
ABOVE: one of the stunning Serra Pelada images that brought Salgado to international attention.

SEBASTIÃO SALGADO

One Brazilian photographer is in a class of his own: Sebastião Salgado, who has made his home in Paris. He began his career in the 1970s but it was his photographs of workers in the Serra Pelada, a vast open-cast gold mine in the Amazon region, that brought him to world prominence in 1986. Whether photographing Bolivian tin miners, Ruhr valley steelworkers or the crowds at football matches, Salgado has a truly compassionate eye. Appointed a UNICEF Special Representative in April 2001, he concentrates on chronicling the lives of the downtrodden and dispossessed. A stunning series of pictures of displaced people, called *Migrations*, was published in book form in 2000.

Modern Architecture

Brazil's major cities have some stunning examples of modern architecture, designed by men with a vision. Perhaps their greatest achievement is Brasília, the capital created in the 1950s at the instigation of President Kubitschek

Aselect group of Brazilian architects, all born in the early years of the 20th century, created a fresh "tropical" aesthetic and became the most influential in their profession. The controversial urban planner Lúcio Costa, precursor of modernism in Brazil, the tropical landscape magician Roberto Burle Marx, and the architect Oscar Niemeyer, have left dozens of monuments in Brazil's major cities. Niemeyer also counts among his achievements the sweeping French Communist Party Headquarters in Paris, the National University Campus in Algeria, the facade of the United Nations Building in New York, and the Serpentine Gallery Pavilion in London, designed in 2003. Burle Marx's work can be seen in far-flung places from Venezuela to Japan, and his home in Rio was bequeathed to the nation on his death.

The culmination of these architects' talents is undoubtedly the gleaming capital of Brasília, founded in 1960, but the first seeds of modern Brazilian architecture were sown in 1931, when the legendary French architect Le Corbusier gave a lecture series in Rio on functionalism.

The influence of Le Corbusier

Le Corbusier's key themes of simplicity in design, economy in materials, and open spaces made their first appearance in Brazil in the Education Ministry building in Rio de Janeiro, the Palácio Capanema, built 1937–45 by a team including Costa, Niemeyer, and Burle Marx, who landscaped the broad esplanade. The Ministry incorporates a patio made possible by raising the main structure by 9 meters (30 ft) on concrete pillars called pilotis. Inside, the floor spaces were left entirely open for flexibility. A

sense of space and a magnificent view of Guanabara Bay were achieved by nearly doubling the normal window size.

Juscelino Kubitschek, then mayor of Belo Horizonte, brought the same team together again in the 1940s to create in that city what is acknowledged as Brazil's most pleasing park – Pampulha. With its expansive recreational area built around an artificial lake, Pampulha combines the landscaper's art with the discreet placement of public buildings. These include an art museum, a dance pavilion, and the Capela de São Francisco, with striking frescos by Cândido Portinari *(see page 117)*.

Niemeyer, fascinated by the "plasticity" of concrete, erected in Pampulha elegant monuments using curves, ramps, and undulating roofs. His low-rise, subtropical constructions include great stretches of ground-floor patios and breezy esplanades. The overall effect is an architecture of fresh, light structures that seem to hover over the green parkland and blue waters of the lake. Kubitschek was delighted and critics stood in awe.

Building Brasília

As Brazil's president in the 1950s, Kubitschek reunited the Pampulha team for an even bolder project, for which he had a personal vision – a new capital city for Brazil *(see page 301)*. An

the main buildings on the Plaza of Three Powers emulate the texture of the clouds in the sky above. Great fields of glass reflect the sky to create a similar effect. City and sky seem to be one. "I sought forms distinctly characterizing the buildings, giving them lightness, as if they were only tentatively attached to the ground," said Niemeyer years later.

Burle Marx died in 1994, Costa four years later, but Niemeyer, now well into his nineties, is still working, and remains Brazil's premier architect, responsible for Rio's Sambódromo and the stunning Contemporary Art Museum across the bridge in Niterói.

international competition was held to select the best urban plan for Brasília. But, said Burle Marx, "Everybody knew in advance who was going to win."

Costa's submission consisted of only a few sketches scratched on notepaper. However, as predicted, this crude effort was enough to win him the contract. Kubitschek himself recruited Niemeyer to design the main public buildings.

The new capital represented the last stage in Niemeyer's march towards austere design and spare construction. The searing white walls of

In 1988 he was awarded (jointly with US citizen Gordon Bunshaft) the Pritzker Prize, the world's most prestigious award for architecture. The citation read: "There is a moment in a nation's history when one individual captures the essence of that culture and gives it form. It is sometimes in music, painting, sculpture, or literature. In Brazil, Oscar Niemeyer has captured that essence with his architecture."

A lifelong communist, Niemeyer has often been in trouble, but remained true to himself. In his memoir *The Curves of Time*, he wrote: "I created [my work] with courage and idealism, but also with an awareness that what is important is life, friends, and attempting to make this unjust world a better place in which to live." ❏

LEFT: Oscar Niemeyer, the grand old man of Brazilian architecture, has never compromised his beliefs.
ABOVE: the National Congress building in Brasília.

PLACES

A detailed guide to the entire country, with main
sites cross-referenced by number to the maps

razil is a giant package with a multitude of gifts. Travelers looking for warm water, white sand, and tropical beauty will be overwhelmed by the Brazilian coastline – the longest, and one of the most beautiful, in the world. The options range from isolated, palm-fringed inlets to vast stretches backed by sand dunes. Brazilians argue eternally over which of the beaches is the best, but reach no consensus.

In the north and northeast, colonial monuments dot the state capitals, most of which are located by the sea. Salvador and Recife offer the best combination of beach and history. In addition, Salvador has developed a particularly rich culture from its special mix of African and Portuguese influences.

The succession of beautiful beaches continues south, reaching its zenith in the all-time leading beach city of the Americas, Rio de Janeiro. But Rio is more than the sum of its beaches. It is spectacular scenery, samba, Carnival, and a relaxed, carefree existence. By contrast, in São Paulo Brazil stops playing and gets down to the serious stuff. The center of the developing world's largest industrial park, São Paulo is the most dynamic city in South America, its hodge-podge of nationalities making it a wonderful Brazilian version of New York.

The further south you travel, the more European are the influences, culminating in the states of Paraná, Santa Catarina, and Rio Grande do Sul, where Italian, German, and Polish settlers have left their mark. Here, too, the accent is on sand and water, but not all of Brazil is located on the coast. Inland travelers will discover some of the world's most remarkable natural wonders. Occupying one-third of the nation's territory is the Amazon rainforest, and below the Amazon region, in an area drained by its rivers, is the Pantanal, a natural sanctuary for fish, birds, and mammals. In the south, the wildly beautiful Iguaçu Falls is considered by many to be the greatest natural attraction of Brazil.

This guide will introduce you to some of Brazil's greatest wonders, and encourage you to discover more about them for yourself. ❏

PRECEDING PAGES: Salvador, capital of Bahia; selling sunhats
on Ipanema beach; sparkling Rio de Janeiro at night.
LEFT: Jabaquara beach, Ilhabela.

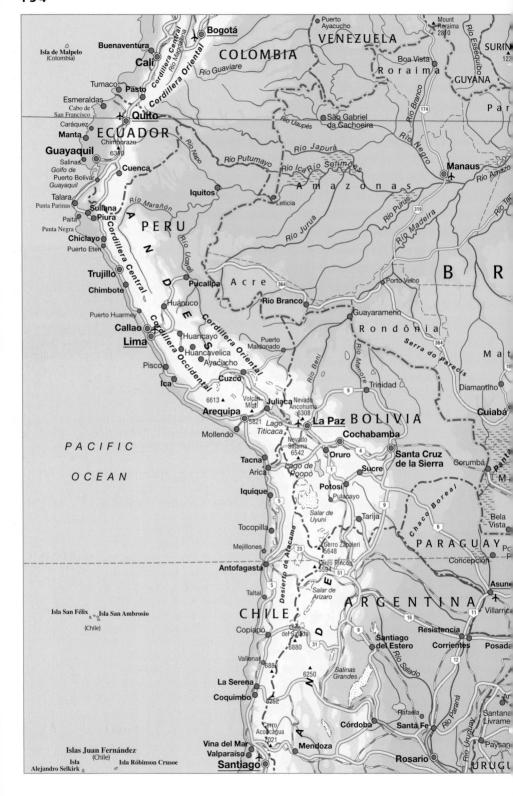

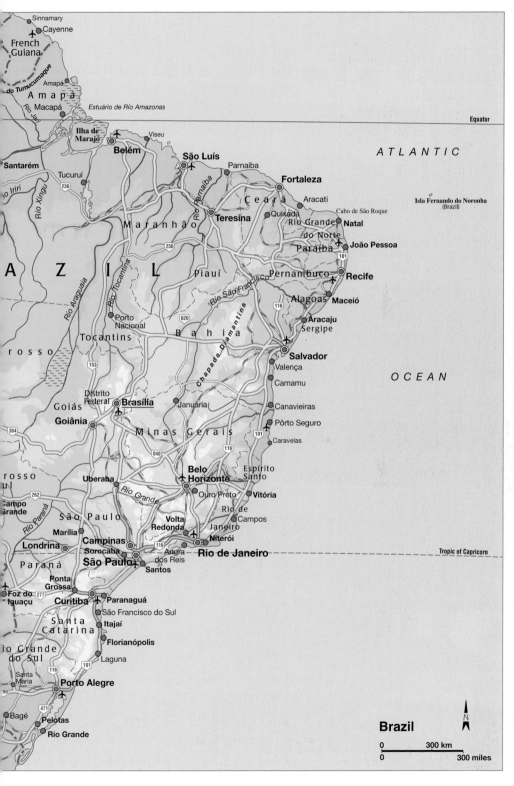

Sinnamary
✈ Cayenne
French Guiana
do Tumucumaque
Amapá
A m a p á
Río Iari
✈ Macapá
Estuário de Río Amazonas

Santarém
Ilha de Marajó
✈
Viseu
Belém
São Luís ✈
Parnaíba

Tucuruí
230
Río Xingu
Rio Iriri
Rio Araguaia
Rio Tocantins
230

M a r a n h ã o
Rio Parnaíba
Teresina
C e a r á
Aracati
Quixadá
Fortaleza
Rio Grande do Norte
Cabo de São Roque
Natal
✈ João Pessoa
101

Piauí
Pernambuco
✈ Recife
Rio São Francisco
Alagoas Maceió
116
Aracaju
Sergipe

Porto Nacional
020
B a h i a
Chapada Diamantina
✈ Salvador
Valença
Camamu

T o c a n t i n s
153
Goiás
Distrito Federal
Brasília
Januária
Canavieiras
Pôrto Seguro
101
Caravelas
Goiânia
M i n a s   G e r a i s

364
040
116

Uberaba
Belo Horizonte ✈
Ouro Prêto
Espírito Santo
Vitória
Río de Campos
262
Rio Grande

rosso ul
Campo Grande
Rio Paraná
S ã o   P a u l o
Marília
Volta Redonda ✈
Niterói
Rio de Janeiro

Londrina
Campinas
Sorocaba
116
Angra dos Reis
Rio de Janeiro
São Paulo ✈
Santos
P a r a n á
Ponta Grossa
277
Foz do Iguaçu
Curitiba ✈
Paranaguá
São Francisco do Sul
S a n t a   C a t a r i n a
Itajaí
Florianópolis
io Grande do Sul
Laguna
116
101
Santa Maria
90
Porto Alegre ✈
471
Bagé
Pelotas
Rio Grande

A T L A N T I C
Equator

Isla Fernando do Noronha
(Brazil)

O C E A N

Tropic of Capricorn

Brazil

N

0   300 km
0   300 miles

THE SOUTHEAST

Highlights of this regon include the hedonism of
Rio de Janeiro, the fast-paced nightlife of São
Paulo, and the baroque jewels of Minas Gerais

Though not large by Brazilian standards, this region contains the nation's most important metropolitan centers and, with its superior infrastructure, services, and leisure facilities, is economically streets ahead of the rest of the country. Partly because of this, and because of the allure of sun and sea, the southeast is also Brazil's premier tourist destination.

The industries that have generated wealth and comfortable lifestyles for many people in the region, operate mainly inside a triangle of three state capitals – also the three most populous cities in Brazil – Rio de Janeiro, São Paulo, and Belo Horizonte.

Alongside the manufacturing successes of São Paulo in particular, agriculture (from coffee plantations to cattle ranches) is still a major player in the southeast's economy. Sugar cane was the region's first money-spinner in the 16th century, followed by gold and diamonds in Minas Gerais, coffee in Rio state (and banking, when Rio de Janeiro was the capital city of Brazil), and, most recently, soybeans. The mines of Minas Gerais now yield mainly iron ore, feeding the region's steel industry, and securing the port of Vitória as the world's biggest exporter of the mineral. The downsides to all this, however, are pollution and shocking social inequality.

For visitors, the southeastern experience is rich with treasures, both natural and man-made. There is the incomparable city of Rio, with gorgeous beaches and an appealing laid-back lifestyle, and lush, forested mountains looming above. Strung along the coast to either side of the city are hundreds more beautiful beaches and tropical islands. São Paulo state has more stretches of perfect sand, and an infrastructure to match; and in landlocked Minas Gerais there is history and culture to lure those with a yearning to relive the romance of the pioneering days.

The colonial towns of this state are showcases for the best of Brazil's baroque art and architecture, a lasting legacy of the spectacular riches amassed by mineral prospectors. ❑

LEFT: colorful houses in Santa Teresa, Rio de Janeiro.

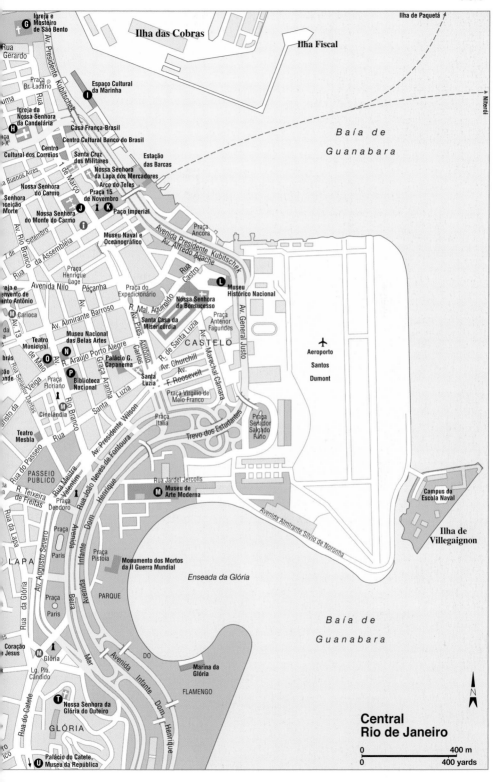

Ilha de Paquetá

Ilha das Cobras

Ilha Fiscal

Niterói

B a í a   d e
G u a n a b a r a

Igreja e
Mosteiro
de São Bento

Rua
Gerardo

Praça
Br. Ladário

Espaço Cultural
da Marinha

Igreja da
Nossa Senhora
da Candelária

Casa França-Brasil

Centro Cultural Banco do Brasil

Centro
Cultural dos Correios

Santa Cruz
dos Militares

Estação
das Barcas

Nossa Senhora
da Lapa dos Mercadores

Nossa Senhora
do Carmo

Arco do Teles

Praça 15
de Novembro

Senhora
nceição
Morte

Nossa Senhora
do Monte do Carmo

Paço Imperial

Museu Naval e
Oceanográfico

Praça
Âncora

Avenida Presidente Kubitschek

Av. Alfredo Agache

Rua
Castro

Praça
Henrique
Lage

Avenida Nilo   Pécanha

Praça do
Expedicionário

Nossa Senhora
do Bonsucesso

Museu
Histórico Nacional

R. Mal. Aguirado

Praça
Antenor
Fagundes

Av. General Justo

·eja n
·nvento de
anto Antônio

Carioca

Av. Almirante Barroso

Santa Casa da
Misericórdia

R. de Santa Luzia

CASTELO

Av. Pres. Antônio Carlos

da
a

Av. 13

Teatro
Municipal

Museu Nacional
das Belas Artes

R. Araújo Porto Alegre

Palácio G.
Capanema

Graça Aranha

Av. Churchill

Av.
F. Roosevelt

Aeroporto
Santos
Dumont

brás
são
onde

Biblioteca
Nacional

Praça
Floriano

Santa
Luzia

Santa
Luzia

Praça Virgílio de
Melo Franco

Cinelândia

Rio Branco

Av. Presidente Wilson

Praça
Itália

Trevo dos Estudantes

Praça
Senador
Salgado
Filho

Teatro
Mesbla

Rua

Rua do Passeio

PASSEIO
PÚBLICO

R. Teixeira
de Freitas

Rua Mestre
Valentim

Rua João Neves de Fontoura

Av. Dom. Henrique

Rua Jardel Jercolls

Museu de
Arte Moderna

Campus da
Escola Naval

Ilha de
Villegaignon

Praça
Deodoro

Praça

Avenida
Infante

Dom.

Praça
Paris

Praça
Pistoia

Monumento dos Mortos
da II Guerra Mundial

Enseada da Glória

LAPA

Rua da Lapa

Rua da Glória

Av. Augusto Severo

Praça
Paris

PARQUE

DO

Avenida   Beira

B a í a   d e
G u a n a b a r a

Coração
e Jesus

Glória

Lg. Pta.
Cândido

Avenida   Infante   Dom.   Henrique

Mar

Marina da
Glória

FLAMENGO

Nossa Senhora da
Glória do Outeiro

Rua do Catete

GLÓRIA

Av. Almirante Silvio de Noronha

**Central
Rio de Janeiro**

0		400 m
0		400 yards

Palácio do Catete,
Museu da República

N

RIO DE JANEIRO

Although no longer Brazil's capital, Rio de Janeiro is the country's most iconic and beautiful city. Everything, from its spectacular natural landmarks to its busy, glitzy beach scene must be seen to be believed

Sprawling in majestic disarray across a strip of land between granite peaks and the South Atlantic Ocean, Rio de Janeiro is a victory of fantasy over fact. Each day, Rio's streets and sidewalks support 12 million people, transported by a million cars, trucks, buses, motorcycles, and scooters, all competing for room in a space designed for less than one-third their number. This spectacular chaos, though, is normal, and does nothing to dampen the enthusiasm of the *cariocas*, Rio's imperturbable residents. For the *carioca*, all things are relative, except for one – the wonder and beauty of their city.

There are just over 6 million residents of Rio proper, but an additional 6 million live in suburbs ringing the city. Many are poor by American or European standards – at least 70 percent. But there is the beach and there is the samba and there is Carnival. And, not least of all, there is the comforting presence of Rio's extraordinary beauty.

Nothing quite prepares you for Rio, not the postcards, not the films, not the comments, nothing, not even living in Rio really does it. There are other cities that have grown up backed by mountains and fronted by the sea, but there are none where the play of light, the shifting of shadows, the mix of colors and hues are so vibrant and mobile. Each day in Rio is slightly different from the previous one, and all are strikingly beautiful.

Early history

The first tourists officially arrived in Rio on January 1, 1502. They were part of a Portuguese exploratory voyage headed by Amerigo Vespucci. He entered what he thought to be the mouth of a river, hence the name Rio de Janeiro or River of January. Vespucci's river was in reality a 380-sq. km (147-sq. mile) bay, still known by its Amerindian name, Guanabara or "Lagoon of the Sea."

As the Portuguese slowly settled their colony, they concentrated on

Main attractions
MUSEU NACIONAL DAS BELAS ARTES
SANTA TERESA
SUGAR LOAF MOUNTAIN
COPACABANA
IPANEMA
CORCOVADO
PARQUE NACIONAL DA TIJUCA
LAGOA RODRIGO DA FREITAS

LEFT: visitors having fun on Corcovado.
BELOW: off to the beach in style.

Crossing the bay these days is far more peaceful than it was in the 16th century.

BELOW: cooling waters in a Praça Floriano fountain.

regions to the north and south of Rio, leaving in peace the Tamoio Amerindians who at that time inhabited the land surrounding the bay. This peace was eventually broken by raids launched by French and Portuguese pirates who prowled the Brazilian coast in search of riches.

In 1555 a French fleet arrived with the intention of founding France's first colony in the southern half of South America. The efforts to colonize the coastline were largely unsuccessful, and in 1560 the Portuguese attacked, driving out the last remnants of the French colony in 1567.

From then on, Rio de Janeiro received increasing attention from Brazil's Portuguese masters. With the expulsion of the French invaders, the city of São Sebastião de Rio de Janeiro was officially founded on January 20, 1567. While named in honor of St Sebastian (having been established on his feast day), the city soon became simply Rio de Janeiro.

By the end of the 16th century, Rio was one of the four largest population centers of the Portuguese colony, and from its port sugar was exported to Europe. Its importance grew steadily over the next 10 years, challenging that of the capital of the viceroyalty of Brazil, Salvador, in the northeastern state of Bahia.

In the 18th century a gold rush in the neighboring state of Minas Gerais turned Rio into the colony's financial center. Gold became the main export item, and much of Brazil's gold went through Rio to Portugal. In 1763 the colonial capital was transferred from Salvador to Rio as recognition of Rio's newly won status.

Capital city

Until the 1960s, Rio was Brazil's pre-eminent city. When the Portuguese royal family fled from Napoleon's conquering army in 1808, Rio became capital of the Portuguese Empire. With Brazil's independence in 1822, Rio's title shifted to capital of the Brazilian Empire, changing again in 1889 to capital of the Republic of Brazil. Throughout these years the city was the economic and political center of Brazil, home to the pomp of the monarchy and the intrigue of the republic.

But the 20th century brought a surge of economic growth in the state of São Paulo. In the 1950s São Paulo surpassed Rio in population and economic importance, a lead that it has never relinquished. Then, in 1960, President Juscelino Kubitschek formally moved the nation's capital to Brasília, a city he had purpose-built for the role in the center of the country, less than five years after taking office in 1956.

Since losing its status as the nation's capital, Rio has suffered on a number of fronts. Its previous rankings as the country's leading industrial and financial center had already been taken over by the upstart São Paulo, and, although Rio's ruling classes refused to recognize the fact, the city to a large extent had become dependent on tourism, both domestic and international. But, even in the unaccustomed

role of number two, Rio remains at the heart of the nation's unending political intrigue. Decisions may be made in Brasília and São Paulo, but as the *cariocas* note with some pride, the plots are still hatched in Rio de Janeiro.

The remains of history

For visitors there is little sense – except in the city center – of Rio's historical past, a result of sporadic construction booms and the *carioca*'s insatiable thirst for the new and modern. With space limited by the contours of the city, something must usually come down before something else can go up. The wrecking ball has done away with much of the original Rio, but there are still unique treasures hidden along the old downtown streets.

In the heart of Rio de Janeiro's downtown area, at the **Largo da Carioca Ⓐ**, is the **Convento de Santo Antônio Ⓑ**. This convent was built over several colonial periods starting in 1608. The main church was completed in 1780, and next to it stands the **Igreja de São Francisco da Penitência Ⓒ**,

built between 1657 and 1772, the interior of which is rich in gold leaf and woodcarvings.

South of the Largo da Carioca is a modern area dominated by the Roman Catholic **Catedral Metropolitana Ⓓ** on Avenida Chile, which was inaugurated in 1976. This huge cone-shaped structure can cram in up to 20,000 people. Four 60-meter (197-ft) high stained-glass windows throw jewel-bright rainbows of light on the interior. The late Pope John Paul II twice visited the cathedral.

Situated north of the cathedral is **Praça Tiradentes Ⓔ**, a public square named after Brazil's most famous revolutionary, Joaquim José da Silva Xavier, better known as Tiradentes (Tooth-Puller). Tiradentes, who came from Minas, was hanged on April 21, 1792, a date that is now celebrated as a national holiday.

Praça Tiradentes is home to two of Rio's principal theaters, Teatro Carlos Gomes and Teatro João Caetano, as well as the **Real Gabinete Português de Leitura**. Opened in 1887, it has the largest and most valuable

Although much of old Rio has been lost, there are still some lovely buildings to be discovered.

BELOW: the modern Metropolitan Cathedral.

TIP

It is possible to take a cruise in the bay aboard the beautifully restored tug, *Laurindo Pitta*, built in England in 1910. The one-and-a-half hour cruises leave from the Espaço Cultural da Marinha at 1.15pm and 3.15pm Thursday to Sunday.

BELOW:
baroque splendor in the Mosteiro de São Bento.

collection of Portuguese-language literature outside Portugal, with more than 350,000 rare works.

Northeast of Praça Tiradentes, along Rua do Teatro, is Largo de São Francisco, in which stands the **Igreja da Ordem Terceira de São Francisco de Paula 🅕**, built in 1801. The exterior of the church is rococo, and the chapels inside are renowned for paintings by the baroque master Valentim da Fonseca e Silva.

São Bento to Arco de Teles

One kilometre (½ mile) north, uphill from Rua Dom Gerardo, is the **Mosteiro de São Bento 🅖**, parts of which date from 1633. This monastery overlooks the bay, but more impressive and spectacular than the view from the hill is the splendor of the monastery's gold-leaf woodcarvings.

The hill on which the monastery stands is one of the few that survive in downtown Rio. The others that existed during the colonial period have fallen victim to one form of *carioca* progress – a penchant for removing hills to fill in the bay. The

most tragic example of this trend took place in 1921–2 when the downtown hill of Castelo was carted off, together with most of Rio's remaining 16th- and 17th-century structures. Before the hill disappeared it formed a solid backdrop to Rio's most elegant street, Avenida Central, now better known as Avenida Rio Branco.

The city's most striking church, the **Igreja da Nossa Senhora da Candelária 🅗**, is situated three blocks south of the Mosteiro São Bento, along Avenida Rio Branco. Built between 1775 and 1811, the domed Candelária stands like a guardian at the head of Avenida Presidente Vargas. The church once stood close to the water, but is now far removed from the shoreline, due to the landfills formed by earth from the flattened hills.

The area designated as the **Espaço Cultural da Marinha 🅘** (Naval Cultural Center; Avenida Alfredo Agache; open Tues–Sun noon–5pm; admission charge) can be found between Candelária and the bay. The center features a number of nautical exhibits that include the imperial barge, built in Sal-

vador in 1808; the torpedo-boat *Bauru*, constructed in the US in 1943, and which took part in World War II; and the submarine *Riachuelo*, built in England in 1973 and decommissioned in 1997. Cruises round the bay (*see margin note opposite*) visit the Ilha Fiscal, the palace built in 1889 that resembles a 14th-century French castle.

Continuing parallel to the curve of the bay, along Rua Primeiro de Março, you come to **Nossa Senhora do Carmo** ❶, completed in 1761. This spectacular church, once the Metropolitan Cathedral, was the site of the coronations of both Brazilian emperors, Pedro I and Pedro II. Next door, separated by a narrow passageway, is the **Ordem Terceira do Monte do Carmo** church, dating from 1770.

Both churches sit on the western side of **Praça XV de Novembro**, home of the **Paço Imperial** ❸. This classic structure dates from 1743; it first served as the capital building for Brazil's governor generals, and was later used as the imperial palace. Restored in the 1980s, it is now a cultural center incorporating a theater, movie house, library, exhibition spaces, and restaurants. Across Rua da Assembléia is the recently restored **Tiradentes Palace**, seat of the State of Rio de Janeiro Parliament. Admission is free, and there are displays in English. The building is an impressive example of the *belle époque* style – don't miss the Grand Salon.

A good way to get to know a bit of old-style Rio is to enter **Arco do Teles** next to Praça XV, opposite the Paço Imperial. Here you'll find narrow, traffic-free streets, colorful mid-18th century buildings, quaint restaurants, and storefronts leading to high-ceilinged interiors.

Fine museums

Less than 500 meters (550 yds) southeast of Praça XV is the **Museu Histórico Nacional** ❶ (Praça Marechal Ancora; open Tues–Fri 10am–5.30pm, Sat–Sun 2–6pm; admission charge),

whose collection of colonial buildings holds Brazil's national archives of rare documents and colonial artifacts, along with a collection of photographs by Spaniard Juan Gutiérrez, who documented Rio at the end of the 19th century.

The **Museu de Arte Moderna (MAM)** ⓜ (Parque do Flamengo; open Tues–Fri noon–6pm, Sat–Sun noon–7pm; admission charge) is close to the downtown airport, Santos Dumont. The museum complements its own national collection with a series of visiting international exhibits. It is also the venue for a number of concerts and shows, and has recently inaugurated a new concert hall. The city's annual jazz festival is held here in October.

The Modern Art Museum is located just off the southern end of Avenida Rio Branco, which was inaugurated in 1905 as Avenida Central, in response to President Rodrigues Alves's vision of a tropical Paris. Unfortunately, Alves the visionary overlooked the fact that downtown Rio de Janeiro, unlike Paris, had no room to grow other than vertically. Through the years, the ele-

TIP

The lovely two-story buildings in historic Arco do Teles are known as *sobrados*.

BELOW: a peaceful corner in the São Bento complex.

BELOW: the reading
room of the
National Library.

gant three- and five-story buildings of
Avenida Central were replaced by 30-
story skyscrapers. In the process, the
avenue also underwent a name change.

Of the 115 splendid buildings that
flanked the avenue in 1905, only 10
remain. One of the most impressive,
five blocks north of the Modern Art
Museum, is the **Museu Nacional das
Belas Artes** (Museum of Fine
Arts; open Tues–Fri 10am–6pm,
Sat–Sun 2–6pm; admission charge). It
houses one of Latin America's finest
art collections, begun by Dom João
VI, and includes paintings by the
great 20th-century painter Cândido
Portinari (see pages 119–20).

The other fine buildings include the
Teatro Municipal , a splendid replica of the Paris Opera House, built in
1905; and the **Biblioteca Nacional**
(National Library; open Mon–Fri
9am–8pm, Sat 9am–3pm), an eclectic
mixture of neoclassicism and art nouveau. Holding around 15 million
works, it is the largest library in Latin
America and the eighth-largest in the
world. These buildings border the area
known as **Cinelândia**, where the city's

first movie houses were built in the
1920–30s. The Rio Film Festival is
today centered on the beautifully
restored Odeon BR, which first opened
its doors in 1926.

Most of Rio's principal museums
and cultural centers are either downtown or near by, such as the **Museu do
Indio** (Indian Museum; Rua das
Palmeiras 55; open Tues–Fri 9am–
5.30pm, Sat–Sun 1–5pm; admission
charge).

In the Botafogo neighborhood, 10
minutes from downtown, this is an
excellent source of information on
Brazil's indigenous people. The **Casa
Rui Barbosa** (open Tues–Fri
10am–5pm, Sat–Sun 2–6pm; admission charge), in Rua São Clemente,
near the Indian Museum, was home to
one of Brazil's famous scholars and
politicians. Rui Barbosa (1848–1923)
was an abolitionist who twice ran
unsuccessfully for the presidency. The
Museu Villa-Lobos (open Mon–Fri
10am–5.30pm; admission charge) in
Rua Sorocaba honours Heito Villa-
Lobos (1887–1959), considered one of
Latin America's greatest and prolific

Heito Villa-Lobos

Heito Villa-Lobos, born in Rio in
1887, showed great musical talent
from an early age, and learned to play
the guitar, cello, and clarinet as a boy.
After his father died in 1899, Heito
began playing in theater orchestras and
with street bands. He began composing
seriously in 1912, and his works drew
on many influences, from tango and
street music, to indigenous Brazilian folk
material. European influences were also
strong, from Debussy and Satie to his
great friend, French composer Darius
Milhaud. The nationalistic works he
composed during the Vargas era
engendered some criticism among
European musicians, but he later
returned to favor. His state funeral was
the last major civic event in Rio before
the capital was transferred to Brasília.

composers, whose body of work includes the *Bachianas Brasileiras*.

Fifteen minutes west by car from downtown is the **Museu Nacional** (Quinta de Boa Vista; open daily 10am–4pm; admission charge), the residence of the Brazilian imperial family during the 19th century. The palace is impressive and houses exhibits on natural history, archaeology, and minerals. It is located next door to Rio's zoo, the **Jardim Zoológico** (open daily 9am–5pm; admission charge), where the exotic and vividly colored birds are the main attraction.

Soccer and samba

The Museu Nacional and the zoo are not far from the **Maracanã**, probably the most famous stadium in the world. This is the country's temple of soccer, built for the 1950 World Cup, and is where Pelé scored his 1,000th goal in 1969. Major games take place here on Sunday afternoon and Wednesday evening. Trips to matches and to the stadium's hall of fame (on non-match days) can be arranged through the concierge of most hotels.

Maracanã in its prime could host crowds of around 200,000, and while the capacity has been reduced (it now has a capacity for 103,000 spectators), the stadium was totally refurbished for the 2007 Pan American Games. As well as soccer games, Maracanã is also the venue for major concerts. Artists who have played the stadium include Frank Sinatra, Paul McCartney, Sting, Madonna, Tina Turner, the Rolling Stones, Kiss, and the Rock-'n'Rio festival.

Soccer is one Brazilian passion, and samba and Carnival are two others. Between the Maracanã and downtown Rio are found two key elements of both samba and Carnival. In Avenida Marquês de Sapucai is located the Passarela do Samba or **Sambódromo**, where the major samba schools parade on the Sunday and Monday nights of Carnival *(see page 85)*. Designed by Oscar Neimeyer, the facilities double as a school during the rest of the year.

In 2006 the **Cidade de Samba** (Samba City; open Wed–Mon noon–8pm, special show Thur 8pm) opened in Rua Rivadavia Corrêa,

The brilliantly colored, noisy birds at Rio's zoo are a delight.

BELOW: the massive arch at the Sambódromo.

A ride on the packed Santa Teresa trolleys is great fun, but take care of your purses, cameras and wallets, as they are targeted by pickpockets.

close to the docks. The purpose-built facilities give visitors an opportunity to visit the workshops of the major samba schools and see how they prepare for carnival, and to listen to live samba music.

Trolley to Santa Teresa

Departing from downtown in front of the **Petrobrás** building (Brazil's state oil company), and close to the Metropolitan Cathedral, are open-sided yellow trolley cars that make the picturesque climb up the mountain and along the surprise-filled streets of the Santa Teresa neighborhood. The highlight of the trip is the crossing of the **Carioca Aqueduct**, known to locals as the **Arcos da Lapa Q**, one of downtown Rio's most striking landmarks. Built in the 18th century to carry water from Santa Teresa to the downtown area, the aqueduct became a viaduct in 1896 when the trolley-car service began operating.

Santa Teresa R is a tranquil nest of eccentricities perched atop the mountain spine that presses against the city down below. According to legend,

black slaves used Santa Teresa's mountain trails to escape to freedom during the 18th century, when Rio was Brazil's leading slave port. The neighborhood began to receive more permanent residents when a yellow fever epidemic forced the city's population to move up into the hills to escape from the mosquitoes carrying the disease. By the end of the 19th century, Santa Teresa became a privileged address for Rio's wealthy, whose Victorian mansions sprouted from its hillsides. Intellectuals and artists were also attracted by its cool breezes and tranquil setting, which were at the same time removed yet close to the hectic downtown area.

One of the neighborhood's most famous 20th-century residents was the "Great Train Robber" Ronnie Biggs. Biggs, the best-known of the gang that stopped a mail train in England in August 1963 and made off with more than £2.6 million (worth over £30 million/US$58 million today), escaped from a maximum security prison in London in July 1965 and made his way to Brazil via Australia. He arrived

in Rio in March 1970, and made it is home until returning to Britain in May 2001 when he was very ill. He first moved to Santa Teresa in 1979 and was a familiar and popular figure in the area.

Distinctive districts

Today, hanging from its hillsides and flanking its winding, cobblestoned streets, the architectural hodge-podge made up of Santa Teresa's homes is one of Rio's most distinctive features. Gabled mansions with wrought-iron fixtures and stained-glass windows stand beside more staid and proper edifices, all perfectly at home atop a mountain that provides a spectacular vista of the Baía de Guanabara. Views are as plentiful as flowers and greenery in Santa Teresa. The best are from the second trolley station.

Many houses in Santa Teresa now offer bed-and-breakfast accommodation, in varying degrees of sophistication and luxury. The majority are part of an organization called Cama e Café (www.camaecafe.com.br), through which reservations can be made.

There are several public stairways that lead from Santa Teresa's streets to the neighborhoods of **Glória** and **Flamengo** hundreds of meters below; and the grounds of the **Museu Chácara do Céu ⑤** (Little House in the Sky Museum; open Wed–Mon noon–5pm; admission charge, free on Wed) that look out over the city, the aqueduct, and the bay.

The museum, at Rua Murtinho Nobre 93, is one of Santa Teresa's main attractions. It contains a collection of works by Brazilian modernists, including paintings by Brazil's greatest modern artist, Cândido Portinari (see page 119), as well as some by a number of European masters.

In the Glória neighborhood southeast of Santa Teresa, perched on a hilltop overlooking Guanabara Bay, is a precious architectural gem, the chapel of **Nossa Senhora da Glória do Outeiro ⓣ** (open Mon–Fri 8am–5pm,

Sat–Sun 8am–noon; free), popularly known simply as the Glória church. This petite 1720s construction, with its gleaming white walls and classic lines, is one of the best-preserved examples of Brazilian baroque and a landmark of downtown Rio.

Near by in **Catete** is the **Palácio do Catete ⓤ**, the residence of Brazilian presidents until the move to Brasília, which now houses the **Museu da República** (Rua do Catete 153; Tues–Fri noon–5pm, Sat–Sun 2–6pm; admission charge, free on Wed), exhibiting historical paintings and items relating to the presidency and the republic. The bedroom of President Getúlio Vargas has been preserved as it was on the night of his suicide on August 24, 1954. Adjoining the palace is the **Museu do Folclore Édison Carneiro** (open Tues–Fri 11am–6pm, Sat–Sun 3–6pm; admission charge), with interesting displays on everyday life and popular religion in Brazil.

The bay

Ever since its "discovery" in 1502, Rio de Janeiro's **Baía de Guanabara**

An old-fashioned postbox outside Rio's central post office. Very few of these ornate ones remain.

BELOW: the sacristy of Nossa Senhora da Glória do Outeiro.

On trips across the bay you will see the green-spired palace on the Ilha Fiscal. Guided tours of the island are organized by the navy (tel: 21-2104 6025 for information).

BELOW: the sweeping entrance to the bay.

has delighted visitors. One Charles Darwin wrote in 1823: "Guanabara Bay exceeds in its magnificence everything the European has seen in his native land." Views of the bay, which had been mistaken for the mouth of a great river, are beautiful, accented by the two forts, one from the 17th century and the other from the 19th, which guard its entrance.

Trips across the bay to the city of **Niterói** on the far side or to the islands within the bay offer spectacular vistas looking back at Rio. The cheapest trip is by ferry boat, but more comfortable aerofoils also make bay trips (both the ferry and the aerofoils leave from Praça XV de Novembro). Schooner trips take in various tourist points and leave every Sunday at 10am, also from the Praça XV. Within the Baía de Guanabara, the favorite stop is the **Ilha de Paquetá**, largest of its 84 islands. Visitors may rent bicycles or take a magical trip around the island by horse-drawn buggy.

Although *cariocas* can be dismissive about Niterói, the city does have attractions: the **Parque da Cidade**, at the end of a winding uphill road through a tropical forest, provides stunning views of the bay and the mountains. At the foot of this hill is the Praia Itaipú, a beach that offers the same panoramic views of Rio. Niterói is also the site of the iconic **Museu de Arte Contemporânea** (open Tues–Fri & Sun 11am–7pm, Sat 1–9pm; admission charge). Designed by Oscar Niemeyer, the spaceship-like building is more of an attraction than the exhibits. See it at night, when it is spectacularly lit.

Sugar Loaf

Undoubtedly the most famous landmark on Guanabara Bay is **Pão de Açúcar ❶**, the solid granite prominence that rises 395 meters (1,300 ft) high at the bay's entrance, and is known to the world as Sugar Loaf. The Amerindians called this singularly shaped monolith *Pau-na-Acuqua*, meaning high, pointed, isolated peak. To the Portuguese this sounded like *pão de açúcar* (sugar loaf), and its shape reminded them of the clay molds used to refine sugar into a conical

Rio–Niterói Bridge

An alternative way to visit Niterói is to take an exhilarating bus ride across the extraordinary Ponte Rio-Niterói – officially called the President Costa e Silva bridge, in honor of the man who ordered its construction. Buses run from the Rodoviária (bus station), and the fare is minimal. When winds are high, the bridge is closed to traffic, for obvious safety reasons. Automobile-drivers should note that a small toll is payable at the Niterói end. Inaugurated on March 4, 1974, the six-lane bridge is a stunning sight. It is more than 13 km (9 miles) long, of which almost 9 km (5.5 miles) is over water. Construction of the bridge, by a British company, began in 1969. It was financed by British banks, and the cost was estimated at around US$22 million.

lump. In 1912, the first cable-car line was built from **Praia Vermelha ❷** at the base of Sugar Loaf to its top in two stages, the first stopping at the rounded **Morro da Urca** (Urca Mountain), which stands 224 meters (705 ft) high.

Today, visitors are whisked up in Italian-made bubble-shaped cars, each of which holds up to 75 passengers and offers 360-degree vision. Each stage takes just three minutes, with cars starting out from the top and the bottom simultaneously and zipping past each other in the middle of the ride. Departures from the Praia Vermelho station, where tickets are sold, are every half-hour from 8am to 10pm.

From both the Morro da Urca and Sugar Loaf, visitors have excellent views on all sides, with paths leading to viewpoints. To the west lie the beaches of **Leme ❸**, Copacabana, Ipanema, and Leblon and the mountains beyond. At your feet are **Botafogo** and **Flamengo** leading to downtown, with **Corcovado** peak and the statue of Christ the Redeemer behind. To the north, the bridge across the bay connects Rio de Janeiro and Niterói, with the latter's beaches stretching away to the east. At any hour of the day or night, the view is quite extraordinarily beautiful.

The beaches

While not all the bay's water is fit for swimming, the beaches that encircle it were once the principal attraction for *cariocas*. At the start of the 20th century, tunnels were constructed linking bayside Botafogo with the ocean beach of Copacabana, and Rio's beach life found a new home. Since then, the *cariocas'* endless search for the best beach has carried them constantly south, first to Copacabana, then to Ipanema and Leblon, then São Conrado, Barra da Tijuca, and beyond.

With the passage of time, a day on the beach has evolved from a tranquil family outing into an all-encompassing cradle-to-grave lifestyle of its own. Today, the beach is not part of the life of Rio, it *is* the life. The beach is a nursery and a schoolyard, a reading room, a soccer field, and a volleyball court. It serves as a singles bar, restaurant, and rock concert hall; an exercise center

TIP

Try to avoid visiting Sugar Loaf between 10am and 11am, and between 2pm and 3pm, as this is when many of the tourist buses arrive. The best time to go is an hour before sunset, when you can see the city as the light changes.

BELOW: cable cars make the trip up to Sugar Loaf every half an hour.

and office all at the same time. Occasionally, someone goes into the water, but only for a refreshing pause before returning to more important beach-based activities.

Cariocas read, gossip, flirt, jog, exercise, dream, think, and even close business deals on the beach. On a glorious summer weekend, nearly the whole of Rio spends some time on the beach. And this isn't to say they aren't on the beach during the week as well. One of the great mysteries of Rio is how anything ever gets done on a warm, sunny day.

The great equalizer

Carioca sociologists claim that the beach is Rio's great equalizer in addition to being its great escape valve. According to this theory, the poor who make up the majority of the city's residents, the inhabitants of its mountainside *favelas*, its housing projects and northern slums, have equal access to the beach and are therefore satisfied even though they are poor. Surprisingly enough, there is some truth to this simplistic and romantic notion, al-

though the rising crime rate indicates that not all of the poor are satisfied with their lot. The beach, though, remains open to all and it is free.

But while they are democratic and integrated, Rio's beaches are not entirely classless. A quick passage along the sands of Copacabana and Ipanema will take you past small "neighborhoods" of bathers, each congregating in its own social type or group – gays, couples, families, teenagers, yuppies, celebrities, and so on. If you return the next day, you will find the same groups in exactly the same places. These "beach corner societies" have become a permanent characteristic of life in Rio de Janeiro.

Copacabana

Although aged, and in some places somewhat the worse for wear, **Praia de Copacabana ❹** remains the centerpiece of Rio de Janeiro's beaches and the international tourist trade. Its classic crescent curve anchored at one end by the imposing presence of Sugar Loaf has made Copacabana a world-class picture-postcard scene for decades. Copacabana beach first gained fame in the 1920s after the opening of the high-class **Copacabana Palace Hotel**. It was also in the early 1920s that gambling was legalized in Brazil, and Copacabana subsequently became home to many of Rio's liveliest casinos.

With gambling facilities and the continent's best hotel, Copacabana evolved into an international watering hole for the world's most glamorous celebrities. Black-tie evening at the Copa, as the hotel was baptized by the *cariocas*, became de rigeur for internationally famous figures, including such luminaries as Lana Turner, Eva Perón, Ali Khan, Marlene Dietrich, and Orson Welles. Even John F. Kennedy dropped in for a visit once in the 1940s.

Casino gambling was finally outlawed in Brazil in 1946, but the party rolled on into the 1950s. Copacabana

TIP

The Copacabana Palace, which opened in 1923, was South America's first luxury hotel, and the first hotel in Rio built on the Atlantic shore rather than within the bay.

BELOW:
Copacabana sparkles by night.

suffered a slump in the 1960s, but with the construction of three major hotels and the refurbishing of others, including the landmark Copacabana Palace, the beach staged a comeback in the 1980s. Today, Copacabana beach has been widened by landfill, and still retains its magic, although Ipanema is an altogether more attractive and safer neighborhood to stay in.

Across its steaming sands on hot summer days pass literally hundreds of thousands of sun and water worshipers. Hawkers of beverages, food, suntan lotions, and hats sway across the beach, adding a musical accompaniment to the flow of colors with their singsong voices and the frantic rhythms with which they beat on small drums and whirl metal ratchets. Bathers linger beneath multicolored beach umbrellas or canopies, then briefly wet themselves in the ocean before parading across **Avenida Atlântica**, the beach drive, for a cool beer at one of the sidewalk cafés.

On any given summer weekend, up to half-a-million *cariocas* and tourists will descend on the locale to prom§-enade on Copacabana; while on New Year's Eve more than 3 million take to the streets and the sand to see in the new year. In February 2006 a crowd estimated at close to 2 million turned up to watch a free concert given by the Rolling Stones. The crush of the beach is an extension of the crush beyond the beach. The quintessential Rio neighborhood, Copacabana is made up of 109 streets on which more than 350,000 people live, squeezed close together into high-rises by the mountains at their back and the Atlantic in front. For this urban mass, the beach is their final backyard escape into open spaces.

At the Ipanema end of Copacabana beach is a section called **Arpoador ❺**, which is famed for its surfing. At the far end, standing sentinel, is the imposing **Dois Irmãos** (Two Brothers) mountain, a feature in one of Rio's most spectacular natural settings.

Ipanema

Ipanema ❻ is an Amerindian name meaning dangerous waters. It is home to a mixture of the traditionally

Cold drinks are among the most popular of the numerous things that vendors sell on Copacabana beach.

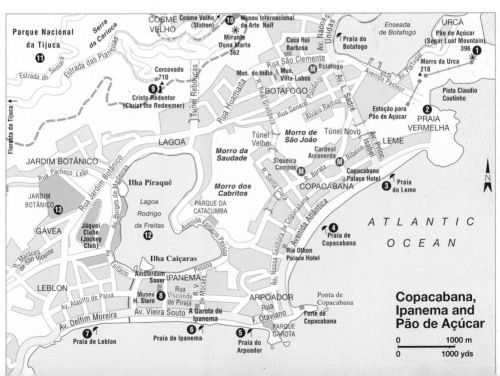

Copacabana, Ipanema and Pão de Açúcar

Despite the prevalence of cell phones, there are plenty of phone kiosks along the beaches.

BELOW LEFT: impromptu entertainment on the beach. **RIGHT:** sand sculptures are works of art.

wealthy and the nouveau riche, although many of the latter have now moved on to Barra. The area began as an adventure in land development in 1894, marked by dirt roads running through the existing sand dunes with a handful of bungalows along the sides of the roads. The neighborhood was mostly ignored until the crush of Copacabana became too much for its well-to-do residents, and they moved to the next beach south.

From the 1950s to the present day, Ipanema has undergone an extraordinary real-estate boom and population explosion, and since the 1960s, a surging army of high-rises have turned the Ipanema skyline into a smaller version of Copacabana.

In the 1960s, the neighborhood was swept by a highly romanticized wave of liberalism. Rio's bohemians and intellectuals gathered at Ipanema's sidewalk cafés and bars to philosophize over the movements of the decade – the hippies, rock 'n' roll, the Beatles, drugs, long hair, and free love. Humor was also present, expressed monthly through a satirical newspaper that proudly announced the founding of the Independent Republic of Ipanema. Two of the Republic's prominent members were the poet Vinicius de Moraes and the songwriter Tom Jobim. One day, Jobim, in the spirit of the period, became enchanted with a beautiful *carioca* girl who walked by his habitual perch in an Ipanema bar. Each day for weeks, he followed her daily passage, and even invited his friend Moraes to join him. Inspired by her beauty, the two put their feelings into words and music, the result being the bossa nova classic, *The Girl from Ipanema*.

This mystical blend of Camelot and Haight Ashbury received a severe blow with the 1964 military coup and the subsequent crackdown on liberals. Now, Moraes and Jobim are both dead, and the girl, Heloisa Pinheiro, is a middle-aged businesswoman and mother of four. However, the story of the song's origin is commemorated in place names: the street down which Heloisa walked is now named after Moraes and the bar is called A Garota de Ipanema (The Girl from Ipanema).

Despite its brevity, this period de-

fined the modern *carioca* spirit – irreverent, independent, and decidedly liberal toward matters of the flesh and spirit. It also propelled Ipanema into the vanguard in determining *carioca* style, pushing Copacabana back into second-class status.

Sand and shops

In the morning, joggers and cyclists rub shoulders, the former on the sidewalk and the latter in the *ciclovia* (cycle lane) that runs the length of the beach, while exercise-class participants go through their public gyrations. During the day, and for much of the evening, the beautiful people of the city hang out here.

Palm trees add to the intimate setting of Ipanema, as does the lack of beachfront hotels and bars. At sunset, the paved sidewalk is crowded with lovers of all ages, often strolling along hand in hand. Ipanema is less boisterous than the beachfront of Copacabana, and it preserves the romance of Rio more than any of the city's 22 other beaches.

Ipanema and **Leblon** ❼ are essentially the same neighborhood; a canal linking the lagoon with the ocean divides the two, giving rise to separate names, but there is a shared identity. They remain Rio's center of chic and sophistication. If it's not "in" in Ipanema and Leblon then it's simply not in. The city's poshest boutiques line the streets, and the trendiest are located on the main street, **Visconde de Pirajá**, and adjoining side streets running in both directions. Of these, **Rua Garcia d'Avila** is one of the best. Ipanema's shops cater to all tastes and all ages, offering leather goods and shoes in addition to clothing and gifts. Although this is not the cheapest area to shop in the city, prices are very reasonable compared to Europe and the United States.

Ipanema in recent years has become Rio de Janeiro's center for jewelry. Brazil is the largest producer of colored gemstones in the world, and samples of every variety and hue can be found on the block of Visconde de Pirajá between Garcia d'Avila and Rua Anibal Mendonça. This block is home to a number of jewelry stores, including the world headquarters of H. Stern, Brazil's leading jeweler and one of the largest in the world. The **Museu H. Stern** ❽ (Rua Garcia d'Avila 113; open Mon–Fri 8.30am–5.30pm, Sat 8.30am–12.30pm; admission free and free taxi to museum from major hotels) houses a fascinating exhibition about everything to do with jewelry, and a free guided multilingual tour is available. There is also the option – which many visitors take up – to buy exclusive jewelry at H. Stern prices.

Christ the Redeemer

Overlooking Rio's beach and city life is the world-famous statue of **Cristo Redentor** ❾ (Christ the Redeemer), standing with his arms outstretched atop **Corcovado** or Hunchback Mountain. To reach the 710-meter (2,330-ft) summit you could go by rented car or taxi, but the recommended method is the 3.7-km (2.3-mile) Corcovado Rail-

TIP

A reputable operator for tours in the Tijuca National Park is Jeep Tour, at Rua João Ricardo 24, São Cristóvão. For information, tel: 21-2108 5800 from 7am to 9pm (www.jeeptour.com.br).

BELOW:
exercising on Ipanema's colorful sidewalk.

Cosme Velho station, from where a quaint little cog train takes you up to Corcovado.

BELOW: the swan pedalos on Lagoa Rodrigo have an enduring popularity.

road, with trains leaving every 20 minutes (daily 8.30am–6.30pm) from the station in the **Cosme Velho** neighborhood, halfway between downtown and Copacabana.

The scenic ride climbs through tropical foliage, with views of the mountain and city below. From the upper station, a recently installed escalator takes visitors the short distance to the summit – although it's easy enough to walk as long as you are fit.

Located close to the train station in Cosme Velho is the **Museu Internacional de Arte Naif** ❿ (Rua Cosme Velho; open Tues–Fri 10am–6pm, Sat–Sun noon–6pm; admission charge, halved if you have a Corcovado train ticket). The museum holds one of the world's largest and most complete collections of naïve art, with more than 6,000 works dating back as far as the 15th century. Many paintings feature images of Rio and Brazil, including the huge canvas by Lia Mittarakis that you see as soon as you walk in.

On the top of Corcovado, the granite statue is visible day and night from most parts of Rio, as long as there is no mist. Standing 38 meters (125 ft) tall, it is the work of a team of artisans headed by French sculptor Paul Landowsky and was completed in 1931. Since then it has competed with Sugar Loaf for the titles of symbol of Rio and best viewpoint. One decided advantage that Corcovado has over Sugar Loaf is that it provides the best view possible of Sugar Loaf itself. Towering over the city, Corcovado also looks down on Niterói, the southern ocean beaches, and the beautiful Lagoa Rodrigo de Freitas *(see next page)*. For an even more spectacular panorama, take to the skies in a helicopter. Helisight (tel: 21-2511 2141; www .helisight.com.br) has four helipads and eight different flights available.

Enveloping Corcovado is one of Rio's most enchanting natural attractions, the **Parque Nacional da Tijuca** ⓫, a tropical reserve that includes 100 km (60 miles) of narrow, two-lane roads, winding through the forest's thick vegetation, interrupted periodically by waterfalls.

Along the way are several excellent viewpoints not to be missed. The

Mesa do Imperador, according to legend, is where Dom Pedro II brought his family for royal picnics so that they could look down directly at the lagoon and southern neighborhoods. The **Vista Chinesa** (Chinese View) looks toward the south with a sidewise glance at Corcovado; while the **Dona Marta Belvedere**, at 362 meters (1,190 ft), just below the summit of Corcovado, gives views directly toward Sugar Loaf and back to Corcovado.

Away from the beaches

Inland from Ipanema lies the **Lagoa Rodrigo de Freitas** ⓬, often referred to simply as Lagoa. This natural lake, originally part of a 16th-century sugar plantation, provides a breathing space from the crowded southern beaches of the city. Around its winding shore, joggers, walkers, and cyclists beat a steady path, while at the same time enjoying the best of Rio's mountain scenery – Corcovado and the Tijuca Forest, Dois Irmãos mountain and the distant flat top of of Pedra da Gávea.

Toward the mountains, on the western edge of the lagoon, can be found Rio's **Jardim Botânico** ⓭ (Botanical Garden; open daily 8am–5pm; admission charge), an area of 140 hectares (340 acres) containing 235,000 plants and trees representing nearly 8,000 species. Created by Portuguese prince regent Dom João VI in 1808, the garden was used to introduce plants from other parts of the world, including tea, cloves, cinnamon, and pineapples. Many species of birds and other wildlife can also be seen. The tranquil garden is a refreshing respite from the heat and urban rush and tumble of Rio, and it deserves a long, studied walk through its many and varied examples of tropical greenery. The majestic avenue at the garden's entrance is lined with a double row of 134 royal palms all more than 160 years old.

Located between the Jardim Botânico and the Lagoa is the city's magnificent Jockey Club, which offers race fans action on Saturday and Sunday afternoon and Monday and Friday evening. Foreign visitors are normally offered access to the palatial members stand, which, like the course, dates from 1926.

Follow the signs, and make sure you don't get confused by the similarity of the names.

BELOW: the Japanese Garden in the Jardim Botânico.

São Conrado

More beaches extend south of Ipanema. The first, **São Conrado ❶**, rests in an idyllic natural amphitheater, surrounded on three sides by thickly forested mountains and hills – including the Pedra da Gávea *(see opposite)*, a massive block of granite more impressive in shape and size than even Sugar Loaf, though it doesn't have the same iconic status.

São Conrado beach closes the circle on this small, enclosed valley and is popular among the affluent youth of Rio. São Conrado can be reached from Ipanema by a tunnel underneath Dois Irmãos mountain, but a far more interesting route is **Avenida Niemeyer**, an engineering marvel that was completed in 1917. The avenue hugs the mountain's cliffs from the end of Leblon to São Conrado. At times, it looks straight down into the sea with striking vistas of the ocean and Ipanema looking back. But the best view is saved for the end, where the avenue descends to São Conrado and suddenly, the ocean, the beach and the towering presence of Gávea emerge into sight. In Rio de Janeiro, the spectacular can become a commonplace, but this is a view that startles with its suddenness and unmatched beauty.

On the cliff side of Avenida Niemeyer is the neighborhood of **Vidigal**, an eclectic mix of the super-rich and those who live in abject poverty. The smart mountainside homes of the former have been surrounded slowly by the ever advancing shacks of the Vidigal *favela*.

Space, and the absence of the crush of Copacabana and Ipanema, are the main factors that separate the outlying beach areas from their better-known neighbors. Although it is compact in area, the relative lack of people means São Conrado has an uncrowded openness that is further guaranteed by the 18-hole **Gávea Golf Course**, which runs right through the middle.

Conrado contrasts

São Conrado is a near perfect microcosm of Rio society. On the valley floor live the middle- and upper-middle-class *cariocas* in luxurious apartments, houses, and condominium complexes, which line the beachfront and flank the golf course. The privileged location of the links makes it one of the most beautiful in the world, and adds to the dominating presence of greenery in São Conrado.

But as lush as São Conrado is, the beauty of the whole area is marred by a development that contrasts starkly with its wealthier face. There is a swath cut out of the hillside vegetation where **Rocinha**, South America's largest *favela (see page 162)*, spreads

Lifeguards keep an eye on unwary swimmers on Rio's beaches.

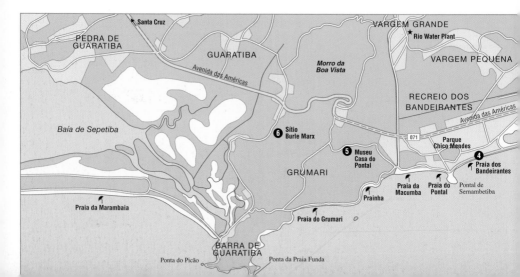

across the mountain from top to bottom. In this swarming anthill of narrow alleys and streets, at least 150,000 people live – and some estimates put it at double that number. Most of them inhabit tumbledown brick houses and shacks, pressed tightly together, side by side.

Flying over Rio

At the end of São Conrado, a highway surges past the massive **Pedra da Gávea**, where hang-gliders soar overhead. On the right, another road leads to the Tijuca National Park and Corcovado, passing through the thick tropical forest and providing memorable views of the beaches below. You may wish to experience the exhilarating sensation of jumping off a runway 510 meters (1,680 ft) above sea level, soaring above the bay, and then gliding down to the beach. To fill this need, several of Rio's more experienced and trustworthy hang-glider pilots offer tandem rides. It is safer not to take rides with hang-gliders touting on the beach. Paulo Celani of Just Fly has nearly 20 years' experience in taking people on tandem flights (tel: 021-2268 0565; cell phone: 9985 7540; www.justfly.com.br).

Barra da Tijuca

From São Conrado, an elevated roadway continues on to the far western beaches, twisting along the sharply vertical cliffs where the mansions of the rich hang suspended at precarious angles. Emerging from a tunnel, you are suddenly face to face with the **Barra da Tijuca ❷**, firmly established as the city's fastest and most prestigious middle- and upper-middle-class suburb.

Since the mid-1980s, the height and density of the buildings in Barra, as it is commonly known, have increased dramatically. Prestigious high-rise blocks march toward the mountains on the western horizon. It is now a US-style city within the city, dubbed Brazil's Miami. Everything is more expensive here, and a car is pretty much a necessity for getting around. Barra is also where Latin America's largest shopping center, **Barra Shopping ❸**, is located. This is a thriving, opulent consumer paradise that acts as a magnet for Rio's discerning shoppers, and also includes a sizeable entertainment center and modern multiplex cinema.

Barra's 18-km (11-mile) beach fills up during the weekend. All along the beach drive, the **Avenida Sernambetiba**, the traffic is bumper to bumper as Rio's middle classes seek to escape the city streets.

At night, like the other Rio beaches, Barra comes alive. There are a number of popular nightclubs and bars in

A hang-glider soars over São Conrado beach. If you want to try, there are plenty of qualified instructors who will accompany you (see page 355).

São Conrado and Barra da Tijuca

ATLANTIC OCEAN

0   2 km
0   2 miles

TIP

As well as the beach, the modern condominiums and the massive shopping centers, Barra is also home to the city's motor-racing circuit (which hosted the Brazilian Formula One Grand Prix throughout the 1980s), and Rio Centro, Latin America's largest exhibition and convention center.

BELOW:
watching the sun go down at Leblon.

the neighborhood, along with the Hard Rock Café Rio. There are also plenty of places to eat, from smart international restaurants, to fast-food outlets, to the multitude of shacks and trailers that line Avenida Sernambetiba (*see page 165 for recommendations*).

Barra's trailers

Barra's answer to Copacabana's sidewalk cafés are the beachfront trailers that sell cold drinks and hot food during the day to beachgoers. But on weekend nights these same trailers become convivial meeting points. Large crowds gather around the more popular trailers, some of which are converted at nights into samba centers called *pagodes*.

Originally confined to backyards in the city's lower-class northern neighborhoods, *pagodes* were no more than samba sing-alongs where musicians, both professional and amateur, engaged in lively midnight jam sessions. In the move to the affluent southern zone of Rio, the *pagodes* have maintained their purist samba qualities, but have acquired commercial overtones, becoming in effect open-air samba bars.

For romantics, however, there can be no quibbling over the splendid image of Barra's beachside trailers. With the surf crashing behind them, guitar and percussion instruments pounding out the samba in the night and scores of fun-seekers singing along, it is just right for an evening out in Rio de Janeiro.

Dozens of motels have sprung up in the Barra region over the years. In Rio – as in the rest of the country – motels are designed for lovers, not for tourists, and rooms are rented out by the hour and furnished with all the facilities a loving couple might desire, including saunas, whirlpools, and mirrored ceilings. Some of the motels in Barra outshine even the city's five-star hotels for unadulterated luxury and sheer indulgence.

Surf and shrimps

At the end of Barra is the **Praia dos Bandeirantes ❹**, a small beach with a natural breakwater creating the effect of a quiet bay. From Recreio

the road climbs sharply along the mountainside, descending to Prainha, a beach that is popular among surfers, and then to **Grumari**, a marvelously isolated beach where part of the movie *Blame It on Rio* was filmed.

From Grumari, a narrow, potholed road climbs straight up the hillside. At the top you will be treated to another of Rio's unforgettable views – the expanse of the **Guaratiba** flatlands and a long sliver of beach stretching off into the distance, the Restinga de Marambaia, a military property that is unfortunately off limits to bathers.

Down the hill is **Pedra da Guaratiba** (60 km/37 miles southwest of Rio), a quaint fishing village with excellent seafood restaurants (Candido's and Quatro Sete Meia). From Barra to Guaratiba is an exhilarating day trip that can be topped by a leisurely two-hour lunch of shrimp or fish dishes at any of the Guaratiba restaurants, which are the favorites of the Rio in-crowd.

There are two other attractions in the Barra and Guaratiba neighborhoods. The first one is the **Museo Casa do** **Pontal ❺** (Estrada do Pontal 3295; open Tues–Sun 9.30am–5.30pm; admission charge), which has a collection of more than 8,000 works of Brazilian folk art, collected over a period of 50 years. The second is the **Sítio Roberto Burle Marx ❻** (tours, booked in advance, Tues–Sun 9.30am and 1.30pm; admission charge), the house and garden of the late, great landscape architect. This was his home from 1949 to his death in 1994, when it was bequeathed to the nation.

Out on the town

For all *cariocas* an evening out is serious business. For many, in fact, it is more serious than the working day. To be in step with Rio time, a night out begins with dinner at 9pm or later. Most popular restaurants are still receiving dinner guests into the morning hours on weekends. Meals fall into two categories: small and intimate or sprawling and raucous. For an intimate dinner, French and Italian restaurants with excellent views are favored. For a sprawling, raucous evening, you will be best served by

TIP

When you visit the Sítio Burle Marx, consider wearing long trousers and sleeves, and adding an extra layer of insect repellent, especially if the weather is humid.

BELOW: a corner of the Burle Marx garden.

Roberto Burle Marx

Roberto Burle Marx was a leader of opinion and style, who did much more than design gardens; he also transformed the way people looked at spaces, through his use of varied textures and unusual plant groupings. The garden has more than 3,500 plant species, some of them extremely rare. Burle Marx, a flamboyant man with an adventurous approach to life, and a legendary quick temper, was a daring collector of non-plant material, too, and displayed old doors from demolition sites, bowsprit figures, clay pots, and chunky rocks to incredible effect around his house. Other examples of his work can also be seen in Flamengo Park and on the sidewalks of Copacabana, whose hallmarks are the undulating paving stones in alternating colors.

Rio's *Favelas*

The *favela*, or shantytown, has become so much a feature of life in Rio that a visit to Rocinha, the largest, is sometimes included in tourist itineraries. Rocinha first sprouted in the 1940s, and is now a swarming anthill of narrow alleys, built on the side of a steep hill. Up to 150,000 people live in Rocinha, most of them in shacks.

In many ways the *favela* is the heartbeat of Brazil's cities, a hotbed of musical talent and home of many of its most creative residents. The cultural input of the *favela* is rarely acknowledged. In fact, the Carnival would not exist if it were not for these communities. All the main samba schools come from or are named after Rio's *favelas*. All Brazilian cities have *favelas*, but those in Rio are the most visible. They sprang up as a response to the chaotic expansion of the city. Property prices exploded, making it impossible for a poor family to buy or rent a house downtown. At the same time, it was too expensive for poorly paid workers to take the two or three buses required to travel in from the cheaper suburbs. So, in the early 1900s, families began to build illegally on Rio's steep hillsides.

Around 70 percent of the people who live in Rocinha are from the impoverished northeast of Brazil. Often a family of six will live in one room with one bed for the adults, while the children sleep on the floor. Life expectancy is low – just 48 years, compared to the national average of 68 years. Illnesses such as bronchitis are common, and although medical care is available at no cost, essential medicines are not. Some 80 percent of people in Rocinha are employed, and the vast majority have nothing to do with the drugs and violence for which their community is famous. However, drug-traffickers, armed with sophisticated, modern weapons, have moved into many *favelas*, not infrequently resulting in gun battles with police troops sent in after them. Innocent bystanders, including children, have been killed by stray bullets.

A visit to a *favela* can be an enlightening experience, but should only be done with a reputable operator. The better agencies are allied with charitable organizations and plow at least some of their profits back into social projects, such as schools and teaching handicrafts. Marcelo Armstrong (tel: 21-3322 2727; www.favelatour.com.br) is a recommended operator, trusted by the communities he visits.

Today, there are an estimated 800 *favelas* in Rio, inhabited by about 3 million people. Over the years, many of the *favelados* have improved their property, so that many today have electricity and running water. Despite the harsh living conditions, almost all houses have a color television, and most have a stereo and the use of a mobile phone. There is even a thriving property business, with richer *favelados* moving on to better houses and selling their rougher shacks to newcomers.

A handful of *favelados* have become national figures. Benedita da Silva, Brazil's first black woman senator, still lives in the Chapeu Mangueira shanty town in Rio de Janeiro. Like most shantytowns, it is located on a hillside, and you have to climb 56 steps to reach Benedita's house.

What makes the Rio *favelas* extraordinary is their close proximity to some of the world's richest neighborhoods. Sprawling across a mountainside, Rocinha looks down on five-star hotels, luxury condominiums, and sophisticated restaurants, where *favelados* are employed as cheap labor. Most middle-class Brazilians would never dream of going anywhere near a *favela*, but they are happy to employ their residents as nannies to look after their children. Their stance is partly due to fear generated by the national media, which is quick to pounce on the more dramatic, inevitably negative, aspects of these communities. ❑

LEFT: Favela das Canoas clambers up the hillside.

steak houses called *churrascarias*, where *cariocas* gather with small armies of friends around long tables practically overflowing with food and drink. At night, Copacabana is traditionally the king of Rio, although a better and more sophisticated selection of bars, clubs, and restaurants can now be found in Ipanema, Leblon, and around the Lagoa.

Copacabana Beach is a good starting point. Sidewalk cafés run the length of Avenida Atlântica, and they act as gathering points for tourists and locals where cold draft beer is the favorite order. Copacabana at night is like an Eastern bazaar. Street vendors will be hawking souvenirs, paintings, wood sculptures, and T-shirts along the avenue. Prostitutes (female, male, and transvestite) prowl the broad sidewalk, with its serpentine designs.

The famous Copacabana Palace Hotel, known affectionately among the inhabitants of the city as "the Copa," was sympathetically refurbished in the 1990s, returning it to its glory days of the 1920s and 1930s, when it attracted the rich and famous from all over the world *(see page 152)*. Make sure you indulge in a cocktail by the pool, or a meal in the Cipriani Restaurant, even if you can't afford to stay here. The Sofitel Rio Palace also has a cocktail bar, from where you can watch the sun set over Ipanema.

Changing scenes

Between Copacabana and Leme is the infamous red-light district. In the dark bars and clubs, and even on the sidewalks, you will see Western men openly curb-crawling – seemingly oblivious to the risk of Aids, the desperation that causes individuals to become prostitutes, and the fact that many of the most attractive women working here are, in fact, men.

Lapa, in downtown Rio, was once the red-light district, but in recent years it has become an exciting area studded with live music bars. The crowd tends to be fairly young. You shouldn't stray from the main streets if you want to be absolutely safe. Some recommended venues include Carioca da Gema, Semente, and Rio Scenarium, which should not be missed for their varied program of Brazilian music, from samba to bossa nova, in atmospheric settings.

Circus and extravaganzas

Lapa is also home to the **Circo Voador** (Flying Circus) music venue, originally a large tent where many leading Brazilian acts got their first break in the 1980s and 1990s. A new, purpose-built venue opened in 2000 and has given Circo Voador a whole new lease of life.

For full-scale extravaganzas, Rio's leading show houses are Canecão, which is located next to the Rio Sul Shopping Center, close to Copacabana, and in Barra, the ATL Hall, showcasing the best in Brazilian and international attractions; while Plataforma I, in Leblon, presents a nightly review of Brazilian song, dance, and Carnival that is pitched quite firmly at the foreign visitor.

In case you need help, there are plenty of police kiosks.

BELOW: A Garota de Ipanema, a bar named after the celebrated song.

Barra Shopping is the largest in Latin America. To attract visitors, free buses are laid on from many hotels.

BELOW: the Sunday Hippie Fair sells crafts and souvenirs of all kinds, and the atmosphere is fun.

Popular nightclubs include Baronneti on Rua Barão da Torre, Ipanema; Bukowski on Rua Paulo Barreto, Botafogo; Six on Rua das Marrecas, Centro; and The Ball Room on Rua Humaitá, Botafogo. It goes without saying, however, that as in any large city, what is hot and what is not will change on a monthly if not a weekly basis. If you are looking for jazz and bossa nova the best call is Mistura Fina on Avenida Borges de Medeiros, Lagoa, and Vinicius Bar on Rua Vinicius de Moraes, Ipanema. To find out what is on and what is popular ask a local person or a hotel concierge, or look in the weekly Rio supplement of *Vejá* magazine.

Going shopping

Although Rio de Janeiro's first major shopping center wasn't constructed until the 1980s, *cariocas* quickly adopted the idea of shopping in air-conditioned malls, happy to escape from the summer temperatures, which average around 95°F (35°C). Nowadays, many of the city's best shops and boutiques have gravitated away from Ipanema toward the city's top malls and shopping centers, especially Rio-Sul and the giant Barra Shopping. The following are the principal shopping centers in Rio.

Rio-Sul (open Mon–Sat 10am–10pm, Sun 3–9pm; free buses from Copacabana hotels) is located in Botafogo, a short distance from Copacabana. It has been completely refurbished and has high-level security. The Rio-Sul is a good option for entertainment, too, with a nightclub, food courts, and several cinemas.

Barra Shopping (open Mon–Sat 11am–9.30pm, Sun 3–9pm; free buses to and from major hotels), Latin America's largest shopping center is in Barra da Tijuca. It closely resembles an American suburban mall.

Cassino Atlântico (open Mon–Fri 9am–9pm, Sat til 8pm) is situated on Copacabana's beachfront drive, Avenida Atlântica, at the Sofitel Rio Palace Hotel. It is smaller, but has a good selection of souvenir and antique shops, as well as art galleries.

Rio Design Leblon (open Mon–Sat 10am–9pm) has designer clothing stores and excellent food outlets, as well as home decor and furniture, which are perhaps of less interest to visitors.

São Conrado Fashion Mall (open Mon–Sat 11am–10pm, Sun 3–9pm) is not far from the Sheraton and Inter-Continental hotels in São Conrado. It is smaller but more stylish than most of the others, and has boutiques, restaurants, and art galleries.

Hippie Fair

The Ipanema Hippie Fair at Praça General Osorio (open Sun 9am–6pm) is something entirely different – a lingering reminder of the flower-children days of the 1960s. On sale is a wide variety of woodcarvings, paintings, hand-tooled leather goods, and other gifts. Many of the vendors also set up stalls and sell their wares in the evening along Copacabana's Avenida Atlântica, an atmospheric place to browse when walking home after dinner. ❑

RESTAURANTS

Albamar
Praça Marechal Ancora 184,
Centro
Tel: 21-2240 8428
Open: L&D daily.
This is one of the city's
oldest restaurants, in a
historic building.
Seafood and typically
Brazilian dishes. **$$**

Bar Lagoa
Avenida Epitácio Pessoa
1674, Lagoa
Tel: 21-2523 1135
Open: L&D daily.
A *carioca* institution
since 1934. Good-value
art deco bar for full
meal or a drink. **$$**

Cais do Oriente
Rua Visconde de Itaboraí 8,
Centro
Tel: 21-2233 2531
Open: L&D daily.
Offers an eclectic mix of
cuisine in the restaur-
ant, as well as bars, a
garden area, and a
lounge with nightly
music shows. **$$$**

Carlota
Rua Dias Ferreira 64, Leblon
Tel: 21-2540 6821
Open: L&D daily.
Small, laid-back bistro,
one of Rio's most popu-
lar with the in-crowd.
Dishes mix innovation
with the classics. **$$$**

Casa da Feijoada
Rua Prudente de Morais 10
loja B, Ipanema
Tel: 21-2247 2776
Open: L&D daily.
Specializes in Brazil's
national dish, *feijoada*,
made with black beans
and various cuts of
pork. **$$**

Celeiro
Rua Dias Ferreira 199,
Leblon
Tel: 21-2274 7843
Open: L&D Wed–Sat, L only
Mon–Tues.
Original and delightful
salads made with
organic vegetables plus
quiches, pies, and good
desserts. **$**

Colombo Tearooms
Goncalves Dias 32, Centro
Tel: 21-2232 2300
Open: Mon–Fri 8am–8pm,
Sat 10am–5pm.
A Rio institution, art
nouveau decor with
mirrored walls. Light
meals and a buffet, but
most famous for its
afternoon teas. **$$**

Garcia & Rodrigues
Avenida Ataulfo de Paiva
1251, Leblon
Tel: 21-3206 4100
Open: L&D Mon–Fri, L only
Sat–Sun.
A high-quality French
restaurant, bakery, wine
cellar, delicatessen, coffee house and snack
bar. **$$**

Gero
Rua Anibal de Mendonça
157, Ipanema
Tel: 21-2239 8158
Open: L&D daily.
Opened in 2002, Gero
is one of the hotspots
on Rio's gastronomic
map. Sophisticated
Italian cuisine. **$$$+**

Grottamare
Rua Gomes Carneiro 132,
Ipanema
Tel: 21-2523 1596
Open: D only Mon–Fri, L&D
Sat–Sun.

Popular and busy
seafood restaurant. **$$**

Hard Rock Café
Citta América, Avenida de las
Americas, Barra da Tijuca
Tel: 21-2132 8000
Open: L&D daily.
Three bars, a restaur-
ant, terrace area, and
dance floor. Brazilian
music memorabilia mix
with international stan-
dards. **$$$**

Margutta
Avenida Henrique Dumont
62, Ipanema
Tel: 21-2259-3887
Open: D only Mon–Fri, L&D
Sat–Sun.
Come to this cozy
restaurant for beautifully
prepared lobster,
shrimps, and a variety of
other seafood. **$$$**

Marius
Rua Francisco Otaviano 96
and Avenida Atlântica 290
Tel: 21-2104 9000
Open: L&D daily.
Adjoining restaurants
serve superb all-you-can-
eat seafood and *rodizio*
respectively in elegant
surroundings. You must
book, and even then be
prepared to wait up to
an hour for a table. **$$$**

Olympe (ex-Troisgrois)
Rua Custódio Serrão 62,
Jardim Botânico
Tel: 21-2537 8582
Open: L&D Mon–Sat.
According to many, this
is the best food in Rio.
Creative French cuisine
from friendly owner/chef
Claude Troisgros. **$$$**

Porcão
Avenida Infante Dom Hen-

rique, Aterro do Flamengo
Tel: 21-3389 8989
Open: L&D daily.
If you choose one barbe-
cue house, this is it. On
the Flamengo Park bay
side, with glorious views
over the bay. Wonderful
food. Equally good
branches in Ipanema
and Copacabana. **$$$**

Quadrifoglio
Rua J.J. Seabra 19, Jardim
Botânico
Tel: 21-2294 1433
Open: L&D Sun–Fri, D only
Sat.
Excellent, light, aromatic
Italian cooking in com-
fortable and friendly sur-
roundings. **$$$**

Quinta do Bacalhau
Rua do Teatro 5, Largo de
São Francisco
Tel: 21-242 8205
Right in the center of
historic Rio, this simple
but extremely good
Portuguese restaurant
specializes in *bacalhau*
(dried, salted cod). **$**

Siri Mole
Rua Francisco Otaviano 50,
Copacabana
Tel: 21-2267 0894
Open: L&D Tues–Sun, D Mon.
One of the city's best for
genuine Brazilian cook-
ing. A number of Bahian
specialties. **$$**

PRICE CATEGORIES

Prices for a two-course
meal for two. Wine costs
around US$20 a bottle.
$= under US$40
$$ = US$40–70
$$$ = US$70–100

RIO DE JANEIRO STATE

In the cool mountains above the city nestles Petrópolis, the imperial summer retreat, while the coast is blessed with a string of gorgeous beaches and tropical islands

Main attractions
PETRÓPOLIS
NOVA FRIBURGO
BÚZIOS
ARRAIAL DO CABO
ANGRA DOS REIS
ILHA GRANDE
PARATI

While the city of **Rio de Janeiro ❶** has captured most of Brazil's glory through the decades, the state of which it is the capital (also called Rio de Janeiro) is replete with attractions of its own. Like its capital, the state of Rio is an exciting contrast of forested mountains and sun-drenched beaches, all located within a few hours of the city.

Into the mountains

Dedicated as they are to beach life, Rio's residents also have the option of getting away from it all and making their escape to the cool, refreshing air of the mountains. This is especially appealing during the hottest months, and was the principal reason behind the founding of Rio's two leading mountain resorts, Petrópolis and Teresópolis. The pastel hues and green gardens of these two *carioca* getaways are a 19th-century imperial inheritance left by independent Brazil's first two rulers, emperors Pedro I and Pedro II.

Petrópolis ❷, a city of 280,000 only 65 km (40 miles) from Rio, is a monument to Pedro II, emperor of Brazil from 1831 until his exile in 1889 (he died in France two years later). The city was first envisioned in the 1830s by Pedro I, who purchased land in the spectacular **Serra Fluminense** mountain range for a projected summer palace. But it was his son, Pedro II, who actually built the palace and the quaint town surrounding it,

starting in the 1840s. The idea was to maintain a refreshing refuge from the wilting summer heat of Rio.

The road to Petrópolis is itself one of the state of Rio's prime scenic attractions. An engineering marvel, its concrete bridges soar over green valleys as the road curves around mountains and the flatlands below. From sea level in Rio, the highway climbs 810 meters (2,660 ft) during the hour-and-a-quarter drive. Along the way, visitors can still glimpse traces of the old Petrópolis Highway, a perilous, cobblestoned

LEFT: diving from the prow of a boat near Angra dos Reis. **BELOW:** the Museu Imperial, Petrópolis.

roadway that used to keep workers constantly busy the whole year round making repairs.

Life in Petrópolis is centered around **Rua do Imperador**, a busy street, and the only part of town with buildings more than five stories tall. Temperatures are lower here than in Rio, and the city's sweater-clad inhabitants give it an autumnal air during the cool months from June to September.

Perpendicular to Rua do Imperador is the Avenida 7 de Setembro, the city's lush boulevard that was used by Brazilian emperors of the past. The partially cobbled avenue is divided by a slow-moving canal, and horse-drawn carriages lined up for rent by the hour form an attractive old-fashioned taxi stand on its sun-dappled stones.

The area around the former royal Summer Palace, which is now the **Museu Imperial** (Rua da Imperatriz 220; open Tues–Sun 11am–6pm; admission charge), is crowded with trees and shrubs and criss-crossed by carefully kept pathways. There is a spectacular sound-and-light show here on Thursday, Friday and Saturday at 8pm;

admission charge). The rose-colored palace is one of Brazil's most interesting museums. Only 300 people are allowed into the museum at a time, so you may have to wait a little while. Visitors are asked to wear specially provided felt slippers, in which they pad quietly over the gleaming jacaranda and brazilwood floors. The museum's humble furnishings, as well as its outward appearance, attest to the character of Pedro II, who for the most part avoided the traditional trappings of nobility. Its second-floor collection of personal artifacts, including a telescope and a telephone, is a reminder of Pedro's scientific dabblings.

Among other items of interest in the palace museum are the spectacular **crown jewels** – a glistening frame of 77 pearls and 639 diamonds – and the colorful skirts and cloaks of the emperor's ceremonial wardrobe, including a cape of bright Amazon toucan feathers. Royal photographs on the second floor, however, show that independent Brazil's last two emperors felt more at home in their conservative business suits than in flowing robes.

TIP

The telephone in the Museu Imperial was given to the emperor by Alexander Graham Bell, inventor of the instrument. It was the first telephone to be used in Brazil.

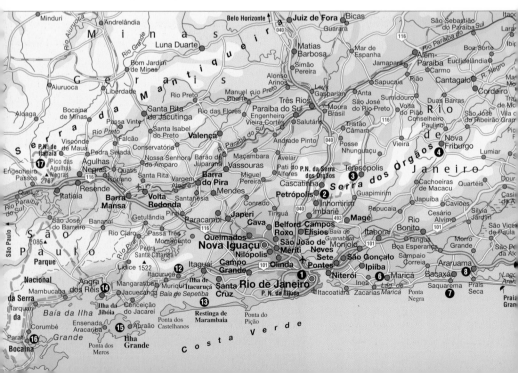

Cathedral and culture

A few blocks away at Rua São Pedro de Alcântara is the towering, French Gothic-style **Catedral de São Pedro de Alcântara** (open Tues–Sun 8am–8pm; free). This imposing structure was begun in 1884 but it took 37 years to finish the first stage, and another 48 years to complete the whole building.

The tombs of Dom Pedro II and his wife Dona Teresa Cristina are here, carved of exquisite Carrara marble. Both died in exile, and their bodies were returned here only in 1939, two decades after the decree banishing the royal family had been revoked.

The city is notable for its delightful rose-colored houses, including many that were once the dwellings of members of the royal family. Petrópolis is also known for its many overgrown private gardens and public parks, and the simple beauty of its streets. **Casa de Pétropolis – Instituto de Cultura** (open Tues–Sun; tel: 24-2242 0653) at Rua Ipiranga 716 is one of the few mansions open to the public. Go to marvel at its exquisite interior, to view its quality art exhibitions, and to have a coffee or lunch in its lovely restaurant.

A few blocks beyond the cathedral, on Rua Alfredo Pachá, is the 1884 **Palácio de Cristal** (Crystal Palace), a glass-and-iron-framed edifice still used for gardening and art exhibitions. The palace was built almost entirely of panels shipped from France. Near by is the unusual **Casa de Santos Dumont** (Rua do Encanto 22; open Tues–Sun 9am–5pm; admission charge), which displays a collection of eccentricities reflecting the unusual personality of its former owner, the pilot and inventor *extraordinaire*, Alberto Santos Dumont. The house, which he designed himself, has just one room, no tables or kitchen (his meals were delivered by a hotel), and no interior staircases. There are all kinds of shelves, each designed for a specific purpose, and a special chest of drawers that the inventor used as a bed.

Other attractions include the sprawling Normandy-style **Hotel Quitandinha** (open Tues–Sun 9am–5pm; admission charge), a luxuriously appointed structure completed in 1945

Santos Dumont, engineer and eccentric, a brilliant but troubled man.

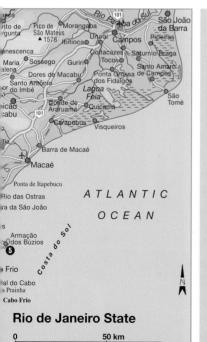

Rio de Janeiro State

| 0 | 50 km |
| 0 | 50 miles |

Alberto Santos Dumont

The downtown Santos Dumont Airport in Rio commemorates Brazil's most famous inventor. The son of a wealthy coffee-grower, Alberto Santos Dumont moved to Paris at the age of 17 in 1891 to study engineering. There he led the life of a playboy until, seven years later, he took his first flight in a balloon. Santos Dumont was enthralled, and went on to design a series of airships. He won the Deutsch Prize for flying from Saint-Cloud, round the Eiffel Tower and back – and gave half his winnings to the poor.

Later, he built 14-bis also know Oiseau de proie (Bird of Prey) ungainly aircraft resembling a series of linked box kites. In this craft, on October 23, 1906, he made the first fully documented heavier-than-air flight – in fact, the first self-powered flight, since the Wright Brothers used a catapult system to get their craft airborne three years earlier. Santos Dumont subsequently designed a monoplane, but lost interest in aviation soon afterward. Sometimes he used his inventions to visit friends in the Paris suburbs, and he would tether a small airship to convenient lamp posts near bars he wished to visit.

Santos Dumont spent his last years back in Brazil. Tragically, he committed suicide in 1932, unable to come to terms with the use of aircraft in warfare.

Souvenirs are for sale, along with fresh produce, at the Brejal market, near Itaipava.

BELOW:
the courtyard of a typical colonial *fazenda*.

as Brazil's leading hotel casino. But only a few months after its inauguration, gambling was outlawed, and has remained so ever since. Today, the striking complex, on the Rio–Petrópolis Highway 8 km (5 miles) from downtown Petrópolis, is a combination condominium and private club.

Mountain gems

Just 57 km (35 miles) from Petrópolis, at the end of a one-hour drive along steep and winding mountain roads, is Rio de Janeiro's other mountain gem, **Teresópolis** (pop. 138,000) ❸. Named after Pedro II's wife, the empress Teresa Cristina, Teresópolis was planned in the 1880s but only incorporated in 1891, two years after the royal couple's exile.

The picturesque town, which is 92 km (57 miles) from Rio on the broad **Rio–Teresópolis Highway**, clings to the edge of the **Serra Fluminense** at 870 meters (2,850 ft). The main attractions, besides the cool air, are an encompassing, though distant, view of Rio's **Baía de Guanabara** and the city's proximity to the spectacular

Parque Nacional da Serra dos Orgãos. The park is dominated by a ridge of sharp peaks, the tallest, **Pedra do Sino**, rising to 2,260 meters (7,410 ft) above sea level. But the range's most striking summit is the rocky spike called **O Dedo de Deus** (The Finger of God). On clear days, the chiseled profile of the Serra dos Orgãos can be seen from many points in Rio itself. Walking trails, waterfalls, and swimming areas make the park a delightful place to spend a day.

Nova Friburgo ❹ (pop. 180,000) is a bustling city two-and-a-half-hours' drive from Rio. It was first settled by a group of 400 Swiss (and later German) immigrant families in the 1820s, who came from the Swiss canton of Fribourg at the invitation of exiled Portuguese king João VI. Today the Brazilian lingerie industry capital, it is notable for excellent cuisine (not all Germanic), dramatic views and trail hikes in nearby, near-virgin Atlantic forest areas, many reachable from the Lumiar–São Pedro da Serra-Sana region. The excellent 65-km (40-mile) road that connects Nova Friburgo with Teresópolis is renowned

Brazil's Colonial *Fazendas*

In the 19th century, when Brazil's major export was coffee, production was centered on large farms, or *fazendas*, in the hinterland behind Rio de Janeiro; land was often hacked out of the lush Atlantic rainforest of the Paraíba valley by slaves. The wealth generated turned the coffee barons into a new elite, who established luxurious and beautiful homes. When coffee production in the area began to decline in the 1880s, to be replaced by cattle, many *fazendas* changed hands, surviving as seats for new owners with independent incomes. Some of the handful of opulent *fazendas* remaining in the valley have been converted into country hotels and restaurants that offer an experience very different from the fast life of Rio city. Set in extensive grounds, they provide relaxation and comfort, with delicious home-produced food served in the silver-plate style of a bygone age. Several have facilities for pursuits such as horse-riding and canoeing. Particularly recommended are two establishments in the former coffee- growing center of Valença: Pousada Fazenda São Polycarpo (tel: 24-9969 0060), beautifully decorated with 19th-century furniture and objets d'art; and Fazenda Pau d'Alho (tel: 24-2453 3033), which has no accommodation but serves an incomparable colonial-style afternoon tea (for which you should reserve in advance).

for its many attractions, and fine restaurants and resort hotels, such as Rosa dos Ventos (tel: 21-2644 9900), Hotel Village Le Canton (tel: 21-2741 4200), and Fazenda Vista Soberba (tel: 22-2529 4053). Recently, it has become faster and easier to drive between Nova Friburgo and the Sun Coast via a newly paved, spectacular mountain highway connecting Lumiar with Rio das Ostras near Búzios.

Paradise found

Located 190 km (115 miles) east of Rio on the Costa do Sol (Sun Coast), **Armação de Búzios 5** is a sophisticated international resort that for much of the year still manages to retain the air of a fishing village – although word has got around, and it's nothing like as quiet as it used to be, even off-season. The really busy time is the high summer season, just before, during and after Carnival, when tranquil Búzios (as it is always known) is overrun by tourists, including many cruise-ship passengers, and the population of 20,000 swells to 100,000. It is best avoided at these times.

Its tranquility was partly due to the fact that it took so long to get there, but major road improvements, following the privatization of the highway linking Rio to Búzios, have reduced traveling time significantly, and the scenic drive can now be done easily in two and a half hours, though holiday weekends still see massive traffic jams.

Búzios has undergone a major real-estate boom since the 1970s, but, fortunately, the city fathers have kept a firm hand on developers. Strict zoning laws limit building heights, with the result that Búzios has escaped the high-rise invasion that has scarred many Brazilian beaches. The fashionable homes that dot the beach-scape blend, for the most part, with the picturesque houses of the fishermen. Much of the tourist accommodation in Búzios is foreign-owned *pousadas* or inns, small and quaint, although very sophisticated and often with pools, and fancy restaurants.

The Bardot connection

According to the history books, **Búzios** was "discovered" by the Por-

TIP

If you don't want to drive, take one of the regular flights run by Team Airlines that link both Rio and São Paulo with Cabo Frio, some 23 km (15 miles) away. Comfortable buses run between Rio and Búzios at regular intervals, from the Rodoviária Novo Rio (tel: 21-3213 1800).

BELOW: a boat full of refreshments on a Búzios beach.

A bronze statue of Bardot gazes wistfully out to sea.

BELOW: children at play in Búzios.

tuguese at the beginning of the 16th century. Local people, however, know better. Búzios was actually discovered in 1964 by French actress Brigitte Bardot who spent two well-documented stays in Búzios, parading her famous bikini-clad torso along the unspoiled beaches and, in the process, spreading the fame of the little town across the globe. Búzios hasn't been the same since. After Bardot, it became a synonym for all that splendor in the tropics is supposed to be – white-sand beaches, crystalline water, palm trees and coconuts, beautiful people, and a relaxing, intoxicating lifestyle of careless ease.

What is amazing about Búzios is that all this is true. It is one of only a handful of super-hyped travel destinations that doesn't delude or disappoint. It is not just as good as the posters. It is even better.

The beaches

Altogether, there are 23 beaches in the Búzios area, some fronting quiet coves and inlets, others the open sea. The main distinction, though, is accessibil-

ity. Beaches close to the town, such as **Ossos**, **Do Canto**, and **Ferradura**, are easily reached on foot or by car.

As might be expected, the best beaches are those that require the most effort to reach, either via long hikes, sometimes over rocky ground, or by a drive along a potholed dirt road. At the end are treasures like **Tartaruga**, **Azeda**, and **Azedinha**, **Brava**, and **Forno**, known for their beautifully calm waters.

Visiting all the beaches by land is not only tiring but also unnecessary. The fishermen of Búzios have become part-time tour operators, and tourists can rent their boats by the hour or by the day. Sailboats can also be hired, as can cars and dune buggies, bicycles, motorcycles, and horses. Enthusiastic divers will find they can rent all the necessary equipment in town.

A typical Búzios day begins late (few people wake up before 11am) with a hearty breakfast at a *pousada*. Daytime activities center around the beach. Swimming, leisurely walks, or the exploration of distant beaches can be enjoyed, with the occasional break for fried shrimp or fresh oysters washed down with ice-cold beer or *caipirinha*, Brazil's national drink,- composed of *cachaça* – a sugar-cane liquor – slices of lime, and lots of ice.

As far as shopping is concerned, there is a variety of fashionable boutiques along cobblestoned **Rua José Bento Ribeiro Dantas**, better-known as **Rua das Pedras**, or Stone Street, and also on **Rua Manuel Turibe de Farias**. And as many Brazilian and foreign-born artists have taken up residence in the town, it has also turned into a booming art mart.

Nightlife in Búzios

At night, the bohemian spirit of Búzios takes charge. Though small in size, the city is considered to be one of the best in Brazil for dining out, with more than 20 quality restaurants, some of which are rated among the country's finest. Gourmets have a wide array of

cuisines from which to choose, including Brazilian, Italian, French, and Portuguese, as well as seafood and crêpes – a local favorite.

Estáncia Dom Juan (barbecued meats), Cigalon (fine French cuisine), Sawasdee (Thai cooking) and S'Essa Rua Fosse Minha (seafood and a spectacular view) are among the top restaurants in Búzios. Other eateries – many superb – are constantly popping up *(see page 179)*. A word of caution, though: the bargain prices of some of Rio's restaurants are not to be found in Búzios these days.

After dinner, the Búzios in-crowd gravitates to the city's bars, many of which have live entertainment. Both bars and restaurants are as well known for their owners as for their offerings. The city's numerous charms have waylaid dozens of foreign visitors since Bardot's first promenade. She left, but many of the others have stayed, opening inns, restaurants, and bars, and providing Búzios with an international air. Natives of Búzios have been joined by French, Swiss, Scandinavian, and American expatriates, who vow they will never leave.

The lake region

Most people go straight to Búzios from Rio, but between the two places are several beautiful beach areas worth exploring, starting with what is known as the lake region: a series of lagoons separated from the sea by lengthy sand-bars. This is a favorite surfing area, as the sea along this unbroken coastline is marked by strong currents and large waves.

Close to **Maricá ⑥** is the **Ponta Negra** beach, a spectacular, nearly deserted stretch of white sand and wild blue water. Major surfing competitions are held in nearby **Saquarema ⑦**, one of the four beach resorts in the lake region. Here, horseback riding through scenic countryside is offered at Nosso Paraíso (tel: 22-9906 8172 or 22-2653 6278). **Araruama ⑧** and **São Pedro da Aldeia ⑨** are popular among *cari-*

ocas during vacation periods (especially Carnival), when the lake region's hotels and numerous campgrounds are filled to overflowing.

Salt flats are also visible off the side of the road along this stretch, culminating in a large area of flats at **Cabo Frio ⑩**. This is officially the end of the lake region and the beginning of the Sun Coast.

Located 29 km (18 miles) from Búzios, Cabo Frio is famed for the white, powdery sand of its beaches and dunes. In vacation season, Cabo Frio's population of 110,000 swells with *cariocas* on holiday. Unlike Búzios, Cabo Frio is a historic city. Its 17th-century ruins include the **Forte São Mateus** and **Nossa Senhora da Assunção** church (both built around 1616), and the **Nossa Senhora dos Anjos** convent (built in 1686).

Undiscovered paradise

Only 18 km (11 miles) from Cabo Frio is **Arraial do Cabo ⑪**, next to Búzios the most beautiful attraction of the Sun Coast. Arraial has been discovered by the tourist trade. Once vacationers pre-

Búzios Trolley tours start from Praia da Armação (tel: 22-2623 2763). They cost about US$15, which includes fruit, soft drinks, and snacks.

BELOW:
Praia do Forte beach, Cabo Frio.

TIP

The rare resurgence ocean current maintains the water at extremely low temperatures, forcing deep, cold water from Antarctica to the surface. Plants and animals deposited on the ocean floor come into contact with sunlight and become nutrients, forming the basis of a food chain for fish, and creating an ideal underwater micro-environment for scuba-divers.

BELOW: Angra dos Reis, once a busy port, is now a seaside resort.

ferred to stay in Búzios and Cabo Frio, and just make day trips to Arraial, but now there is a range of *pousadas* and hotels to choose from.

Arraial has the clearest water in southern Brazil, making it the preferred site of scuba-divers. The city is located at the tip of a cape with a variety of beaches, some with quiet waters and lush green mountain backdrops, while others, the surfer beaches, are swept by strong winds that drive the waves high up the beach.

There are 10 licenced operators running diving tours from Arraial, which receives some 12,000 divers a year, attracted by the abundant underwater fauna, which benefits from the resurgence phenomenon *(see margin)* that provides rich nutrients for the underwater food chain, and ensures visibility even at depths of 30 meters (100 ft). Boat trips leave from the Marina dos Pescadores, at Praia dos Anjos.

Off the coast is the **Ilha do Farol**, site of a lighthouse but better-known for the **Gruta Azul**, an underwater grotto with bright blue waters. The island, accessible by boat, also offers excellent views of the mainland.

Like Búzios, Arraial began as a fishing village, and is still known for the quality of the fresh catches brought in each day. The local fishermen climb to the top of sand dunes, from where they look into the water below in search of schools of fish, a testimony to the unspoiled clarity of the waters.

The Green Coast

On the southwestern side of the city of Rio lies a string of beaches and islands known collectively as the **Costa Verde** (Green Coast). This coast stretches for 260 km (160 miles), as far as the border with São Paulo state. Named for the dense vegetation that dominates the coastline and descends right down to the sea, the Costa Verde is nature at its best: a splendid tropical mix of mountains, rainforest, beaches, and islands. Green, in every imaginable shade, surrounds you, invading even the sea with a soft turquoise hue.

Access to the Green Coast is along coastal highway BR 101, known as the **Rio–Santos Highway** after the two port cities that it connects. The scenic drive compares with the one down Spain's Costa Brava or California's State Road 1. At times, it seems almost as if you are going to take flight as the road rises high up a mountainside for a wide panoramic view, before winding steeply back down to the shoreline. This memorable route takes you past a national park, two nuclear power plants, tourist resorts, fishing villages, ocean-liner tanking stations, cattle ranches, a shipyard, and the town of Parati – a stunning monument to Brazil's colonial past.

The most enticing attractions along the Green Coast are the beaches. Some are small, encased by rocky cliffs, with clear, tranquil lagoons, while others stretch on for miles, pounded by rough surf. The entire area is a haven for sports enthusiasts, offering everything from tennis, golf, and boating to deep-sea fishing, diving, and surfing.

Although it is just about possible to see the Green Coast in a single day, to explore it thoroughly and truly enjoy its beauty, plan on two or three days, or more. Over the past 20 years, tourism has become the leading activity of the region, and there are a growing number of fine hotels and restaurants, even on some of the islands.

Tropical islands

The Green Coast begins 100 km (60 miles) outside Rio de Janeiro city at the town of **Itacuruçá** ⓬ (pop. 3,700). From the town harbor, schooners holding up to 40 people depart every morning for one-day excursions to the nearby tropical islands in the surrounding **Baía de Sepetiba** ⓭. The trips are reasonably priced, and you can buy a seafood lunch or buffet for an extra charge. The schooners stop at several islands, such as **Martins**, **Itacuruçá**, and **Jaguanum**, to allow passengers to swim or snorkel. Some of the smaller islands can be visited by hiring a boat and guide, usually a local fisherman (the islands of **Pombeba** and **Sororoca** are recommended). Also, for visitors

who wish to stay on the islands, there are several good hotels, including the Hotel Elias C and the Hotel do Pierre.

The highway continues past **Muriqui** to **Mangaratiba**, site of a large Club Mediterranée. Further down the road is **Angra dos Reis** ⓮ (Kings' Cove), the Green Coast's largest city (pop. 130,000), which sprawls across a series of hills at the beginning of a 100-km- (60-mile-) long gulf.

There are some 365 islands and 2,000 recognized beaches in the myriad of inlets, coves, and waterways around Angra dos Reis, including the large bays of Sepetiba and Ilha Grande. The water is warm and clear year-round, and still a perfect sanctuary for marine life, despite evidence of gradually rising pollution from over-building, poor regulation of sanitation, and increased shipping traffic and commercial boatyards.

Spearfishing on the rocky shores and fishing in deeper waters are favorite pastimes. The tourist information center, opposite the bus station near the harbor, provides maps and information on hotels and boat tours. The Hotel do

TIP

There are fast-track ferries that run passengers in small boats from Ilha Grande to Mangaratiba, where buses wait to deliver them to Rio hotels or direct to the airport. You can find current information on the harbor front in Abraão.

BELOW:
fishing boats
in Itacuruçá.

TIP

There are *capoeira* classes held in the Casa de Cultura in Abraão. Visitors are welcome to join in, although the energetic mix of dance and martial arts may defeat all but the very fittest.

BELOW: sarongs and hammocks for sale in Vila do Abraão. The Parrot's Beak is in the background.

Frade has the coast's only golf course (18 holes), where international tournaments are held in June and November.

Angra's tourist and accommodation infrastructure has improved significantly over the past few years, but it does not have the frenetic nightlife of Búzios. While there is a growing network of improved restaurants and bars in the city, most visitors tend to remain in their hotels or *pousadas* in the evening, sometimes going by speedboat to islands such as Ilha do Arroz, Ilha de Itanhangá and Chivas, where special night-time events and parties take place during peak season.

Ilha Grande

Some 90 minutes from Angra by boat is the paradisiacal **Ilha Grande ⑮**, a nature reserve with 192 km (120 miles) of coastline, spectacular flora and fauna, 106 beautiful beaches, idyllic coves, waterfalls, and mountain-trail walks. The island can be reached by ferry boats that operate from Mangaratiba and Angra and disembark at **Abraão**, the only town on the island – and a tiny one at that, with only about 500 permanent inhabitants. Abraão is a delightful little place, its few streets lined with wooden-shuttered houses, painted in bright primary colors.

Ilha Grande has become a very popular destination for well-heeled tourists and backpackers alike, with a recent increase in the number of chic *pousadas* and simple campgrounds, excellent restaurants, good, modest eateries, and atmospheric bars. From Abraão, small boats can be rented if you wish to visit more distant beaches such as Lopes Mendes, Mangues, and Saco do Céu. Or you can take off on your own to explore one of the many well-marked nature trails that lead over the hills.

If you are fit and healthy you could climb the 960-meter (3,150-ft) peak called the **Bico do Papagaio** (Parrot's Beak), which resembles its name. If you do so, take water and mosquito repellent, and make sure somebody knows where you've gone. It's not particularly difficult climb, but the weather can change rapidly, and clouds and mist descend in no time.

There is a strong emphasis on "ecologically aware" tourism on Ilha

Grande. A company called Body and Soul Adventures (www.bodysouladventures.com) offers a program of sea-kayaking and hiking along the island's spectacular trails, combined with yoga sessions and massage.

History preserved

From Angra, the coastal highway flanks the gulf, running past two nuclear power plants, and the picturesque fishing village of **Mambucaba**. At the far end of the bay, about three and a half hours' drive from Rio (265 km/165 miles), is **Parati** (pop. 32,000), a colonial jewel that in 1966 was declared a national monument by UNESCO and today delights visitors from other parts of Brazil and around the world.

Parati was founded in 1660, and in the 18th century gained fame and wealth as a result of the discovery of gold and diamonds in the neighboring state of Minas Gerais. The precious stones were transported by land to Parati and from there either on to Rio de Janeiro or by ship to Portugal. The city also served as the main stopping-off point for travelers and commerce moving between São Paulo to the south and Rio de Janeiro. For more than a century, Parati flourished and its citizens prospered. Opulent mansions and large estates attest to the wealth of its residents.

After Brazil declared independence in 1822, the export of gold to Portugal ceased and a new road was eventually built, bypassing Parati and connecting Rio to São Paulo directly. Parati lost its strategic position and was forgotten. Although the town then became less prosperous, neglect meant that its colonial heritage was preserved. Today, that heritage awaits visitors in the form of colonial churches and houses in the relaxed, laid-back atmosphere of a town trapped contentedly in a time warp. Be careful how you go when exploring the town: the shiny, uneven paving stones in narrow roads that slope towards the center can easily throw you off balance.

Standing out among Parati's churches is **Santa Rita** (built in 1722), a classic example of Brazilian baroque architecture that was built for the freed mulatto population. Today the church

TIP

Parati is a respected producer of *cachaça*, the sugar-cane liquor that forms the basis of the *caipirinha*, and its shops are filled with bottles of the stuff, in all shapes, sizes, and colors.

BELOW: all the streets in Parati are lined with brightly painted houses.

Literary Festival

In August 2003 Parati became the latest city to host an international literary festival, comparable with those at Hay-on-Wye, Adelaide, Toronto, Berlin, and Edinburgh. The literary festival was begun by Liz Calder, a co-founder of Bloomsbury Publishing, whose love for Brazil stems from the years she spent in São Paulo in the mid-1960s, working as a model. Several years on, Parati's annual FLIP festival, held in August, has become a very prestigious event, consolidating a reputation as one of the world's leading and truly international literary jamborees, and attracting some of Brazil's, and the world's, finest authors, including Salman Rushdie, Ian McEwan, Martin Amis, Margaret Atwood, Paul Auster, Ariano Suassuna, and Ruy Castro, among many others.

Shopping opportunities in attractive surroundings.

BELOW:
Parati's colonial architecture bathed in golden sunlight.

also houses the small **Museu de Arte Sacra** (Museum of Sacred Art; open Wed–Sun 9–11am, 2–5pm; free).

Parati and its people have a great sense of identity, and this is well displayed in the stunning **Casa de Cultura** (Sun–Mon and Wed–Thur 10am–6.30pm, Fri–Sat 1–9.30pm; admission charge). This is a monument to Parati, and to its people, their simplicity, and dignity.

All Parati's streets contain hidden surprises: art galleries, handicraft shops, quaint *pousadas*, and colonial houses. From the outside, the *pousadas* look like typical whitewashed Mediterranean-style houses, with heavy wooden doors and shutters painted in bright colors. Inside, however, they open up onto delicately landscaped courtyards with pots of ferns, orchids, rosebushes, violets, and begonias.

Parati is not known for its beaches, but schooners such as the 24-meter (80-ft) *Soberno da Costa* make day trips to the nearby islands. There are about 65 islands and 300 beaches to choose from. Hotels and travel agents sell tickets for trips out, or you can just walk along the pier and make a deal with a local fisherman to take you.

Inland detour

If heading towards São Paulo, there is an interesting detour on the state border to the **Parque Nacional de Itatiaia** ⓱ (off the Rio–São Paulo highway). This beautiful nature reserve on the slopes of the Mantiqueira range was established in 1937. It was Brazil's first national park, and has a good infrastructure for tourists. Its forests are rich in wildlife, orchids, and bromeliads; it is a paradise for birdwatchers and has beautiful waterfalls and lakes.

Higher up in the mountains, the vegetation changes to grassland and brush, then to the lunar rocky landscape of the **Pico das Agulhas Negras** (2,787 meters/9,150 ft). This is a great place for rock-climbing and trekking. Near the park entrance, there is a natural history museum (open Tues–Sun 10am–4pm). Recommended places to stay are the Hotel Simon (tel: 24-3352 1230/2214) and the Hotel do Ypê (tel: 24-3352 1453). ❑

The Gold Trail

From Parati, you may like to follow the **Gold Trail** (Caminho do Ouro), which is now open to visitors, retracing the routes taken by gold prospectors in the 18th century. This combines a bit of history, a bit of activity, and some splendid scenery. Specially adapted open trucks take you to the village of Penha, from where there is a 2.5-km (1½-mile) hike to a local farmhouse, accompanied by a *frigo-burro* (cooler-donkey), which carries cold drinks to keep you refreshed on the journey.

Departures are from the Teatro Espaço at Rua Dona Geralda 327 (Wed–Sun 10am). Further information can be had on tel: 24-3371 1575. The cost is approximately US$10, with a further US$5 if you want the lunch provided at the farmhouse.

RESTAURANTS

Petrópolis

Locanda della Mimosa
Alameda das Mimosas 30,
Vale Florido
Tel: 24-2233 5405
Open: L only Fri, L&D
Sat–Sun.
Danio Braga is rated as
one of Brazil's best
chefs, with good reason.
The fact that he's off
the beaten track doesn't
deter his fans. $$$+

Majorica
Rua do Imperador 754
Tel: 24-2242 2498
Open: daily 11am–late.
A traditional steak
house. Rump steak
remains the best-seller,
but there are dishes
with sauces, and good
fish options, too. $$

Pousada Alcobaça
Rua Dr Agostinho Goulão
298, Corrêas
Tel: 24-2221 1240
Open: daily 8am–late.
A delightful guest house
on the outskirts of
Petrópolis. Simply pre-
pared home cooking of
the highest standard.
Most vegetables are
home-grown. $$$

Solar do Imperio
Avenida Koeler 376
Tel: 24-2103 3000
Open: L&D daily.
Located in downtown
Petrópolis, this hotel's
restaurant is beautifully
appointed, and offers an
attractive menu, includ-
ing a very reasonably
priced *prix fixe* lunch
during the week. $$

Búzios

Bar do Zé
Orla Bardot 382, Centro
Tel: 22-2623 4986
Open: D only daily.
Gourmet fare. Menu
varies according to
what's fresh in the mar-
ket – a good sign. $$$

Brigitta's
Rua das Pedras 131, Centro
Tel: 24-2623 6157
Open: daily 5pm–late.
Brigitta's is a landmark.
Shrimp and lobster fig-
ure prominently, but
there are less expensive
choices to be had, and
all are good. $$$

Chez Michou
Rua das Pedras 90, Centro
Tel: 22-2623 2169
Open: daily 5pm–late.
A Búzios monument and
meeting place. Inexpen-
sive crêpes, imagina-
tively filled, lots of
noise. No credit cards. $

Cigalon
Rua das Pedras 265, Centro
Tel: 22-2623 6284
Open: Mon–Sat 6pm–late,
Sun 1pm–late.
Enterprising menu in a
sophisticated setting.
Great desserts. $$$

Estância Dom Juan
Rua das Pedras 178, Centro
Tel: 22-2623 2169
Open: daily noon–late.
Melt-in-your-mouth beef.
Delightful setting, occa-
sionally livened up by a
tango evening. $$$

Sawasdee
Orla Bardot 422, Centro
Tel: 22-2623 4644
Open: Thur–Tues 6pm–late.
A touch of Thai: plenty
of ginger and tamarind
accompany freshly
caught seafood. $$$+

Parati

Banana da Terra
Rua Dr Samuel Costa 198
Tel: 24-3371 1725
Open: D Mon, Wed, Thur,
L&D Fri–Sun.
Seafood partnered with
local ingredients. Brave
combinations make for
memorable meals.
$$–$$$

Bartholomeu
Rua Dr Samuel Costa 176
Tel: 24-3371 5032
Open: daily D only.
A touch of class. Fine
dining in an 18th-
century setting. Argen-
tine beef a specialty.
$$–$$$

Merlin o Mago
Rua do Comércio 376
Tel: 24-3371 2157
Open: D only Thur–Tues.
A touch of magic and
whimsy in a 1780s
building. Emphasis is on
fresh ingredients and
respect for their prepar-
ation. This really is very
special. $$$

Porto Entreposto Cultural
Rua do Comércio 14
Tel: 24-3371 1058
Open: L&D daily.
Creative menu, and an
attractive setting.
$$–$$$

Refúgio
Praça da Bandeira 1
Tel: 24-3371 2447
Open: L&D daily.
Comfortable, traditional
surroundings in which to
enjoy fine fish and other
dishes. Lots of shrimp,
which pushes the price
up. $$$

PRICE CATEGORIES

Prices for a two-course
meal for two. Wine costs
around $20 a bottle.
$= under $40
$$ = $40–70
$$$ = $70–100

RIGHT: outside Chez Michou restaurant in Búzios.

SÃO PAULO: CITY AND STATE

São Paulo state is Brazil's economic powerhouse.
Its capital is a vibrant place with an enormous
cultural mix, and some great restaurants.
And not far from the city lies a mountain
retreat and a number of splendid beaches

Brasília

São Paulo ● Rio de Janeiro

The state of São Paulo – Brazil's largest (pop. 40 million), most economically diverse, and wealthiest, includes a little bit of everything, from the smoky industries of São Paulo city, to beach resorts that rival Rio; from a string of pleasing mountain resorts, to a fertile farm area that is the most productive in Brazil.

The most striking element of São Paulo's modern development has been its startling velocity. During the first three and a half centuries of recorded Brazilian history (1500–1850) São Paulo was a backwater, home to a few mixed-race traders and pioneers. Today, the state of São Paulo is Brazil's economic powerhouse and as such provides one-third of the country's GNP. Half of all Brazilian manufacturing concerns are members of the Sao Paulo industrial federation (FIESP), and around half of Brazil's 50 biggest privately held corporations and private banks are headquartered in the state. The state is also responsible for federal tax revenues well in excess of the average per capita in Brazil, and a disproportionately high consumption of such items as electrical power.

First settlements

São Paulo's story is as old as Brazil's. The coastal settlement of São Vicente was founded in 1532, the first permanent Portuguese colony in the New World. A generation later, in 1554, two courageous Jesuits, José de Anchieta

and Manuel da Nóbrega, established a mission on the high plateau 70 km (42 miles) inland from São Vicente. They called the colony **São Paulo de Piratininga**. Much of São Paulo's traditional dynamism can be traced to the early isolation of settlements like São Vicente and Piratininga, located far away from the administrative and commercial center of the colony in the northeast region.

Since few European women were willing to accept the hardships of life on the wind-blown plateau, male

Main attractions
MONASTEIRO E BASILICA DE SÃO BE
TEATRO MUNICIPAL
PINACOTECA DO ESTADO
MUSEU DE ARTE DE SAO PAULO
IBIRAPUERA
PARANAPIACABA
EMBU
SAO SEBASTIAO

PRECEDING PAGES:
the city at night.
LEFT: São Paulo is
a high-rise city.
BELOW: excitement
on the trading floor.

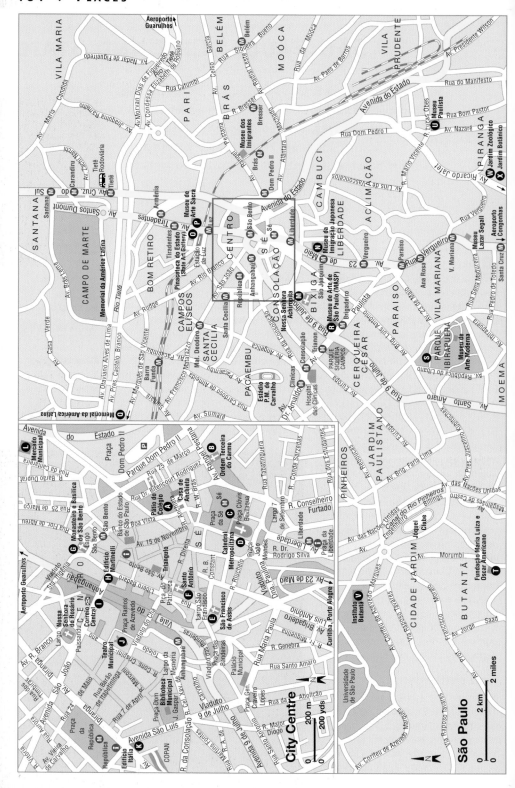

colonists married Amerindian women and fathered hardy, mixed-race children who were accustomed to the privations of a frontier life and felt no attachment to faraway Portugal.

Within two generations, the remote colony of São Paulo de Piratininga had produced its own brand of frontiersman, known as the *bandeirante*. On his Amerindian side, the *bandeirante*'s heritage included pathfinding and survival skills. From his Portuguese father, he inherited a thirst for gain and a nomadic streak that would send him roaming across half a continent moved by the desire to find gold, diamonds, and indigenous people to be sold as slaves to the colonists. Despite his less than noble motives, the *bandeirante* was instrumental in the conquest and establishment of the country's frontiers.

Bandeirante individualism was carried over to the political arena during the 19th century. Pedro I, the Portuguese emperor, was greatly influenced by his *paulista* advisers, led by José Bonifácio de Andrade e Silva. *Paulistas* are people born in São Paulo state; later in the century they led the fight against slavery and helped to establish the 1889 republic.

Economic growth

But São Paulo's true vocation was business. Attracted by the growth of British textile manufacturing, *paulista* plantation owners first cultivated cotton in the early 19th century. Lacking a large slave population, however, the state's plantations soon faced a manpower shortage, and cotton production fell behind the American competition.

So, with money from the cotton boom, they diversified into coffee, a product enjoying increased world demand and little producer competition. São Paulo's climatic conditions and the fertile red soil called *terra roxa* proved ideal for the finicky coffee bush, and the stage was set for the state to become Brazil's richest.

Within a decade, coffee surpassed cotton as São Paulo's chief cash crop.

Meanwhile, the labor-shortage problem was solved with large-scale European immigration, which began in the 1870s following a systematic campaign to attract settlers. Between 1870 and 1920, the campaign successfully attracted some 5 million immigrants. About half settled in São Paulo, most working for set contractual periods as coffee-plantation laborers.

Industry and migration

Coffee money rebuilt the once sleepy outpost of São Paulo de Piratininga. At the same time, the coffee barons began to look for investment hedges to protect themselves against a drop in world coffee prices. Their chief strategy, as in the past, was diversification, this time into manufacturing. Key elements were an innovative, dynamic business elite; ready capital from booming coffee exports; an enviable network of railroads; a first-class port; skilled, literate workers from the ranks of European immigrants; and, because of the web of rivers flowing down the coastal mountains, the Serra do Mar, ample sources of cheap hydroelectric power.

The Obelisk is a monument to the tenentes *revolt in 1924.*

BELOW: the other side of São Paulo – the Paraisopolis slum of 60,000 people in the Morumbi district.

TIP

São Paulo's international airport is 30 km (18 miles) east of the city center in Guarulhos. There are efficient airport service buses (US$10) every 30 to 45 minutes from 5.30am to 11.40pm, stopping at Praça da Republica, the Terminal Tiete bus station, and the domestic Congonhas Airport. A taxi to the city center costs about US$20. Leave at least 1½ hours before check-in time, longer at rush hour.

BELOW: a fruit vendor in downtown São Paulo.

The stage was set for São Paulo's leap toward becoming both an industrial and a financial giant. World War I was the spark: lack of European manufactured imports left a vacuum eagerly filled by a rising class of entrepreneurs. The 1930s Depression began a process of internal migration that further fed the rapidly industrializing state's hunger for labor, and made São Paulo city the world's fastest-growing major city during most of the 1960s and 1970s, with as many as 1,000 new residents arriving every day.

Independent streak

Meanwhile, São Paulo's tradition of political and intellectual independence continued into the 20th century. One of the first stirrings against the conservative old republic was a 1924 São Paulo barracks revolt led by some young army officers. In 1932, the entire state mobilized in a three-month civil war against federal intervention in state affairs.

Paulistas were also at the forefront of a nationalist intellectual movement that erupted in 1922, when the Bra-zilian government organized an exhibition in Rio de Janeiro marking the 100th anniversary of independence. A group of São Paulo artists and writers boycotted the official event, staging a parallel **Modern Art Week** at São Paulo's **Municipal Theater**.

This generation of intellectuals – the painter Anita Malfatti, novelist Mário de Andrade, critic Oswald de Andrade, sculptor Victor Brecheret, and composer Heitor Villa-Lobos – came to dominate 20th-century Brazilian arts and literature, and the continued mix of disparate elements, old and new, foreign and indigenous, is probably São Paulo's greatest charm.

São Paulo city

The state capital, also **São Paulo ❶**, is a city of contrasts. Its vast industrial park, one of the biggest and most modern in the world, attests to the force of the city's dynamo, its elegant apartment buildings and mansions demonstrate the wealth of its powerful business elite, and its cultural and gastronomic scenes rival those of New York and London. But it also reflects

Religious Mixture

This ethnically diverse city has correspondingly diverse religious beliefs. Despite its strong Catholic base, it is one of Brazil's least Catholic cities, with one-third of its population following other faiths. Due mainly to the several different waves of immigration, you now find many branches of Protestantism as well as Shinto and Buddhism among the large oriental population, Islam among the 1 million-strong community of Lebanese origin, and around 100,000 Jewish worshipers. Traditional African creeds such as *umbanda e candomblé* *(see page 70)* are also very much in evidence at all levels of society, often juxtaposed with more formalised religions. Such diversity makes São Paulo a brilliant example of Brazilian cultural and religious syncretism.

Brazil's strong socio-economic disparities. While the areas close to the city center are rich and developed, the periphery suffers from a lack of infrastructure and severe poverty. Half the population survives on a total family income of only US$100 or less a month. Yet, even for its poor, São Paulo is a "carousel," according to one of the city's most respected journalists, Lourenço Diaféria. "São Paulo is a migrant city," he notes. "Many people manage to rise here, if only because their origins were so humble."

Ethnic make-up

Despite the economic contrasts of São Paulo, its inhabitants share the usual Brazilian friendliness and *joie de vivre*. Much of this conviviality is attributed to Brazil's enormous ethnic diversity, which can be seen at its best in São Paulo. The city's 20 million inhabitants, almost 11 percent of Brazil's population, make it the fifth-largest city on earth, smaller only than Tokyo, Mexico City, Seoul and New York, and home to more ethnic communities than any other city in the region.

São Paulo is the third-largest Italian city in the world, the largest Japanese city outside Japan, the biggest Portuguese city outside Portugal, the major Spanish city outside Spain, and the third-largest Lebanese city outside Lebanon. In contrast to other large Brazilian cities, black and mixed-race people make up less than 10 percent of São Paulo's population.

The business dynamo

São Paulo is the largest center of business-oriented tourism in the country, as well as its main entrance point. The city receives around 20 million visitors a year, 57 percent of whom come here on business. The city hosts 120 of the 160 largest trade shows in the country, and stands out for its sophisticated infrastructure, geared to the business traveler, with large hotel chains established in several of its neighborhoods.

Such a large influx of business travelers is mostly due to the fact that São Paulo is not only the headquarters of several of Brazil's main national and multinational banks and corporations

Some people reckon that Liberdade, São Paulo's Japanese quarter, is more Japanese than Tokyo. While the latter has become progressively more Westernized, this small district seems to inhabit a time warp. (For more on Liberdade, see page 190.)

BELOW: seen from the air, the city is a maze of interlinked highways.

BELOW: an angelic stance outside the Cathedral.

(as has already been mentioned), but also has a modern, highly diversified industrial park that houses international blue-chip companies from important sectors such as automobile manufacturers, telecommunications, electronics, and food.

Agricultural activity is equally significant, and the Greater São Paulo region has a concentration of important agricultural distribution centers such as Mogi das Cruzes (40 km/25 miles east of the city), and Biritiba Mirim, some 70 km (45 miles) away.

In addition to this industrial and agricultural activity, São Paulo has been leaning more and more toward the the provision of medical facilities and educational establishments, as well as specializing in the service sector, with large shopping malls, and leisure and cultural centers that attract numerous visitors.

Historical center

The hard knot marking the center of São Paulo is a breezy esplanade and a handful of white-walled structures called the **Pátio do Colégio A**. It was here that the hardy Jesuits Anchieta and Nóbrega founded the São Paulo de Piratininga mission in 1554. The houses and chapel were substantially reinforced during restoration work in the 1970s. The **Casa de Anchieta**, part of the complex, is now a cramped **museum** (open Tues–Sun 9am–noon and 1–5pm; admission charge) displaying artifacts belonging to the village's earliest settlers.

It took nearly 100 years to add the first ring around São Paulo's humble settlement. In 1632, the **Igreja da Ordem Terceira do Carmo B** was built about 200 meters (660 ft) from Anchieta's chapel, just behind the historic square, **Praça da Sé C**. The Mannerist facade of the Carmo church is well preserved, although largely hidden by office buildings and a fire station. On the south side of the Praça da Sé, the present **Catedral Metropolitana D**, whose Gothic-Byzantine facade and 100-meter (330-ft) spires were built in 1954, replaced a tottering 18th-century cathedral that was torn down by the city's Roman Catholic diocese in 1920.

In 1647 a building with another appealing Mannerist facade went up at one of the outlying points of the village – the pretty **Igreja de São Francisco de Assis E**, located about 400 meters/yds from the Pátio do Colégio. A convent was attached in 1676. The complex is still bustling, and displays colonial-era woodcarvings and gold-leaf decoration.

In 1717 the **Igreja de Santo Antônio F** was completed about halfway between the Pátio do Colégio and São Francisco. Recently restored, Santo Antônio's bright yellow-and-white facade is a pleasing contrast to the gray office towers rising around it.

To the northeast of the center, in Largo São Bento, from where thousands of *bandeirantes* expeditions were launched, is one of the city's oldest buildings, the **Monasteiro e Basilica de São Bento G**, built in 1598. Its monks still sing angelic Gregorian chants, accompanied by one of the largest pipe organs in the country. These popular recitals can be enjoyed during some of the basilica's daily masses if you don't mind getting up early: Monday to Friday at 7am, Saturday at 6am and Sunday at 10am. Afterwards make sure to try the fresh bread prepared by the monks at the monastery's bakery.

Building boom

The 20th century brought a sweeping transformation to the old downtown. The peak coffee year of 1901 coincided with the inauguration of the brick-and-iron Luz train station, marked by an English-style clock tower and expansive gardens. The postwar years brought the **Banco do Estado de São Paulo**, modeled after New York's Empire State Building. Near by, on **Avenida São João**, is the 30-story office building, the **Edifício Martinelli** ; the first great status symbol of São Paulo's Italian population, it was inaugurated in 1929. Just the other side of the tunnel stands the imposing **Correio Central** ❶ (Central Post Office), built in 1920.

A few blocks south, on Rua Toledo, is the **Teatro Municipal** ❶, an eclectic building whose Italian Renaissance and art nouveau styles evoke a miniature Paris Opera House. It was designed by the noted architect Francisco Ramos de Azevedo, and inaugurated in 1911 (a square close by is named after the architect). Isadora Duncan, Anna Pavlova, and Enrico Caruso performed under the 1.5-tonne Swiss crystal chandelier, and must have been impressed by the marble, bronze, and onyx decor. The spirit of an Italian opera singer is said to belt out forlorn solos from an upper window as his equally ghostly girlfriend clasps a lily and weeps.

West of here, on the southern corner of Praça de República, is one of the most potent symbols of the new São Paulo, the 42-story **Edifício Itália** ❶, dating from 1965.

To see another building designed by Ramos de Azevedo, this one in the Depression year of 1933, you must go to the northeast edge of the city center behind Praça Dom Pedro II. Here you will find the sprawling German-Gothic **Mercado Municipal** ❶. This market is still in use, and worth a visit for its 55 pretty stained-glass windows and wonderful displays of fresh produce.

On the mezzanine level, the recently added food court offers Spanish, Portuguese, Italian, Brazilian, Japanese, and Arab specialties (open Mon–Sat 7am–6pm, Sun 7am–4pm).

City expansion

Until the mid-19th century the quadrilateral of churches, embracing a dozen or so streets of one-story dwellings, was the full extent of the "city." The 1868 inauguration of the Jundiaí–Santos railroad to transport the cotton crop changed the face of São Paulo for ever. Red brick and wrought iron crept into the city's previously rustic architecture. Workshops and warehouses grew up around the train station, near today's Luz commuter rail terminal.

Fast food for a fast city: a hot-dog seller waits for trade.

BELOW: getting a haircut in the Plaça da Sé.

The rise of coffee presaged even more growth. From 1892, when the first iron footbridge was flung across the downtown **Anhangabaú Valley**, through the 1920s, São Paulo added another ring of busy business districts and colorful neighborhoods. The coffee barons themselves were the first to build on the north side of the Anhangabaú, in a district called **Campos Elíseos**. Some of their Art Nouveau mansions, surrounded by high iron gates and gleaming with bronze and stained-glass finishings, can still be seen although, overall, the neighborhood today is a shabby remnant of its glittering past. Later, more mansions were erected in nearby **Higienópolis** and then in an elegant row along **Avenida Paulista**.

Meanwhile, thousands of immigrants poured into neighborhoods that sprouted up around São Paulo's old downtown. Vila Inglesa, Vila Economizadora, and others, their rows of red-brick houses and shops still neat and tidy, were civilized efforts to meet the city's urgent housing needs. But they didn't work.

By the time São Paulo's World War I industrial expansion began, Italian, Japanese, and Portuguese immigrants were crowded into cheek-by-jowl tenements in a ring of slums – **Brás, Bom Retiro, Bela Vista**, and **Liberdade** – circling the historic downtown. Even today these now cleaned-up neighborhoods contain tenements housing strong ethnic communities.

Distinctive communities

Bela Vista (popularly known as **Bixiga**), to the south of the center, is São Paulo's Little Italy. **Rua 13 de Maio**, Bixiga's heart, is a row of green-and-red *cantinas* and pretty little two-story houses. The parish church, **Nossa Senhora Achiropita** , is a squat mini-basilica graced by ornate columns and topped by an oversized dome. Achiropita is the site of an annual festival (which takes place during the weekends of August) celebrating wine, pasta, and music. Rua 13 de Maio is roped off as thousands gather for dancing, drinking (5,000 liters of wine is consumed), and eating (3 tonnes of spaghetti and 40,000 pizzas).

TIP

Bela Vista's nickname – Bixiga – is not very flattering. In Portuguese it means bladder, and refers to an early 20th-century market here that sold tripe to immigrants who could not afford anything better.

BELOW:
Liberdade, where East meets West.

Liberdade

A sprawling neighborhood centered around Rua Galvão Bueno, Liberdade, São Paulo's lively Japanese quarter, is home to 1.5 million Japanese, the largest population outside Japan. Liberdade's history began in June 1908, when the steamer *Kasato Maru* docked in Santos harbor with 830 Japanese immigrants on board. Their journey from the coffee farms in the interior of the state to the founding of their own quarter in the city of São Paulo is recounted at the exceptional **Museu da Imigração Japonesa**  (open Tues–Sun pm; admission charge) on Rua São Joaquim. The building also houses a school that teaches the ritual of the tea ceremony.

Today Liberdade is cherished by locals and tourists alike for its trendy shopping, top-quality oriental food and unbeatable atmosphere. To sample the cuisine, pay a visit to Kinoshita (Rua da Glória 168), a traditional restaurant with innovations orchestrated by fashionable chef Tsuyoshi Murakami; or Sushi Yassu (Rua Tomás Gonzaga 98), which offers the best sushi in town, and a huge menu. Or try one delicacy at a time at the Oriental Street Fair on Sunday (9am–7pm) at Praça Liberdade (by Liberdade Metro). Day or night, Liberdade is full of life, color, and surprises. Visitors typically have only one complaint – they find it hard to believe they're in the heart of South America.

Bom Retiro, north of the historic center, near the Luz train station, retains vestiges of its past as São Paulo's Arab and Lebanese Christian neighborhood. Twisting Rua 25 de Março packs fabric and rug stores side by side in a noisy bazaar. Jewish, Muslim, and Christian merchants sip coffee together and chat as if Middle East tensions did not exist.

East of the city center, surrounding the cavernous Roosevelt commuter train terminal, is Brás. Predominantly Italian at the turn of the 20th century, Brás today houses thousands of migrants from the impoverished northeast. They are São Paulo's bus drivers, sun-seared road workers, and construction laborers. Their culture, rich with the sap of Brazilian folklore, can be seen on every street corner. *Nordestino* (northeastern) accordion players perform nightly at the shabby north end of Praça da Sé. During the day, *repentistas* (guitar players who make up clever, rhyming lyrics on any subject suggested by onlookers) hold forth on the breezy São Bento esplanade. Bahian *capoeira* (Afro-Brazilian martial dance, *see page 106*) performers move to the eerie sound of the single-string *berimbau* outside the Anhangabaú subway station, and at Praça do Patriarca, a *nordestino* herb salesman deals in alligator skins, colorless elixirs, and Amazon spices sold from burlap sacks spread on the sidewalk.

From the 1940s onwards, São Paulo added more and more commercial and residential rings as it spiraled outward. Higienópolis and the Jardins, south of Avenida Paulista, became middle- and upper-class, high-rise apartment neighborhoods. Later, offices, apartments, and shopping centers formed another ring around elegant Avenida Faria Lima, just to the south of Paulista. In the 1970s, São Paulo jumped the Pinheiros River to start an even glitzier ring in hilly Morumbi, where strikingly landscaped mansions include the official residence of the state governor.

Museums and galleries

Although São Paulo's citizens are known as workaholics, the city offers plenty of leisure pursuits. It has the best cultural attractions in the country, as well as excellent parks.

Behind the Luz train station and park (north of the center; Metro Luz or Tiradentes) is the Pinacoteca do Estado ⊙ (State Art Gallery; Praça da Luz 2; open Tues–Sun 10am–6pm; admission charge, free on Sat), a beautiful neoclassical building designed by Ramos de Azevedo in 1905. What MASP *(see page 192)* does for Western art, the state gallery's 5,000-piece collection does for its Brazilian counterpart. Highlights include sculptures by Vitor Brecheret, creator of the *Bandeirantes Monument*, and Júnior's *A Leitura*, a portrait of a girl reading against a background of palm trees and striped awnings.

Across Avenida Tiradentes from the Pinacoteca do Estado is São Paulo's most important collection of colonial art and artifacts. The Museu de Arte Sacra ⓟ (Avenida Tiradentes 676; Metro Armenia or Tiradentes; open

TIP

Admission charges for most museums and galleries are very small – usually US$1–3 except for MASP *(see page 192),* which currently charges US$10.

BELOW: the city's shopping streets are always busy.

The sober facade of the Catholic University.

BELOW: the massive Bandeirantes Monument.

Tues–Fri 11am–6pm, Sat–Sun 10am–7pm; admission charge) contains 1,000 pieces displayed in the former cloisters and chapel of the labyrinthine **Mosteiro da Luz**, and represents the evolution of sacred art in Brazil.

The main baroque structure of the monastery was completed in 1774, although portions date from the late 17th century. The collection is completed by oil portraits of São Paulo's first bishops, gold and silver altar accoutrements, carved gold-leaf fragments of churches torn down by the juggernaut of 20th-century progress, and rare woodcarvings by Brazil's great 18th-century sculptor Antônio Francisco Lisboa, better known as Aleijadinho *(see page 203).*

To the west, the **Memorial da América Latina** ❑, designed by Oscar Niemeyer on his traditional bold arcs of concrete, was built in 1989 (Metro: Barra Funda). The buildings house an important **Latin American Cultural Center** (open Tues–Sun 9am–6pm; free) with a museum, a library, an auditorium, and an exhibition center.

You need to go to the south of the city center (Metro Trianon-MASP) to visit MASP, the **Museu de Arte de São Paulo** ❑ (Avenida Paulista 1578; open Tues–Sun 11am–5pm; admission charge). This is São Paulo's cultural pride, with nearly 1,000 pieces originating from ancient Greece and contemporary Brazil. The unusual display arrangement – rows of paintings encased in smoked-glass slabs – was designed chiefly as a teaching aid. Detailed explanations on the back of each display put the artists and their work into historical perspective.

The museum is like an art history book – but offering the real thing instead of color plates. Raphael, Bosch, Holbein, Rembrandt, Monet, Van Gogh, Goya, Reynolds, and Picasso are just a few of the artists representing major European trends. The museum also includes a survey of Brazilian art from 19th-century court painters Almeida Júnior and Pedro Américo, to 20th-century modernists Portinari, Di Cavalcanti, and Tarsila do Amaral.

Further south is São Paulo's most important park and modern art venue. **Ibirapuera** ❑ (Metro Vila Mariana or Paraiso and a short taxi ride) is a huge area of trees, lawns, and handsome pavilions, completed to celebrate São Paulo's 400th anniversary in 1954. Today, some 200,000 *paulista* use its playgrounds, picnic areas, and sports complex on sunny weekends. At the front of the park are two of São Paulo's most noted monuments: the 72-meter (235-ft) **Obelisk and Mausoleum** honoring heroes of the 1932 civil war, and Vitor Brecheret's **Bandeirantes Monument**, a tribute to the 17th-century pioneers *(see page 34).* Ibirapuera's low-slung curving pavilions, designed by Oscar Niemeyer, constitute São Paulo's most important cultural center *(see box opposite).*

Off to the west, across from the imposing state governor's palace in Morumbi, the **Fundação Maria Luiza e Oscar Americano** ❑ (Avenida Morumbi 4077; open Tues–Fri

11am–5pm, Sat–Sun 10am–5pm; admission charge) is São Paulo's most bucolic setting for art appreciation. It's a lovely spot, but you'll have to take a taxi to get there. Oscar Americano was a noted architect and collector who willed his estate to the public as an arts foundation when he died in 1974. The discreet glass-and-stone mansion displays works by Di Cavalcanti, Portinari, Guignard, 17th-century Dutch painter Franz Post, and many others, against a lush background of broad lawns and landscaped woods. A tearoom overlooks the ground-floor patio and is open until 6pm. String quartets and soloists perform in a small auditorium on Sunday afternoon.

Imperial reminders

In the tranquil suburb of Ipiranga, the sprawling **Museu Paulista ⓤ** (Metro Vila Mariana and a short taxi ride; Avenida Nazaré s/n; open Tues–Sun 9am–4.45pm; admission charge) marks the spot where Pedro I declared Brazilian independence. An equestrian monument stands on the site where Pedro shouted, "Independence or death!" before a small entourage. The emperor's remains are buried beneath the bronze-and-concrete landmark.

The massive, neoclassical museum building is a hodge-podge of historical and scientific exhibits. One wing displays artifacts relating to Pedro and his family. Another includes furnishings, farm implements, and even horse carts from São Paulo's colonial past. Research by the University of São Paulo on Brazil's Amerindians has yielded material for several galleries, including an interesting display of pre-Columbian pottery from the Amazon island of Marajó.

Other exhibits honor the aviation pioneer Alberto Santos Dumont (who was born in Petrópolis), and the state militiamen who fought in the 1924 *tenentes* military revolt *(see page 34).* A separate gallery displays Pedro Américo's 1888 painting *Independencia ou Morte,* a romanticized portrayal of Pedro I's famous declaration quoted above.

To the southwest of the city, in the grounds of the São Paulo University, is the **Instituto Butantã ⓥ** (Avenida

TIP

Most museums and attractions can be reached conveniently by Metro, but for the few that can't, you need to take a taxi. The city's buses are overcrowded, slow, and not very safe. Taxis are metered and quite expensive – around US$12 for a 15-minute journey. It's always best to take a taxi when going out at night.

BELOW: sculpture at the 26th São Paulo Bienal.

Art in the Park

The main showcase of the Ibirapuera pavilions is a three-story rectangle of ramps and glass, which hosts São Paulo's prestigious Bienal art shows (Oct–Dec in even-numbered years; (www1.uol.com.br/bienal). Held since 1951, this is the world's largest regularly scheduled arts event, bringing together all that's new, experimental, and weird in the worlds of art and music. The pavilion also hosts industrial and cultural fairs. The third floor displays a permanent collection of contemporary Brazilian art. Linked to the pavilion by an undulating breezeway, the **Museu de Arte Moderna** (open Tues–Wed, Fri–Sun 10am–6pm, Thur 10am–10pm; admission charge) hosts changing exhibits of work by Brazil's contemporary sculptors and painters.

If you are fascinated by snakes, the Instituto Butantã is the place to go – it's got about 1,000 of them.

BELOW: most of the animals in the city zoo are kept in natural habitats.

Vital Brasil 1500; Metro Clínicas and a taxi ride; open Tues–Sun 9am–4.30pm), founded in 1901, is one of the world's leading centers for the study of poisonous snakes. The slithery reptiles are everywhere – coiled behind glass in ornate kiosks, piled one on top of the other in grassy habitats, stuffed and mounted in display cases next to hairy spiders and scorpions. Altogether, there are some 1,000 live snakes on the premises. Periodically, staff members will milk venom from their fangs.

Dining and shopping

For most *paulista* as well as foreign visitors, São Paulo is above all else a restaurant city. With its many ethnic communities, each with their own national dishes and restaurants, São Paulo has raised food appreciation to the level of worship. For the *paulista*, the substitute for Rio's beach life is an active nightlife centered on wine and dinner at one of the city's many restaurants. The largest concentration of good restaurants is in Jardim Paulistano, Cerqueira Cesar and Itaim Bibi

(see page 201). Although most restaurants open early, they do not fill up until 9 or 10pm on weekdays and even later on the weekends. Wednesday and Saturday are *feijoada* days in São Paulo. *Feijoada* is one of the most traditional Brazilian dishes, and some say that it started with the African slaves who added bread and offal to the pieces of pork left over by their masters. Another theory is that it derives from European recipes such as Portuguese stews. This irresistible calorific bomb of black beans and several types of meat is best eaten at lunchtime, preferably when a digestive nap can be taken afterwards.

When *paulista* are not working or dining out, they are usually shopping. **Rua Augusta**, around Rua Oscar Freire in Jardim Paulista, is the traditional headquarters for fashionable but pricey men and women's wear. Forum, Zoomp, and Ellus are famous boutiques. There are more boutiques in various galleries spread along Rua Augusta. **Rua Oscar Freire** and its surroundings (Rua Bela Cintra and Rua Haddock Lobo) are known as São

Further Afield

For those with time to go further afield (and who don't mind a relatively expensive taxi ride), there's a completely different side to São Paulo. The city has one of the world's largest zoos, with no fewer than 3,200 animals and 444 species, mostly occupying natural habitats. The **Jardim Zoológico** Ⓦ (Avenida Miguel Stéfano 4241; open Tues–Sun 9am–5pm; admission charge), noted for its tropical bird collection, attracts several million visitors annually.

On the same street as the zoo is the **Jardim Botânico** Ⓧ (Botanic Garden; open Wed–Sun 9am–5pm). There is public access to 360,000 sq. meters (430,000 sq. yards) of gardens, with two glasshouses containing hundreds of delicate plant species, including an orchid collection. The Botanic Institute here educates the public on the various ecosystems of Brazil.

North of the city, there's a delightful open space, the **Horto Florestal**, also known as Parque Albert Löefgren (Rua do Horto 931; open daily 6am–6pm). Founded in 1896, the park has a playground, good walking trails, and the Pedra Grande viewpoint, offering a beautiful view of the north of São Paulo city. Within the park the **Museu Florestal Octavio Vecchi** (open Mon–Fri 9–11.30am, 1.30–4pm) displays a huge variety of native woods.

Paulo's 5th Avenue, where you can find designer names including Versace, Fendi, Montblanc, Armani, Kenzo, Thierry Mugler, Cartier, and Tommy Hilfiger. A Saturday morning stroll through this area allows a fascinating glimpse into the lifestyle of the Brazilian rich and famous.

For antique-lovers the best bet is to visit one of the fairs that take place in museums and city squares on the weekend. The most famous are the MASP fair every Sunday at the Museu de Arte de São Paulo (Avenida Paulista 1578; 9am–5pm); and the fair at Shopping Center Iguatemi's parking lot, also on Sunday (Avenida Faria Lima; 9am–5pm).

But the *paulistano*'s first love is the shopping center. The priciest is **Morumbi**. The oldest, the most elegant, and, for many, the best, is **Iguatemi**, on Avenida Faria Lima; and the most traditional is **Ibirapuera**, a boxy structure near the park. The newest is **Shopping Light**, an upmarket mall with boutiques and eateries near the Anhangabau Metro station in the center of town.

Nightlife

São Paulo has a seemingly infinite number of bars *(botecos)*, nightclubs, and discos. The choice of where to go depends on taste, money, season, age, and what is or is not currently trendy. São Paulo's nightlife comes alive around midnight. Be warned that instead of an entrance fee, many venues use a card with a pre-set minimum amount that you pay at the end of the night. Even soft drinks can be expensive, and some places also charge an "artistic cover" to pay for the cost of the band.

The most varied nightlife, packed with the young and beautiful, can be found in Itaim Bibi, Vila Olímpia and Vila Madalena, where artists, university students, and alternative minds meet for some of the best "see and be seen" ambience in town. The best draft beer is at Original (Rua Grauna 137, Moema, in the south of the city), but for an incredible night view of the city Skye is champion. Attached to the restaurant of the same name, Skye is located on the roof of the Hotel Unique (Avenida Brigadeiro Luis Antonio

As in most city markets, the art on sale may be good, bad, or indifferent, but most of it is the work of local artists.

BELOW:
São Paulo has lots of good restaurants, and they always seem to be busy.

Ayrton Senna died in May 1994, aged only 34, but the legend lives on.

4700, Jardim Paulista). Varied live music can be found at Grazie a Dio! (Rua Girassol 67, Vila Madalena), and great dancing at the CB Bar (Rua Brigadeiro Galvao 871, Barra Funda). But for those looking for a truly romantic and classy venue, the Baretto at Hotel Fasano is unbeatable (Rua Vitorio Fasano 88, Jardim Paulista). Bars on Rua da Consolaçäo (between Alameda Jacé and Alameda Tietê) generally cater to a gay clientele.

Cigar aficionados should head for the Havana Club in the Hotel Renaissance (Alameda Santos 2233, Cerqueira César) – a comfortable cigar lounge and bar with its own dance floor. For cowboys and cowgirls (even the Brazilian ones, of whom there are many), there is Jardineira Beer (Avenida dos Bandeirantes 1051, Vila Olímpia).

Diverse entertainments

São Paulo's postwar growth (and money) has made it a magnet for world-class performers. A typical season might bring the Bolshoi Ballet, the New York Philharmonic, James Taylor, and many other stars to venues including the **Anhembi Convention Center**, the state-of-the-art **Credicard Hall**, **Ibirapuera Gymnasium**, the **Teatro Municipal**, or the **Direct TV Music Hall** in Moema. The **Alfa Real Theater**, next to the Transamérica Hotel, offers modern and comfortable facilities for the performing arts. Top musical acts perform at **Tom Brasil** in Vila Olímpia. (Check the local press for details or go to www.gringoes.com and follow the links.)

São Paulo competes head-to-head with Rio when it comes to X-rated entertainment. Glitzy strip bars featuring explicit "erotic" acts start on Rua Augusta near the Caesar Park Hotel, extending all the way to Rua Nestor Pestana downtown. Others are located on Rua Bento Freitas near the Hilton. In Itaim Bibi, near Ibirapuera, there is also the renowned Café Photo.

Mountain resorts

Like the inhabitants of Rio de Janeiro, São Paulo residents can vacation in the mountains or on the shore without leaving their home state. At 1,628 meters (5,600 ft), and 167 km (103 miles) from São Paulo, in a lush valley of the Mantiqueira range, **Campos do Jordão ❷** is São Paulo's chief mountain resort, with alpine chalets and winter weather. The month-long July Music Festival at the modern **Claudio Santoro Auditorium** features classical and popular programs, and has become the most important musical event in the country.

Next door is the pleasantly landscaped **Felícia Leirner sculpture garden** (open Tues–Sun 10am–6pm). On display are magnificent bronze and granite works by the Polish-born artist whose name it takes.

The hub of Campos do Jordão's busy downtown is a row of chalet-style restaurants and shops. Local products include metal, wood, and leather crafts. Near by is a tranquil lake circled by horse-drawn carriages for hire. Yellow and brown trollies carrying tourists occasionally rattle past.

Formula One Magic

Brazil's Formula One world championship reputation bears comparison with its record for soccer success. Since Emerson Fittipaldi started the trend in 1972, armed with what was arguably the greatest Formula One design of all time, the Lotus 72D Emmo, Brazilians have won more championships than drivers of any other nationality. Fittipaldi was followed by Nelson Piquet, winner of three world titles, and then by Brazil's most celebrated driver, Ayrton Senna. Senna was second only to Alain Prost in the number of Formula One victories (he won 41 times against Prost's 51) and in the total number of Formula One championship points. He died aged 34 during the San Marino Grand Prix at Imola in May 1994, and became one of Formula One's greatest legends.

One motivating factor for Brazilian drivers must be that Brazilians worship success, and world-conquering sportsmen become instant national heroes. Yet it cannot be denied that, at its best, Brazilian driving, like Brazilian soccer, is nothing short of magical. And that magic is more than capable of galvanizing the crowds into a frenzy whenever a local driver wins at home – as happened when Felipe Massa won the Brazilian Grand Prix on São Paulo's Interlagos circuit in October 2006 , the first Brazilian to do so since Senna in 1993.

Ringing the downtown area are around 50 hotels and dozens of summer homes belonging to the *paulistano* elite. The largest such abode, bearing the impressive name **Palácio Boa Vista**, is the state governor's winter retreat. A portion of this Tudor-style mansion has been converted into a **museum** (open Wed–Sun 10am–noon, 2–5pm; admission charge). Attractions of the museum include 19th-century furnishings and oil paintings by *paulista* artists, including Tarsila do Amaral, Di Cavalcanti, and Cândido Portinari.

About 12 km (7 miles) from downtown, Itapeva Peak offers an impressive view of the Paraíba River Valley, where São Paulo coffee bushes first took root more than a century ago.

Somewhat closer to São Paulo, 60 km (40 miles) north on the Fernão Dias Highway, but better organized for visitors, is the mountain resort of **Atibaia ❸**, São Paulo's peach and strawberry capital. A winter festival honors the lowly strawberry, selling everything from strawberry jam to pink strawberry liquors.

At 800 meters (2,600 ft) above sea-level, Atibaia's crisp, clean air attracts families in search of hotels with sports and leisure facilities, such as the Village Eldorado and the Estancia Atibainha. The younger crowd comes to Atibaia to practice hang-gliding or paragliding from the platforms of the stunning Pedra Grande.

The city's delightfully landscaped Parque Municipal features mineral water springs, lakes, and a **railroad museum** (open weekends and holidays 10am–6pm; admission charge). Near the center is Atibaia's white-walled **Museu Historico Municipal João Batista Conti** (Praça Bento Paes; open Tues–Sun 10am– 5pm; free), dating from 1836.

Railroad outpost

Some 60 km (40 miles) from São Paulo, traveling toward the coast, is a quaint railroad outpost frozen in time,

Paranapiacaba ❹. Built in 1867 by British railroaders, the brick-and-board station and row houses are a portrait of Victorian England. The tall clock tower is reminiscent of Big Ben at Westminster. At a height of 800 meters (2,500 ft), Paranapiacaba (which means Sea View in the Tupi-Guarani language) was the last station on the Jundiaí–Santos line before the breathtaking plunge down the Great Escarpment.

A half-hour train ride, on a creaking, huffing engine, brings tourists through tunnels and across narrow viaducts to the edge of the sheer mountainside for a spectacular view of the Santos lowlands. Paranapiacaba offers few amenities, however. There are no hotels or restaurants, only a few fruit and soft-drink stands. A **museum** (open Sat–Sun only) displays 19th-century train carriages and memorabilia.

Strolling by the river.

Day trips

Quaint, prosperous **Itu ❺**, 100 km (60 miles) from São Paulo on the Castelo Branco Highway, is another fresh-air paradise. The town's delights include 18th- and 19th-century row houses on

BELOW:
the alpine-style
Campos do Jordão.

pretty pedestrian streets, and a handful of cluttered antique stores. The **Museu Republicano da Convenção de Itu** (open Tues–Sat 10am–4.45pm, Sun 9am–3.45pm; free) off the main square exhibits colonial and imperial-era furnishings and artifacts. A small **Museu da Energia** (open Tues–Sun 10am–5pm; free) tells the story of electricity.

Closer to São Paulo, 28 km (17 miles) on the Regis Bittencourt Highway, is the state handicrafts capital of **Embu ⑥**. Most stores open Tuesday to Sunday, 8am–6pm, and every Sunday the town's two main squares, and a network of pedestrian streets linking them, become a vast primitive arts, handicrafts, and Brazilian food festival, when cars are not allowed in the town's center.

Ceramics, leather- and metal-worked handicrafts, woolen goods, lacework, knitted items, and colorful batiks are for sale at wooden stalls. On Largo dos Jesuitas, woodcarvers practice their craft in the open air, often surrounded by an audience. Rows of quaint 18th-century houses serve as

antique and rustic furniture stores.

Visitors can sample Bahian delicacies like *vatapá* (a seafood or chicken stew) or coconut sweets at outdoor stalls, or choose from among a dozen interesting restaurants. Near by, O Garimpo and Casa do Barao specialize in varied Brazilian cuisine.

Beaches

The beach resorts of São Paulo are not something for which the state is famous. Nevertheless, its stretch of the Rio–Santos Highway, one of the most beautiful in the country, offers the visitor more than 400 km (240 miles) of beaches, which are regular retreats for affluent city workers during weekends and holidays.

Ubatuba ⑦, only 70 km (40 miles) from Parati in southern Rio de Janeiro (*see page 177*, is convenient for both São Paulo and Rio, although its charms are low-key rather than picturesque. A total of 85 km (50 miles) of beaches curl around Ubatuba's inlets and islands. Boat trips take visitors to the Anchieta Prison ruins on one of the main islands, then continue up the coast

At the Embu handicrafts market you can see craftsmen at work, so you know that goods are locally made.

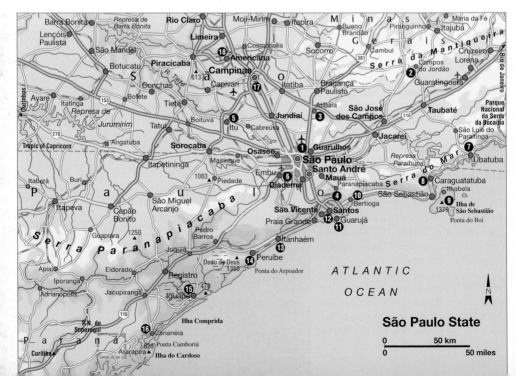

São Paulo State

0   50 km

0   50 miles

to the eerie remains of Lagoinha Sugar Plantation, which was partially destroyed by fire during the 19th century.

Caraguatatuba ❽, 50 km (30 miles) south of Ubatuba on State Highway 55, has almost as many beaches but fewer historical attractions than its northern neighbor. Its excellent Pousada Tabatinga offers several sports facilities just a step away from the sand.

São Sebastião ❾, 25 km (15 miles) south from Caraguatatuba on Highway 55, has an eclectic clutch of beaches distributed over some 100 km (60 miles) of coast. Maresias and Camburi beaches are good for surfing and eating out, with a very lively nightlife. Boicucanga has more accommodation options and Barra do Una has good fishing, boat trips, and dining. The center of São Sebastião is where historical buildings and services are concentrated.

From São Sebastião ferry boats take visitors to the village of **Ilhabela**, also called São Sebastião Island. The startling mountain scenery, waterfalls, beaches, and azure sea have made the island popular with São Paulo's wealthy set. Ilhabela is also a byword for water sports, and every July it hosts the largest sailing event in South America.

Another 100 km (60 miles) down Highway 55 is peaceful **Bertioga** ❿, where there is some interesting flora and fauna. The **Forte São João**, with blazing white walls and miniature turrets, guards a narrow inlet. Its ancient cannons bear down on passing pleasure craft. The fortress dates back to 1547, and is considered the oldest in the country.

Thirty kilometers (18 miles) south of Bertioga is one of the most frequented towns on São Paulo's coast, the resort of **Guarujá** ⓫. **Enseada** is the most popular beach, a horseshoe of spray, sand, and gleaming hotels recalling Copacabana. Near by is the more isolated **Pernambuco** beach. São Paulo's monied elite have made this their Malibu. Mansions of every archi-tectural style – surrounded by broad lawns and closed in by fences, hedges, and guards – look out over surf and green and gray offshore islands.

Like São Paulo, Guarujá is a city for restaurant-goers. Highly recommended are Il Faro for Italian cuisine and Rufino's for seafood, and the bar and restaurant of the Casa Grande Hotel, a sprawling colonial inn on **Praia da Enseada**. Just a few blocks from the Casa Grande is the narrow area of **Praia de Pitangueiras**. Streets near the beach have been pedestrianized so people can browse unhindered among dozens of boutiques, handicraft and jewelry stores.

Island port

From downtown Guarujá, visitors can catch the car ferry across an oily inlet to **Santos** ⓬, São Paulo's chief port. *Santistas* don't try to hide the business end of their island – hulking tankers ply the narrow channels spewing oil; freight containers are piled in ugly pens or next to dilapidated warehouses. Unfortunately, this decay has spread from the port to the

TIP

The name Bertioga comes from the Tupi word Buriquioca, which means "the home of big monkeys."

BELOW: the São Sebastião canal at Ilhabela.

The history of coffee production can be traced at the Bolsa Oficial de Café.

city's old downtown area. Historic **Igreja do Carmo**, with portions dating from 1589, is a gray facade next to a broken-down train station. Near by, a slum district has sprung up around the 17th-century **São Bento** church and its **Museu de Arte Sacra** (Rua Santa Joana D'Arc 795; open Tues–Sun 2–5pm; free). The recently restored **Bolsa Oficial de Café** in Rua 15 de Novembre houses a small but interesting coffee museum and café. There is also a football memorial dedicated to the city's greatest players.

The ocean side of Santos, however, shows the same whitewashed face as Guarujá. The **Museu de Pesca** (Fishing Museum; open Tues–Sun 10am–6pm; admission charge), near the Guarujá ferry landing, exhibits stuffed fish killed in nearby waters, an immense, 91-kg (200-lb) octopus, and the bones of a 23-meter (76-ft) whale, as well as fishing boats.

São Vicente, Brazil's oldest settlement, is only 5 km (3 miles) from Santos and was the first Portuguese permanent settlement (1532). The main Gonzaguinha beach is lined with white and pastel-colored apartment houses, bars and outdoor restaurants. São Vicente is the gateway to Brazil's most crowded beach – **Praia Grande**, in season a seemingly endless stretch of spray, grayish-brown sand, and bobbing human bodies.

Another 60 km (35 miles) south on Highway 55 is a very different scene, slow-moving **Itanhaém** ⓭, another one of Brazil's oldest settlements. Parts of the gray, spooky Nossa Senhora da Conceição chapel date back to 1534.

Other beach towns south of São Vicente include pretty **Peruíbe** ⓮ (80 km/50 miles); **Iguape** ⓯ (200 km/120 miles), on a quiet inlet formed by Ilha Comprida; and remote **Cananéia** ⓰ (280 km/170 miles), which has a nature reserve and also offers boat excursions to nearby islands, which have some isolated beaches.

Northern towns

Two urban centers in the northern interior of the state are worth a brief visit (if you are passing that way). One is industrial **Campinas** ⓱ (100 km/60 miles from São Paulo), which became wealthy from sugar and coffee. It is now the site of one of Brazil's best universities, Unicamp, which was a refuge for left-wing teachers during the years of military repression.

The city has a fine cathedral, the neoclassical **Catedral Metropolitana**, dating from 1883, on Largo do Rosário. The main cultural venue, which has a noted symphony orchestra, is the **Centro de Convivência** (Praça Imprensa Fluminense).

Nearby **Americana** ⓲ was the most successful of the Brazilian communities settled by Confederates fleeing the southern states of the United States after the Civil War (1861–5). They were drawn here by the prospect of cheap land, religious freedom, and the fact that slave labor – an institution that the war had brought it to an end in the United States – was still legal in Brazil. ❏

RESTAURANTS

Arabia
Rua Haddock Lobo 1397,
Cerqueira Cesar
Tel: 11-3061 2203
Open: L&D daily.
Spacious, comfortable
restaurant that serves
wonderful Lebanese
food. **$$**

Baby Beef Rubaiyat
Alameda Santos 86, Paraíso
Tel: 11-3141 1188
Avenida Brigadeiro Faria
Lima 2954, Itaim Bibi
Tel: 11-33078 9488
Open: L&D daily.
Elegant *churrascarias*,
considered among the
city's best. **$$**

Cantaloup
Rua Manuel Guedes 474,
Itaim Bibi
Tel: 11-3078 3445
Open: L&D Mon–Fri, D only
Sat, L only Sun.
A real favorite. Can-
taloup serves creative
contemporary food in a
beautifully refurbished
old bread factory. **$$**

Capim Santo
Alameda Ministro Rocha
Azevedo 471, Cerqueira
Cesar
Tel: 11-3068 8486
Open: L&D daily.
Particularly good value
is the lunchtime buffet
with seafood, salad, and
meat. On Sundays the
buffet includes shrimp
or lobster. **$$**

Cheiro Verde
Rua Peixoto Gomide 1413,
Jardim Paulista
Tel: 11-289 6853
Open: daily.

Vegetarians can have a
tough time in Brazil, but
here they are well
catered for in a simple,
friendly restaurant. **$**

Fasano
Rua Vitorio Fasano 88,
Cerqueira Cesar
Tel: 11-3062 4000
Open: Mon–Sat D only.
If you can afford it, go to
one of the most luxuri-
ous restaurants in São
Paulo. Finest Italian
cooking in the Fasano
Hotel. **$$$+**

Gero
Rua Haddock Lobo 1629 Tel:
11-3064 0005
Open: L&D daily.
A bistro version of the
Fasano, offering the
same quality for a lower
price, in a younger, more
informal setting. **$**

Jardim de Napoli
Rua Dr Martinico Prado 463,
Higienópolis
Tel: 11-3666 3022
Open: daily, all day.
Typical Italian *cantina*
serving good pasta and
pizzas. **$**

Koyama
Rua 13 de Maio 1050, Bela
Vista
Tel: 11-283 1833
Open: L&D Mon–Sat.
Exceptionally good
Japanese food in tradi-
tional surroundings. **$$**

Le Coq Hardy
Rua Jeronimo da Veiga 461,
Itaim Bibi
Tel: 11-3079 3344
Open: L&D Mon–Fri, D only
Sat.

The best French restau-
rant in town. Chocolate
tasting for dessert. **$$**

Massimo
Alameda Santos 1826,
Cerqueira Cesar
Tel: 11-3284 0311
Open: daily.
Top-class Italian and
international cuisine in
spacious, elegant sur-
roundings; excellent
wines. A favorite with
top executives and polit-
icians. **$$$**

Panino Giusto
Rua Augusta 2963, Jardim
Paulista
Tel: 11-3064 9992
Open: daily.
Deliciously elaborate
sandwiches and light
meals. **$**

Portucale
Rua Nova Cidade 418,

Vila Olímpia
Tel: 11-3845 8929
Open: L&D Tues–Sat, L only
Sun.
Traditional Portuguese
specialties, always
nicely presented. **$$**

Vinheria Percussi
Rua Conego Eugenio Leite
523, Pinheiros
Tel: 011-3088 4920 Open:
L&D Tues Sat, L only Sun.
A delightful restaurant
serving exquisite, deli-
cately flavored Italian
food. **$$**

PRICE CATEGORIES

Prices for a two-course
meal for two. Wine costs
around US$20 a bottle.
$= under US$40
$$ = US$40–70
$$$ = US$70–100

RIGHT: the chic Quinta do Mandioca restaurant.

THE SPLENDOR OF BRAZILIAN BAROQUE

Brazil's exuberant tradition in baroque art and architecture is one of the most memorable sights in the east of the country

Unlike the monumental structures that sometimes overwhelm many of the Latin American capitals, Brazil's earliest public works of art are fresh, noble, and lively. The baroque movement had three main centers in 18th-century Brazil: Salvador, Rio de Janeiro, and Minas Gerais.

The Jesuits, who sponsored the colonial explosion of baroque in Bahia, were noted for their openness to new ideas and local trends, encouraging what many in Europe regarded as "the secular opulence" of the baroque. Brazilian themes were brought to the decorative arts, and great bunches of tropical fruits and wavy palms formed an incongruous background to the traditional Bible stories depicted in paintings and wood carvings. In Rio de Janeiro the baroque experience was less intense, as Rio was then secondary to the vice-regal capital of Salvador; and many colonial buildings were destroyed during an early 20th-century construction boom. The best surviving example is the Igreja de Nossa Senhora da Glória do Outeiro, dating from 1714.

It was in Minas Gerais that Brazilian baroque reached its apex. Ouro Preto, the former state capital, is an architectural delight. The secret is the substitution of the curve for the line. The purest example, Ouro Preto's Rosário dos Pretos chapel (see page 210), has a convex facade, ending in two delicate bell-tower curves. Inside, the nave is an oval. Doors and windows are framed by elegant archways.

ABOVE: Brazil is keen on preserving its rich history. The 16th-century town of Cachoeira in Bahia has been declared a World Heritage Site by UNESCO because it retains so much fine baroque architecture (see page 225).

BELOW: Churches in the multicultural northern state of Bahia, such as Nossa Senhora da Conceição do Monte in Cachoeira, had to appeal to European, Amerindian, and Afro-Brazilian worshipers alike.

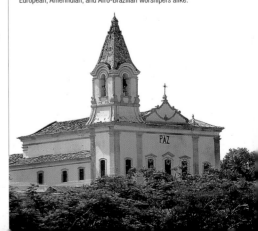

TOP LEFT: Decorative art was a major feature of baroque. Fine attention to detail, such as this spout on a fountain dating from 1749, is typical of the preserved colonial town of Tiradentes, in Minas Gerais.

LEFT: Wood carvings are another important factor in Brazilian baroque. Local themes gradually crept into Bahian decorative arts in the 18th century, and resulted in interesting representations of saints with Amerindian faces, but depicted in typically European styles.

BRAZIL'S BAROQUE GENIUS

One reason for the artistic unity of *mineiro* churches is the dominance of one baroque artisan – Antônio Francisco Lisboa (1730s–1814). The uneducated son of a Portuguese craftsman and a black slave woman, he became an individualistic sculptor and architect.

Struck by a crippling disease that left his hands paralysed, he was known as Aleijadinho – "The Little Cripple." Undaunted, however, he continued working by strapping a hammer and chisel to his wrists. Lisboa applied the principles of European baroque that he learned from books and missionaries. His greatest achievements are in Ouro Preto, and the 12 soapstone figures of the Old Testament Prophets, and the 66 wood carvings of the Stations of the Cross, at Congonhas do Campo in eastern Minas Gerais *(see pages 208 and 212).*

ABOVE: Situated at the southern tip of Rio de Janeiro state, the pretty little 18th-century town of Parati, another UNESCO site, is lined with colorful colonial buildings, both in the historic center and along the waterfront.

LEFT: Colonial Salvador is now one of Brazil's most visited cities. The baroque architecture and pastel-colored facades in the Pelourinho district are a typical blend of European and Brazilian styles.

BELOW LEFT: Sculptures and carvings of Christ and other biblical figures abound, such as this example in Minas Gerais. The Jesuit missionaries, who were responsible for much ecclesiastical architecture, were aware that ornate baroque art would attract and awe the religious Brazilian people. Although the Jesuits were expelled in the mid-18th century, they left behind a rich legacy.

MINAS GERAIS AND ESPÍRITO SANTO

Minas Gerais made its fortune from gold and diamonds, and spent much of it on splendid baroque architecture. The less-visited state of Espírito Santo is home to three impressive nature reserves

The state of Minas Gerais is a Brazilian giant. It covers 587,000 sq. km (352,200 sq. miles), is the fifth-largest state in the area, and has nearly 19 million inhabitants. It is rugged and isolated, with a central plateau rising sharply from an escarpment that rims the entire eastern frontier. The land of this once heavily wooded province is ragged now.

Minas means mines, and everything from gold and diamonds to iron has flowed from its veins of mineral ore to the world. Even today, the streets of its quaint, ancient towns are pink with iron-ore dust and its rivers red with it.

Folklore contrasts the *mineiro* sharply with the extravagant *carioca* and the industrious *paulista*. The *mineiro* is said to be stubborn, cautious, hard-working, and thrifty. He is also an assiduous preserver; he has kept not only the music-box churches of his baroque past, but also saved family heirlooms and trinkets, which clutter his attic rooms. São João del Rei residents have preserved the music, and even the musical instruments, of the 18th century, performing a liturgy of baroque orchestral pieces every Holy Week. Yet *mineiros* are both conservative and progressive. The state contains Brazil's best-preserved colonial towns, but *mineiros* also built the nation's first planned city, Belo Horizonte.

And it was a group of *mineiros,* led by President Juscelino Kubitschek, who built Brasília.

Colonial isolation

Much of the *mineiro* traditionalism can be traced back to the state's isolation during colonial times. Minas Gerais was established only when the gold rush began in 1695 *(see page 35)*. The only line of communication with the rest of the world until the 19th century was by way of mule down the perilous Escarpment.

Isolation was so great that the *mineiros* started their own farms and cottage industries. This versatility gave many of them a taste for democracy.

LEFT: Aleijadinho's *Prophet*, in Congonhas do Campo.
BELOW: colonial Ouro Preto.

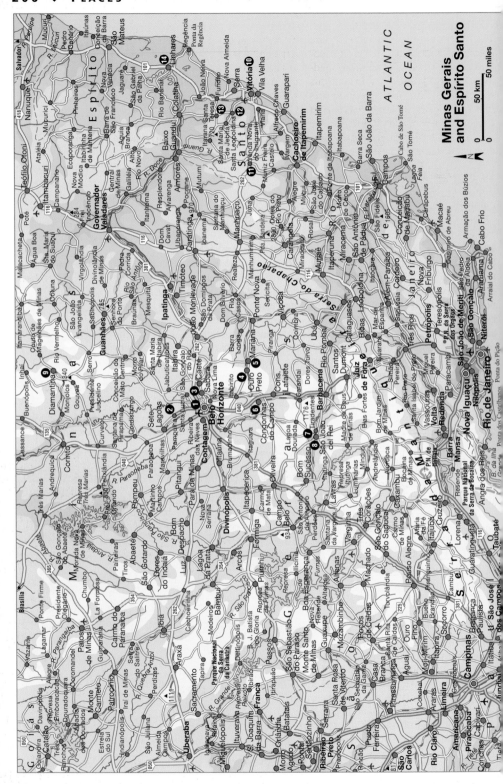

Minas Gerais
and Espírito Santo

The French traveler Saint-Hilaire noted that "there were scarcely any absentee landowners in Minas. The landowner worked side by side with his slaves, unlike the aristocratic owners in the rest of Brazil." And *mineiro* poet Carlos Drummond de Andrade *(see margin)* said: "Minas has never produced a dictator and never will."

Gold and diamond fever

In the 18th century, the gold of Minas Gerais was a colossus bestriding the world of commerce. About 1,200 tonnes of it were mined from 1700 to 1820. This fantastic amount made up 80 percent of all the gold produced throughout the world during that period.

Prospectors became spectacularly wealthy almost overnight. There were even some slaves who enriched themselves by clandestinely clawing the earth from underground mines. The legendary Chico Rei, who was a king in Africa before being brought to Brazil as a slave, vowed that he would recover his crown in the New World. That's exactly what he did, working feverishly in order to earn enough gold to purchase his own freedom and that of his large brotherhood.

The gold rush in Minas had ramifications abroad. Lisbon was flooded with gold coins minted at Ouro Preto's Casa dos Contos. But instead of investing their newfound wealth securely, the monarchy frittered away the fortune on opulent "improvements."

By the time Brazil's gold rush gave way to diamonds a few years later, Portugal had learned its lesson. The Tijuco diamond mines were closed to prospectors. A governor was appointed, and a garrison sent to back up his decrees. But the plan didn't work. The prospect of riches makes men greedy. Governors like João Fernandes – who spent a vast sum building an artificial lake and a Portuguese sailing ship for his slave mistress, Xica da Silva – dealt in contraband. The diamonds themselves brought renewed wealth for only a short time.

Today, most visitors to the state fly to Belo Horizonte, and travel from there to Ouro Preto and other places of interest, so this is where this suggested route will begin.

Carlos Drummond de Andrade (1902–87) is regarded by many as the most influential of Brazil's 20th-century poets. You can see a life-sized statue of him by Copacabana beach in Rio, the city he later made his home.

BELOW:
Capela de São Francisco, designed by Oscar Niemeyer.

*Watching street life
in Ouro Preto.*

BELOW:
an ornate window
and balcony in
Ouro Preto.

Towns around the capital

Ouro Preto was Minas Gerais's capital until 1897, when *mineiro* statesmen inaugurated Brazil's first planned city, **Belo Horizonte ❶**. Compared to Ouro Preto, the bustling metropolis, with a population of 2.4 million, possesses little for sightseers, but it is a good base for visiting surrounding historic towns.

In chic **Pampulha ❷** is the striking **Capela de São Francisco**, with its undulating roof and blue tiles, designed by Oscar Niemeyer in collaboration with Brazil's greatest modern artist, Candido Portinari *(see page 119)*, who was responsible for the starkly painted images of St Francis and the 14 Stations of the Cross.

Lying in a wooded valley 23 km (14 miles) north of Belo Horizonte is **Sabará ❸**, a baroque treasure. A leafy suburb hides the town's bizarre, musty jewel, the oddly shaped chapel of **Nossa Senhora do O**. O's humble exterior belies its exuberant decor; every inch of wall and ceiling space is covered by woodcarvings, gold leaf, darkly mysterious paintings that depict various Bible stories, and delicate gold-hued oriental motifs. The Far Eastern figures reflect the experiences of Portuguese Jesuits in the Orient.

A few blocks from the chapel is Sabará's larger **Nossa Senhora da Conceição** parish church. Its squarish facade is redeemed by an explosion of rich interior decoration. The oriental theme is frequently used, especially on the design-crowded sacristy door.

Presiding incongruously over Sabará's main square is the ghostly stone shell of the **Igreja do Rosário dos Pretos**, which was abandoned when the gold mines ran down. A few blocks away is the precious **Igreja do Carmo**, a treasure trove of Aleijadinho works, including intricate soapstone pulpits and a bas-relief frontispiece. A pair of muscular male torsos, bulging with woodcarved veins, hold the ornate choir loft in place.

The town of black gold

Although the riches produced by mining disappeared, the art remained. Today, the best place to see it is **Ouro Preto ❹**. Located 100 km (60 miles) from Belo Horizonte, Ouro Preto was

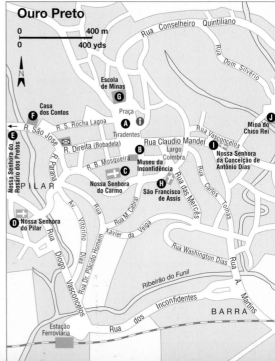

Ouro Preto

0   400 m
0   400 yds
N

Rua Conselheiro Quintiliano
Rua Dom Silvério
Escola de Minas **G**
Casa dos Contos **F**
Praça **A** ℹ
Mina do Chico Rei **J**
R. São José
R. S. Rocha Lagoa
R. Direita (Bobadela)
Tiradentes
Rua Claudio Manuel **B**
Rua Vasconcelos
Nossa Senhora da Conceição de António Dias **I**
R. Paraná
R. B. Mosqueira
Largo Coimbra
Museu da Inconfidência **C**
Nossa Senhora do Rosário dos Pretos **E**
PILAR
Nossa Senhora do Carmo
São Francisco de Assis **H**
Rua das Mercês
Rua Carlos Tomás
Nossa Senhora do Pilar **D**
Av. Vitorino
Rua M. Cabral
Xavier da Veiga
Rua Diogo Vasconcelos
Rua Dr. Plácido Homem
Rua Washington Dias
Ribeirão do Funil
Rua A. Martins
BARRA
Estação Ferroviária
Rua dos Inconfidentes

the center of the late 17th-century gold rush. First known as Vila Rica, it was just a mountain village when bands of adventurers from the Atlantic coast came in search of slaves and gold. Near Vila Rica they found a strange black stone and sent samples to Portugal. What they had unwittingly discovered was gold (the black coloration was from iron oxide in the soil). Vila Rica was swiftly renamed Ouro Preto (Black Gold), and the gold rush was underway.

By 1750, Ouro Preto had a population of 80,000, which at that time was larger than that of New York City. Jesuit priests also arrived, bringing ideas and artistic concepts from Europe; they insisted that their churches, financed by the gold from the mines, be built in the baroque style. Today, Ouro Preto has Brazil's purest collection of baroque art and architecture. Six museums and no fewer than 13 churches set among low hills and picture-book cottages make Ouro Preto resemble a Grimm Brothers' fairy-tale town. In 1981, UNESCO declared Ouro Preto a World Cultural Monument, a title it well deserves.

The fall of Tiradentes

At the center of town is spacious **Praça Tiradentes** **A**, fronted by the imposing **Museu da Inconfidência** **B** (open Tues–Sun noon–5.30pm; admission charge). The cobbled plaza is rich in history. The severed head of patriot Joaquim José da Silva Xavier, nicknamed Tiradentes (Tooth-Puller) was displayed on a pole there in 1792. Xavier and six of his co-conspirators had plotted a coup to bring about Brazilian independence, but spies infiltrated the group and exposed the plan, and Tiradentes was executed.

The museum once served as the town hall. Art and history are its current focuses. A macabre exhibit displays portions of the gallows used for Tiradentes's execution. Near by is a copy of his death warrant. Some of Tiradentes's fellow conspirators are buried beneath masonry slabs on the first floor.

A family affair

Another important building on Praça Tiradentes is the impressive church of **Nossa Senhora do Carmo** **C** (open

April 21, the date on which Tiradentes was executed, is commemorated as a national holiday.

BELOW: lovely Ouro Preto nestles in the hills.

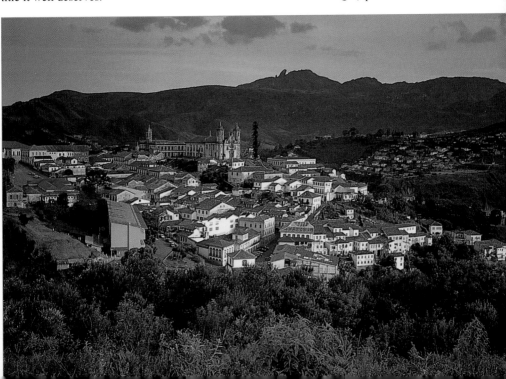

These are the typical figurines you find on sale in Ouro Preto.

BELOW: an expressive 18th-century fountain.

Tues–Sun noon–5pm), where the work of Aleijadinho *(see below)* can be seen.

This sturdy edifice was designed in 1766 by Aleijadinho's father, the engineer Manuel Francisco Lisboa. His son altered the plan while work was under way in 1770, incorporating the bell towers into the facade and adding an elegant archway over the main door. The changes were a compromise between conservative Mannerist traditions and the emerging baroque style that Aleijadinho championed. The exuberant stone carvings of curlicues and soaring angels above the main entrance are particularly fine.

Sacred treasures

Next to the church is Carmo's richly endowed collection of sacred art, housed in the **Museu do Oratório** (open daily 9.30–11.50am, 1.30–5.30pm; admission charge). Aleijadinho's wood carvings are prominent here, along with illuminated manuscripts and gleaming gold and silver altar accoutrements. A piece of bone labeled "St Clement" floats eerily in a glass-and-gold reliquary.

Golden decor

Three blocks west of Carmo is the deceptively simple parish church of **Nossa Senhora do Pilar ⒟**. The squarish facade hides Ouro Preto's most extravagant baroque interior. Partly the work of the sculptor Francisco Xavier de Brito, Pilar's walls explode with rosy-cheeked saints and angels, their garments fluttering against the gold-leaf background.

Nossa Senhora do Rosário dos Pretos ⒠, in the Rosário district farther west, produces the opposite effect. Its bold baroque facade houses an almost bare interior. Rosário was built by slaves, who had accumulated enough gold to erect its stunning shell, but not to decorate the interior. But what a shell it is; the convex walls, curved facade, and shapely bell towers make Rosário Brazil's most brashly baroque architectural monument.

Two other museums mark the route along cobbled streets back to Praça Tiradentes. The **Casa dos Contos ⒡** (open Tues–Sat 12.30–5.30pm, Sun 9am–3pm; admission charge), at the base of steep Rua Rocha Lagoa, was

Local Hero

Tiradentes is one of Ouro Preto's colonial heroes. The other is a very different figure, the sculptor and architect Antônio Francisco Lisboa (1738–1814), always referred to as Aleijadinho. He was given this nickname, which means "Little Cripple," because of a debilitating disease he contracted in midlife – probably arthritis – but which he did not allow to prevent him working, however painful it must have been *(see page 57)*.

Aleijadinho was extremely prolific, and his exquisite work can be found in churches throughout the state of Minas Gerais. There is also a room full of his eccentric, richly detailed woodcarvings in the Museu da Inconfidência *(see previous page)*. Of particular note is the moving figure of Christ at the Pillar.

the tax authority during the gold-rush era. Gold coins, and the surprisingly sophisticated foundry for minting them, are displayed. At the top end of the street is Ouro Preto's sprawling **Escola de Minas** (College of Mine Engineering) **G**. The mineralogy museum inside (open Tues–Sun noon–5pm) has an extremely interesting collection of precious stones, ores, and crystals – 23,000 pieces in total.

Aleijadinho's masterpiece

Just east of Praça Tiradentes is an Aleijadinho architectural masterpiece, the jewel-box chapel of **São Francisco de Assis** **H** (open Tues–Sun 8.30–11.45am and 1.30–5pm). The church's baroque lines resemble those of Rosário dos Pretos. Extravagant relief work above the main entrance is a continuation of similar works at Carmo. Inside are rare wood and soapstone carvings by Aleijadinho, characterized by the almond eyes, shapely anatomical features and ruffled garments of the high *mineiro* baroque. The wall and ceiling paintings are by Manuel da Costa Athayde (1762–1837), whose works feature distorted human figures and realistic backgrounds. Painted surfaces and architectural features blend at the margins as if the painted sky ceiling could open up for God's inspection.

Two blocks east of São Francisco chapel is Ouro Preto's monument to Aleijadinho, the museum and church of **Nossa Senhora da Conceição de Antônio Dias** **I** (open Tues–Sat 8.30am–11.30pm, 1.30–4.45pm, Sun noon–4.45pm). Aleijadinho is buried beneath a wooden marker near a side altar. The galleries behind the sacristy display his wood and soapstone carvings and the richly illustrated bibles and missals he used to study European artistic models.

Still in Ouro Preto, you can visit the **Mina do Chico Rei** **J** (Rua Dom Silvério 108; open daily 8am–5pm), a gold mine built by slaves in 1702, which fell into disuse following the

abolition of slavery in 1888. A small stretch of the 1,300-meter (4,265-ft) gallery is accessible to visitors.

Between Ouro Preto and Mariana (8 km/5 miles from Ouro Preto) is the more interesting **Mina da Passagem** (open daily 9am–5pm; substantial admission charge), which was in use until the late 1980s. Demonstrations of the processing of gold ore are held here. This mine was dug out in the 18th century and has an 11-km (7-mile) gallery, going down to a depth of 120 meters (394 ft). Visitors can go down into the gallery by train as far as an underground lake.

Athayde's birthplace

The fascinating colonial town of **Mariana** **5**, birthplace of Athayde, is 12 km (7 miles) from Ouro Preto. The twin chapels of **Carmo** and **São Francisco**, and the magnificent **Catedral de Nossa Senhora da Assunção**, are smothered in the dark colors and mulatto figures of Athayde's opulent art. Especially noteworthy is *The Passion and Death of Saint Francis*. Athayde is buried under a wooden marker at the rear of

A painted wooden frieze in the Igreja de São Francisco.

BELOW: the florid baroque interior of a Mariana church.

A delicate decorative shrine in the Igreja de Santo Antônio.

BELOW: the twin-towered Santo Antônio church in Tiradentes.

Carmo. The cathedral has a German organ, built in 1701 and dragged by mule from Rio de Janeiro. Concerts are held on Friday at 11am and Sundays at 12.15pm. Behind the cathedral is Mariana's sacred art museum, **Museu Arquidiocesano de Arte Sacra** (Rua Frei Durão; open Tues–Sun 9am–noon, 1.30–5pm; admission charge), which contains the largest collection of baroque painting and sculpture in Minas Gerais.

Congonhas do Campo

Eastern Minas Gerais, more economically developed than the bleak *sertão,* offers artistic treasures of the late *mineiro* baroque. **Congonhas do Campo ❻**, 80 km (48 miles) from Belo Horizonte, is the site of Aleijadinho's two greatest masterworks of sculpture: the 12 life-sized outdoor carvings of *The Prophets,* located on the esplanade of the **Bom Jesus de Matosinhos Sanctuary**; and the 66 painted woodcarvings of *The Stations of the Cross,* housed in a series of garden chapels near by. Carved entirely from soapstone, *The Prophets* are stolid, gray, and severe. In their stylized postures and costumes, they possess a mythic quality, as if sculpted entirely from imagination.

While *The Prophets* seem suitably remote, the carved figures of *The Stations of the Cross* are vibrant and filled with emotion. The Christ statue, with its almond eyes and half-open mouth, skin pale and veined, and muscles strained, is as haunting as *The Holy Shroud.* The 12 Apostles, with their worried, working-class faces, probably sculpted after local residents, could well be an 18th-century jury.

Tiradentes

A further 80 km (50 miles) to the south is the 1746 birthplace of Joaquim José da Silva Xavier. The town, appropriately named **Tiradentes ❼**, preserves the colonial-era feeling better than almost any other in Minas Gerais. Pink slate streets, an occasional horse-drawn cart, lace curtains, and brightly painted shutters contribute to a feeling of tranquility. The spacious **Museu Padre Toledo** (Rua Padre Toledo; open daily Wed–Mon 9–11.30am, 1–4.40pm; admission charge) contains period furnishings and sacred art. Near by is the imposing **Igreja de Santo Antônio**, with gold-plated decoration and a stone frontispiece carved by Aleijadinho. Inside there is an 18th-century organ, a companion piece to the instrument in Mariana.

Railroad town

Only 12 km (7 miles) from Tiradentes is bustling **São João del Rei ❽**. The São João train station, on Avenida Hemílio Alves 366, has been turned into a gleaming museum, the **Museu Ferroviário** (open Tues–Sat 9–11.30am and 1–6pm; admission charge), a fascinating reminder of old-fashioned rail travel. Hulking black and red Baldwin locomotives, dating as far back as 1880, are lined up in the roundhouse like oversized toys around a Christmas tree. Wood-paneled excursion cars feature porcelain fixtures and etched win-

dows. The Victorian-style station is clean and authentic, right down to the ear-splitting steam whistle and syncopated huff and puff of the old train that still makes tourist trips.

The town has seven churches. **Igreja do Carmo** recalls the baroque masterpieces of Ouro Preto. The nearby cathedral, the **Basílica de Nossa Senhora do Pilar**, presents a blocky facade on the outside, and richly decorated walls and ceilings within. But the pleasing proportions and rounded towers of the **Igreja de São Francisco**, which has been justifiably hailed as Aleijadinho's most mature architectural triumph, is the town's proudest treasure. Double rows of swaying palm trees lead to a graceful esplanade of wide steps and curving balustrades.

Diamantina

Heading north from Belo Horizonte (about 280 km/175 miles), you will come to a rugged hamlet that many consider the equal of Ouro Preto in austere beauty and history – **Diamantina ❾**. Bordering Brazil's semi-arid

sertão, Diamantina is surrounded by iron-red hills rising to a rocky plain. This area is particularly rich in orchids. In fact, there are almost 300 species in the area, some of them very rare. The town's white-walled cottages and churches cascade down an irregular slope, producing a stark profile of wooden steeples.

The ornate wood and stone **Igreja do Carmo** across the square, was another gift from the diamond czar to his lover. Fernandes ordered the bell tower to be moved to the rear of the church when Silva complained its tolling kept her awake. Carmo's ceiling is covered by dark-hued paintings depicting Bible stories, which were favored by 18th-century *mineiro* painters, including José Soares de Araujo, whose work at Carmo and the nearby **Igreja do Amparo** recalls that of Athayde.

Colorful **Nossa Senhora do Rosário**, a block from Carmo, was built entirely by slaves, and the woodcarvings of the saints are black. Outside, the roots of a tree near by have split Rosário's wooden crucifix, leaving only the bar and tip of the cross visible. Folklore says

Diamantina was the headquarters of the diamond contractor João Fernandes and his slave mistress, Xica da Silva. Her stately home is located on Praça Lobo Mesquita.

BELOW: scarred hillsides surround the pretty town of Diamantina.

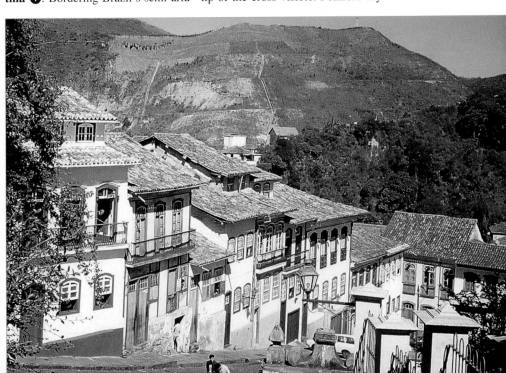

a slave accused of stealing was executed on the spot while protesting his innocence. He told onlookers: "Something extraordinary will occur here to prove my truthfulness." Soon after, buds appeared on the cross, eventually snaking into the ground and producing the sturdy tree.

Across from Diamantina's cathedral is the informative **Museu do Diamante** (Diamond Museum; open Tues–Sat noon–5.30pm, Sun 9am–noon; admission charge). Period mining equipment, documents, and furnishings are displayed. Grisly implements of torture used against the slaves are kept in a back room.

Also near the square is Diamantina's Public Library, noted for its delicate trellis and *muxarabiê* (a lattice-work casing covering an entire second-story balcony). A few blocks away, on **Rua Direita**, is the humble birthplace of President Juscelino Kubitschek (1902–76). Near by is the **Casa da Glória**, a pair of blue and white stone structures linked by a wooden bridge. The site was the headquarters of Diamantina's royal governors.

Kubitschek's early life in Diamantina was none too easy. His father died when Juscelino was just two years old, and he was brought up by his mother, a schoolteacher of Czech descent – hence the un-Brazilian name.

BELOW:
orchids proliferate in many parts of Espírito Santo.

Espírito Santo

The coastal city of **Vitória** ❿, capital of the state of **Espírito Santo**, was founded in 1551, and has remained a relatively small town (pop. 313,000), its heart comprising an island connected to the suburbs by a series of bridges. There are a few buildings recalling its colonial past, and some beaches along the coast north and south of the city that are quite pretty. However, this state has not, as yet, been affected by the tourist boom that has brought so many changes to its neighbors Bahia and Minas Gerais, and, of course, to Rio de Janeiro.

The **Teatro Carlos Gomes** (Praça Costa Pereira) in Vitória was built as a copy of La Scala in Milan. It frequently hosts music festivals as well as putting on plays. The **Catedral Metropolitana** (Praça Dom Luis Scortegagna), built in 1918, has beautiful stained-glass windows.

Outdoor pursuits

The lovely alpine-like countryside around the village of **Venda Nova do Imigrante** (known simply as Venda

Nova) **⓫**, 113 km (70 miles) west of Vitória, is popular for walking and mountaineering. About 70 km (44 miles) northwest of Vitória is the Swiss-founded town of **Santa Leopoldina ⓬**, which offers a pleasant day trip from the capital.

A further 21 km (13 miles) north lies the charming hill town of **Santa Teresa ⓭**. Just outside it, the **Museu Biológico Professor Mello Leitão** (Avenida José Ruschi 4; open Tues–Sun 8am–5pm; admission charge) is a natural history museum founded by Augusto Ruschi, a world-famous expert on humming birds, who died in 1986. Set in an area of forests in which a vast variety of orchids proliferate, the museum has a small zoo attached, a humming-bird and butterfly garden, and grounds containing a wide variety of plants and trees.

Nature reserves

Close to **Linhares ⓮**, 135 km (84 miles) from Vitória, is the **Reserva Biológica Comboios** (open daily 8am–noon, 1–5pm; www.projetotamar. org.br), a fascinating nature reserve set up to protect marine turtles. There are a number of hotels and restaurants in Linhares itself.

There are two other nature reserves near Linhares. The **Linhares Reserve** (e-mail: floresta@tropical.com.br), a private reserve; and the IBAMA-run **Sooretama Biological Reserve** (contact José Olimpio Vargas on e-mail: olimpio@es.ibama.gov.br). Both these reserves have been established to protect the rainforest and its incredible variety of plants (including numerous orchids), birds, and other wildlife. More than 370 species of birds have been recorded, including the red-billed curassow. To visit either of these reserves, you will need special authorization, obtainable from the e-mail addresses above.

Further north, near the border with Bahia state, is **Conceição da Barra**, a small town from which you can reach **Itaúnas** with its lonely beaches and enormous sand dunes, some of them more than 30 meters (90 ft) high. The dunes have buried the old town of Itaúnas, and only the church tower can still be seen above the sand. ❑

TIP

IBAMA is the acronym for the Brazilian Institute of Environment and Renewable Natural Resources (www.ibama.gov.br).

BELOW: a hawksbill turtle, oblivious of the photographer.

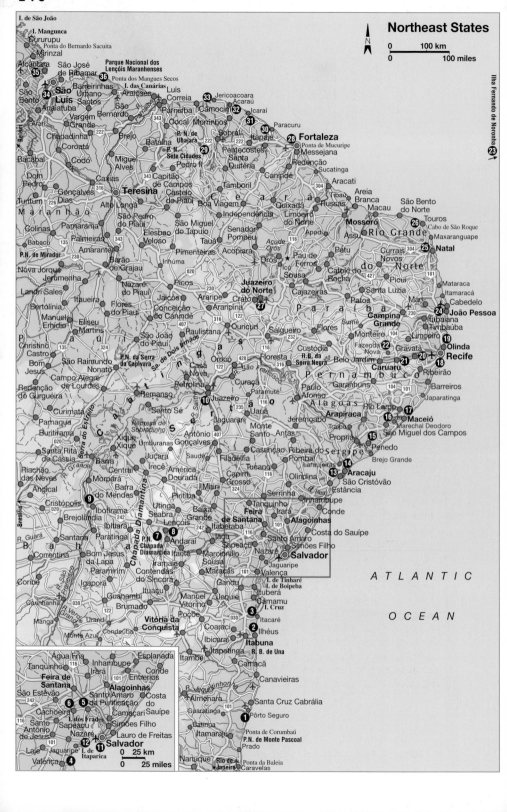

Northeast States

0   100 km
0   100 miles

THE NORTHEAST

Northeastern Brazil comprises vast areas of
scrubland, idyllic beaches, and beautiful
colonial towns, and its vibrant culture is
reflected in its festivals and music

The world is waking up to the potential of the northeast of
Brazil as a tourist destination: communications have
been greatly improved in recent years, and you can now
fly direct to Salvador and Recife from a number of foreign
cities. The attraction is obvious: quite simply, the northeastern coast is a paradise. It is warm and sunny all year round,
the glorious beaches are perhaps the best in Brazil, and certainly the least spoilt, the wilderness areas are magical, and
then there is the culture. The colonial towns are the oldest in
the country, and *nordestinos* are a vibrant people whose distinctive Carnival and religious festivals rival Rio's.

Bahia, set apart from the rest of the northeast by its strong African
roots, has a wonderfully rich heritage. Salvador, Bahia's capital, and
once the capital of the whole country, is now one of the most favored destinations in Brazil, since word has got around about the food, the music,
and the festivals, as well as the colonial architecture.

The most populous and prosperous areas of the northeast are concentrated along the coast, where there is a strip of fertile land – as there is
along the course of the São Francisco River, which runs through Bahia,
Pernambuco, Sergipe, and Alagoas. The coastal economy therefore benefits from agriculture, and from the income gained from tourists who
visit the tropical beaches.

There is another aspect to the northeast, though: this is a predominantly
parched territory of nine states, making up 18 percent of Brazil. It had its
short-lived glory days at the beginning of the colonial period, when its
economy was based on sugar cane and cotton plantations.

After competition killed off the sugar trade, the northeast went into
decline, and was for many years neglected due to its general lack of productive potential: the vast, arid *sertão* (scrubland) of the interior is a
hard place to eke out a living. Today, state-funded development schemes
are attempting to benefit those in greatest need, and stem the tide of
migration to the cities, and the social problems this brings. ❏

PRECEDING PAGES: fishermen haul in their nets on a Bahian beach.

BAHIA

Bahia, where the Portuguese first landed, is said to be the most Brazilian of states. Today, its laid-back, colorful lifestyle attracts visitors, who come to explore the historic towns and arid interior landscape, and relax in idyllic beach resorts

Bahia is the soul of Brazil. In this northeastern state more than anywhere else, the country's cultures and races have mixed, producing, many believe, what is most authentically Brazilian.

It was at **Porto Seguro**, on the southern coast of Bahia, that Pedro Álvares Cabral first "discovered" this land in 1500. A year later, on November 1 – All Saints' Day – the Italian navigator Amerigo Vespucci arrived in what is now **Salvador**, the capital of Bahia and, until 1763, also the capital of Brazil.

Bahia is the site of the country's first medical school, its oldest churches, its most important colonial architecture, and one of the largest collections of sacred art. Bahia is also the birthplace of many of Brazil's outstanding writers, politicians, and composers. Bahia-born novelist Jorge Amado's works have been translated into nearly 50 languages, and several of his books have become major films (including *Dona Flor and Her Two Husbands* and *Gabriela*). The music of Bahians João Gilberto, Caetano Veloso, Baden Powell, and Gilberto Gil is enjoyed by aficionados all over the world.

There is another side to Bahia, one that appeals to the spirit and the senses. The mysticism of Bahia is so strong, it pervades every aspect of life: it can be perceived in the way people dress, in their speech, their music, their way of relating to each other,

even in their food. This mysticism is another reason Brazilians say that in Bahia lies the soul of their country.

The source of this mysticism was the original culture preserved by enslaved Africans. Today, the Pantheist religion of the African Yoruba tribe is still alive and well in Bahia, and many white Bahians who are self-professed Catholics can be seen making their offerings to the deities of the *candomblé* religion.

The phenomenon of syncretism, the blending of Catholicism with African

Main attractions

PORTO SEGURO
ILHÉUS
ITACARÉ
SANTO AMARO DA PURIFICAÇÃO
SÃO FELIX
P. N. CHAPADA DIAMANTINA
LENÇOIS

LEFT: Bahian man wears the colors of his *orixá* (African god).
BELOW: cycling on a rural road in Porto Seguro.

TIP

You can fly to Porto Seguro with TAM from a number of US cities, with a stop-over in São Paulo, from where there are daily flights.

religions, resulted when the slaves, forbidden to express their own religious beliefs, did so by worshiping their deities disguised as Catholic saints. Nowadays, you can see the devout worshiping the African goddess Iemanjá as Our Lady, or the god Oxumaré as St Anthony.

Southern Bahia

The Portuguese first landed and established contact with the original inhabitants near today's **Porto Seguro ❶**, in the south of Bahia. Pataxo Amerindians still live near the town, fishing and fashioning handicrafts to sell to tourists. The area around **Monte Pascoal**, where the Portuguese had their first sighting of Brazil in 1500, is a densely forested nature reserve of original Atlantic rainforest. There are four national parks in the area: Descobrimento, Monte Pascoal, Pau Brasil and Abrolhos – the last a marine national park.

The town of Porto Seguro (pop. 128,000) is 600 km (373 miles) north of Vitória, in the state of Espírito Santo, and 722 km (448 miles) from the state's capital, Salvador. It is one of the main

tourist destinations for Brazilians; international travelers, too, have been coming here for many years. There are innumerable restaurants, bars, and dance halls and dozens of hotels and *pousadas* to suit every preference and budget. Some rather nice, sophisticated hotels, large and small, are now emerging all over the southern part of Bahia, attracting large numbers of the so-called "discerning traveler." Nightlife is particularly lively during the summer months and local holidays. Carnival here is a major celebration.

Across the bay by ferry is **Arraial d'Ajuda**, with *pousadas* and bars that swing with lively *forró* dancing. Twenty-five kilometers (15 miles) further south by *kombi* or bus is **Trancoso**, with colorful houses and a colonial church (1656) built around a grassy square, the Quadrado, with commanding views over the Atlantic. The magnificent beaches here attract droves of national and international tourists in the summer, and the whole area is an oasis of peace during the off season.

Some 264 km (164 miles) north of Porto Seguro lies the most important

city on Bahia's southern coast – the cocoa capital of Brazil, as well as one of the major export ports. **Ilhéus ❷** (pop. 220,000), some 468 km (290 miles) from Salvador, was founded in 1534 and had its heyday in the early 20th century, due to the wealth produced by the cocoa plantations. Beaches abound in the region, and the city's Carnival celebration is one of the liveliest in Bahia. Jorge Amado *(see panel below)*, the foremost Bahian writer, was born near by, and the city became the inspiration and the setting for *Gabriela Clove and Cinnamon*, one of his best-known works.

Olivença, 20 km (12 miles) south of Ilhéus, is an excellent place to camp and "take the waters." Besides Carnival, major festivals in Ilhéus include St Sebastian (January 11–20), the city's birthday (June 28), and the cocoa festival (the entire month of October). Further south, Comandatuba Island has one of Brazil's best resorts; set in tropical gardens and blessed with 21 km (13 miles) of beaches, it has its own airport, spa, and a golf course.

Sought-after destinations

Itacaré ❸, 70 km (43 miles) north of Ilhéus, has become one of the most sought-after destinations in Bahia. The little town (pop. 18,000) lies at the mouth of Rio das Contas, which starts at Chapada Diamantina *(see page 227)*. Many restaurants and *pousadas* cater for the visitors who come here for the magnificent beaches and scenery. All forms of ecotourism are encouraged: diving, surfing, and walks through the Atlantic rainforest and the region's many deserted beaches. There are also excellent *pousadas* and some very exclusive resorts in the area.

Continuing north, the Maraú Peninsula is still a pristine and remote area, as access is not particularly easy. The magic of Maraú is its remoteness; it is ideal for those seeking peace and quiet. Some small *pousadas* and one sophisticated resort serve the area. At the extreme north of the peninsula is Barra

Grande, which can get very busy during the season (by local standards), but nearby Taipús de Fora, considered by many to be the finest beach in Brazil, can be remarkably quiet and peaceful. The area can be visited on day trips from Itacaré.

Morro de São Paulo is a fishing village on the island of Tinharé, situated some 270 km (168 miles) south of Salvador. Once a hippy hang-out, the village has become increasingly fashionable with Brazilian and international tourists, though it is still wonderfully relaxed, and there are no roads. Another island with great beaches is nearby **Boipeba** – reminiscent of Brazil 50 years ago, it is very quiet, with a laid-back lifestyle.

Further north, towards Salvador, 270 km (168 miles) away is the town of **Valença ❹** (pop. 83,000), where the Una River meets the Atlantic Ocean. The town is the site of one of Brazil's first textile factories to use hydroelectric power. One of the best beaches in the region, 15 km (9 miles) from Valença, is **Guaibim**, with a number of good seafood restaurants and bars.

A Pataxo Amerindian girl selling tribal artifacts by the roadside.

Jorge Amado

Jorge Amado is Brazil's best-known 20th-century writer, and his work has been published in 52 countries. He was born in the town of Itabuna, 38 km (24 miles) from Ilhéus, on August 10, 1912, one of four children. His father was a cocoa farmer, which gave Jorge his in-depth knowledge of rural life in Bahia. At the age of 10 he started a newsletter called *A Luneta*, which he distributed to family and neighbors, and only five years later, he was living in Pelourinho *(see page 234)*, working as a crime reporter on a newspaper in the capital. In December 1933 he married Matilde Garcia Rosa, but it was Zélia Gattai, whom he met in 1945, after he and Matilde had separated, who was the great love of his life. Also a writer, she was his constant companion until his death. His prolific output was only matched by his political convictions. His strongly held views, his writings, and his connections with the Brazilian Communist Party, landed him in prison a number of times. He was a keen traveler and a devotee of *candomblé*. Jorge Amado died on August 6, 2001 in Salvador, where, in accordance with his wishes, he was cremated and his ashes scattered around a mango tree in the gardens of his house in Rio Vermelho, where Zélia, aged 91 at the time of writing, still lives. There is a museum dedicated to him in Salvador *(see page 235)*.

TIP

The *sertão* is a land that lionizes its folk heroes, and also has its own distinctive brand of music. The two-part harmony of *música sertaneja* is simple and linear, the chords rarely numbering more than three. Themes are of lost love, homesickness, bad weather, and death. This music is no longer restricted to the *sertão*: popular variety shows on Brazilian television are now dedicated to this genre.

BELOW: a sculpture at the TAMAR turtle reserve.

North from Salvador

North from **Salvador** *(see page 231)* the Estrada de Coco (Coconut Road) takes you from the city's most distant beach, Itapoã. Along this road, lined with coconut palms, you will pass virtually unspoiled tropical beaches, including **Jaua**, **Arembepe**, **Jucuípe**, **Abaí**, **Guarajuba** (where a brand-new international resort has just opened), and **Itacimirim**.

Some 85 km (53 miles) from Salvador, at **Praia do Forte** thousands of coconut palms stand on 12 km (7 miles) of white sandy beach, protected against threats to the environment by a private foundation. Praia do Forte was once just a small fishing village. The high street has recently been paved, cafés, restaurants, shops, *pousadas* and hotels abound, and an increasing number of international tourists visit the village. Even so, it remains a delightful place and, like most resorts, it can be blissfully quiet in the low season.

Praia do Forte is also the site of a major preservation center for sea turtles. The eggs are collected from nests on the beach at night and protected from predators (both humans and other animal) until the young are old enough to be set free in the sea and fend for themselves.

Continuing along from Praia do Forte the road, now known as **Linha Verde** (Green Line), follows the coastline past spectacular, semi-deserted beaches all the way to the border with the state of **Sergipe**. It passes **Costa do Sauípe**, a purpose-built resort with five luxury international hotels. The first phase was completed in 2000, at a staggering cost of US$600 million. Fifty more hotels are planned in a series of five further building phases. Worth noting for golfers is the 18-hole golf course (open to non-residents; daily 7am–6pm; to play 18 holes, last tee-off is 2.30pm, to play 9 holes tee-off is 3.30pm; tel: 71-2104 8523).

The *sertão*

Situated inland, 200 km (124 miles) from the coast, is the *sertão*, the northeast's drought-ridden scrubland region. This area has been the setting for a great deal of Brazilian tragedy. Periodic droughts drive local farm laborers from the *sertão* to the coastal cities in search of food and work. When the rains return, so do the *sertanejos*. But often, the rains do as much damage as good: torrential downpours can easily cause massive flooding over this severely parched earth, which is too dry to absorb the rainwater. The *sertanejos* are a hardy people, loyal to their birthplace, and their land holds surprises for those willing to discover them.

A good place to start a trip to the *sertão* is in the Recôncavo da Bahia, the term used for the hot and humid region that surrounds Salvador's Baía de Todos os Santos. This region was once the source of much wealth, created by the sugar cane and tobacco booms. Over several centuries slaves were brought from Africa to work the land. This heritage can be seen in the many historic towns in the region: Santo Amaro, São Félix, Jaguaripe,

and, above all, Cachoeira. **Santo Amaro da Purificação** ❺ (pop. 60,000), a colonial town located some 80 km (50 miles) from Salvador, was once a center of tobacco and sugar production. The town is revered by fans of Brazilian popular music as the home of singers and siblings Caetano Veloso and Maria Bethânia. While their international careers have taken them away from Santo Amaro, they return regularly, and their mother, Dona Cano, is a national figure in her own right, and the nearest Brazilians have to royalty. Now moving towards her centenary, she is a deeply religious woman, modest and still amazingly active, and is much loved and revered. She will host and entertain a visiting friend of one of her many children with the same charm and ease with which she will sit and talk with the president of Brazil. An artistic vein runs through the family, and the eldest son, Rodrigo, has for more than 50 years now been organizing an annual event in Santo Amaro which takes place on the first Saturday after Epiphany (January 6) and attracts scores of visitors.

Along Santo Amaro's cobblestone streets and tiny *praças* (squares), pink and white stucco colonial homes alternate with art deco facades painted in pastel colors, and decorated with raised geometric outlines in glittering white. These facades, testimony to the area's development and prosperity in the early part of the 20th century, can be seen in many of the small towns in the interior of the northeast.

A tour through history

Colonial churches and monuments abound in **Cachoeira** ❻ (pop. 32,000), 120 km (74 miles) from Salvador, and is a center of tobacco, cashew nut, and orange production. One of the main sites is the church of **Nossa Senhora da Conceição do Monte**, an 18th-century structure with a lovely view of the Paraguaçu River, and the village of São Félix on the opposite bank. The church is open to the public only in November.

Don't miss the **Correios e Telégrafos**, the post office, which has the best example of an art deco facade in town. Cachoeira also has souvenir shops, inns, and restaurants. The **Pou-**

Rural people in Bahia often have hard lives.

BELOW:
Praia do Forte beach and church.

TIP

Samba de roda is always a feature of the Irmandade da Boa Morte celebrations, but you may also see spontaneous performances at other times. Groups, mainly of young men, mark the rhythm, while women, dressed in typical costumes, dance the samba in a circular formation. Now and then, one of the dancers will go to the center and demonstrate her dancing abilities.

BELOW: carrying the shopping home in São Felix.

sada do **Convento**, a 17th-century convent converted into a guest house, is especially interesting: the guest rooms were once nuns' cells, and the mausoleum is now a television lounge.

One of the most fascinating *festas* in Brazil is celebrated by the **Irmandade da Boa Morte** (Sisterhood of Our Lady of Good Death). It is not clear when this sorority was established, but it is certain that it goes back to the early 19th century and the days of slavery. Created to provide social assistance, particularly the provision of a dignified funeral, it lives on to this day. Membership is open only to black women over the age of 40, who must be devotees of both *candomblé* and the Virgin Mary. New sisters follow a strict three-year admission process. The sisterhood's main celebrations take place in the first fortnight in August, with an extensive program that includes processions to celebrate the death, burial, and resurrection of the Virgin. The celebrations combine African and Catholic rituals in a striking example of syncretism.

São Félix

Across the river, over the 300-meter (985-ft) iron bridge that bears the grandiose name of Imperial Ponte D. Pedro I, is sleepy **São Félix**, with colonial architecture from the 17th–19th centuries. Some landmarks are the churches of Deus Menino and Senhor São Félix, the town hall, and the **Centro Cultural Dannemann** (open Tues–Sun 8am–5pm) on the river front, with art exhibitions and displays of old machinery used for making *charutos* (cigars). You can see the skill involved in the making of hand-rolled cigars, and, of course, you can also buy the finished product.

In the **Casa da Cultura Américo Simas** (open Mon–Fri 9am–noon, 2–5pm), located in a 19th-century cigar factory, a number of courses are offered to the local population.

Jaguaripe and Nazaré

Jaguaripe (River of the Jaguar, in the Tupi-Guarani language) lies on the eastern banks of the river of the same name, 240 km (148 miles) from Salvador. It is fast becoming a center for ecotourism, and is also of historical interest, with religious and secular buildings, some dating from the early 17th century. From here you can go on a 45-minute cruise downstream to **Maragogipinho**, where pottery was first introduced by the Jesuits more than 300 years ago. Today, though still a cottage industry, it is regarded as the largest in Latin America, and you can visit the workshops.

Once a year, during Holy Week, there is a large exhibition at nearby **Nazaré das Farinhas**, one of the busiest towns in the Recôncavo. Nazaré is also home to the oldest working cinema in Brazil, Cinema Rio Branco, recently restored by a local football player, Vampeta, who made it to the national team, and also played in the Netherlands, Italy, and France.

The Recôncavo is one of the major centers of Bahia's strong agricultural economy. The state of Bahia produces

grains, sugar cane and coconuts, and 95 percent of the country's cocoa output is harvested here. The town of **Camaçari** is home to one of Brazil's three petrochemical complexes, and industry in the region is booming.

Chapada Diamantina

The **Parque Nacional Chapada Diamantina** ❼ was formed in 1985 and covers an area of 152,000 hectares (600 sq. miles). Altitude in the park varies from 400 meters (1,300 ft) and 1,700 meters (5,600 ft) above sea level. The rainy season is from November to April, with the heaviest rainfall between November and January. The driest time, and the best time to visit, is from August to October.

This region is one of the most beautiful in the Bahian countryside, and will appeal to all nature enthusiasts. Mountain springs help keep the drought away. Chapada is a mountain wilderness, best explored with a local guide. Orchids abound near the waterfalls, some of which can only be reached on foot. The **Cachoeira da Fumaça**, 66 km (41 miles) from

Lençóis, is 400 meters (1,300 ft) high. It can be reached only by a very steep 7-km (4-mile) walk. The **Gruta das Areias**, a grotto just over 1 km (½ mile) long, is lined with colored sands, which artisans use to fill glass bottles, creating delightful patterns. A stunning view of the region can be seen from on top of the **Pai Inácio Mountain**, where a host of exotic plants thrive. Small towns and villages, such as Mucugê and Igatú, give visitors an interesting insight into the history and lives of of the people who inhabit this unusual region.

Diamond boom town

Situated in the heart of Bahia, 425 km (265 miles) west of Salvador, just outside the national park, and serving as its main gateway, is one of the state's most distinctive attractions, the town of **Lençóis** ❽ (pop. 10,000). Resting in the foothills of the **Sincorá Mountains**, Lençóis dates back to 1844, when diamonds were first discovered in the region. Hoards of fortune-seekers descended on the site, improvising shelters out of large cloth

Colored sand from the Gruta das Areias is used to make intricate pictures in bottles.

BELOW: the majestic Pai Inácio mountain in Chapada Diamantina.

TIP

At 320 km (199 miles) long, with a surface of 4,220 sq. km (1,630 sq. miles) the Sobradinho Dam is one of the largest artificial lakes in the world. The wall is 41 meters (134 ft) at its highest and 12.5 km (7.7 miles) long. The lock measures 120 meters (394 ft) by 17 meters (56 ft), allowing navigation between towns in Minas Gerais and Pernambuco states.

sheets, called *lençóis* in Portuguese, a name that has stuck.

The diamond rush turned the little settlement into a boom town. Lençóis society wore the latest Parisian fashions and sent their children to study in France. The French government even opened a consulate here. There are some interesting buildings in Lençóis, but its main attractions are the natural wonders near by.

Though its folklore is unmistakably Bahian, Lençóis has its own peculiarities. Carnival is not a major event, but the Feast of São João in June is widely celebrated. Lençóis also has *jarê*, its own unique version of *candomblé*. *Jarê* celebrations occur in September, December, and January, in *candomblé* temples or the homes of its devotees.

Local handicrafts include lace, crochet, and earthenware. Lençóis has accommodation to suit all budgets and preferences, from campsites and inns to attractive hotels such as the Canto das Águas, with large tropical gardens by the river. Lençóis can be reached from Salvador by car and by a six-hour comfortable coach service (usually twice a day, depending on season). There are organized tours to the region, and there's a limited air service.

Due west of Lençóis, 252 km (157 miles) further along Highway 242, is the city of **Ibotirama** ❾, on the legendary São Francisco River *(see page 246)*. A fisherman's paradise, its 24,000 inhabitants raise cattle and plant cassava, corn, beans, and rice, but when the drought comes, they depend on the river for food. Dozens of species of fish, including the piranha (seen as a delicacy), are here for the taking. Boats and canoes can be rented at the wharf.

Keen photographers can take a canoe out at the end of the day to photograph the spectacular sunset over the river's left bank. From March to October, the dry season, the water level drops, exposing sandy beaches on the river islands of **Gado Bravo** (40 minutes upstream) and **Ilha Grande** (25 minutes downstream).

From Ibotirama, the São Francisco flows northeast to the **Sobradinho Dam** *(see margin note)*. Close to the northern edge of the lake is the city of **Juazeiro** ❿ (pop. 200,000), 566 km (352 miles) northwest of Salvador. During the colonial period, Juazeiro was a stopover for travelers and pioneers on their way to Salvador from the states north of Bahia. A township was officially founded in 1706, when Franciscan monks built a mission, complete with a chapel and a monastery, in a Cariri Amerindian village. By the end of the 18th century, Juazeiro had become the region's most important commercial and social center. Local fish, caught in the São Francisco River, is served in the restaurants here. The folk art of the Juazeiro region is dominated by the *carranca*, the half-man, half-dragon wooden figurehead placed on boats to keep the devil at bay. The *carrancas*, with their teeth bared in a silent roar, are carved from tree trunks and painted in bright colors. You will see miniature versions of them on sale as souvenirs. ❑

RESTAURANTS

Lençóis

Beco da Coruja
Rua da Rosário 172
Tel: 75-3334 1652
Open: L&D daily.
A recommended vegetarian restaurant which takes it for granted that vegetarians like interesting food as much as carnivores do. **$$**

Burritos y Taquitos Santa Fé
Rua José Florêncio 5
Tel: 75-3334 1083
Open: D only daily.
The place for tasty and reliably good Mexican food. **$$**

Neco's Bar Restaurante
Praça Maestro Clarindo Pacheco 15
Tel: 75-3334 1179
Open: L&D daily (until last customer).

Delicious, home-made typical food in simple surroundings – but it must be ordered a day in advance. **$$**

Os Artistas da Massa
Rua da Baderna 49
Tel: 75-3334 1886
Open: D only daily.
Excellent, authentic Italian pasta. **$$$**

Restaurante Canto das Águas
Avenida Senhor dos Passos 01
Tel: 75-3334 1154
Open: L&D daily.
A concise menu of tasty, well-cooked dishes, and attentive service. **$$$**

• • • • • • • • • • • • • • • • • •

Prices for a two-course meal for two. Wine costs around US$20 a bottle.

$ = under US$40, **$$** = US$40–70, **$$$** = US$70–100

Bahian Cuisine

Bahian cooking is a unique Afro-Brazilian cuisine that is delicious and satisfying. Some dishes can be very peppery or rather heavy, so it is worth experimenting.

Though it contains contributions from the Portuguese colonists and the Brazilian native Amerindians, by far the most important influence on Bahian cuisine came from the enslaved Africans, who not only brought their own style of cooking with them, but also modified Portuguese dishes with African herbs and spices.

Bahian cuisine is characterized by the generous use of *malagueta* chili peppers and *dendê* oil extracted from an African palm that grows well in the northeastern climate. Several Bahian dishes also contain seafood (usually shrimp), coconut milk, banana, and okra (ladies' fingers).

Moqueca is one of the region's most popular dishes. It is a mixture of shrimp – perhaps with other seafood as well – coconut, garlic, onion, parsley, pepper, tomato paste, and the ubiquitous *dendê* oil. These ingredients are all sautéed over a low flame and served with rice cooked in coconut milk – a creamy, delicious dish.

Other traditional dishes are *vatapá* – a spicy shrimp puree made with palm oil and nuts – and *carurú de camarão*, which contains both fresh and dried shrimp, as well as sliced okra.

In the better Bahian restaurants, these dishes are served with a hot *malagueta* sauce. Sometimes this is added directly to the dish in the kitchens, and the cook may ask you if you like your food *quente* (spicy hot). Until you get used to the strong flavors of the *dendê* and *malagueta*, it is best to say no. If the sauce is placed in a bowl on the table, as it often is, you can try a little at a time. Bahian hotels are a good place to kick off your culinary adventure, since they tend to go a little easier on the *malagueta*.

The women of Bahia are among the world's great confectioners. They concoct sweets from coconut, eggs, ginger, milk, cinnamon, and lemon. *Cocada*, a sugared coconut sweet flavored with ginger or lemon, is a favorite. *Ambrosia*, made with egg yolks and vanilla, and *quindim* (glistening little yellow desserts made from egg yolks, sugar, and ground coconut) are sweet delights. You can buy *cocada* from *baianas* throughout Salvador.

RIGHT: *acarajé* bean patties for sale.

Baianas, usually dressed in white, set up shop daily in special shelters or at improvised tables where they sell *cocada*, *abará*, and *acarajé*, a traditional street food. You really should try this typical food, but do so at a place that has been recommended to you, or where you see plenty of local people eating, to be sure you are getting a fresh and well-prepared product.

Acarajé is made from shelled *fradinho* beans (similar to black-eyed peas), which are mashed together with ground shrimp and other ingredients and formed into a ball, then deep-fried in *dendê* (palm) oil. It is served split in half and then stuffed with *vatapá*, or *caruru*, shrimps and salad, and hot chili pepper if you wish. *Abará* is made from the same ingredients, but is not deep-fried. *Acarajé* is a wonderful treat to have between meals, especially if you have it with a beer at one of the beachfront bars.

Poverty has forced many Bahians to leave their state and go to Rio de Janeiro and other cities in search of work, and, of course, their cuisine has gone with them, so you are likely to find Bahian food in many other parts of Brazil.

For a Bahian culinary and cultural experience, however, you can't do better than go to one of Salvador's restaurants, many of which offer local cuisine, together with a folklore show *(see page 241 for some recommendations)*. ❑

SALVADOR

The capital of Bahia has a festive atmosphere and much to admire, from beautiful colonial churches to events like Carnival *afoxé* dance groups and numerous processions and rituals

S alvador was first colonized some 30 years after Brazil was discovered. In 1530, King João III sent a group of colonists to stake claim to this new land and thereby strengthened the Portuguese presence against French and Dutch invaders. Salvador became the first capital of Brazil in 1549, when the Portuguese court sent Tomé de Souza as the country's first governor general.

Perched atop cliffs, the tiny settlement was an ideal national capital because of its natural defenses. **Salvador ⑪** has since lost economic and political importance but is renowned as the center of Afro-Brazilian culture, with a mixture of black and white races descended from Africans, Europeans, and Amerindians. With a population of 2.6 million, Salvador, capital of the state of Bahia, is Brazil's fourth-largest city. Because life in Bahia revolves around Salvador, Brazilians frequently intermix the two, saying Bahia when they mean Salvador.

The religion and mysticism that are so much a part of Bahian life are reflected in the name Salvador, which means savior. The peninsula where the city was built, first discovered by Amerigo Vespucci in 1501, faces **Baía de Todos os Santos** (All Saints' Bay), named in honor of November 1, the day it was discovered.

What is most striking about Salvador is the way it assaults the senses: the sight of the gold-encrusted altars and panels of its churches; the inviting scent and exotic taste of the African-influenced food; the sounds of the street vendors' cries, the roar of traffic, the chant of fans at a soccer game, or enthusiasts at a political rally; and, most of all, the distinctive sounds and rhythm of Bahian music.

City of music

Throughout Salvador, and certainly on any beach, weekends are a time for music-making. Though much of the music today is commercial, some of it is influenced by *candomblé* (Afro-

LEFT: welcome to Salvador.
BELOW: the elevator links the upper and lower towns.

TIP

Some people prefer to
to spend a Carnival
evening in a camarote
(box) along the route.
Camarotes range from
the simple, affording a
space from which to
see the various bands
pass by, to the more
sophisticated, with air-
conditioning, drinks, a
buffet supper, and a
disco/nightclub, guaran-
teeing a party until
dawn. Prices vary
according to the night
of the week and the
facilities on offer.

Brazilian ritual worship), in which the pulsating, hypnotic rhythm calls the gods into contact with their devotees. Groups of native Bahians, known as *baianos*, gather in bars to sing their favorite songs.

Other clusters of amateur musicians play small drums and other percussion instruments, as well as the occasional guitar or *cavaquinho*, which has four strings and resembles a ukulele. Music and religion are as essential a part of the people's lives here as eating and sleeping. The year is organized around religious holidays. Street processions mark the celebrations. The religious calendar culminates in Carnival *(see page 87*, traditionally a last fling before the 40-day Lenten period of prayer and penance preceding Easter.

Carnival and *candomblé*

Officially, Carnival lasts for four days, from the Saturday to the Tuesday before Ash Wednesday, but in Salvador the festivities start on the previous Wednesday and continue for a week. Preparation for the Carnival is practically a summer-long event.

Salvador's Carnival

Carnival in Salvador is a highly organized affair. The Carnival *blocos* (blocks) are formed of a *trio elétrico* – national and local stars, soloists and bands, performing on stages perched atop enormous trucks, belting out music for dancing in the streets. They are followed by a support truck, which provides a bar, toilets, and a medical post. Each *bloco* permits around 3,000 participants to dance and have fun in a roped-off area with security protection as it makes its way through the streets at a slow pace, taking from five to seven hours to reach its destination. In order to join a Carnival *bloco* an *abadá* kit is required: this comprises shorts and a T-shirt printed with the *bloco*'s security symbol. The *abadá* is the access ticket, and is inspected carefully by the security team to prevent non-members joining in. They go on sale well in advance, and prices range from affordable to very high, depending on the popularity of the band.

Some revelers, known as *foliões pipoca* (popcorn dancers – an allusion to their jumping-up-and-down style of dance) follow behind the *bloco*, outside the roped area, enjoying the music without paying, but not enjoying the privileges or safety of *bloco* members. It is all great fun, and quite exhilarating, but remember that care should be taken in such large crowds.

Clubs host pre-Carnival balls and hold *ensaios* (rehearsals).

If you visit during Carnival, don't expect to get much sleep: local people generate enough energy to keep going practically non-stop. Salvador's Carnival is a completely different experience from its counterparts in Rio de Janeiro and other parts of the country. There are no samba schools competing for government money, and none of the extravagant costumes worn in Rio's samba parades. Here, the celebration is pure, wild fun: drinking, dancing, and music.

Though Carnival is an outgrowth of Christianity, mysticism also has its place. During Carnival, *afoxés*, groups of *candomblé* practitioners, take to the streets with banners and images of their patrons, usually African deities to whom they dedicate songs and offerings. One of the most famous and original *afoxés*, however, has chosen a different patron. Based in the center of the historical Pelourinho district, it is called *Filhos de Gandhi* (Sons of Gandhi), in honor of the Indian leader, and is dedicated to peace.

It is not only at Carnival time, though, that Salvador is home to joyful religious or popular celebrations. There is at least one important holiday per month, and if there is no holiday during your stay, you can usually arrange to attend a *candomblé* ceremony (though they are not open to the public all year round), or a *capoeira* display *(see opposite)*. Travel agencies and some hotels can make reservations for folklore shows (including *capoeira*) and those *candomblé* ceremonies that are open to the public. You could also contact Bahiatursa, the state tourism board (tel: 71-3117 3000), where operators, some of whom may speak English, can assist in making reservations.

Candomblé ceremonies are lively, spirited events with much music and dancing, but they are serious religious rituals and, as such, require respectful behavior and conservative dress –

preferably in white or light colors – and no shorts or halter tops. Also, cameras are strictly forbidden. Ceremonies usually take place at night and last at least three hours.

Capoeira, a martial art developed by the slaves, is a foot-fighting technique disguised as a dance *(see page 106)*. Forbidden by their owners to fight, the slaves were forced to hide this pastime behind the trappings of a gymnastics display. Today, you can see this rhythmic exercise performed on street corners and in the Mercado Modelo in Salvador to the music of the *berimbau*, a one-stringed instrument resembling an archer's bow.

Saints' days

Among Salvador's festivals is that of **Procissão do Senhor Bom Jesus dos Navegantes**, a New Year's Day procession in honor of Our Lord of the Seafarers, when a flotilla of boats escorts the image of Christ to the **Boa Viagem beach**. Another takes place on the second Thursday in January, when *baianas* in brilliant-white costumes ritually wash the steps of the church of **Nosso Senhor do Bonfim** (Our Lord of Good Ending), Salvador's most frequently visited church.

Iemanjá, the *candomblé* goddess of the sea, is honored on February 2, when *baianas* in white lace blouses and skirts send offerings, such as combs, mirrors, and soaps, out to sea on small handmade boats. This *orixá* (goddess), who is perceived as vain, is placated to guarantee calm waters for the fishermen.

Festivities in June to celebrate the saints' days of St Antony, St John and St Peter are collectively called *festas juninas* (June festivals), St John's day being the most important, and even rivaling Christmas. Finally, Nossa Senhora da Conceição da Praia (Our Lady of the Beach) is honored on December 8 with a Mass, a procession from the church dedicated to her, and popular festivities. *(For more on all these festivals, see page 89.)*

The best way to orient yourself in Salvador is to think of the town as divided into four: beaches, suburbs, and upper and lower cities. Downtown Salvador encompasses both the historical **Cidade Alta** (Upper City) and the newer **Cidade Baixa** (Lower City).

The Upper City

A walking tour of the Cidade Alta starts at the **Praça da Sé Ⓐ** opening onto **Terreiro de Jesus**, home to three of Salvador's most famous churches. The largest, the **Catedral Basílica Ⓑ**, is a 17th-century Jesuit structure built largely of stone, with beautiful examples of gold-leaf work in its main altar. Next to it are the 18th-century **São Pedro dos Clérigos Ⓒ** (St Peter's) and the 17th-century **Ordem Terceira de São Domingos Ⓓ** (Dominican). Shops in the area sell handmade lace and leather goods, and lovely primitive paintings.

Rising majestically from the adjoining square, **Praça Anchieta**, is one of the world's most opulent baroque churches. Paradoxically, it is dedicated to a saint who preached the

Candomblé *figures are for sale in all the shops.*

BELOW: lovely Pelourinho has some of the best colonial architecture in the Americas.

simple, unencumbered life. The **Igreja de São Francisco** E (St Francis) is an impressive 18th-century structure built of stone imported from Portugal. Its interior is covered from floor to ceiling with highly intricate carvings, thickly encrusted with gold leaf. In a side altar is the splendid statue of St Peter of Alcântara, which was carved from the single trunk of a jacaranda tree by Manoel Inácio da Costa, one of Brazil's most important baroque artists. Blue and white hand-painted *azulejos* (tiles) depicting scenes from the life of St Francis, imported from Portugal in the late 18th century, adorn the porch.

The Franciscan monastery, which may be visited, is annexed to the church, and surrounds a delightful courtyard.

Next door, the **Ordem Terceira de São Francisco** F (Church of the Third Order of St Francis) is noteworthy for its Spanish-style baroque facade and the 18th-century tiles in the courtyard.

Returning to the north side of Terreiro de Jesus, you will find the **Museu Afro-Brasileiro** G (Afro-

Brazilian Museum; open Mon–Fri 9am–5pm; admission charge) in the old medical faculty. It has a fascinating collection of objects that highlight the strong African influence on Bahian culture, including musical instruments, masks, costumes, carvings, and other artifacts that are part of the *candomblé* religion. There are also some beautiful wooden panels carved by Carybé, an Argentinian artist who fell in love with Brazil and adopted Salvador as his home.

Largo do Pelourinho

A short distance along **Rua Alfredo Brito**, on your right facing away from Terreiro de Jesus, you reach the **Largo do Pelourinho** H (Pillory Square), site of Salvador's best-preserved colonial buildings, whose colorful facades line the steep, meandering cobble-stoned streets. The name recalls a time when pillories were set up here to punish slaves and criminals.

Today, Pelourinho is considered by UNESCO to be the most important grouping of 17th- and 18th-century colonial architecture in the Americas.

TIP

It is said that Salvador has 365 churches, one for each day of the year. You could try counting, but you may be too busy enjoying the city.

Although once a fashionable district of Salvador, the fortunes of its inhabitants gradually deteriorated. However, Pelourinho is charming and distinctive. Many of the buildings have been renovated in recent years, and the area is well policed.

The center of Praça José Alencar square is occupied by the **Casa de Jorge Amado ❶** (open Mon–Sat 9am–6pm), a small museum-cum-library-cum-café, replete with books by one of Brazil's most famous novelists (his works have been translated into nearly 50 languages). The collection also includes photographs, memorabilia and a video about the life of Amado (1912–2001), one of Bahia's most beloved sons *(see page 223)*.

Next door is the tiny **Museu da Cidade** (City Museum; open Mon, Wed–Sat 9.30am–6.30pm, Sun 9am–1pm; admission charge), with a collection of Afro-Brazilian folkloric items. On the top floor are mannequins dressed as the most important *orixás* (gods) of the *candomblé* faith, identified by their African names as well as their equivalent Catholic saint's name.

The **Senac Restaurant ❶** (open Mon–Sat 11.30am–3.30pm, 6.30–11pm, Sun 11.30am–3.30pm) in the square, which is run by a government hotel and restaurant school, is an excellent place to try the local food and see a Bahian folklore show (Thur–Sat at 7pm). The restaurant serves lunch and dinner and has a buffet section (Mon–Fri 11.30am–2.30pm) where your chosen food is charged by weight.

Just down the street from Pelourinho Square is the church of **Nossa Senhora do Rosário dos Pretos ❿** (Our Lady of the Rosary of Black People). Because slaves were not permitted to go inside their masters' churches, they erected their own places of worship. At the bottom of Pelourinho Square is a flight of steps called the Ladeira do Carmo, which leads to the **Largo do Carmo ❶** (Carmelite Square). Scene of the resistance against the Dutch invaders, this block of buildings is the site of the Dutch surrender. The most interesting building is the **Igreja do Carmo ⓜ** (Carmelite Church and Convent), dating from 1585. The convent has been partially transformed into a small **museum** (open Mon–Sat 9am–1pm and 2–6pm). This area, called Santo Antônio, has enjoyed a renaissance in recent years. Several of the once run-down buildings have been restored and now house small hotels and inns.

Art and opulence

Still in the upper city, but in the opposite direction, are two museums that can be visited in an afternoon. The **Museu de Arte Sacra ⓝ** (Museum of Sacred Art; open Mon–Fri 11.30am–5.30pm; admission charge) at Rua do Sodré 276 is housed in the 17th-century church and convent of **Santa Teresa**. *Baianos* claim this is the largest collection of sacred art in Latin America. Whether or not this is the case, it is easily the most impressive of the city's museums, and one of the most fascinating in Brazil.

An icon in the Museu de Arte Sacra.

BELOW: sidewalk styling in Pelourinho.

TIP

You may well be besieged with street vendors offering hand-made jewelry and trinkets for sale. You can pick up some nice souvenirs very cheaply, but don't be afraid to say no very firmly if you want to be left alone. The sellers are usually very good-natured and friendly.

BELOW LEFT: Internet access behind a crumbling facade. **RIGHT:** cheerful local boy.

The baroque and rococo art is displayed in large, airy rooms, many of them lined with blue, white and yellow tiles brought from Portugal in the 1600s. Proving that contraband was a part of secular life in the 17th and 18th centuries, many of the larger images of saints, carved from wood, have been hollowed out to hide smuggled jewels and gold. Paintings, ivory sculptures, and works in earthenware, silver, and gold are also displayed.

Going toward the Barra beach area, at Avenida Sete de Setembro 2490, one of the city's main thoroughfares, you will find the **Museu Carlos Costa Pinto** 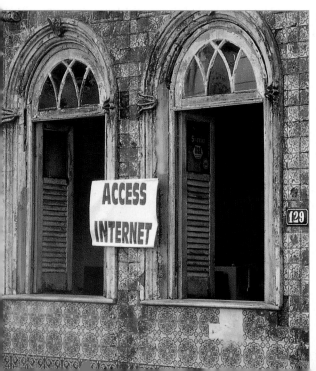 (open Mon and Wed–Fri 2.30–7pm, Sat–Sun 3–6pm; admission charge), in the **Vitória** district. Carlos Costa Pinto (1885–1946) was a wealthy businessman and art collector, and the museum houses his family's collection of colonial furnishings, porcelain and jewelry, including crystal, hand-painted porcelain dishes, and opulent silver *balagandans* – clusters of charms that were pinned to the blouses of slave women to indicate their owners' personal wealth. Much

of the flooring in the main rooms downstairs is of pink Carrara marble. At the entrance, museum employees place cloth slippers over your shoes to protect the floor.

Around Praça da Sé

Starting once more at the Praça da Sé, but heading toward the Lower City, walk down Rua da Misericórdia to the church of **Santa Casa da Misericórdia** 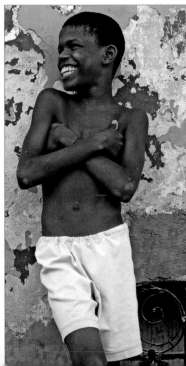, which is decorated with lovely 18th-century Portuguese tiles. Inside is a **museum** (open Mon–Fri 8am–5pm; tel: 71-3322 7666), recently renovated and reopened, containing church treasures and sacred art.

A short way down the street is the **Praça Municipal** 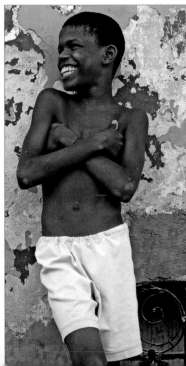, where the town council and city hall are housed in splendid colonial buildings. The square leads you to Salvador's famous **Elevador Lacerda**, a massive elevator built in 1930 to link the Upper and Lower cities. From here there are excellent views of Baía de Todos os Santos (All Saints' Bay). The elevator whisks you down to the **Cidade Baixa**, the Lower City.

The Lower City

Straight ahead as you leave the elevator is the **Mercado Modelo ®**, which has occupied the former customs house, in its present form, since 1971, having twice been destroyed by fire. In this three-story building you will find stalls selling all kinds of local handicrafts and souvenirs.

The Mercado Modelo is one of Salvador's not-to-be-missed sites. Although it's undeniably touristy, it is the best place in town to purchase your souvenirs. As you stroll among the stalls, you will spot vendors of musical instruments playing their wares to entice you to buy. You may hear percussion instruments, or the single-stringed *berimbau*. There are also good displays of *capoeira*. You will be pressed to give them money, but the entertainment is well worth it. For refreshment, try one of the many types of fresh fruit juices.

Across the road from the market, keeping the bay to your right, walk down the street to the church of **Nossa Senhora da Conceição de Praia ®**. Planned and built in Portugal in the early 18th century, this church was brought to Brazil piece by piece. It is the site of the annual religious procession held on December 8, one of the most important feast days in Salvador's Catholic calendar.

The Bonfim church

About 10 km (6 miles) in the opposite direction stands the famous church of **Nosso Senhor do Bonfim** (open Tues–Sun 6.30–11.30am, 1.30–6pm). On the way to the church, you will pass the rustic **São Joaquim Market** (open Mon–Sat 6am–6pm, Sun 6am–noon). The market is fascinating, and has been improved recently following years of neglect, which left it dirty and run-down.

The Bonfim church was built in 1745 and is one of the most popular sites for religious pilgrimage in the country. People come from throughout Brazil to pray for jobs or cures, or to give thanks for miracles attributed to Our Lord. As you enter the church, boys and women will try to sell you a colorful ribbon printed with the words *Lembrança do Senhor do Bonfim da*

TIP

The best way to get to Bonfim is by taxi. It shouldn't be too expensive – around US$12–14. Some hotels have "special" taxis parked outside. Convenient, but their rates are higher.

BELOW: looking at the upper city from below.

TIP

Inexpensive, air-conditioned buses run between Rio Vermelho and Pelourinho. There is also a good bus service from the airport all the way to Pelourinho, which is excellent value for money at about R$5 (US$2.50) for a 30-minute scenic journey.

BELOW: bangles for sale – the choice seems limitless.

Bahia (Souvenir of Our Lord of Good Ending of Bahia). The custom is that a friend should give you a ribbon and tie it around your wrist in three knots, representing three wishes: when the ribbon falls off, it is said, your wishes will come true.

Lacking the ornateness of Salvador's other churches, Bonfim is a favorite with both Catholics and *candomblé* practitioners. Don't miss the **Miracle Room**, which is filled with photographs of those who have reached a state of grace, and plaster castings of limbs or organs belonging to devotees cured through divine intervention.

Further down this same road is the church of **Monte Serrat**, a simple 16th-century chapel with Portuguese tiles. Near by is the **Boa Viagem** church, which is the destination of Salvador's Our Lord of the Seafarers procession held every New Year's Day.

The beaches

A series of interconnecting streets and roads provides a non-stop promenade along Salvador's beaches, from the near-downtown Barra beach to the distant north coast beaches that are considered among Brazil's most beautiful. The city beach, **Barra** is famed less for its beauty than for the conviviality of its bars and sidewalk cafés. Barra is where many local people stop for a beer after work, and stay late into the evening. Barra is also good for shopping and has some apart-hotels, which can be rented by the week or month and are usually much cheaper than hotels. The beach is protected by the gallant old fort **Santo Antônio da Barra**, with a lighthouse and oceanography museum.

The next beach northward from Barra is **Ondina**, home to some big hotels. Inland from the beach, in the same neighborhood, is the **Salvador Zoo** (open Tues–Sun 9.30am–5pm; admission charge). Next is **Rio Vermelho**, a picturesque and up-and-coming neighborhood where several good restaurants and new hotels have opened. The writer Jorge Amado lived here for six months of the year, until his death in 2001 (he used to spend the summer in Paris). There are coconut palms along the beaches as you travel

northward, passing by **Mariquita** and **Amaralina**, where several local restaurants are located.

At **Pituba**, you may see *jangadas*, primitive sail-driven fishing boats made of split logs roped together. Other beaches along this route include **Jardim de Alá**, **Armação de Iemanjá**, **Boca do Rio**, **Corsário**, **Pituaçu**, and **Patamares** (where there are also some good restaurants).

Piatã and **Itapoã**, the last beaches before the airport, are considered to be among Salvador's best. Itapoã may be slightly less crowded than Piatã, especially during the week, but in terms of natural beauty and opportunities for eating and drinking, they are equal. The statue of Iemanjá marks the border between the two beaches. One of the most beautiful sights in Salvador is the sunset viewed from Itapoã beach.

After dark

Nightlife in Salvador is concentrated in the cobblestoned streets of Pelourinho, where live music fills the air on most nights of the week, but particularly on Tuesday, and there are concerts every night in summer – most of them free to enjoy. There are nightclubs in the Barra area and along the beach drive. The Rio Vermelho district has good restaurants, bars, and nightlife.

The **Teatro Castro Alves**, located at **Campo Grande** across from the **Hotel Tropical da Bahia**, is the place for ballet, theater, and musical performances, and has a seating capacity of 1,400. Large signs outside the theater list the current events. Occasionally, the Castro Alves is host to a Brazilian or foreign symphony orchestra, and you may find one of Brazil's top recording artists performing there. Look out for names such as Caetano Veloso, Maria Bethânia and Gal Costa – *baianos* who, along with Gilberto Gil, are among Brazil's most popular singers and songwriters.

Soccer is a major form of entertainment in Salvador, as it is throughout Brazil. The local team, Esporte Clube Bahia, play at the city's **Otávio Mangabeira Stadium** (often referred to as Fonte Nova), usually on Wednesday night and Sunday afternoon. Book

You usually find live music on the streets of Salvador.

BELOW:
capoeira is an art, but it takes lots of practice.

Map on
page 218

TIP

Salvador restaurants
often have live music
during the evening, loud
enough to be lively, but
not so loud that you
can't have a conversa-
tion. The music that
belts out in the streets,
however, commands
your full attention.

BELOW:
relaxing in the
shade by the sea.

a seat in the reserved area *(cadeiras especiais)*; it is more expensive but worth it. Tickets are available at the stadium from 8am on the day of the game.

You are advised to avoid the port area and the streets surrounding Pelourinho at night. For the very best in entertainment, day or night, do what local people do: go to the beach. Pick one of the thatched-roof huts that function as bars on Pituba or Piatã beach, sit on a sawed-off trunk used as a stool, order your *batida* or *caipirinha* (cocktails made with fruit and *cachaça* – sugar-cane alcohol), and listen to the music played by your neighbors as you watch the waves roll in.

Day trips from Salvador

Ilha de Itaparica ⑫ is a tropical island set in the Baía de Todos os Santos, where Club Med built its first hotel in Brazil. About 19,000 people live on the island, divided mainly into fishermen and wealthy weekenders, whose beachfront mansions can often be reached only by boat. As it is a popular bolt-hole for middle-class Brazilians, hotels tend to be expensive, and

the island gets very crowded during weekends and holidays.

There are several ways to reach the island. Ferry boats leave Salvador's port at regular intervals for the 45-minute crossing. You can also drive around to the other side of the bay to the bridge that links Itaparica to the mainland. This is a three-hour trip that may be extended to include stops at the fascinating historical towns of Santo Amaro and Cachoeira. Or you could take the passenger ferry from the Mercado Modelo in Salvador, which is great fun as long as you have good sea legs. Once on the island, you can rent a bicycle to do some exploring along its many beaches.

If time is limited, take the day-long bay cruise sold by the top travel agencies in Salvador. The cruise includes transportation to and from your hotel and free *batidas* and soft drinks. Aboard the double-masted schooner *(saveiro)*, you're in for a delightful surprise: the guide and crew are also musicians. As the boat gently skims the calm waters of the bay between stops, the crew gathers at the prow to sing and play popular songs. Later in the day, after a fair number of *batidas*, nearly everyone is enthusiastically singing along and dancing.

After leaving Salvador, most of these boats make two stops. The first, in the late morning, is at **Ilha dos Frades**, a tiny and all but deserted island inhabited by fishermen who have found a second, more lucrative source of revenue: tourists. The boat anchors offshore, and visitors are brought ashore 10 at a time in rowing boats. Those who are not afraid of the jellyfish ("Their sting is just a little nip," the locals say) can swim to the shore.

After an hour of exploring, drinking, or eating a snack at one of the improvised bars, or purchasing souvenirs, you're taken onto Itaparica Island for lunch and a walking tour. Then it is back to the boat for the return trip to Salvador, with a splendid view of the sunset over the city. ❑

RESTAURANTS

Salvador has a wide variety of restaurants, many with tables set in flower-decked courtyards. You can find some authentic Bahian cooking, often served in extremely large portions – some dishes are made for sharing – and prices are generally very reasonable.

Al Carmo
Rua do Carmo 66, Pelourinho
Tel: 71-3242 0283
Open: D only Mon, L&D Tues–Sat.
Good, well-priced food in old colonial house with picturesque views over harbour. **$**

Alfredo di Roma
Rua Morro do Escravo Miguel s/n, Atlantic Towers, Ondina
Tel: 71-3331 7775
Open: L&D daily.
A branch of the renowned Rome original, located in the Caesar Towers Hotel. **$$$**

Escola do Senac
Praça José de Alencar 13, Largo do Pelourinho
Tel: 71-3324-4552/3324-4550/3324-4551
Open: L&D Mon–Sat, L only Sun, folklore show Thur–Sat evening.
This self-service place is the city's catering school, so a wide variety of dishes is offered. There is a buffet section where food is charged by weight. **$$**

La Lupa
Rua das Laranjeiras 17, Pelourinho
Tel: 71-3322 0066
Open: L&D daily.
This reputable Italian restaurant is set in a historic building in the Pelourinho district. **$$**

Mama Bahia
Rua Portas do Carmo 21, Pelourinho
Tel: 71-3322 4397
Open: L&D daily.
Meat is a speciality. **$$**

Manjericão
Rua Fonte do Boi 3-B, Rio Vermelho
Tel: 71-3335 5641
Open: L only Mon–Sat.
Natural food served in a very pleasant garden at lunchtime. **$**

Maria Mata Mouro
Rua da Ordem Terceira de São Francisco 8, Pelourinho
Tel: 71-3321 3929/4244
Open: L&D daily.
An eclectic menu of well-prepared contemporary cuisine in the heart of the historic district. **$$**

Pizzeria Romolo e Remo
Rua das Laranjeiras 27, Pelourinho
Tel: 71-3321 8060
Open: D only Tues–Sun
There are 32 different pizzas on the menu of this Italian-owned restaurant. **$$**

Quattro Amici Pizzeria
Rua Dom Marcos Teixeira 35, Barra
Tel: 71-3264 5999/2709
Open: L&D daily.

A good pizzeria in a restored 19th-century building. **$**

Restaurante Conventual
Convento do Carmo Hotel, Rua do Carmo s/n, Pelourinho
Tel: 71-3327 8400
Open: L&D daily.
In the most luxurious hotel in the city. There is a mix of Portuguese and Bahian influences on the excellent food. **$$$+**

Sorriso da Dadá
Rua Frei Vicente 5, Pelourinho
Tel: 71-3321 9642
Open: L&D daily.
Great Bahian food in lovely surroundings. **$$$**

Trapiche Adelaide
Praça dos Tupinambas 2, Avenida do Contorno
Tel: 71-3326 2211
Open: L&D Mon–Sat, L only Sun.
Serves international cuisine in a wonderful location, right by the Baía de Todos os Santos. **$$$**

Yemanjá
Avenida Octávio Mangabeira 4655, Jardim Armação
Tel: 3461 9010
Open: L&D daily.
Authentic Bahian dishes and a pleasant atmosphere. **$$$**

PRICE CATEGORIES

Prices for a two-course meal for two. Wine costs around US$20 a bottle.
$= under US$40
$$ = US$40–70
$$$ = US$70–100

RIGHT: great food and friendly service in Salvador.

MISTURA FINA: AFRO-BRAZILIAN CULTURE

The mix of races in Brazil is mainly European and African, but with Amerindian and many more exotic races, this is a truly multicultural society

Mistura Fina (Exquisite mixture) is a proud term often used to describe Brazil's multiracial origins.

When the Portuguese founded Brazil, they had problems with trying to populate an area almost one hundred times larger than their mother country. To solve this, they adopted a policy of interbreeding with other races, and imported black Africans as slave labor to build the colony. Slavery in Brazil was long lasting, but it was less rigorous than in the British colonies, and Afro-Brazilians were therefore able to preserve much of their culture. The result, many generations later, is that the majority of Brazilians are of mixed blood and in Brazilian culture, African roots are still very much alive.

Candomblé, *umbanda*, *macumba*, and spiritism all derive from African religions, and are often practiced in parallel with Christianity. A follower may go to church on Sunday and to the *terreiro*, where the African religions are practiced, on Friday.

Carnival was an institution that had been practiced in Portugal, but was also intended to give slaves an annual respite, and an opportunity to express their heritage. Today, the whole population gets involved, but it still bears the hallmark of Africa. The rhythms of Brazilian music have strong African roots, transmuted into a distinctly Brazilian sound. The sensual bossa nova and samba, and their derivatives such as lambada are reminiscent of African dances.

Brazil today without its African roots would be unthinkable; its culture would be incomparably poorer for the absence of the African essence, which is now part of every Brazilian soul.

ABOVE: Olodum, the world-famous drum group, combine native African rhythms with a typically up-tempo Brazilian interpretation.

LEFT: Religious offerings take various forms. At the Festival of Iemanjá, offerings of flowers and cosmetics are made to the vain goddess of the sea to guarantee calm waters. The festival is celebrated on New Year's Eve in Rio, in early February in Salvador.

LEFT: A *umbanda* priestess, an example of blended spiritual cultures. *Umbanda* is a mystical movement that combines worship of African, Brazilian, and European figures. This syncretism is part of Brazilian life, and many people pay allegiance to Afro-Brazilian religions and Christianity without any apparent compromise.

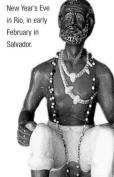

RIGHT: Black effigies of various kinds are frequently seen. This effigy of Preto Velho (the "Old Black Man") is typical of the clay figurines reflecting local African heritage that are made in the Recife area of Pernambuco, in northeast Brazil.

AFRO-BRAZILIAN ART AND CRAFTS

A great deal of Brazilian art and local crafts reflect an African heritage, and many pieces are derived from the skills and traditions that the slaves brought with them over the centuries. Wooden sculptures from the northeast region, in particular, are strongly reminiscent of African works.

The *carranca* figureheads that traditionally were believed to protect the river boats of the São Francisco River, and which today can be found in the region as souvenirs, come from the figurative art of Africa. Stylized statues in the same area are strongly reminiscent of the masks that proliferate in much of West Africa.

The faithful followers of *candomblé* are usually richly adorned with strings of beads in the colors of the African gods, as part of their religious costume. These are made of seeds or shells, and are similar to those which can be found in Africa. The beach-side stalls that sell them, largely in the northeast of the country, also carry a vivid range of T-shirts bearing traditional African designs.

RIGHT: Lucky ribbons are popular in Brazil. Many Afro-Brazilians are very superstitious, and various objects are deemed to have a good or bad omen. In Bahia these ribbons have been incorporated into the Catholic Bonfim tradition, and bring good luck if received as a present.

BELOW: Holy icons play a role in worship. Here, the symbol of Oxum, who is the goddess of the Osun River in Yoruba mythology, is held by a black *candomblé* priestess from the northeast. Oxum is believed to be the goddess of fresh water, and of love and money.

ABOVE: These Bahian women, attending Friday prayers, are dressed in long robes and headdresses of traditional white lace. They are followers of the *candomblé* ritual, the most African of all the Brazilian religious cults.

SERGIPE AND ALAGOAS

Great beaches, colonial towns, delicious seafood, and a host of festivals are luring increasing numbers of visitors to these two relatively unexplored states

Main attractions
SÃO CRISTÓVÃO
LARANJEIRAS
ARACAJU
PENEDO
MARECHAL DEODORO
MACEIÓ

BELOW: graceful palms are a typical feature of the northeast coast.

Sergipe and Alagoas played a part in the rich sugar-cane period of Brazilian history, which began in the late 16th century. As in neighboring Bahia and Pernambuco, the population was divided between landlords and slaves – the latter brought here in growing numbers to work in the sugar mills and plantations. But there were numerous rebellions, and runaway slaves went into hiding in the forests where they formed independent communities, or *quilombos*, some of which flourished and lasted for decades.

The most famous, and largest, of these *quilombos* was the Republic of Palmares in the state of Alagoas, which lasted for 65 years, and had at one time almost 30,000 inhabitants. In 1694 the *quilombo* was destroyed and its inhabitants killed or taken back into slavery. The site of the republic has become a pilgrimage center, and a bust of its last leader, Zumbi, who was executed in 1695, now stands in Brasília.

Vestiges of the state's colonial past can also be seen in the sugar mills and once grand farmhouses in the region, and in the ornate churches and other buildings in some historic towns.

Coastal attractions

Whereas neighboring northeastern states have largely substituted a tourist boom for the sugar-cane industry, Sergipe and Alagoas have yet fully to capitalize on this sector, but tourism is beginning to take off. Between Recife and Salvador, the two most important cities in the northeast, lie 840 km (525 miles) of beautiful coastline, which attract increasing numbers of visitors, and much of it lies in these two states.

The state capitals Aracaju and Maceió both have good urban beaches, and the stunning, unspoiled palm-ringed sands and deep blue sea of Alagoas are among the best in the northeast. The dark green of Sergipe's waters are not as inviting, but the state more than compensates with two attractive historic towns.

São Cristóvão

Lying about 34 km (20 miles) south of Aracaju, the capital, is **São Cristóvão** ⑬, founded in 1590 by Cristóvão de Barros. It is the fourth- oldest city in Brazil, and has a number of well-preserved elegant colonial structures, including the lovely Convento de São Francisco (1693), the Igreja e Convento do Carmo (1743–66), and Nossa Senhora da Vitória (late 17th century). There are also some museums, including the **Museu de Arte Sacra**, housed in the São Francisco convent; and, next door, the **Museu Histórico de Sergipe** (both open Tues–Sun 1–6pm; admission charge).

The Igreja do Carmo also houses a striking **museum of votive offerings** (open Mon–Fri 8am–noon, 2–7pm). A visit to São Cristóvão is not complete without trying the biscuits, made by nuns, that are sold in the orphanage next to the church of Nossa Senhora da Visitação.

Most visitors come to São Cristóvão for the religious procession of Senhor dos Passos, which takes place two weeks after Carnival. Accommodation in the town is very simple, and there is just one restaurant.

Laranjeiras

Nearby **Laranjeiras** (23 km/15 miles west of Aracaju) is another town that was founded on the sugar industry, and has preserved its heritage. It has the highest concentration of folkloric groups in the state, most notably the Grupo Folclórico São Gonçalo. It also has a rich Afro-Brazilian culture, and plays host to the first Afro-Brazilian museum in Latin America, the **Museu Afro-Brasileiro de Sergipe** (open Tues–Sun 9am–noon, 2–6pm; admission charge), which opened in the 1970s. A number of groups in the town practice *candomblé*, and visits can be arranged through the museum.

Although only a small town, it has seven churches, notably Sant'Aninha (1875) and Comendaroba (1734). In the late afternoon you will see local people selling *acarajé* and other regional snacks in the town center. If you are thinking of staying in Laranjeiras, be aware that accommodation is hard to find.

Local people have seen a lot of changes in recent years.

BELOW LEFT: a home-made surf board in Maceió.
RIGHT: coconut milk for sale.

São Francisco River

Born from a spring in the hills of Minas Gerais, the São Francisco, the third-largest river in Brazil, has been important in shaping the country's economic and cultural development. In the 19th century, the 3,000-km (1,800-mile) river played a vital role in the development of the northeast, through which its reddish-brown waters flow, defining the border between Sergipe and Alagoas, where it empties into the Atlantic Ocean. It was virtually the only major thoroughfare in the region, which lacked roads and railways. The river's role as primary mover of people and products has given it a place in Brazilian history and legend somewhat equivalent to that of the Mississippi in the US. From the 19th century until well into modern times, riverboats plied the São Francisco, carrying essential supplies to backwoods towns.

The villages and settlements that sprang up along the river banks during the colonial period had become important trading centers and commercial outposts by the mid-19th century. Today, the valley still serves as an agricultural oasis in an otherwise arid terrain. Along the banks you encounter farms producing fruits for export, including grapes, papaya, and mango. The Vale do Rio São Francisco is the only region in the world producing fine wines at a latitude of 8º from the Equator, most notably the Rio Sol vineyard run by Portuguese grower João Santos. Since its inception in 2003, Rio Sol wines have been rivaling the vineyards of southern Brazil, winning important national awards. Visits can be arranged through the restaurant Maria Bonita (Areia Branca, Petrolina) run by João's wife Denise. The vineyard forms part of the São Francisco Wine Route, 50 km (32 miles) outside Petrolina.

One of Brazil's most curious native art forms has its origins in the São Francisco. Known as *Velho Chico* (Old Chico) to the local inhabitants, the river is both admired and feared as the home of evil spirits. In order to protect themselves from these spirits, boatmen in the 19th century made wooden figureheads for their vessels, depicting fierce, ugly creatures which could warn a boat's crew of danger by emitting low moans. These figureheads, half-man, half-beast, are called *carrancas*. Only the older boatmen still believe in the powers of *carrancas*, but the legend lives on, and the figures are still attached to modern boats as curios.

Two of the best places to purchase authentic *carrancas*, carved from cedarwood, are Petrolina in Pernambuco (750 km/465 miles from Recife) and neighboring Juazeiro in Bahia state (5km/3 miles from Petrolina). Oficina do Artesão (Final da Avenida Cardoso de Sa, Vila Eduardo, Petrolina) sells *carrancas* and other interesting wooden sculptures produced on-site by resident artists.

Many boatmen offer day-long cruises to visitors. Trips begin in Penedo in Alagoas, Paulo Afonso and Juazeiro in Bahia, and, directly across the river, Petrolina in Pernambuco, Ibotirama in Bahia, and Januária and Pirapora in Minas Gerais.

From Petrolina one can also visit a number of river islands, the most interesting of which is the Ilha de Massangano, where you can see Samba de Veio, one of the oldest folk groups in the region, established more than 100 years ago. The best time to see them is on the Dia dos Reis (January 6), when the group play until dawn.

One gallant old paddlewheel steamboat, built in the US in 1913 for use on the Mississippi, still makes jaunts down the São Francisco. For many years it made the trip from Pirapora to Juazeiro, serving tourists and the people who live along the route. Today it is used exclusively for tourists, and goes only as far as Januária (reservations from Unitour, Rua Tupis 171, Belo Horizonte; tel: 31-3201 7144; fax: 31-3226 7152). ❏

LEFT: loading up for a river trip.

Aracaju

A short way further north, **Aracaju** ⑭, lies in the center of the Sergipe coastal strip. Founded in 1855, Aracaju (pop. 290,000) has a small but well-maintained historic center, with buildings that include the Cathedral of Nossa Senhora da Conceição. Opposite the cathedral, in a delightful colonial building, is the Tourist Center (Praça Olimpio Campos) which, apart from the local tourist office, also houses a number of artisan stores with a varied selection of local crafts for sale at reasonable prices.

There is better accommodation at nearby Atalaia beach than in the center of town. With an extensive promenade and a variety of restaurants, Atalaia makes a good base for exploring Aracaju, and for day trips to other beaches, such as Do Rabalo and Mosqueiro.

Festivals galore

Aracaju is noted for the beauty of its beaches and the hospitality of its people, whose festival calendar is one of the fullest in the northeast. The numerous festivals are nearly always based on religious holidays, though they may often appear more secular then sacred. They include Bom Jesus dos Navegantes, a maritime procession of gaily decorated boats (January 1); São Benedicto, celebrated with folk dances and mock battles (the first weekend in January); the Festas Juninas, in honor of the three saints John, Anthony and Peter (vibrant celebrations throughout the month of June); Expoarte, a handcraft fair (the whole month of July); and Iemanjá, a religious procession in honor of the *candomblé* goddess, which is celebrated at different times in different cities, but here is held on December 8.

Seafood center

Delicious seafood abounds here, among which is Aracaju's main claim to fame, its freshwater shrimp (similar to crayfish in appearance), caught in the Sergipe River. Crab is another of this city's specialties, and for dessert, breadfruit compote or stewed coconut. The obligatory appetizer is a *batida*, made from sugar-cane liquor *(cachaça)* and any one of a variety of local fruits – the best are mango, cashew, coconut, and mangaba.

Crossing the state border

Moving north along the BR-101 highway from Aracaju, you cross the state border between Sergipe and Alagoas, delineated by the immense São Francisco River *(see opposite)*. Here, the town of **Penedo** ⑮, built in the 17th and 18th centuries, is a good place to stop on your way to the state capital, Maceió *(see page 248)*.

Penedo's baroque and rococo churches are its main attractions, in particular Nossa Senhora dos Anjos (1759) and Nossa Senhora da Corrente (1764). River trips downstream to the mouth of the São Francisco can be taken from Piacabucu (22 km/14 miles from Penedo), or take the ferry across the river to Neópolis, where boat trips can be arranged at Brejo Grande (27 km/17 miles from Neópolis).

The tourist office in the Praça Olimpio Campos.

BELOW: excellent seafood is a local specialty.

Santana do São Francisco (3 km/1½ miles from Neópolis) is a good place to buy handmade earthenware and porcelain goods at the Centro de Artesanato, a project run by members of the local community.

Tranquil beaches

The road from Penedo to Maceió passes a variety of quiet, often deserted beaches, such as Japu, Miai de Cima, and Barreiras. Closer to Maceió, Praia do Gunga (45 km/28 miles to the south) is a popular choice in the summer months. The beach is located at the point where the Roteiro lake meets the sea. It has a good infrastructure for visitors, with a number of stalls offering food and drinks. One of the busiest beaches close to the city limits is Praia do Francês, which is near the historic old town of Marechal Deodoro, the first capital of Alagoas.

Marechal Deodoro

Marechal Deodoro ⓰ itself is home to some lovely examples of Brazilian colonial architecture. Among the gems are the Convento de São Francisco (Monastery of St Francis), dating from 1684, and the church of Nossa Senhora da Conceição (1755).

Originally called Alagoas, the town was renamed after its most famous son, Field Marshal Manuel Deodoro da Fonseca (1827–92), who became, briefly, the first (non-elected) president of Brazil in 1891. He heading the military coup that deposed Emperor Dom Pedro II two years earlier, but his time in office was turbulent. Faced with strong opposition from the Congress, he handed over power to Vice-President Floriano Peixoto after a few months, and died the following year.

Maceió

Between Sergipe and Pernambuco (to the north) lies the state of Alagoas, whose capital is **Maceió** ⓱, with a total population of 880,000. The city, founded in 1815, grew gradually out of a sugar plantation established there in the 18th century.

Maceió beaches are famous for the transparent bright emerald green of the water, especially at low tide on downtown **Praia Pajuçara**. Trapped

These attractive figures are made all over the region.

BELOW: an idyllic lunch by the sea – only the donkey is left out.

between the beach and offshore sandbars, the water becomes an enormous wading pool. For a small sum, fishermen will take you out to the sandbars in their *jangadas* (outrigger boats).

The city is struggling to keep up with the flow of tourists who descend upon it every year in summer. December is an especially busy month, when Maceió holds its Festival do Mar (Festival of the Sea) at Pajuçara. It is celebrated with a giant street and beach party that includes sporting events, folk dancing, and booths selling native handicrafts.

Maceió is a mostly modern town, but a few old buildings survive, including the **Pierre Chalita Sacred Art Museum** (open Mon–Fri 8am–noon, 2–6pm; admission charge), in the Palácio do Governo; the church of Bom Jesus dos Martirios (1870); and the Catedral de Nossa Senhora dos Prazeres (1840) on Praça Dom Pedro II.

North along the coast

Continuing north of Maceió towards the state border with Pernambuco is one of the most beautiful stretches of coastal road in the region. The palm-tree-lined road hugs the coast for most of the distance, allowing easy access to a number of beaches. The section from Barra de Camaragibe to Porto de Pedras is reminiscent of bygone days, with little to disturb its serenity. The road passes through a series of small villages where local people sell craft goods, cakes, and tapioca from their porches. A series of discreet, easy-to-miss dirt tracks take you down to isolated beaches, which see few tourists at the busiest of times.

The small town of **Porto de Pedras** makes a good base for visiting the beaches. The local restaurant here run by Dona Marinete specializes in excellent home-cooking. Her signature dishes include lobster stew and a regional crab omelette *(see below).*

Beaches worth visiting include Praia do Toque and Tatuamunha. North of Porto de Pedras, almost on the border with Pernambuco, are the beaches of Japaratinga and Maragogi. The latter was recently rated one of the top 10 beaches in Brazil by a respected national publication. ❑

TIP

In the little resort of São Miguel dos Milagres, near Porto de Pedras, you could pamper yourself at the lovely Pousada do Caju (tel: 82-295 1103), a luxury retreat with just 13 guest rooms, all with verandas, private pools, and Jacuzzis.

RESTAURANTS

Aracaju

Casquinha de Caranguejo
Avenida Santos Dumont 751, Atalaia
Tel: 79-3243 7011
Open: L&D daily.
Popular beachfront crab restaurant. Other dishes include *badejo* fish cooked with banana. **$**

O Miguel
Avenida Antonio Alves 340, Atalaia Velha
Tel: 79-3243 1444
Open: L&D daily.
Down-to-earth restaurant; does a great *carne de sol* and *pirão de leite.* **$$**

Laranjeiras

Nico's Restaurante
Praça da Matriz
Tel: 79-281 2883
Open: L&D daily.
In the center of town, specializing in regional dishes. Simple and friendly atmosphere. **$**

São Cristóvão

O Sobrado
Praça Getulio Vargas 40
Tel: 079-3261 1310
Open: L&D daily.
Luckily, the only restaurant in town is a good one. Local food in an attractive colonial house. **$**

Maceió

Carne de Sol do Picui
Avenida da Paz 1140
Tel: 82-3223 5313
Open: L&D daily.
A dozen variations of the local specialty, *carne de sol*. One dish is easily enough for two. **$**

Divina Gula
Rua Engenheiro Paulo Brandão Nogueira 85, Stella Maris
Tel: 82-3235 1016
Open: L&D Tues–Sun.
Highly recommended. Set in a colonial building, the restaurant serves a variety of local dishes. **$$**

Penedo

Esquina Imperial
Avenida Floriano Peixoto 61

No phone bookings.
Open: L daily.
Long-established family-run restaurant in historic building. Kilo (pay by weight) system. **$**

Porto de Pedras

Peixada da Marinete
Rua Avelino Cunha s/n
No phone bookings.
Open: L&D daily.
Simple setting and great food. Go for *lagostada* – baby lobster stew – or *fritada de aratu* – crab omelette. **$–$$**

• • • • • • • • • • • • • • •

Prices for a two-course meal for two. Wine costs around US$20 a bottle. **$** = under US$40, **$$** = US$40–70, **$$$** = US$70–100

RECIFE AND PERNAMBUCO

Bustling Recife and beautiful, baroque Olinda
are the main focuses of a state whose other
attractions include art and handicraft centers,
and some gorgeous sandy stretches of beach

W hen sugar was king in the late 16th and early 17th centuries, Pernambuco was the richest state in Brazil. Sugar plantations and mills – *engenhos* – were centered in the region around Olinda, and Recife quickly developed as the ideal port for the export of the product. Slave labor was easy to come by, and political power came in the wake of economic dominance. When the economic importance of sugar dwindled, it was largely replaced by cotton, but by the mid-17th century, finds of gold and precious metal in the state of Minas Gerais were getting all the attention. The capital of the country was moved south, from Salvador near the sugar plantations to Rio de Janeiro, closer to the rich gold-mining areas, and Pernambuco and its capital, Recife, never regained their former glory.

Although political and economic power have moved south, Recife is once again becoming a booming center, this time for the fast-growing tourism industry. Good hotels and restaurants are attracting growing numbers of Brazilian and international visitors looking for beautiful beaches, colonial gems like Olinda, and a year-round warm climate.

Coral-reef city

Recife ⓲, capital of the state of Pernambuco, is a metropolis of 1.4 million inhabitants. Its name comes from the Arabic word for "fortified wall,"

which in Portuguese has acquired the meaning of "reef." Recife's coastline, like much of the northeast, is characterized by barnacle and coral reefs running parallel to the mainland, between 90 meters (330 ft) and 1 km (½ mile) from the shore. The waves break on the far side of the reefs, making the water on the near side a shallow, salt-water swimming pool, tranquil and safe for bathers. On **Boa Viagem** beach in Recife you can wade out to the reefs at low tide, and barely get your knees wet.

Main attractions

RECIFE:
TEATRO SANTA ISABEL
CAPELA DOURADA
BOA VIAGEM
ILHA ITAMARACÁ
OLINDA
CARUARU
FAZENDA NOVA

LEFT:
selling coconut
milk on the beach.
BELOW:
Pernambouco
state market.

Ornate, if crumbling, architecture in Recife.

In 1537, the Portuguese settled the coastal area of Pernambuco. A Dutch invasion a century later, under Prince Maurice of Nassau, brought with it a new era of art, culture, and urbanization to the town. Recife was once a maze of swamps and islets that Prince Maurice made habitable through the construction of canals. Now there are 39 bridges spanning the canals and rivers that separate the three main islands of Recife.

Walking tour

A walking tour of Recife's historical district begins at the **Praça da República ⒜** with the **Teatro Santa Isabel ⒝** (open Mon–Fri 1–5pm), a neoclassical building dating from 1850, and one of the most beautiful in the city. Other 19th-century buildings on this square include the governor's mansion, the palace of justice, and the law courts, which double as the Catholic University's law school (the oldest one in Brazil).

Just across the street from the palace of justice is the baroque **Capela Dourada ⒞** (Golden Chapel; chapel and adjoining sacred art museum open Mon–Fri 8–11.30am, 2–5pm, Sat 8–11.30am; admission charge). According to legend, it contains more gold than any church in Brazil, except Salvador's Igreja de São Francisco. Built in the late 17th century by laymen attached to the Franciscan Order, this is one of the most important examples of religious architecture in Brazil.

Eight blocks from the Santa Isabel Theater, down Rua do Sol, is the **Casa da Cultura ⒟** (open Mon–Sat 9am–7pm, Sun 10am–2pm), a three-story structure that served as a penitentiary for more than 100 years. In 1975 it was remodeled to become Recife's largest handicraft center. The prison cells have been turned into booths displaying articles ranging from leather and straw accessories to clay figurines, silk-screened T-shirts, and fruit liqueurs. On Praça Visconde de Mauá, opposite the Casa da Cultura and next to the **Estação Central ⒠** (1888), is the **Museu do Trem** (open Mon–Thur 1–6pm, Fri 8am–noon; admission charge), which traces the history of Brazil's railroads.

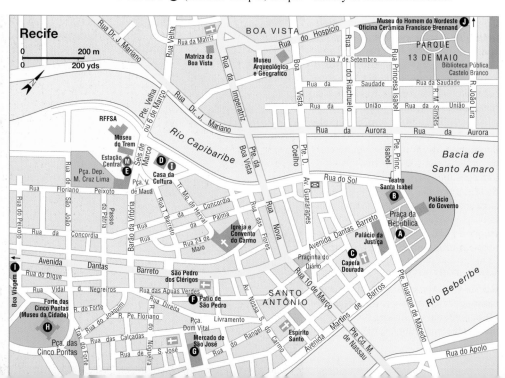

Four hundred meters (440 yds) away, southeast along Rua T. Barreto, is the **Patio de São Pedro ❻**, the artists' corner of Recife, with music and folklore performances on weekends. It is a good place to buy local craftwork. The **Igreja de São Pedro** near by is an interesting example of baroque architecture. Continuing southeast, across Praça Dom Vital, you come to the **Mercado de São José ❼**, a busy market (open Mon–Sat 5am–3.30pm, Sun 6am–noon) in a 19th-century building.

At the southern end of the downtown area, the massive, star-shaped **Forte das Cinco Pontas ❽**, built by the Dutch in 1630, houses the **Museu da Cidade** (Largo das Cinco Pontas; open Mon–Fri 9am–6pm, Sat–Sun 1–5pm; admission charge), with displays on the history of Recife.

Walking southwest from the Museu da Cidade along Avenida Dantas Barreto, you will eventually come to **Boa Viagem ❶**. Most of the better restaurants and bars and nearly all the city's fine hotels are located on or near the beach here. It is Recife's most beautiful beach, and also the center of its social life.

In the evening, the action is concentrated along the beach itself, and on Avenida Conselheiro Aguiar, one block inland. The street is home to a number of small bars and sidewalk cafés offering inexpensive drinks, nibbles, and live music.

There are a dozen museums in Recife, but one stands out: the **Museu do Homem do Nordeste ❿** (Museum of Northeastern Man; open Tues–Wed and Fri 11am–5pm, Thur 8am–5pm; Sat–Sun and holidays 1–5pm; admission charge) at Avenida 17 de Agosto 2187. Founded by the late Gilberto Freyre (1900–87), Brazil's most reputable anthropologist, the museum is a tribute to the cultural history of this fascinating and unusual region. The museum has bilingual guides and is located in the **Casa Forte** district, 6 km (4 miles) from downtown.

Another diverting stop in the same part of town, in the working-class district of **Várzea**, is the **Oficina Cerâmica Francisco Brennand** (open Mon–Fri 8am–5pm), the workshop and studio of one of the northeast's best-known artisans. This immense atelier was a brick and tile factory until Francisco Brennand took it over. Brennand (b. 1927) is famed in Recife for his beautiful, hand-painted tiles, pottery, and vaguely erotic statuary, all eagerly bought by local people and tourists. You can visit the workshop, and if you call ahead for a tour you may be lucky enough to be escorted by Mr Brennand himself (for details tel: 81-3271 2466).

Glorious beaches

The name Pernambuco comes from the indigenous Tupi word *paranampuka*, which means "the sea that beats on the rocks." Indeed, the sea has played a major part in Pernambuco's history. Now, it's the beaches that attract large numbers of visitors, generating an additional and much-valued source of income. Pernambuco's coast stretches for 187 km (116 miles) between the

The Igreja de São Pedro in Recife is an interesting example of baroque architecture.

BELOW:
Porto de Galinhas, popular for its soft, white sand.

*Pernambuco
coconuts: the milk is
one of the most
refreshing drinks
imaginable in hot
weather.*

BELOW:
Porto de Galinhas
has a thriving
center, as well as
excellent beaches.

states of Paraíba to the north and Alagoas to the south. Visitors will find many glorious beaches, with sunshine and warm waters for most of the year.

As already mentioned, the best and most famous beach in Recife is Boa Viagem. Outside Recife, the most beautiful beaches lie to the south. **Porto de Galinhas**, next to the town of **Ipojuca**, 50 km (30 miles) from downtown Recife, is fast gaining an international reputation for its 18-km (12-mile) extension of soft, white sand, some world-class hotels, an attractive village, and excellent restaurants. A little further south, there are frequent surfing competitions during the summer months at Maracaípe. Continuing further, you will find Praia dos Carneiros; one of the most beautiful beaches along Pernambuco's coastline, it can be visited from Porto de Galinhas on a day tour.

To the north, the best beaches are found on **Ilha Itamaracá**, 53 km (33 miles) from Recife, where local people spend their weekends. On the way, along highway BR-101, is the historical town of **Igarassu**, much of which has

been declared a National Monument. It is home to one of the oldest churches in Brazil, built in 1535, and dedicated to the twin saints of Cosme and Damião. The adjoining Franciscan monastery has one of the largest collections of baroque religious paintings in the country, comprising more than 200 works. There are also a number of colonial houses, and Brazil's first Masonic hall.

Halfway across the bridge to Itamaracá sits a police checkpoint, a reminder that part of the island serves as an open prison for model inmates serving time at a nearby penitentiary. Married prisoners are allowed to live with their families, and all the inmates are engaged in some form of commerce. As you start down the island road, you will see lines of booths and small shops run by prisoners, selling postcards and crafts. Each man is identified by a number stenciled on to his T-shirt.

Before you reach Forte Orange, built by the Dutch in 1631, take the side road to **Vila Velha**, the island's first settlement, founded in 1534. This iso-

lated village is tucked away in a coconut grove on the southern coast.

A number of colonial buildings, crowned by the 17th-century Nossa Senhora da Conceição church, line the square. If you're looking for a midday break, there are several regional and seafood restaurants. Splendid beaches line most of the island's shore.

Downtown Itamaracá and the historical Forte Orange district have some simple hotels and restaurants. Next to the old fort, there is a visitor center with displays on the work of the Manatee Project, which looks after injured manatees before returning them to the open sea.

A cultural wonder

Time has stood still in **Olinda** ⑲, which stretches like an open-air museum across the hills overlooking Recife. The town is a treasure trove of baroque art and architecture and, as such, was declared a World Heritage Site by UNESCO in 1982. However, many of the buildings are still awaiting restoration.

Legend has it that the first Por-tuguese emissary sent to govern the region was so enthralled by the beauty of these hills that he said "*O linda situ-ação para uma vila*" (What a beautiful site for a settlement) – hence Olinda's name. By far the best way to explore Olinda is on foot. Narrow streets lined with brightly colored colonial homes, serenely beautiful churches, sidewalk cafés, and shops displaying ornate signs wind through the 17th-century setting of Olinda's hills.

Starting off at the **Praça do Carmo**, site of Brazil's oldest Carmelite church (built in 1580), continue up Rua São Francisco to the **São Roque** chapel, **Nossa Senhora das Neves** church, and the monastery of **São Francisco** (open Mon–Fri 7–11.30am, 2–5pm, Sat 7am–noon), dating from 1585, with baroque frescoes depicting the *Life of the Virgin Mary*. Turn left on Rua Bispo Coutinho to visit the **Seminário de Olinda** and the **Nossa Senhora da Graça** church – both well-preserved examples of 16th-century Brazilian baroque architecture. This street opens out on to Alto da Sé, a hilltop square overlooking the ocean,

TIP

The coast here is a great place for oysters. On the beach, vendors carry buckets full of them, packed in ice. They are opened in front of you, topped with a drop of lemon, oil, and salt, and you have an instant snack.

BELOW:
beautiful baroque São Francisco.

and Recife, 6 km (4 miles) away.

The **Igreja da Sé**, the first parish church in the northeast, was built at the time of Olinda's founding in 1537 and today is the cathedral of the archdiocese. Across from the cathedral, housed in the **Palácio Episcopal** (1676) is the **sacred art museum** (open Tues–Fri 8am–noon, 2–6pm, Sat–Sun 2–5.30pm), which contains a collection of panels portraying the history of Olinda. On weekend evenings, the Alto da Sé comes alive with outdoor cafés and bars.

As you turn down the Ladeira da Misericórdia, on your right is the church of the **Misericórdia** (open daily 11.45am–12.30pm, 6–6.30pm only) dating from 1549. Its richly detailed wood-and-gold engravings are reminiscent of the French Boucher school. The building from which the **Mercado da Ribeira** operates, on Rua Bernardo Vieira de Melo, was used in the 16th century as a slave market; the market is now an excellent place to buy art. On the corner of Rua 13 de Maio is the **Museu de Arte Contemporânea** (open Tues–Fri 8am–6pm,

A cheerful mural in Olinda.

BELOW:
Olinda – the name means "beautiful."

Sat–Sun 2–5.30pm; admission charge), an 18th-century structure that was originally designed to house prisoners of the Inquisition.

Most of Olinda's other historical buildings are open daily to visitors, with a two-hour lunch break, usually noon–2pm. Accommodation can be found in luxury hotels and small inns, many housed in historic mansions.

Mountain resort

The twice-weekly Caruaru handicrafts fair, and the backwoods town of Fazenda Nova (190 km/118 miles from Recife), are the final destinations of an excellent day trip from Recife along the BR-232 highway that winds up the coastal mountain range to the resort town of Gravatá, and beyond.

Halfway to Gravatá, near **Vitória de Santo Antão**, looming on the left, is an enormous bottle with a crayfish on the label: the symbol of the Pitú *cachaça* distillery. The distillery hardly needs its bottle sign: its product, Brazil's distinctive sugar-cane liquor, can be smelled long before the bottle appears. Tours of the plant are

available, and there are free tastings of the most famous brand of *cachaça* in the northeast.

From here to Gravatá it's 32 km (20 miles) along a tortuous mountain road. The air becomes noticeably cooler, the vegetation more sparse. **Gravatá ⑳** is where Recife's wealthy have summer homes, and the fresh mountain air attracts visitors to its hotels and inns at the weekend. This is practically the last you will see of anything green, except for scrubland plants and lizards, until you return to the coast.

Eclectic trading post

Ideally, a visit to Fazenda Nova should be made either on a Wednesday or a Saturday. On these two days the next-door city of **Caruaru ㉑** turns into one great trading post, with rich and poor rubbing shoulders at the stalls. At one stand, a wealthy Recife matron may be choosing her hand-painted earthenware tea set, while at another, a toothless old man from the *sertão* will try to exchange a scraggly goat for a few sacks of rice, beans, and sugar. People from outlying villages pay the

equivalent of a few cents apiece for a place in a truck or a jeep to come to Caruaru just to do their weekly shopping. Others travel from distant states or foreign countries to purchase some of Brazil's most beautiful and artistic handicrafts.

The gaily painted figurines, first created by the late Mestre Vitalino, are among the most popular items for sale, but beware of vendors who try to charge high prices, alleging that their figurines were made by the Mestre himself. Vitalino wasn't *that* prolific. What's on display here, and in Recife's Casa da Cultura (where many of the same items are sold, but with less variety), was probably made by students of Vitalino. Caruaru's fair opens at about 9am and goes on until 5pm, and is considered the best of its kind in South America.

Fazenda Nova ㉒, a sleepy village that survived for years on what it could scratch out of the parched earth, took its place on the map in 1968 when the Pacheco family, with support from the state government, inaugurated **Nova Jerusalem**. This

TIP

You can also visit the Casa-Museu de Mestre Vitalino in Caruaru's Alto do Moura district (open Mon–Sat 8am–noon, 2–5pm), where the great ceramicist lived and worked.

BELOW: doll-making is a local tradition that remains popular.

Master Ceramicist

The Caruaru ceramicist known as Mestre (Master) Vitalino – an acknowledgement of his status – was Vitalino Pereira dos Santos (1909–63), who lived in the Alto do Moura district, and became famous for his distinctive clay figures, mostly portraying poor rural workers of the northeast.

A group of other *bonequeiros* (doll-makers), who had also come to Caruaru from the surrounding countryside, gathered around him, making models in a similar style. Vitalino's five children worked with their father, and after his death continued the family tradition.

Two other interesting ceramicists whose work you can see in Caruaru are Luís Antônio and Manoel Galdino (the latter died in 1996), whose work has a more contemporary feel.

Buses cover long distances on the sun-baked roads of Pernambuco.

BELOW: carrying the cross in the Passion Play.

open-air theater, which is designed to resemble the Jerusalem of AD 33, comes to life once a year, during Holy Week, when the Passion of Christ is re-enacted before tens of thousands of spectators.

The setting is perfect: huge stages, each depicting a station of the cross, rise out of the sandy soil, looming over actors and spectators. The audience follows the players (500 in all, most of them village residents) from scene to scene, and becomes part of the Passion Play. Audience participation is at its height when Pontius Pilate asks the crowd, "Who shall it be – the King of the Jews or Barabbas?" The actors do not speak. Instead, they mouth the recorded dialogue.

Giant statues

Just a short walk from the theater is the no less impressive **Parque das Esculturas** (open daily 7am–5pm), a mammoth tribute to the northeast. In the park you'll find immense stone statues, weighing up to 20 metric tonnes, representing both folk heroes and the ordinary people of the northeast. In one section, there is a washerwoman, a cottonpicker, a sugar-cane cutter, and a lacemaker – each of them 3–4 meters (10–13 ft) tall. In another section, Lampião, the legendary Robin Hood of the northeast, and his beloved, Maria Bonita, stand tall. There is also a collection of figures taken from Pernambuco's folk dances and celebrations, including an immense sea horse and his rider; a *jaraguá*, half-man, half-monster; and a *frevo* dancer.

Frevo (from the Portuguese *ferver* to boil) is the centerpiece of Pernambuco's Carnival combining a range of musical styles. In this festival there are no samba schools like those found in the south, and no electric instruments such as are found in Salvador. People dance in the streets, holding up parasols to help keep their balance. Groups portray *maracatu*, a typical northeastern legend that tells the history of the *candomblé* religion and its roots in the times of slavery.

The center of northeastern Carnival is Olinda, whose narrow streets are packed with delirious celebrants throughout the four-day festival. ❑

The New Jerusalem

Nova Jerusalem Is regarded as the largest open-air theater in the world. It occupies an area of 10 hectares (25 acres), and is surrounded by 3.5 km (2.2 miles) of stone walls, with seven gates and 70 towers. There had been a local Passion Play here for some time, but the huge theater was initiated by Plínio Pacheco. He was born in 1926, at the other end of the country, in the southernmost state of Rio Grande do Sul, and went to Fazenda Nova to visit a friend who was playing the part of Jesus in a production performed in the streets of the tiny village. There, he met Diva Mendonça, daughter of the performance's organizer; they fell in love and married, and in 1962 Plínio had the idea of building a miniature Jerusalem for the play. For more details, check www.novajerusalem.com.br.

RESTAURANTS

Recife

Boi Preto Grill
Avenida Boa Viagem 97,
Pina
Tel: 81-3466 6334
Open: L&D daily.
This is the place for carnivores – a great barbecue spot. **$$$**

Chez Georges
Avenida Boa Viagem 1906,
Terceiro Jardim
Tel: 81-3466 6334
Open: L&D Sun–Fri.
Excellent French cooking, with some local influences. **$$$**

Chica Pitanga
Rua Petrolina 19,
Boa Viagem
Tel: 81-3465 2224
Open: L&D daily.
The best self-service place in Recife. **$$**

Famiglia Giuliano
Avenida Engenheiro
Domingos Ferreira 3980,
Boa Viagem
Tel: 81-3465 9922
Open: L&D daily.
In a replica medieval castle; famous for its *feijoada*. **$$$**

Mingus
Rua Atlântico 102,
Boa Viagem
Tel: 81-3465 4000
Open: D Tues-Wed, L Thur & Sun, L&D Fri–Sat.
Mingus offers excellent and refined contemporary dining. **$$$**

Pomodoro Café
Rua Capitão Rebelinho 418,
Pina
Tel: 081-3326 6023
Open: D daily.

This is considered by many people to be the best Italian restaurant in the city. **$$$**

Taberna Japonesa Quina do Futuro
Rua Xavier Marques 134,
Aflitos
Tel: 81-3241 9589
Open: L&D Mon–Sat.
Offers an excellent oriental alternative to regional food. **$$$**

Olinda

A Manoá
Rua Bispo Coutinho 645,
Alto da Sé
Tel: 81-3429 6825
Open: L&D daily.
Fantastic views from the second-floor windows while you enjoy a variety of good meat and seafood. There's live music most Saturday nights. **$$**

Oficina do Sabor
Rua do Amparo 355
Tel: 81-3429 3331
Open: L&D Tues–Sun.
Creative mix of international and regional cuisines produces excellent results. **$$$**

Porto de Galinhas

Beijupirá Restaurante
Rua Beijupirá s/n, Qd. 9
Tel: 81-3552 2354
Open: L&D daily.
A landmark in Porto de Galinhas. Seafood is a specialty, but there are also good rice and chicken dishes. **$$$**

Domingos
Rua Beijupirá, Galeria Paraoby
Tel: 81-3552 1489
Open: L–late daily.
Run by a well-known owner-chef with many years' experience in top restaurants in Rio de Janeiro. It's a pleasant setting and there's an excellent, reasonably priced menu. **$$**

La Crêperie – Crepes e Saladas
Rua Beijupirá (opposite Banco do Brasil)
Tel: 81-3552 1831
Open: L&D daily.
This is a good place to go if you want an informal meal. **$$**

Munganga Bistrô
Avenida Beira-Mar 32,
Galeria Caminho da Praia
Tel: 81-3552 2480

Open: L&D (until last client) daily.
Munganga Bistro is known for its reputable wine list and reliably good menu. **$$**

Petrolina

Maria Bonita
Areia Branca
Tel: 87-3864 0422
Fantastic Portuguese food, plus a fine selection of Rio Sul wines, all served in a relaxed and friendly setting. **$$**

PRICE CATEGORIES
Prices for a two-course meal for two. Wine costs around US$20 a bottle.
$= under US$40
$$ = US$40–70
$$$ = US$70–100

RIGHT: oysters with lemon – a local delicacy.

FERNANDO DE NORONHA

Fernando de Noronha is a little bit of paradise on earth, and those who visit never forget it. Although the island now encourages tourism, it is part of a protected reserve, and efforts are made to ensure that it is not spoiled

TIP

There are two daily 1-hour flights from Natal and two 1½-hour flights from Recife with Nordeste (tel: 0300 788 7000) or Trip (www.airtrip .com.br).

BELOW: a school of squirrel fish.

rystal-clear waters and an exuberance of corals, dolphins, lobsters, and colorful tropical fish, as well as wonderfully preserved beaches and virtually no pollution, make **Fernando de Noronha** ❷ a paradise for divers, surfers, and all nature-lovers, and a reminder that the world can still be a beautiful and peaceful place.

The island is formed from the tip of a mountain whose base is 4,000 meters (13,125 ft) below sea level, and is part of a volcanic archipelago of 21 islands covering an area of 26 sq. km (10 sq.

miles). It was discovered in 1503 by the Italian explorer Amerigo Vespucci, and given to Fernando de Loronha in 1504 by the Portuguese king, hence its name (with one letter changed). Because of its strategic position, the island was invaded in turn by the French, the Dutch, and the French again, before returning to Portuguese domination.

In 1938 it was turned into a prison, and during World War II Fernando de Noronha served as an American base. The army barracks from that period have been converted into the island's only classified hotel.

In 1988 Fernando de Noronha became part of a Marine National Park covering an area of 112 sq. km (43 sq. miles), and protected by IBAMA, the Brazilian Institute for the Environment. This is the largest of the islands, and the only one that is inhabited. To visit any of the others, you need a special permit from IBAMA.

Wildlife highlights

Thousands of migratory birds stop off at the island on their way south. On a boat trip to the Enseada dos Golfinhos, hundreds of playful dolphins can be seen out at sea. Swimming is allowed only at the entrance to the bay so as not to disturb them, but lucky divers sometimes encounter the dolphins as they enter or leave the bay in the early mornings or late afternoons.

Between January and June, tourists

can observe marine turtles laying their eggs in the sand at night at Praia do Leão, and – with permission from the Tamar Project, they can help monitor the baby turtles going out to sea.

But the greatest marvels are underwater, so it is unsurprising that scuba-diving and snorkeling are the most popular activities for visitors. The sight of a myriad of multicolored fish and corals, sponges, and plants is unforgettable, and there are also wrecks of sunken ships to visit. For the more adventurous, there is the possibility of meeting sharks on a night dive.

Riding, mountain-biking, or trekking to some of the more remote beaches is also popular. There are interesting natural rock sculptures at the Baía dos Porcos beach, a waterfall at Praia do Sancho during the rainy season, and a heavenly natural swimming pool among the rocks at Praia do Atalaia.

The 18th-century Igreja Nossa Senhora dos Remédios, in the village of Vila dos Remédios, and the Forte de Nossa Senhora dos Remédios near by, are the only remains of the island's checkered history. The Morro do Pico is the highest point on the island at 323 meters (1,060 ft); it offers a splendid view of the archipelago, especially at sunset. Pleasant temperatures of around of 26°C (79°F) year-round, with a refreshing rainy season from February to July, complete the idyll.

Most of the island's 2,000 inhabitants are employed in local tourism, as guides, boatmen, drivers, or looking after one of the many *pousadas*. The island's main hotel, the Esmeralda do Atlântico (tel: 81-3619 1255), is expensive; the Hotel Dolfhin (tel: 81-3619 1170) is cheaper, as are the *pousadas*. In the evening, watch *forró* dancing at the Mirante do Boldró bar, or try delicious fried shark *(tubarão)* at the Bar do Cachorro.

Green tax

You can travel independently, or book through a travel agency or tour operator who may secure discounts on lodgings. The island has to import food and water from the mainland, so IBAMA discourages lingerers by charging an environmental preservation tax based on length of stay. ❏

TIP

Take local currency when visiting the island. Most places don't accept credit cards, and there are no ATMS or exchange facilities. For more details on Fernando de Noronha, check the official website: www.noronha.pe. gov.br

BELOW: the Morro dois Irmaos, Fernando de Noronha.

THE FAR NORTHEAST

Fishing villages, lunar dunescapes, mestiço culture,
fossil sites, and a place of pilgrimage – these
are some of the images typical of the
communities north of Pernambuco state

Main attractions
JOÃO PESSSOA
NATAL
CANOA QUEBRADA
FORTALEZA
JERICOACOARA
SÃO LUÍS
ALCÂNTARA
P N LENÇOIS MARAHENSES

T he northern coastline stretches along beautiful, semi-deserted beaches from dry Rio Grande do Norte all the way to the borders of the Amazon, and the *babaçu* palm groves of Maranhão state. Rio Grande do Norte and the small state of Paraíba just south of it were part of the sugar-cane boom of the early years of colonization, and declined with the demise of the *engenhos* (sugar mills).

Colonization in Ceará and Piauí came with the cattle ranchers in the late 17th century, though it is Ceará's beaches and fishermen that have made its fame. Maranhão was first colonized by the French, then the Dutch, and only after they were expelled in the mid-17th century did the Portuguese show any interest in the state, developing sugar and cotton plantations. Maranhão's economy now centers on the multi-use *babaçu* plant, parts of which are made into food products (especially cooking oil), or are added to fertilizers, cellulose, timber, and roofing materials.

While these northeast states remain among the poorest in Brazil, tourism, mostly in Ceará, brings hopes of a brighter future. The natural beauties of the region are unparalleled.

A 16th-century city

Just over 100 km (60 miles) north of Recife on the Atlantic coast lies **João Pessoa ㉔** (pop. 625,000), the eastern-most point of the Americas. The

dozens of beaches in this region share two fortunate characteristics: they are protected from the pounding surf by rows of reefs, and from the tropical sun by lines of coconut palms.

Capital of the state of **Paraíba**, João Pessoa is the third-oldest city in Brazil. It celebrated its 400th anniversary in 1985. Tropical greenery is abundant in the city, especially palm trees, bougainvilleas, flamboyants and other flowering trees. The lake in **Parque Solon de Lucena** downtown is ringed with majestic royal palms.

LEFT: taking home the supper.
BELOW: Natal's beaches are stunning.

A wood carving entitled Maternity *in Fortaleza's Museum of Art and Popular Culture.*

BELOW:
cars and bars along the stretch of Ponta Negra beach, Natal.

The lovely baroque architecture exemplified by the church of **São Francisco** and the **Convent of Santo Antônio** contrasts with the futuristic design of the Tropical Tambaú Hotel, which looks like an immense flying saucer set halfway into the Atlantic Ocean. All guest rooms look out onto the sea. At high tide, the waves nearly reach the windowsills. The city receives far fewer tourists than other northeastern states, so it's uncrowded beaches are more attractive.

If you make a pre-dawn trek out to **Cabo Branco** (White Cape), 14 km (8 miles) from the city, you can enjoy the knowledge that you are the first person in the Americas to see the sun rise. Nearby Praia da Penha is a fishing village with a 19th-century church.

One of the best beaches in the region is **Praia do Poço**, just 10 km (6 miles) north of the Tropical Tambaú Hotel. Go there at low tide, when the ocean recedes to reveal the island of **Areia Vermelha** (Red Sand). Rows of *jangadas*, the fishermen's primitive rafts that are an integral part of the scenery, take visitors to the island. Sea

algae and schools of colorful fish glitter in the transparent water.

Further north, toward the border with Rio Grande do Norte, is **Baía da Traição**. The region has a number of deserted beaches and fishing villages, with simple restaurants and *pousadas*. Highlights include Coqueirinho and De Tamba beaches, where Potiguaras Amerindians sell crafts, and sweets made from local fruits.

Around Calcanhar Cape

Rio Grande do Norte, which borders Paraíba to the north, lies on the northeastern curve of the continent. En route to the state capital, Natal, you reach **Pipa** (80 km/50 miles from Natal), the favorite of young, hip, northeastern Brazilians. Pipa started life as an ecological reserve, but during peak season and weekends visitors are equally attracted by the nightlife. It comprises several attractive beaches, including Praia de Amor, where you can often see dolphins.

A more peaceful option is its generally overlooked neighbor, **Tibau de Sul**, a small village located at the point

where the Tibau River reaches the sea. Across the river there is an impressive view of sand dunes, extending several kilometers along Guarairas beach. A small boat ferries tourists across.

Tibau also offers a fantastic gastronomic experience, courtesy of chef Tadeu Lubambo. Working as a photojournalist in the 1980s, Tadeu was the first outsider to live among the Xingu Amerindians. Today he welcomes eight guests into his house each night to enjoy a six-course degustation menu at a meal that kicks off with a tropical *caipirinha*, and lasts about four hours.

Some 60 km (38 miles) further north is **Eduardo Gomes**, home to Barreira do Inferno, the rocket launch center. A view of Barreira can be had from nearby **Cotovelo Beach**, one of the loveliest on the state's southern coast.

Natal ㉕ (pop. 750,000), 185 km (110 miles) from João Pessoa, is not only the state capital but another of the region's beach resorts. **Ponta Negra** is the most popular beach, with a wide variety of hotels, bars, and restaurants. A recent surge in charter flights from Europe has turned Natal into a busy tourist destination during the Christmas to Carnival period.

On Christmas Day 1599, Jerónimo de Albuquerque founded the city of Santiago here. It was later renamed Natal, which is Portuguese for Christmas. In 1633 the town was taken and briefly occupied by the Dutch, who called it New Amsterdam.

Its most famous monument, the star-shaped **Forte dos Reis Magos** (Three Kings Fort) was so named because construction began at Epiphany, January 6, 1600. Natal's **Museu Câmara Cascudo** (Avenida Hermes da Fonseca 1398; open Tues–Fri and Sun 8–10.30am, 2–4.30pm; admission charge), has displays ranging from Amazonian Indian artifacts to objects used in *candomblé* rites.

Ribeira, on the riverfront, forms the oldest part of the city. Here, some of the buildings, including Teatro Alberto Maranhão, have been restored.

En route to Touros beach

The 100-km (60-mile) drive from Natal northward to Touros beach is an adventure, following a succession of semi-deserted beaches marked by sand dunes and coconut palms. You'll pass by Maxaranguape, and Ponta Gorda, the site of Cabo de São Roque, where, on August 16, 1501, the first Portuguese expedition arrived, one year after the discovery of Brazil. The enormous sand dunes at **Praia do Genipabu** attract visitors from all over the country. The increase in tourism, especially the use of beach buggies, is already taking its toll on the dunes, and Morro do Caneca, the iconic dune on Ponta Negra beach, has been temporarily fenced off to avoid erosion.

Touros ㉖, a town of 28,000, gets its name from the bulls that once wandered freely here. There is a handful of small inns, cafes, bars and restaurants where you can enjoy shrimp roasted in garlic butter or fresh broiled lobster. At night, go to Calcanhar Cape, 8 km (5 miles) away, to watch the sun go down and the Touros lighthouse come on. The island of Fer-

A pilgrim touches an image of Padre Cicero in Juazeiro do Norte.

BELOW: the star-shaped Three Kings Fort.

nando de Noronha, a wildlife preserve, lies 290 km (180 miles) northeast off the cape (see pages 260–1).

Going inland

TIP

Juazeiro receives pilgrims all year round, but high points in the devotional calendar are March 24, July 20, and November 1.

Most people continue along the coast from the cape to Fortaleza, but it is possible to make a trip inland by bus from Natal to **Juazeiro do Norte** ㉗. This is a religious center where pilgrims (romeiros) come to pay homage to Padre Cícero Romão Batista, who in 1889 wrought a miracle that earned him excommunication from the Catholic Church five years later. Padre Cícero consolidated his temporal powers, and in 1911 became a political leader whose army of cangaceiros defeated federal troops sent to arrest him. Pilgrims visit a 25-meter (75-ft) statue of Cícero, with his characteristic hat and stick. The devotional tour begins in the **Capela de Socorro** where he is buried, and includes churches and the House of Miracles.

The Cariri valley's other townships are **Crato**, noted for its university, museums, and active cultural life; and **Barbalho**, whose hot springs offer more corporeal pleasures. The hilly **Chapada do Araripe**, due west of Juazeiro, 700 meters (2,200 ft) above sea level, provides welcome relief, with waterfalls and natural pools, protected inside a national park.

East of Juazeiro, across the border in Paraíba, on the BR-230 5 km (3 miles) from the town of **Souza**, is the Vale dos Dinossauros (Dinosaur Valley; open daily 8am–6pm), which has the largest grouping of dinosaur footprints in the world. There is a visitor center here where you can hire a guide.

Ceará's coast

If you are sticking to the coast, you will find that the state of **Ceará** has 560 km (350 miles) of wonderful beaches backed by palms, sand dunes, and freshwater lagoons, where the favored residents of state capital Fortaleza spend strenuous weekends drinking beer, and cracking open crabs and lobsters while watching the jangadas bring the day's catch through the rollers. For the adventurous, the 800-km (500-mile) drive between Natal and Fortaleza can be made almost

BELOW: sliding down sand dunes is always good fun.

exclusively along the shore in a beach buggy, stopping off in small villages on the way. The drive will take you past innumerable beaches, each one more beautiful than the last.

In the coastal villages, where offshore breezes blow constantly, lacemakers and embroiderers still ply their trade. But tourism and the weekend homes of city-dwellers are rapidly altering the coastal area.

Southeastern beaches

The southeastern coast of the state has a selection of attractive beaches, starting with **Canoa Quebrada**, some 60 km (37 miles) from the border with Rio Grande do Norte and 10 km (6 miles) from Aracati. During the 1970s, the lunar dune-scape of Canoa Quebrada attracted a generation of hippies from Brazil and abroad. They settled down in the fishermen's primitive houses, blending natural fruit juices, *forró* and free love with a village lifestyle that had changed little in 300 years. Development and its accompanying ills have followed a tourist influx, and the main avenue, Broadway, experiences an ever-growing trade in bars and restaurants. Fortunately, Canoa Quebrada's broad expanse of beach, the dunes, and the crumbling red sandstone cliffs still retain something of the original magic.

The eroded sandstone cliffs of **Morro Branco**, 70 km (43 miles) north of Aracati and 85 km (53 miles) south of Fortaleza, provide the raw material for craftsmen, while the less crowded beach here offers a welcome relief from Fortaleza's urban sprawl. Late in the afternoon, local fishermen visit the beach bars, proffering cooked lobsters. **Iguape**, 50 km (30 miles) from Fortaleza, is famous for its lacemakers (ask to look at the Renaissance pattern) and the artificially colored sands from Morro Branco packed into bottles to depict landscapes.

Just a 34-km (21-mile) drive south of Fortaleza is **Aquiraz**, which, in the 17th century, was Ceará's first cap-

ital, and contains the ruins of a Jesuit mission. It is home to an 18th-century church with the image of São José do Ribamar, the state's patron saint. The historic church ruins may be reached by way of a rum distillery.

Of the beaches still closer to the city, **Prainha** is the most authentic. There are several seafood restaurants and bars stretching across the sand. The local fishermen here will take tourists for *jangada* rides. These traditional flat rafts with lateen sails are covered in advertising, as if they were racing cars, because in July, professionals compete in the Dragon of the Sea regatta.

The still urban, sophisticated resort of **Porto das Dunas** is worth checking out, as is the Beach Park Hotel, near a water park of the same name.

Inland hardship

In gritty contrast, the hinterland of Ceará is periodically racked by drought. When the crops are ruined and the landlords dismiss their *vaqueiros* (cowboys), they pack their belongings and head for the swollen cities in order to survive as best they

Selling bottles of colored sand makes a little money for local people.

BELOW: fresh fruit juice for sale on the beach.

A fisherman with the first catch of the day.

BELOW: Fortaleza high-rises tower above the sands.

can. Those who remain keep alive a strong oral culture derived from the troubadours. Village poets – *repentistas* – duel for hours to cap each other's rhymes with more extravagant verbal conceits. Traditions are also recorded in the *cordel* pamphlets illustrated with woodcuts, whose humorous rhymes recount deeds of the anarchic cowboy-warriors – *cangaceiros* – of local politics, and religious miracles.

The first attempt to colonize the arid *sertão* of Ceará, which separated the Rio Grande and Maranhão, was in 1603. Amerindian fighter Pero Coelho de Souza led a mob of Portuguese soldiers and Amerindian warriors on a raid for slaves. He returned in 1606 but was driven off by a terrible drought.

Fortaleza's founder

Martim Soares Moreno was on the first expedition and was ordered by the governor general of Brazil to open up the region by befriending the Amerindians. By 1611 he was promoted to captain of Ceará and founded **Fortaleza** ❷⑧ by building the first fortress of São Paulo and a chapel by the Ceará River's mouth. The fortress stood Moreno in good stead when the French attacked that year – as did the Tapuia and Tupinambá tribes whom he had befriended. Fighting alongside the Amerindians, he drove off the French, then succumbed to the charms of Iracema, an Amerindian princess who is the city's muse and patron saint. Brazilian literati, led by José Alencar, rediscovered Amerindian history in a romantic movement that flowered just over a century ago with the novel *O Guaraní*, and a short story retelling the tale of Iracema.

Dutch invaders in 1649 built the foundations of a fort in what is now the center of Fortaleza. By 1654, the Dutch were driven out by the Portuguese, who rechristened the fort Nossa Senhora de Assunção. Fortaleza consolidated itself as a trading center for the cattle country of the interior.

Many of the Amerindian-fighting *bandeirantes* from São Paulo stayed behind, to establish immense cattle ranches that still exist today. In contrast to the sugar plantations of Pernambuco, Ceará's ranches used

almost no African slave labor, and the region's culture is more influenced by its Amerindian-Portuguese *mestiço* past than African roots.

The city seafront

Nothing remains of the original fortress that gave Fortaleza its name. With a population of 2.2 million, the city instead looks forward, as the aptly named **Praia do Futuro** indicates. Here, beachfront condominiums and bars have sprouted up, pushing visitors in search of unspoiled coastline away to beaches outside the sprawling city. Fortaleza's real strength is its selection of out-of-town beaches.

Praia do Futuro is a beach of two halves. The northern section, closer to Meireles, is not recommended for tourists, as it resembles a ghost town after several of the bars closed down. Petty crime is common in this section, and there is little or no policing. Nowadays local people head to the southern part, where there is an appropriate infrastructure. Praia do Futuro is a lively spot on Thursday evening, when all the bars serve crabs.

The city's seafront hotels are situated on Avenida President Kennedy, which runs along the **Praia do Meireles**, the main meeting place. At night, the noisy bars and the broad sidewalks below the Imperial Othon Palace Hotel are packed with people drawn by the handicraft market, offering lace, ceramics, leather goods, colored sand packed into bottles, and a wide variety of souvenirs.

Fortaleza is a major exporter of lobster. Seafood restaurants along the ocean front offer crab, shrimp, lobster, or *peixada* – the local seafood specialty. The best restaurants are located a few blocks back from the seafront and include Cantinho do Faustino, where one should not be misled by the simplicity of the setting and the presentation *(see page 273)*. Northeasterners round off the night at hot, crowded dance halls like Clube do Vaqueiro (Wednesday) and Parque do Vaqueiro (Friday), where couples dance the lively but seductive *forró*, accompanied by accordion music. The restaurants and bars in restored historic buildings around the Centro Cultural Dragão do Mar often host live music.

TIP

Crab *(caranguejo)* is served in most of the *barracas* (kiosks) on the beach, usually boiled in water or coconut milk. It is given to you with a little wooden hammer, and you have to break the shell and extract the meat.

BELOW: salt production is a labor-intensive industry.

Ceará's Salt

The economy of the Ceará region was based for many years on three things: subsistence agriculture and cattle rearing in the interior, and salt production on the eastern coast. The high winds that blow along this coast, and the high salinity of the seawater, make it an ideal area for the production of sea salt, which, in the days before refrigeration, was essential for preserving food, as well as being used in cooking. The happy combination of beef and salt led to the invention of *carne de sol* (sun-dried or jerked beef), which is one of the most typical and most delicious regional dishes, and one which you will find in many local restaurants. Salt is still produced around Fortaleza, although there is no longer such a high demand for it.

A man with a color co-ordinated shirt in São Luís.

BELOW: São Luís is an enchanting place.

MAC (Museum of Contemporary Art) and the Ceará Memorial Museum here have extensive displays of arts and crafts, and items on the history of Ceará; both deserve a visit.

The Praia do Meireles stretches from Mucuripe near the docks, where there's a lighthouse, to the breakwater at Volta de Jurema. The central section, **Praia de Iracema**, is marked by a modern sculpture designed by Morena and his princess, but the beach is too polluted for swimming. However, its bars and restaurants are fun at night.

Handicrafts can be purchased at several locations, including the Tourist Center (Rua Senador Pompeu 350), in the tastefully converted old city jail; or sometimes more cheaply at the Mercado Central, which has more than 1,000 close-packed booths spread over several floors. The Ceart Center (Avenida Santos Dumont 1589, Aldeota) has an excellent selection of arts and crafts from various regions of the state.

Another attraction is the Teatro José de Alencar, a cast-iron structure imported from Britain in 1910. Tours are available for a nominal fee.

West of Fortaleza, in the Ibiapaba hills, is the **Parque Nacional de Ubajara** , with caves that contain interesting stalagmite formations and a cable car that takes visitors up to waterfalls and lush green vegetation.

Northwestern beaches

Northwest of Fortaleza, a series of beaches begins at **Barra do Ceará** – the river's mouth – but **Cumbuco** is the first port of call, 33 km (20 miles) from the city. The attractions are the surfing beach and the dunes stretching inland as far as the black surface of the **Parnamirim** freshwater lagoon. At the beach bars, rides through the surf on sailing rafts are available.

There is no coastal road running north, but 85 km (53 miles) from Fortaleza is **Paracuru** ㉚, reached from inland on the BR-222 federal highway. A lively community that enjoys a week-long Carnival and regular surf and sailing regattas, the town is a favorite weekend spot. A few miles further on is the less sophisticated **Lagoinha**, where rooms are available to rent in village houses. An intersection on the highway leading from BR-222 to Paracuru goes to Trairi, with access to the beaches of **Freixeiras**, **Guajiru**, and **Mundaú**.

Icaraí ㉛ is 140 km (87 miles) from Fortaleza, via the BR-222 intersection leading past Itapipoca, behind the Mundaú dunes and across the Trairi River. Beaches include Pesqueiro, Inferno, and Baleia. **Acaraú** ㉜, a further 90 km (57 miles) from Fortaleza, is one of the most popular beach centers. The adjacent fishing village of **Almofala** also has a fine, unspoiled beach, and an 18th-century church, which for years was covered by sands.

The finest of Ceará's beaches is the remote **Jericoacoara** ㉝, the picture-postcard image of Brazil's northeast. Declared a national park in 2002, it is a beautiful – even magical – spot, with a beach that the *Washington Post Magazine* described as "one of the 10 most beautiful on the planet." A short

while ago it was a paradisaical fishing village, cut off behind the dunes. Now, there is a plethora of *pousadas* and restaurants catering to the influx of visitors that is already bringing changes to a village that still remains small and friendly. The pure horizontals of sea, dunes, and sky are cut by coconut palms, and the village has no electricity or cars. A preservation order means that rare and endangered species are protected in the dunes and lagoons. Sea turtles come up the beach to lay their eggs, and the village has much of the mystique that Canoa Quebrada enjoyed a decade or so ago.

Reaching Jericoacoara (about 300 km/190 miles from Fortaleza), is difficult because it is cut off by the dunes. The trip can be made by bus, then four-wheel-drive (www.jericoacoara.com/br; tel: 88-669 2000/621 0211).

Ancient sites in Piauí

The state of Piauí has impressive geological monuments formed by erosion over millions of years. These can be visited at the **Parque Nacional Sete Cidades**, 180 km (112 miles) from the capital, **Teresina**. The **Parque Nacional da Serra da Capivara**, in the southwest of the state, is the oldest archeological site in the Americas – more than 50,000 years old – and was declared a World Heritage Site by UNESCO in 1991. Besides fossils of mastodons and giant ground sloths, it has the largest set of rock art in the world. The **Museu do Homem Americano** has interesting specimens of fossils and prehistoric tools (pre-arranged visits only, tel: 86-582 1567).

São Luís

At the top of Brazil's northeast region, between the Amazon basin and the *sertão*, perched on the bayside of São Luís Island, is **São Luís ㉞**, capital of the state of Maranhão and another World Heritage Site. Legend has it that a serpent lives under the town, and that one day, once it has grown large enough, it will squeeze the island, causing it to sink. São Luís is enchanting, with a rich mix of history and culture. The city was founded in 1612 by French colonists, who first encountered the Tupinamba Amerindians on

A tiled restaurant sign in São Luís.

BELOW:
Palácio dos Leves, São Luís.

TIP

Both A Diquinha and A Varanda were popular with former Brazilian president José Sarney, and it is said that while in power (1985–90) he requested takeaways from Dona Diquinha to be delivered by plane to Brasília. She proudly displays a plaque in the restaurant, acknowledging services to the Brazilian government.

BELOW: the immaculate sand dunes of Lençois Marahenses.

the island. The two groups lived in harmony until the French were driven out by the Portuguese three years later. In 1641 the Dutch invaded the island but were able to maintain their position for only three years. The mixed heritage manifests itself in the music of *tambor-de-criola* and *Bumba-Meu-Boi*. The *Bumba-Meu-Boi* celebrations on the feast days of São João (June 24) and São Pedro (June 29) form part of the June Festivals, and are on a par with Carnival in other cities. On Friday evening (6–8.30pm) musicians and dancers gather in the Mercado da Praia Grande to perform the sensual *tambor-de-criola* in a tradition that has been handed down over generations.

The city is known for the brightly tiled, two-story homes that line its narrow, sloping streets. The blue, yellow, white, and green *azulejos* (tiles) were originally imported from Portugal, and have become the city's trademark. Cars have been banned from the most important streets, making it ideal for exploring on foot. Major points of interest include the **Cathedral** (1763), **Praça Remédios** (1860), **Capela de**

Santo Antônio (1624), and the **Museu Historico e Artistico do Marãnho** (Maranhão Art and History Museum; open Tues–Fri 9am–7pm, Sat–Sun 2–7pm; admission charge), in an early 19th-century villa. There are numerous stores in the historic center (known as Reviver) selling handicrafts as well as two peculiar local drinks: *Jesus* (a sweet, pink soft drink), and *Tiquira* (a *cachaça* made from manioc).

There is no shortage of good restaurants, but for an authentic gastronomic experience visit a *base*. The term comes from a time when there were no restaurants and workers would visit the houses of local cooks for lunch. These houses were referred to as *bases*, and several still exist today, the most famous of which are A Diquinha and A Varanda *(see opposite)*.

Many of the best hotels in the city can be found in the beach districts of Ponta d'Areia, Santo Antonio, Calhau, and Caolho. The last three form a continuous 5-km (3-mile) stretch with plenty of bars and restaurants. All these beaches have very strong undercurrents so inquire first before diving in.

Alcântara

A trip to São Luís is not complete without a visit to **Alcântara** ❸❺, originally a Tupinambá Amerindian village, which in the 17th century became the favored retreat for the landed gentry of Maranhão. Highlights include the **Alcântara Museum** (open Tues–Sun 9am–1.45pm); Nossa Senhora do Carmo church (1663); and the original Pelourinho (whipping post). The boat trip to Alcântara, 53 km (33 miles) over choppy waters, takes 60 minutes. Boats leave the Terminal Hidroviario (Avenida Vitorino Freire) at around 9am, depending on tides. There are a number of *pousadas* in the town if you want to stay and enjoy the tranquility of Alcântara at night.

In the 1950s drought drove a group of *rendeiras* (lacemakers) from Ceará to set up shop in the small fishing town of **Raposa** (33 km/20 miles north of São Luís). Their simple wooden houses, built on *palafiltas* (stilts) because of flooding from nearby mangrove swamps, serve as shops and homes. From Raposa you can arrange boat trips to the island of Curupu.

Lençois Marahenses

With more than 155,000 hectares (382,000 acres) of sand dunes, **Parque Nacional de Lençois Marahenses** ❸❻ is an ecological paradise. During the rainy season (Dec–May) hundreds of crystalline lakes are formed. In September to October wind speeds can reach up to 70 km/h (45 mph), so it is advisable to wear sunglasses. A new road to **Barreirinhas**, just outside Lençois Marahenses, has cut the journey time from São Luís to three hours. Barreirinhas has become the main portal to the park, with numerous agencies offering a variety of excursions, including boat trips, 4x4 rides, and a 30-minute flight over the park.

To get an idea of the simplicity of life here, take a boat to the tiny fishing village of Cabure along Rio Preguicas, stay at one of the *pousadas*, and eat in one of several good restaurants. But be warned: electricity comes from a generator, which is switched off at 10pm. On the way to Cabure you can stop off at Mandacaru for amazing views of the national park from the top of the lighthouse. ❑

A tempting little crafts shop in Barreirinhas.

RESTAURANTS

Fortaleza

Cantinho do Faustino
Rua Delmiro Gouveia 1520
Tel: 85-3267 5348
Open: L&D Tues–Sat, L Sun.
Innovative Brazilian food with some delicious surprises. **$$**

Cemoara
Rua Joaquim Nabuco 166, Mercure Apartments, Meireles
Tel: 85-3242 8500
Open: L&D daily.
Probably one of the best *bolinho de bacalhau* (cod fish cakes) in Brazil. **$$$**

Colher de Pau
Rua Frederico Borges, 204 Varjota
Tel: 85-3267 3773
Open: L, D daily.
This Fortaleza institution serves excellent regional food. *Carne de sol frita* (fried sun-dried beef) is recommended. **$**

João Pessoa

Bargaco
Avenida Cabo Branco 5160
Tel: 83-3247 9957
Open: L&D daily.
Popular Bahian food specialist. Mini-*acarajé* is an interesting innovation, while the lobster *moqueca* is a must. **$$**

Mangai
Avenida General Adson Ramalho 696
Tel: 83-3226 1615
Open: L&D daily.
Excellent self-service restaurant with plenty of regional dishes including *buchada de bode*. **$**

Natal

Âncora Caipira
Rua Seridó 745, Petrópolis
Tel: 84-3202 9364
Open: L&D daily.
Menu inspired by local recipes such as sun-dried meat and goat. **$$**

Camaroes
Avenida Engenheiro Roberto Freire 2610, Ponta Negra
Tel: 84-3209 2424
Open: L&D daily.
Hugely popular seafood restaurant. Shrimp dishes are the specialty. **$$**

São Luís

A Diquinha
Rua João Luís 62, Diamante
Tel: 98-3221 9803
Open: L&D daily.
Excellent home-cooking in this simple restaurant, just 10 minutes from the center by taxi. **$**

A Varanda
Rua Genesio Rego 185
Tel: 98-3232 8428
Open: L&D Mon–Sat.
Impressive home-cooking served in owners' garden, 15 minutes from center by taxi. You must book. **$**

Prices for a two-course meal for two. Wine costs around US$20 a bottle. $ = under $40, $$ = $40–70, $$$ = $70–100

THE AMAZON

In the north of Brazil, humanity is dwarfed by the continent's greatest river and its magnificent forested basin. Ecotours and river cruises from the once splendid rubber towns of Belém and Manaus ply the Amazon and its tributaries

Brasília

Rio de Janeiro

Though it is not the longest river in the world, the **Amazon** is the world's *greatest* river. At the end of a 6,570-km (4,080-mile) journey that begins in the Peruvian Andes, the river's massive mouth discharges a fifth of all the world's freshwater into the Atlantic, permeating the saltwater over 100 km (60 miles) from the shore. And Amazonia is a vast, open-air greenhouse of global evolution, where a tenth of the world's 10 million living species make their homes. The River Amazon dominates Brazil, yet Brazilians are only beginning to discover it.

Early explorers

Amerigo Vespucci, an Italian adventurer much given to exaggeration, and after whom the Americas were named, claimed to have sailed up the Amazon in 1499. He was followed a year later by the Spaniard Vicente Pinzon, but the credit for the first voyage of discovery down the river goes to Francisco de Orellana.

He set out by boat in 1542 on a short reconnaissance during an expedition in search of the legendary gold of El Dorado, for which he had joined forces with Gonzalo Pizarro, younger brother of Francisco, one of the conquistadors of Peru.

For six months, his boat was swept downriver through "the excellent land and dominion of the Amazons," where his scribe Friar Carvajal was amazed by sightings of a matriarchal tribe, with bare-breasted women "doing as much fighting as ten Indian men." It was these remarkable warriors who later inspired the name "Amazons," after the women of Greek mythology who removed their right breasts to facilitate using a bow and arrow.

Amazonia began to excite scientific interest all over the world a century after its "discovery", when in 1641 Spanish Jesuit Cristóbal de Acuña published *A New Discovery of the Great River of the Amazons,* carefully recording Amerindian customs, farming

Main attractions
BELÉM
ILHA DE MARAJÓ
SOURE
CARAJÁS
MONTE ALEGRE
SANTARÉM
MANAUS
RORAIMA

PRECEDING PAGES:
boat trip on an
Amazon tributary.
LEFT: going up river.
BELOW: unloading
fish at Belém dock.

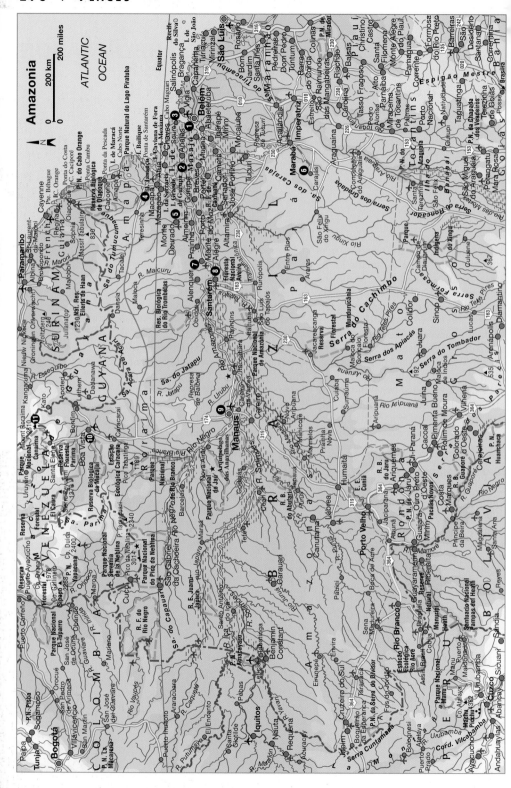

methods, and herbal medicine, and concluding that – mosquitoes notwith-standing – it was "one vast paradise".

Botanical research

Bedrock scientific research about the Amazon was carried out by a trio of English collectors led by Alfred Russell Wallace, whose work on the diversity of Amazonian flora and fauna influenced Darwin's *On the Origin of Species*. Together with Henry Walter Bates and Richard Spruce, he set out in 1848 and discovered more than 15,000 species new to science.

Another Englishman used his botanical skills to provoke the region's economic undoing when he broke Brazil's rubber monopoly. For a fee of £1,000, adventurer Henry Wickham loaded 70,000 seeds of *Hevea brasiliensis* aboard a chartered steamer in 1876, and slipped them past customs in Belém, claiming they were rare plant samples for Queen Victoria. The seedlings sprouted under glass in London's Kew Gardens, and by 1912 had grown into Malaya's ordered, disease-free rubber plantations.

Rubber riches

The properties of rubber, which had been discovered by the Omagua Amerindians, fascinated French travelers in the 18th century. Then Charles Goodyear's 1844 discovery of vulcanization, followed by Dunlop's 1888 invention of the pneumatic tire, caused a commercial explosion. As the price of rubber soared, production rose from 156 metric tonnes in 1830 to 21,000 metric tonnes in 1897. The cities were emptied of labor, and thousands migrated from the northeast to become rubber-tappers or *seringueiros*.

During the last decade of the 19th century, Brazil sold 88 percent of all exported rubber in the world, and for 25 years, around the turn of the 20th century, rubber made the Amazon port of Manaus, 1,600 km (1,000 miles) from the Atlantic, one of the richest cities in the world. A system of debt slavery was used to harvest Brazil's "black gold" over a vast area of Amazon jungle. The hundred or so rubber barons who controlled Manaus sent their laundry to Lisbon, and their wives and children to Paris.

Tibouchina, one of numerous Amazonian species painted by English watercolorist Margaret Mee.

BELOW: Belém's graceful waterfront.

Good-quality, hand-made basketware is worth buying in Belém.

BELOW:
the rare blue
hyacinth macaw.

However, British-controlled plantations in Asia undercut Amazon rubber prices just before World War I, and within a decade Manaus was a jungle backwater again. American industrialist Henry Ford attempted to compete with the British by organizing his own Amazon rubber plantation in 1927, but was unsuccessful *(see page 291)*. You can still see one of Ford's two plantation sites, Belterra, near the Amazon River 825 km (500 miles) from Belém.

Elegant Belém

With its public parks, wrought-iron bandstands, *beaux-arts* buildings, and mango-tree-lined avenues, **Belém ❶** retains more elegance of the bygone rubber era than its rival, Manaus. During its *belle époque*, French visitors to this city compared it favorably with Marseilles or Bordeaux. A city of 1.4 million set on the river's southern bank one degree south of the Equator and 145 km (90 miles) from the open sea, Belém is the gateway to the Amazon.

Between November and April it rains almost every day, but a breeze generally makes the humid climate tolerable.

Belém is the capital of the state of Pará, which covers an area twice the size of France. It was properly linked to southern Brazil by the Belém–Brasília Highway only in 1960, and is still chiefly a port city for the export of tropical hardwoods, Brazil nuts, jute, and other primary products.

A tour of the old city, whose narrow streets still contain old houses fronted with Portuguese tiles, begins at the **Forte do Castelo ❹**, the nucleus of the original settlement of Santa Maria do Belém do Grão Pará, and now sadly run-down. Adjacent is the 18th-century church of **Santo Alexandre ❺**, now a **museum of religious art** (open Tues–Sun 1–6pm; admission charge). The cathedral church, **Catedral de Nossa Senhora da Graça ❻**, opposite the fort, contains sculptures in Carrara marble and paintings by the Italian artist Pietro de Angelis.

One block away, on the south side of Praça Dom Pedro II, is the **Palácio Lauro Sodré ❼**, the former seat of government, which now houses the **Museu do Estado do Pará** (State of Pará Museum; open Tues–Sun 9am–

Amazon Facts

- The official source of the Amazon, found in 1953, is on Mount Huagra in the Peruvian Andes.
- The river is 6,570 km (4,080 miles) long (only the Nile is longer) and its mouth is 330 km (200 miles) wide.
- The Amazon has 1,100 tributaries, including 17 that are more than 1,600 km (1,000 miles) long.
- In places, the Amazon is 110 km (68 miles) wide; its lower course has depths of over 60 meters (297 ft). Ocean-going freighters can travel 3,720 km (2,310 miles) inland from the Atlantic to Iquitos, Peru.
- The river system is the globe's largest body of freshwater. Total water flow is 160,000–200,000 cubic meters (42–53 million US gallons) a second, 12 times that of the Mississippi.
- The Amazon basin is larger than that of any other river, and contains the world's largest, but rapidly diminishing, rainforest. This spreads over nine countries, but most of it lies within the boundaries of Brazil.
- Amazonia supports 30 percent of all known plant and animal species, including 2,500 fish species, 50,000 higher plant species and untold millions of insects.
- The average annual rainfall is over 2,000 mm (79 inches), making the Amazon basin the wettest region in the world.

1pm; admission charge). It was built in the 18th century by the Italian architect Landi, and contains numerous examples of fine 19th-century furniture. Also on Praça Dom Pedro II is the current local government building, **Palácio Antônio Lemos** ❸. Dating from the late 19th century, the height of the rubber boom, it was built in the Portuguese imperial style and houses an **art museum** (open Tues–Fri 9am–1pm, 2–6pm, Sat–Sun 9am–noon; admission charge), with many fine paintings and furnishings.

The **Ver-O-Peso** ❺, Belém's vast dockside market at the northern end of Avenida Portugal, is a store window of Amazonia's prodigious variety of fish and tropical fruit. Fishing boats bring in their catches, which may include 90-kg (200-lb) monsters. The **Feira do Açaí** at the end of the market is the exclusive purveyor of the small açaí berries that are the basis of much of Belém's cooking.

There are few souvenirs to buy inside the two food pavilions, but alongside them is a fascinating covered area of booths selling herbal medicines and charms used in African-Brazilian *umbanda* rituals. Sea horses, armadillo tails, and tortoise shells are piled up beside herbs that local people swear will cure rheumatism and heart problems. Also on sale are perfumes said to be guaranteed to attract men, women, money, and good fortune. Pickpockets can be a problem, and the area is best avoided after dark.

The east side

Continuing along the dockside, you will come to **Estação das Docas**. Here, the dilapidated warehouses have been transformed into an impressive cultural space with restaurants, bars, and a theater. Near the customs house on **Praça Waldemar Henrique** ❼, the state tourism authority, **Paratur** operates a visitor center *(see margin)* and a **Feira do Artesanato** (Handicraft Fair) that is useful if you are looking for souvenirs. **Icoaraci** ❽, about half an hour from the city (the bus stop is two blocks from the Paratur office), is a center for modern ceramic ware that follows the pre-Columbian Amerindian *maroajara* pottery tradition,

TIP

The Paratur office, near the shipping port at Praça Maestro Waldemar Henrique, is open Mon–Fri 8am–noon, 1–6pm. Staff are friendly but most speak little English (tel: 91-212 0669; www.paratur.pa.gov.br).

BELOW: pilgrims join Our Lady of Nazaré procession in Belém.

whose elaborate motifs are believed to have been borrowed from Inca culture.

Continuing along Avenida Presidente Vargas – the main shopping street – away from the port, you will come to the **Praça da República ❶**, then Belém's theater, the **Teatro da Paz ❿** (open Mon–Fri 9am–6pm; tours available). This recently restored theater, built in 1874, is set in a green area complete with bandstand and the Bar do Parque – an agreeable place to sit and drink a Cerpa, the local beer.

About 15 minutes' walk inland from the Praça da República, along Avenida Nazaré, is Belém's most important church, the **Basílica de Nazaré ⓚ**, built in 1852, with impressive marble work and stained glass. It is the center of the Cirio de Nazaré religious procession *(see page 91)* that was instituted by the Jesuits as a means of catechizing Amerindians, and still draws over a million faithful on the second Sunday of every October. The venerated image of the Virgin was found in the forest near Belém in 1700.

Continuing on, you will come to the **Museu Emílio Goeldi ❷** (Rua Maga-lhães Barata 376; open Tues–Thur 9–noon, 2–5pm, Fri 9am–noon, Sat–Sun 9am–5pm; admission charge), which incorporates a fine zoological garden with many tropical species. The museum, founded in 1866, has a superb anthropological collection, and often has excellent temporary exhibitions about Amazon life. Further from the center but also worth a visit are the **Bosque Gardens** (Tues–Sun 8am–5pm), which enclose an area of almost natural forest, and a small zoo.

Ilha de Marajó

Several tour agencies, including Ceotur, operate one-day trips upriver, but they usually simply go up the Guajará River and visit some well-prepared *caboclo* dwellings. A better option is the Acará Lodge, which is two hours up the river and offers two-day stays in very modest accommodation.

One of the world's largest river islands (48,000 sq. km/18,535 sq. miles), **Ilha de Marajó ❷** at the river's mouth, is larger than Switzerland, yet has a population of just 250,000 people. They are far outnum-

TIP

If you want to visit Belém for the festival of Cirio de Nazaré in October, you should make advance hotel reservations because accommodations get booked up early for this event.

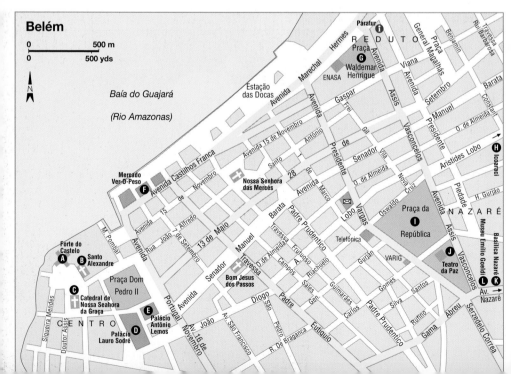

Belém

0   500 m
0   500 yds

N

Baía do Guajará

(Rio Amazonas)

bered by the herds of water buffalo that wallow in the flat, swampy northern area *(see below)*.

A government-owned ENASA ferry makes the four-hour trip to **Soure ❸** on the island's eastern tip (tel: 91-242 6103/257 4915/257 4972). Air taxis from Belém Aeroclub do the trip in about 30 minutes. The best place to stay in Soure is the Hotel Ilha do Marajó. The hotel can arrange trips to the Praia do Pesqueiro and Praia Araruna, beaches washed by water that is part-river, part-ocean. A ferry crosses the river to Salvaterra, where a battered taxi continues to Joanes (where you can stay at the comfortable Pousada dos Guarás).

First called the Ilha Grande do Joanes, Marajó was settled in 1617 by Franciscan monks who built a stone church here in 1665, the ruins of which survive by the lighthouse. At nearby **Monserrat** there is another stone-built church containing baroque images.

From Soure, day trips can be arranged to the **Providencia** and **Santa Caterina buffalo ranches**. However, buffalo farms in the island's interior, reachable only by boat, horse, or tractor, have far more wildlife than the populated coastal region. **Fazendas Laranjeira** and **Tapeira** both have private museums containing archeological relics from ancient Amerindian sites.

Buffalo country

About 70 years ago, water buffalo were imported to the island as beasts of burden and to produce milk, meat, and for hides. They took to the place famously and bred extremely well. The buffalo had advantages over horses, as their widely splayed hooves were much tougher and did not rot. They also had advantages over the delicate-humped zebu cattle often to be found on Marajó, as their hide was much thicker, and that gave them the ability to shake off any hostile fauna.

Marajó is home to dolphins, capybaras, monkeys, birds, and alligators. But it is the great variety of snakes –

from rattlesnakes to boas – that could be troublesome if the buffalos' hides were not so tough.

The animals' qualities also include a gentle, placid outlook on life, which commended them to the local authorities who took some on for duty in the fire service and for the police force. They are sometimes to be seen on parade with the police, a pair yoked together pulling a cart or individually, bearing a constable carrying his ceremonial lance, ready for action in the mud, perhaps to pull a farm implement or even a car out of the oozing ground. Their riders clearly have good relations with them, calling them each by its own name, guiding them gently with reins attached to a nose ring.

Now the Brazilian army is following up a good thing and using the water buffalo as pack animals in their numerous bases in Amazonia. They can easily carry supplies and munitions in remote areas, which may arrive by air but must eventually be moved by other means in the jungle where there are no roads and little fuel, and rivers are often too shallow

TIP

Marajó island is an ecological haven, with its fine unspoiled beaches and abundance of flora and fauna. There are at least 361 species of birds; the rare red ibis can be seen in many places on the island. There have also been finds of Pre-Columbian ceramics.

BELOW: Ilha de Marajó, one of the world's largest river islands.

The Lost City of El Dorado

The search for cities paved with gold is integral to the romance associated with the conquest and exploration of South America. El Dorado, which means The Golden Man, was the name given by Spanish explorers to a fabled Amazon king who ruled over the fantastically wealthy Kingdom of Manoa, deep in the jungle. The king himself was rumored to encrust his powerful naked body daily in gold dust, which he regularly washed off in a sacred lake.

Such tales of limitless riches spread abroad soon after Brazil's discovery. In the early 20th century, Colonel Percy Fawcett (1867–1925), an eccentric English archaeologist and explorer, whose lifelong obsession was to prove the existence of lost Amazonian civilizations, came across records indicating that a 16th-century shipwrecked adventurer, Diego Álvarez, had found numerous mines of gold, silver and precious stones.

So it was that explorers such as Francisco de Orellana, the first European to traverse the entire Amazon basin, were less interested in national glory or the conversion of souls than in the gold of El Dorado. The Spanish Orellana, who had won his spurs fighting alongside Francisco Pizarro in Peru – where the *conquistadores* had helped

themselves to copious amounts of Inca gold – became second-in-command on Gonzales Pizarro's 1540 expedition in search of new territories, gold, and cinnamon.

Pizarro was eventually forced, in the face of starvation and hostile Amerindians, to return ignominiously to his base in Ecuador. But Orellana became separated from his patron, and with a smaller band of men, found favor with some Amazon tribes and glimpsed both tall, white Amazons and female warriors who, according to a captured male, lived in all-women villages and once a year invited men from surrounding tribes to a mating festival. Their leader, Orellana was told, ate with gold and silver utensils, and the villages were littered with golden female idols. However, Orellana was never able to uncover the vast quantities of gold he heard about, or verify the rumors about the local customs.

Portuguese explorer Francisco Raposo may have discovered the remains of El Dorado's kingdom, apparently devastated by an earthquake. His 1754 report describes relics of a great city, with stone-paved streets, elaborate plazas, and stately architecture, beautiful statues, hieroglyphics, and colorful frescoes – and a handful of gold coins.

This fascinating city has never been rediscovered, yet Fawcett, described by colleagues as both a dreamer and a rascal, wrote in 1925: "It is certain that amazing ruins of ancient cities, ruins incomparably older than those of Egypt, exist in the far interior of Mato Grosso." Fawcett obtained a 10-inch (25-cm) black stone image allegedly taken from the ruined city by Raposo, and his irresistible fascination with the stone led him to venture several times into Brazil's deep interior. His final attempt began in May 1925, when he set out with his son Jack and a friend, and all three were lost. Over the decades, a number of expeditions were mounted, at first as rescue attempts, later to try to discover what had happened to the three men. Among many wild rumors was one that Fawcett had lost his memory, and lived the rest of his life as the chief of an Amerindian tribe.

Dreams of El Dorado continue. In the early 1980s and again in 1996, gold was discovered in the Serra Pelada mountains in the Amazon. Each discovery drew thousands of prospectors, sparking a new rush – to the detriment of the indigenous inhabitants – to become rich from the same precious yellow metal that first brought white men to the Amazon. ❑

LEFT: an idealized view of early Amerindian life.

to navigate. "They don't require petrol or special food. Buffalo eat anything," the army says.

Straddling the Equator

Macapá ❹, at the Amazon's northern mouth, stands on the Equator, where you can straddle the marker line or *marco zero*. It has a large fort built of Lisbon brick by the Portuguese in 1782 and a thriving economy based on shrimp fishing and manganese mining. Planes leave Macapá for **Monte Dourado** ❺ and the Jari Project, US billionaire Daniel K. Ludwig's ill-fated attempt to substitute the natural forest with plantations to mass-produce pulp to make paper. Ludwig purchased a huge tract of land in the late 1960s, and the paper mill and factory went into production a decade later. However, a combination of poor soil, destructive insects, and tropical diseases doomed the project to failure.

The Carajás project

The southeastern Amazon occupies a special place in the perennial dreams of economic greatness that have haunted Brasília's government planners: dreams that have become nightmares for conservationists. Development mega-projects that have consumed billions of dollars sprout across the region under the umbrella of the Carajás project.

Conceived around an 18 billion-tonne iron-ore mine in the hills around **Carajás** ❻, 880 km (547 miles) south of Belém, Brazil's "moonshot" in the Amazon includes the Tucuruí hydro-electric dam, an 890-km (560-mile) railroad through the forest, and an immense complex supporting an aluminum smelting plant and a deepwater port. This highly controversial project has caused immense social and environmental damage, having flooded 2,400 sq. km (927 sq. miles) of Amazon rainforest and expelled 30,000 indigenous people from their homes.

Those interested in Brazil's development and the bravura of the entrepreneurs can reach both Tucuruí and the Carajás mine at **Serra Norte** by plane from Belém. The treacherous terraces of the Serra Pelada gold mine, made infamous in the late 1980s, no longer exist. The mine is

The terrible conditions that workers endured in the old Serra Pelada mine were brought to the world's attention by photographer Sebastião Salgado (see page 123).

BELOW: Carajás iron-ore mine, a highly controversial project.

mechanized, and the *garimpeiros* (gold prospectors) are long gone.

Toward Manaus

Along the river from Belém, en route to Manaus, lies **Monte Alegre ❼**, a small village that became famous when American archeologist Anna Roosevelt discovered pictographs and artifacts in caves in the area, which significantly altered existing ideas on human colonization in South America and the Amazon.

About 160 km (100 miles) further upstream, **Santarém ❽** stands exactly halfway between Belém and Manaus, at the junction of the Tapajós and Amazon rivers. Founded in 1661 as a fort to keep foreign interests out of the mid-Amazon before the arrival of the Portuguese, Santarém was the center of a thriving Amerindian culture. Near by lie the remains of the rubber plantations of **Belterra** and **Fordlandia**, the latter now reclaimed by jungle, expensive failures set up by the Ford Motor Company in the 1930s.

This mid-Amazon town has the comfortable Amazon Park Hotel and river-

The grin on a piranha, like the smile on a crocodile, is not to be trusted.

boats that bring produce for the busy daily market along the waterfront. Most one-day boat tours travel up the Tapajós as far as **Alter do Chão**, site of the original settlement, and a superb beach some 38 km (23 miles) from Santarém. The white sand beach forms a long curving spit that almost closes off the **Lago Verde** lagoon from the river. Also reachable by car, the village has a simple fish restaurant, a *pousada*, and a number of weekend homes for Santarém's wealthy.

In Alter do Chão, the **Centro do Preservação de Arte Indígena** (Center for the Preservation of Indigenous Art; open daily) exhibits art and crafts made by a number of Amazon tribes. Most hotels organize trips to the **Floresta Nacional do Tapajós** (National Forest Reserve), a well-preserved area of original forest.

The port city

The city of **Manaus ❾** is an oddity, an urban extravagance that turns its back on the rich surrounding forest and survives instead on federal subsidies, its exotic past, and, increasingly, on

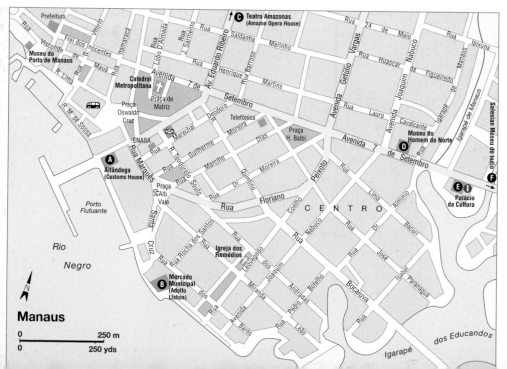

Manaus

0 _____ 250 m
0 _____ 250 yds

tourism. Its moving spirit has always been quick riches. Once it had Art Nouveau grandeur; then, in the latter half of the 20th century, it acquired the image of a tawdry electronics bazaar, justified only by its status as a free port. Now, an ambitious restoration program is breathing new life into the city's architectural and cultural aspects. The port city's strategic position, close to the point where the three greatest tributaries form the Amazon River, means that it has long been the collecting point for forest produce from a vast area, and today is an important base for jungle tours.

Manaus still has reminders of its rubber wealth in the late 19th and early 20th centuries. British engineers in 1906 built the **Alfândega** Ⓐ (Customs House) out of Scottish bricks in an imperial style; and to accommodate the river's 14-meter (40-ft) rise and fall, they assembled foreign-made sections of the floating dock.

The **Mercado Municipal (Adolfo Lisboa)** Ⓑ, on Rua dos Barés, southward along the dockside, is a busy market (open daily 8am–6pm) filled with regional produce, from exotic fruit, to magic herbs to cure all ills. Handicrafts can also be bought there. The market is housed in an interesting cast-iron building, imported from Europe in 1882, which is a replica of the old Les Halles market in Paris.

Culture comes to Manaus

The **Teatro Amazonas** Ⓒ (Amazon Opera House; open for tours Mon–Sat 9am–4pm), located in the northern part of downtown Manaus, was begun in 1881, at the height of the rubber boom, after complaints from European touring companies that had been forced to play in smaller halls. Arriving there to sing during a cholera scare, the Italian tenor Enrico Caruso (1873–1921), one of the greatest operatic stars of his time, returned to Europe without disembarking. After the grand inaugural performance of Ponchielli's *La Gioconda* in 1897, a month after the theater was completed, there were scant records of other operas before the rubber boom collapsed.

The theater has been restored four times since it was constructed. The

Loading bananas in the floating port of Manaus.

BELOW:
the restored Teatro Amazonas at night.

The proud monument outside the Teatro Amazonas, erected when Manuas was a wealthy city.

BELOW:
river cruises are a comfortable way to explore the Amazon.

columns and banisters are of English cast iron, with stage curtains, chandeliers, and mirrors supplied by France. The marble came from Italy and the porcelain from Venice. Decorative motifs show the meeting of the Amazon waters and scenes from romantic literature about the Amerindians.

After many years of neglect, the theater was renovated in the 1990s, and now functions as the venue for ballet, opera, and orchestral performances, as well as being the location of the Amazonas Film Festival each November. Another cultural center is the **Teatro da Instalação** on Rua Frei José dos Inocentes, which hosts free music and dance performances (tel: 92-3234 4096/622 2840; email: teatroinstalaçao @culturamazonas.am.gov.br) in a newly restored historic building.

At Avenida Sete de Setembro 1385, the **Museu do Homem do Norte**  (Museum of Northern Man; open Mon 8am–noon, Tues–Fri 8am–noon, 1–5pm, tel: 92-3232 5373) gives a good idea of traditional Amazonian lifestyles. Also worth a look is the nearby, wedding cake-like **Palácio da Cultura** ❺, a former palace, then seat of the state government, and now the venue for various cultural events.

Commercial hub

Though its rubber industry enjoyed a brief wartime recovery, Manaus was not rescued from lingering decay until 1967, when it was declared a free-trade zone. To take advantage of tax breaks, hundreds of factories were installed in the industrial zone. A Zona Franca, selling electronic consumer goods, also sprang up in the city center, but prices will not excite foreigners.

The narrow streets of the port district are lined with stores selling goods to those who live on outlying tributaries. There is busy trade in some of the 1,500 different varieties of river fish and, in a separate section, Amerindian artifacts, *umbanda* items, and *guaraná* – a ginseng-like herbal energy preparation, which is also hugely popular as a soft drink. More Amerindian artifacts can be found at the **Salesian Museu do Indio** ❼ (Rua Duque de Caxias 296; open Mon–Fri 9am–noon, 1–5pm, Sat 9am–noon).

River Cruises

River cruises are a superb way to immerse yourself in the jungle. They all offer basic comforts such as en suite bathrooms and air-conditioning as you venture into the rainforest. Most have a set itinerary: an early morning excursion into the forest (when it is most lively), followed by a few hours' cruise. In mid-afternoon smaller launches explore the river tributaries and the rainforest in more depth, and in the evening there is a talk on flora and fauna followed by flashlight caiman-spotting by canoe. The *Tucano* offers comfortable cabins on eight-night trips from Manaus along Rio Negro and Rio Branco (www.nature tours.com; info@naturetours.com). The smaller *Desavio* runs three- to four-day trips (www.amazoncruise.net; email: info@amazoncruise.net).

Outside the center

A 20-minute ride out of the city along the Estrada Ponta Negra leads to CIGS, the army's training school for jungle warfare. There is an excellent zoo (open Tues–Sun 9.30am–4.30pm; admission charge) stocked with hundreds of Amazonian animals.

The **National Amazonian Research Institute** (INPA) carries out advanced studies with the help of many top foreign scientists. The aquatic mammals division (open Mon–Fri 9am–noon, 2–4pm, Sat 9am–noon), located about 25 minutes by taxi along the Estrada do Aleixo, has a collection of manatees, freshwater dolphins, and other species.

The **Tropical Hotel** (tel: 092-2123 5000), situated on the Praia da Ponta Negra, 20 km (12 miles) outside the city, has become the social center of Manaus. Its modern architecture is hardly tropical, but the gardens, circular swimming pool, and, above all, the excellent swimming in the **Rio Negro** during the low-water season, make it a major attraction. The hotel operates daily boat tours 9 km (5 miles) up the Rio Negro to **Lago Salvador** and the **Guedes Igarapé**. Visitors may fish, swim, walk the forest paths, and eat at a floating restaurant. An overnight stay at the lake allows time to travel up the *igarapé* (a forest backwater or creek) by motorized canoe, where you can go flashlighting to see alligators.

Day trips from Manaus

Several tour companies operate daylong river trips that follow a well-beaten track toward the **Lago de Janauary** ecological park to see the Victoria Regia giant waterlilies (best from April to September). The boats then turn toward the "meeting of the waters." The warm, clear waters of the Rio Negro collide with the silty Rio Solimões and run parallel without mixing for 20 km (12 miles) in a great churning pattern through which tour boats pass. Some trips pause on **Terra Nova Island**, where river-dwellers demonstrate their rubber-tapping skills and sell souvenirs.

The leading operator is Amazon Explorers (tel: 92-3633 3319). Another reputable tour company for the region

Vivid Heliconia makes a bright splash of color.

BELOW: giant Victoria Regia water lilies in the Lago de Janauary ecological park.

A Thwarted Dream

A mazonia is pock-marked with the ruins of the dreams of rich men, many of them foreigners. There are two of them along the River Tapajós, both memorials of the US automobile mogul Henry Ford, who had the idea that the land he had bought in Amazonia would be able to provide the rubber needed to make tires for the cars he manufactured in Detroit.

He bought 1 million hectares (about 2.5 million acress) of land on the Tapajós in the 1920s, paying a lot more than he needed, to a man who had just received a concession from the government at cut price. Ford called his tract of land Fordlandia. Sadly, the land turned out to be no good for growing rubber trees intensively, and after a few years it was abandoned to leaf blight, and soon sank back into the forest.

However, Ford's dream was not dead yet. He tried again further down the Tapajós near its confluence with the Amazon. Belterra, as it was named, was supposed to be the success that would efface the failure of Fordlandia, and the car magnate was assiduous about taking care of his employees, local and foreign.

Managers from the US were housed in a neighborhood called Vila Americana, in fine bungalows

that were reminiscent of the houses of functionaries of the British Raj in India.

Nor did he exploit his workers, as local bosses had done for decades, notably the rubber barons of the 19th century who had operated a system of slavery. Ford paid good wages, three times what a laborer could earn in the nearby city of Belém, schools were built, and water pipes laid, but as Stephen Nugent relates in his book *Wide Mouth: the Amazon Speaks*, by 1940 there was very little rubber being produced.

One or two survivors of the Ford era linger on. Sabia, an octogenarian whose leathery face shows his Indian ancestry, sits in his tidy little house next to the old sawmill and bears out Nugent's account from his own experience. Sabia remembers the days when he was a foreman and the US planters were in charge.

"There were very few of them and they didn't bring their families," he recalls. "And they weren't much good at the very tricky task of planting trees. You can plant a rubber tree successfully in one spot, yet another one planted just a few meters away may wilt."

More than 3½ million trees had been planted, but the operation was going too slowly, and it is estimated that it would have taken 1,000 years for the new area to be put under cultivation. After an expenditure of more than $10 million, Ford walked away, and eventually the area was sold off to the Brazilian government.

The authorities have kept it as a resource for the neighborhood, and to this day planning regulations decree that new houses have to be built in accordance with the domestic plans that the Fords brought with them from the US. The remains are there to be inspected: there are broad avenues, a sturdy church, and some remaining rubber trees, their trunks bearing the cuts from which the latex seeped out into the little cups that the workers emptied religiously every day. There's also a signpost, almost covered by forest creeper, indicating the way to Vila Americana, and the fire-hydrants still proclaiming that they were manufactured in Michigan.

A mile or two away is the little settlement of Pindobal, which served as a port for Belterra. Very few freight vessels tie up there these days, and the foreshore is left to families pottering about in their canoes, while local children play around the rusting wreckage of a bulldozer. ❑

LEFT: traditional method of rubber-tapping.

is Swallows and Amazons (tel: 92-3622 1246; www.swallowsandamazontours.com); email: swallows@internext.com.br.

Jungle lodges

A two-night minimum is recommended for a stay in a jungle lodge. All of the lodges will include transport, excursions, guides, and meals (but not drinks), and most have a schedule of activities that includes short treks into the forest, canoe trips, piranha-fishing, torchlight caiman-spotting, and visits to local communities. The further into the jungle you go, the more pristine the forest, and the greater number of animal species you are likely to spot. Lodges range in comfort and cost. The following are some of the best:

The **Amazon Village** is three hours downstream from Manaus on the banks of the Purqucuara River. Thatched wooden bungalows are en suite with cold-water showers. There is a generator for limited electricity, an alfresco restaurant, and sun deck (tel: 92-3633 1444; www.amazon-village .com.br; email: info@amazon-village.com.br).

Five hours by road and canoe from

Manaus is the **Amazon Eco-Lodge**, a remote, idyllic floating lodge on the Mamori River. There are 16 rooms with shared cold-water shower facilities, and a limited supply of electricity. A canopy platform allows a fantastic view over the rainforest as it comes alive at dawn and dusk (tel: 92-365 6603; www.naturesafaris.com; email: sales@naturesafaris.com).

The **Uakari Lodge** is located in the Mamiraua Nature Reserve, the largest protected area of floodplain forest in Brazil, on the confluence of the Solimões and Japurá rivers. This floating lodge has 10 en suite rooms with solar-powered electricity. Thanks to the remoteness, you are likely to see some rare Amazon species. Access is by a one-hour flight from Manaus to Tefé, then a four- to five-hour trip upstream by motorized-canoe (tel: 97 3343 4160; www. mamiraua.org.br).

Traveling by boat

Traveling by boat is a means of getting around, and not the same as taking a river cruise. Though a growing number of roads are being built in the Ama-

Messing about on the Rio Negro.

BELOW: armed with laptops, lawyers, police, doctors, teachers, and election workers travel by boat up the Amazon, sleeping aboard in hammocks, and bringing law to jungle communities.

zon, rivers remain by far the most practical form of transport for most people. Locals, and a few intrepid tourists, use the picturesque, cheap, and, in many ways, practical *gaiolas* that ply the waters of the Amazon River system. There is no better way to appreciate the character of the rural people of the Amazon than by travelling aboard a *gaiola*.

Though accommodation on board these riverboats is extremely basic, the open-sided decks festooned with hammocks are a logical solution to the slow, pitching gait of the boats and the sultry, humid climate. The movement of the boat keeps insects away, and many more passengers can be accommodated than by more conventional use of the space.

The trip from Manaus to Belém takes a little over a week – as long as there are no breakdowns. However, there are shorter trips that will give much the same flavor – one or two days is usually enough for most people – for example, **Santarém** to **Obidos**. On any *gaiola* it is advisable to take your own food, hammock, and bottled

water. The food served on board is usually basic, often badly cooked, and occasionally inedible. Toilet facilities are extremely limited, and by the end of the journey they can be unpleasantly smelly. To offset these hardships, you will experience the closeness of the river and the forest at their most magical.

Taking it slowly

You will also be forced to come to terms with the pace of life in Amazonia, which is somewhere between very slow and stationary. It is better to travel upstream, because the boats keep closer to the edge of the river, where the current is slower. Traveling downstream, you may find yourself several hundred yards from either shore, with only a distant view of the vegetation. Bear in mind, however, that these trips are essentially a way of getting from A to B, and you will be lucky to see much wildlife.

For the less intrepid, there are better-equipped vessels with cabins and regular bunks. These are run by the government ENASA line, principally for tourists. These are luxurious by

Pupunha *palm fruit can be found in all the local markets.*

BELOW: craft large and small in Manaus docks.

Cruise-Ship Port of Call

A trip along South America's mighty ocean-river should be high on every explorer's wish-list, for its sheer scale boggles the imagination. Amazon cruise ships will show you the river in rather more comfort than the local boats, and there are plenty to choose from. Most run from Barbados and combine a few Caribbean calls with a stop at Santarém – where you can witness "the marriage of the waters," as the coal-black Rio Negro merges with the café-crème Rio Solimões – before visiting Parentins and Alter do Chão (home to an excellent museum charting Amazonian history and culture) en route to Manaus. If you can, choose a cruise that also calls at Devil's Island, off the coast of French Guyana. Home to the infamous prison described in the novel *Papillon*, it is a fascinating, and horrifying, place to visit, with its lightless isolation cells and haunting guillotine area.

Companies offering Amazon cruises include deluxe small-ship operators Silversea Cruises and Seabourn Cruise Line (tel: 0870 333 7030; www.silversea.com; or 0845 070 0500; www.seabourn.com). If you'd prefer a larger ship (or a lower price), try Fred Olsen Cruises (tel: 01473 742424; www.FredOlsenCruises.co.uk), Saga Cruises (tel: 0800 505030; www.saga.co.uk) or Princess Cruises (tel: 0845 355 5800; www.princesscruises.co.uk).

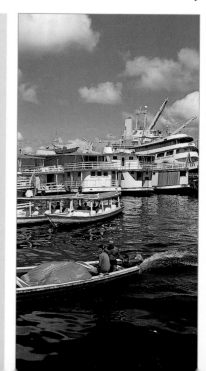

comparison with the *gaiolas*, with a bar, restaurant, and observation deck. They even make stops to allow you to soak up the Amazon experience.

Whichever vessel you choose, a river voyage is an unforgettable experience. But unless you want your trip to include many frustrations and hours, or even days, spent waiting, you would be advised to book and pay for it in advance on one of the tourist vessels.

Those with time to spare can travel up the Solimões as far as **Benjamin Constant** and **Letícia** on the Peruvian-Colombian border, where it becomes the Marañón River. Launches from Manaus – subject to frequent delays – usually take about eight days. The river banks are lined with small homesteads, where people fish, scratch a living from a few cultivated acres, and sell palm-hearts or turtles to passing boats.

Roraima

The Rio Branco drains Brazil's northernmost state, **Roraima**, whose dense forests and unmapped borders divide the Amazon and Orinoco river basins.

Until a highway was built from Manaus in 1977, with considerable loss of life due to clashes with displaced Amerindian tribes, its capital **Boa Vista ⑩** was isolated from the rest of Brazil. Roraima is, according to legend, the location of the mythical El Dorado *(see page 284)*. Mysterious **Mount Roraima ⑪** is believed to have inspired Sir Arthur Conan Doyle's novel *The Lost World*.

The 27,000-strong Yanomami Amerindian tribe – the continent's largest and least acculturated indigenous group – occupies a region straddling the Brazil-Venezuela border in the **Parima** mountain range – a region of jagged, forested peaks and chasms. The rare minerals on the Yanomami's land have attracted the ruthless interests of businessmen and illegal prospectors. It is estimated that 20 percent of the population was wiped out by attacks or disease during the 1970s and 80s. In 1992 Yanomami land was finally demarcated, but, to date, Brazil has not recognized tribal land-ownership, and the military is increasing its presence. ❏

The Yanomami live in huge communal houses called yanos, which can house up to 400 people. They build them in a large ring around an open space for dancing and ceremonies. Each family has its own hearth, and sleeps in hammocks around their fires.

RESTAURANTS

Belém

Blue Marlin Sushi and Sahimi
Rua Governador Malcher 252
Tel: 91-242 5946
Open: L&D daily.
Renowned sushi restaurant. Very popular, and stays open late. **$$**

Circulo Militar
Praça Frei Caetano Brandão
Bafa de Guajará
Tel: 91-223 4374
Open: L&D daily.
Occupying a huge barrack room in the old fort, this place offers a feast not to be missed. There's a

good menu with plenty of choice, and it's served at long tables by good-humored waiters. The dining room overlooks the Amazon River. **$$**

Lá em Casa/O Outro
Rua Governador José Malcher 247 Nazaré
Tel: 91-223 1212
Open: L&D daily.
One of the best restaurants for delicious Amazonian specialties, including ice cream flavored with various exotic fruits. **$$**

Manaus

Canto da Peixada
Rua Emilio Moreira 1677
(Praça 14 de Janeiro)

Tel: 92-234 3021
Open: L&D Mon–Sat
Serves fresh Amazon fish and interesting regional dishes. **$**

Choppicanha Bar and Grill
Rua Marques de Santa Cruz 25
Tel: 92-3631 1111
Open: L&D Mon–Sat, L Sun.
A good *churrascaria*, with lots of tender beef and chicken, as well as local fish. **$$**

Fiorentina
Rua José Pareraguá 44
Tel: 92-3232 1295
Open: L&D daily.
Traditional Italian restaurant serving standard dishes of pizza and

pasta. They are well cooked and presented, making it a good option in this area, particularly if you've had enough of the local fish. **$**

Peixaria Moronguêtá
Rua Jaith Chaves s/n
Tel: 92-615 3362
Open: L&D Mon–Sat.
There's an extensive menu of local fish cooked in an imaginative variety of ways in this pretty little restaurant overlooking Porto Ceasa. **$**

● ● ● ● ● ● ● ● ● ● ● ● ● ● ● ●
Prices for a two-course meal for two. Wine is around US$20 a bottle.
$ = under US$40, **$$** = $40–70,
$$$ = $70–100

THE RICHES OF THE RIVER AMAZON

The world's greatest river and largest rainforest is estimated to contain one-tenth of the plant, animal, and insect species to be found on earth

The River Amazon is one of the greatest symbols of Brazil. It rises in the snows of the Peruvian Andes just a short distance from the Pacific Ocean. It then travels across the heart of South America – a distance of 6,570 km (4,080 miles) – before it flows out into the Atlantic Ocean at the equator. It has about 15,000 tributaries, some of which, like the Araguaia and the Madeira, are mighty rivers in themselves. Just past Manaus, one of the most spectacular river sights is the meeting of the "black waters" of the Rio Negro with the "white waters" of the Rio Solimões, two other Amazon tributaries. The Amazon has a greater flow than any other river, depositing in the ocean each year about one-fifth of the world's freshwater.

At its mouth the Amazon is 300 km (185 miles) wide, a labyrinth of channels and islands, one of which has a greater land mass than Switzerland. The water flows with such force that it still tastes fresh 180 km (110 miles) out into the ocean.

The Amazon's network of dark, dense jungles has often been referred to as The Great Green Hell. In the west of the Amazon basin, it is still possible to fly for several hours and see nothing below you but a carpet of tropical forest, broken only by rivers snaking their way through the trees. The Amazon has remained virtually unchanged for the past 100 million years, for it did not pass through the same ice ages that altered other parts of the world's landscapes. Some of the most remote areas are still inhabited by Amerindian groups who have never had contact with the world outside their own jungle, although such groups are increasingly rare as more and more forays are made into the rainforest.

ABOVE: A boat safari along an Amazonian side-creek, taking in the sights, sounds and smells of the jungle, is one of the highlights for many visitors to the region. There are several reliable operators (see page 289).

ABOVE LEFT: Urucu berries are treasured by Amerindians because they contain a bright red-colored dye that members of some groups use to paint their faces and bodies.

TOP LEFT: The Victoria Regis water lily has enormous, circular leaves that can measure up to 2 metres (6½ feet) across.

LEFT: The brightly colored poison arrow frog belongs to the *Dendrobatidae* family, and there are some 220 species. They are very small, ranging in size from 1–6 cm (0.2–2.5 in). They gained their name because their poison used to be extracted by Amerindians to use on the tips of arrows.

ABOVE: The great Rio Madeira, which the Portuguese named after their Atla island. Though it is just a tributary of the Amazon, the river flows over a distance of more than 1,600 km (1,000 miles).

DEFORESTATION IN THE AMAZON

About 16 percent of the Amazon forest – an area the size of France or twice the size of Colorado – has already been cut down, almost all of it over the past 50 years. Most of the destruction has taken place in the east of the basin, "opened up" in the 1960s and 1970s when the military government built a vast network of roads. Cattle companies then moved in, slashing and burning the forest to sow pasture.

"Avança Brasil" was announced in 2001, a US$40-billion program that included the building of 10,000 km (6,215 miles) of highways, electric dams, and power lines. Some 30 percent of the Trans-Amazon and 40 percent of the Cuiabá-Santarém paving has been completed, but the program has been halted pending reviews by the government.

ABOVE: A black spider monkey: this delightful animal uses its tail to enable it to swing from branch to branch in the forest. The monkeys "play" in groups, and act as if they are having a lot of fun.

LEFT: If you are visiting the Amazon, try to stay in a jungle lodge so that you really feel involved in the experience. You go to sleep listening to the bewitching sounds of the tropical forest at night, and wake up to them in the morning. Pictured is the Ariau Amazon Towers, on the banks of the Rio Negro, but there are a number of others *(see page 291 for recommendations)*, most of which will organize night-time caiman-spotting trips.

LEFT: Tapping a tree to obtain rubber. Thousands of families, living deep in the rainforest, still tap rubber trees to obtain the latex. This was the substance that made the region rich in the 19th century, after the discovery of vulcanization and the invention of the pneumatic tire.

RIGHT: The toucan is a striking-looking bird, and a recognizable image of the Amazon rainforest. Its huge yellow bill can be as much as half the length of its body, and it uses it to crush the seeds and extract the berries that it feeds on. Toucans make their nests in trees, and typically lay about three eggs. They are not at all shy of humans, so you are very likely to see them in the course of your visit.

THE CENTER-WEST

This is a territory of vast open plains, and pockets
of wetlands rich in wildlife, yet it is also the
location of Brasília, the country's futuristic capital

Apart from the federal district – Brasília – this region can truly be described as Brazil's "Wild West," whose parallels with North America's eponymous land in centuries past are manifold. *Bandeirantes* first traveled west to push back the frontiers of discovered territory, seeking gold but, for the most part, surviving by hacking down swathes of jungle so they could run cattle on the land.

The vast *cerrado* (savanna plains, the terrain of most of the region) is still sparsely populated, and many modern-day fortune-hunters still claim their prize from the land and then move on, while others stay to run huge isolated cattle ranches. Dusty frontier towns, like the set of a Western film, are spread thinly. There are even a few Amerindians still living in the region.

Since 1960, the region has been host to Brazil's capital and has expanded rapidly. Intensive soybean cultivation is the principal source of income, with cattle-raising a close second. Today, a staggering 85 percent of the population of 14 million live in urban areas. Most visitors, however, still come for adventure in an untamed land.

The chief attraction, especially for birdwatchers and fishing enthusiasts, is the Pantanal, an enormous, seasonally flooded swamp with a unique population of waterbirds. Tourists might otherwise come to see spectacular canyons and waterfalls; to ride horseback through cowboy country; to view the high plains from a hot-air balloon; to witness pioneering history; or to learn about Amerindian culture.

You may wish to see Brasília. Modern, orderly, architecturally homogeneous Brasília – so incongruous in the middle of the empty *cerrado* – was conceived as a symbol of national unity, located in the geographical center of the country. It was the vision of then-president Juscelino Kubitschek, and was intended to provide the impetus to populate the west, but Brasília today still has few links with the wild country surrounding it. ❑

PRECEDING PAGES: the Palácio de Justicia in Brasília, and the sculpted head of former president Juscelino Kubitschek.
LEFT: land clearance in Mato Grosso.

BRASÍLIA AND GOIÁS

Located in the very center of the country, at the edge of a formerly remote state cut by major river systems, the capital of Brazil is an impressive architectural monument that represents the realization of a dream

For more than two centuries, the aim of Brazilian visionaries was to fill the vacuum in the center of their country. In 1891 Brazil's first republican government sent a scientific team to survey possible sites in Goiás, which is watered by three great rivers – the Amazon, the Paraná, and the São Francisco. For the same purpose, a later commission was sent, in 1946, to conduct an aerial survey. Yet until the election of president Juscelino Kubitschek in 1955, Brasília remained simply an idea.

Kubitschek made the development of Brasília the centerpiece of his campaign to modernize the country. The pace of the project was determined by politics; Kubitschek knew that if the city was ever to be completed, it had to be done by the end of his five-year term. He selected as his architect Oscar Niemeyer, a communist and student of Le Corbusier. An international jury selected the city plan, which was the work of controversial architect Lúcio Costa, and Niemeyer designed all the major public buildings.

Groundbreaking plan

The work began in September 1956 on the highest and flattest of the five sites identified by the aerial survey. The first task was to build a runway, which was used to bring in the initial building materials and heavy equipment. Brasília ❶ thus became the world's first major city conceived in terms of

air access. Only after construction had begun was a road pushed through from Belo Horizonte, 740 km (460 miles) to the southeast. A dam followed, and Lake Paranoá began to emerge. By April 1960, the city housed 100,000 people and was ready for its inauguration as capital. In 1987 it was declared a World Heritage Site by UNESCO, and in 2002 an elegant triple-span steel bridge was built over Lake Paranoá – Juscelino Kubitschek Bridge.

Most visitors will come to Brasília the way Kubitschek first came – by

Main attractions
TORRE DE TELEVISÃO
MEMORIAL JK
ESPLANADA DOS MINISTÉRIOS
CONGRESSO NACIONAL
CATEDRAL METROPOLITANA
PALÁCIO DA ALVORADA
PARQUE CIDADE SARAH KUBITSCHEK
PARQUE CHAPADA DOS VEADEIROS

LEFT: The Warriors honors the laborers who built the city.
BELOW: the iconic Congreso Nacional building towers.

Soldier on guard outside a government building.

plane. After flying over the semi-arid and sparsely inhabited Central Plateau, the city suddenly emerges as a row of white building blocks set along a gentle rise above the artificial lake.

Overland, the most spectacular approach is by road from the northeast. After driving through miles of red dust and gnarled scrub, known as *cerrado,* you reach a eucalyptus-lined ridge just beyond **Planaltina**, the oldest town in this region. Brasília is laid out in a gleaming arc in the valley below.

Like the United Nations Secretariat in New York, the present-day city is trapped in a 1950s vision of the future. Built around the automobile, its urban core is a complex of super-highways, which creates a hostile environment for pedestrians.

While under construction, Brasília captured the world's imagination, but soon afterwards, the world lost interest and Brasília became synonymous with technocracy run wild. Yet to this day, the building of Brasília remains a point of great pride among Brazilians. It was the only postwar project intended to serve the people, not industry; and it was entirely financed and built at the behest of an elected president, in a time of democracy. For all the flaws that are now evident, Lúcio Costa spoke for the majority of Brazilians when he asserted, "The only important thing for me is that Brasília exists."

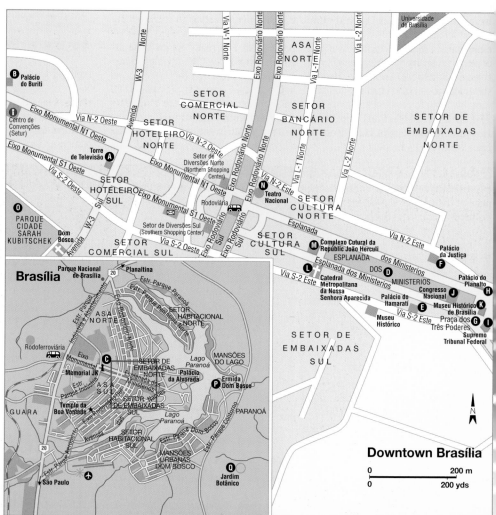

Downtown Brasília

0   200 m

0   200 yds

~tting to know the city

~he first recommended stop in Brasília
~s the **Torre de Televisão**  (Televi-
~ion Tower; open Tues–Sun 8am–8pm,
~on 2–8pm) at the highest point of the
~ixo **Monumental** (Monumental
~xis) that runs through the center of
~he city. A good map at the foot of the
~ower explains how the streets are laid
~ut. An elevator to the top of the tower
~ives a bird's-eye view of Costa's plan:
~wo gently curving arcs indicating the
~esidential areas of the city, bisected
~y the Eixo Monumental containing
~he buildings of government.

Costa's plan has been variously de-
~cribed as a cross, a bow and arrow, or
~n airplane. Costa accepted all these in-
~erpretations, but said he really chose
~ts shape to accommodate the curvature
~f the terrain above the lake, while
~mphasizing the civic buildings at the
~enter of the city. Costa's design was
~elected because of its simplicity and
~uitability for a national capital.

The government sector

~eading west from the center along the
~ixo Monumental, you next come to

the administrative seat of the Federal
District in **Palácio do Buriti** ⑬, in
pretty Praça Municipal. Continuing
westward you come to the **Memorial
JK** ⓒ (open Tues–Sun 9am–5.40pm),
the memorial to Kubitschek. It was the
first building in Brasília that the military allowed Niemeyer to design after
their takeover in 1964. The curious
sickle-shaped structure on top of the
monument in which the statue of
Kubitschek stands seems more like a
political gesture by Niemeyer than a
symbol of Kubitschek's beliefs.

Inside the monument is Kubitschek's
tomb and a collection of memorabilia
about his life and the construction of
Brasília. One showcase contains a sum-
mary of the unsuccessful entries in the
competition to design the city, including a proposal to house most of its
population in 18 enormous tower blocks
over 300 meters (1,000 ft) high, housing 16,000 people.

Heading in the other direction from
the Television Tower, down the hill
past the main bus terminal, the Eixo
Monumental opens onto the
Esplanada dos Ministérios ⓓ (Es-

*Kubitschek stands
aloft the Memorial
JK, a striking
Niemeyer design.*

BELOW: the
curvaceous
JK Bridge at
sunset.

TIP

There are some specialized four-hour tours of Brasília's architectural landmarks. Contact the Bluepoint agency (tel: 61-274 0033).

planade of the Ministries). A row of 16 identical pale-green box-shaped buildings runs down both sides of the vast open boulevard. Each building houses a different government department whose name is emblazoned in gold letters on the front. Since every ministry has long since outgrown its original quarters, they have sprouted additions at the back, connected in mid-air by concrete tubes to their mother ship. In the late 1960s, several buildings were subject to arson attacks, reportedly by disgruntled civil servants protesting against their forced move from Rio, although this was never substantiated.

Niemeyer's best

Flanking the end of the Esplanade are Niemeyer's two finest buildings: the **Palácio do Itamaratí ❸** (open Mon–Fri 2–4.30pm, guided tours only), now housing the Foreign Ministry, which floats in splendid isolation in the midst of a reflecting pool; and the **Palácio da Justiça ❺** (Ministry of Justice; open Mon–Fri 9–11am, 3–5pm), whose six curtains of falling water on the exterior echo

the natural waterfalls around Brasília.

Beyond the Eixo Monumental is the **Praça dos Três Poderes ❼** (Plaza of the Three Powers) – a dense forest of political symbols. Named after the three divisions of power under the Brazilian Constitution, the executive is represented by the **Palácio do Planalto ❽** (open Sun 9.30am–1.30pm), on the left, housing the president's offices, while the judiciary is represented by the **Supremo Tribunal Federal ❾** (Supreme Court; open Sat–Sun and holidays 10am–5.30pm) on the right.

Overshadowing both – architecturally if not politically – are the twin towers and offset domes of the **Congresso Nacional ❿** (Chamber of Deputies open Mon–Fri 9am–noon, 2.30–4.30pm, Sat–Sun and holidays 9am–1pm; Senate open Mon–Fri 9–11.30am, 3.30–4.30pm, Sat–Sun and holidays 10am–2pm). This is the building whose silhouette is the signature of Brasília. Even the former monarchy has a place in the plaza. The rows of tall imperial palms behind the congress building were transplanted from the Botanical Garden that Dom João VI created in Rio.

Around the plaza

There are a number of notable sculptures on the plaza. The basaltic head of Kubitschek protrudes from the marble walls of the small **Museu Histórico de Brasília ⓚ** (open Sun–Fri 9am–6pm; admission charge), which is actually just a series of panels outlining the history of Brasília, and the most memorable sayings of Kubitschek, whose powers of hyperbole rivaled his talent for conceiving new cities.

In front of the supreme court is a blindfolded figure of Justice, sculpted by Alfredo Ceschiatti. Facing the Palácio do Planalto are the figures of *The Warriors* by Bruno Giorgi, a tribute to the thousands of workers and laborers who built Brasília. A note of whimsy is added to the plaza by

BELOW: the sinuous lines of the Congreso Nacional, the signature of Brasília.

Niemeyer's pigeon house, the **Pombal**.

The most recent addition to the plaza is the **Pantheon Tancredo Neves** (open daily 9am–6pm), a tribute to the founding father of the New Republic, who died in April 1985 before he could be sworn in as president. Inside the darkened interior is Brasília's most extraordinary and disturbing artwork. The mural, by João Camara, depicts the story of an uprising in the 18th century led by Brazil's best-known revolutionary, Tiradentes (Joaquim José da Silva Xavier). Painted in seven black-and-white panels (rather like Picasso's *Guernica*), it is heavy with Masonic symbolism.

The **Catedral Metropolitana da Nossa Senhora Aparecida ❶** (open Mon 8am–5pm, Tues–Sun 8am–6pm) at the western end of the Esplanada dos Ministérios is an unusual concrete building with a spectacular, stained-glass domed roof. Near by, the newest buildings on the Esplanada dos Ministérios are the Biblioteca Nacional Leonel de Moura Brizola (National Library) and the Museu Nacional Honestino Guimarães (National Museum), that together make up the **Complexo Cultural da República João Herculino ⓜ**. These two buildings were completed in 2006, following Niemeyer's original plans.

On the north side of the Eixo Monumental, near the Rodoviária, is the pyramid-shaped **Teatro Nacional ❶** (open daily 9am–8pm), where art shows and other exhibitions are held.

Further away, on the shores of Lake Paranoá, is the **Palácio da Alvorada** (open Wed only 3–5.30pm for guided tours). The official presidential residence, the Alvorada is regarded as one of Niemeyer's masterpieces, and one of the first projects to be completed. It is a two-story, rectangular building whose main features are the marble columns that have become a symbol of Brasília.

Residential Brasília

To appreciate Brasília as a living city, you need to leave the center and visit the areas where people actually live – the purpose-built *quadras* that are arrayed along the city's north and south wings. Each *quadra* is made up of six

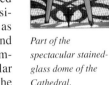

Part of the spectacular stained-glass dome of the Cathedral.

BELOW: the Catedral Metropólitana and its guardians.

TIP

The bustling downtown shopping malls in the northern and southern *conjuntos* provide a welcome relief from the artificiality of the center.

BELOW: a regimented row of ministry buildings.

to eight low-rise residential blocks, grouped around well-landscaped lawns and courtyards. Short commercial streets, which provide a range of basic services for the residents, are evenly interspersed between them. The *quadras* provide an essentially uniform standard of living across the city, which for many residents is a welcome respite from the urban jungles of Brazil's coastal cities.

Satellite cities

Lúcio Costa's original pilot plan for Brasília gives the city a rigid shape. Once all the *quadras* planned for the north wing are built, the city proper can grow no further. The great surprise in the evolution of Brasília has been the explosive growth of the "satellite cities" beyond its green belt. These were originally settled by construction workers from the northeast, who remained after their contracted work in the city finished. Their numbers have since swelled with new migrants and lower-middle-class residents, who have sold the free apartments they were awarded in the pilot plan.

Today, Brasília proper accounts for only 22 percent of the population of the Federal District. Despite the egalitarian architecture of the pilot plan, the class barriers in the wider Federal District are more rigid than in the rest of the country. The population is zoned by income into separate cities.

Leisure and pleasure

If you are looking for leisure and relaxation, go to the **Parque Cidade Sarah Kubitschek** ⊙ (open Tues–Sun 9am–midnight), named after Juscelino Kubitschek's wife, and also known as Parque da Cidade (City Park). This is a vast, green area of 42 hectares (104 acres) in the centre of Brasília, close to Torre de Televisão. Here local people and visitors alike come to exercise, sunbathe, meet friends, or just relax.

Further out, by Lake Paranoá, the **Pontão do Lago Sul** has shops, restaurants, bars, antique fairs, and piers. Younger visitors will probably favor Pier 21 (open daily 11am–11pm), a shopping center full of bars, nightclubs, restaurants, cinemas, and bookshops.

Social Life

Visitors staying in the hotel sector in the center of Brasília often get the mistaken impression that the city is completely dead at night. This is not the case: there is a lively scene in the bars, restaurants, and clubs concentrated along certain commercial streets in the residential wings – notably 109/110 South, 405/406 South and 303/304 North. Brasília's extremely fluid and casual social life is defined by the fact that it is a relatively affluent city and, as a modern, new creation, appeals to upwardly mobile young people. Although those who worked in the government sector in Rio de Janeiro – when that city was the capital – resented moving to Brasília, in recent decades many young professionals have moved here from other parts of Brazil.

Center of spiritualism

Brasília's spiritual life is as unusual as its social mores. Niemeyer's concrete cathedral along the Eixo Monumental represents the official faith. Closer to the city's true faith is the cult of Dom Bosco, an Italian priest and educator who prophesied in 1883 that a new civilization would arise in a land of milk and honey on the site of present-day Brasília. His prophecy provided spiritual legitimacy for Kubitschek's secular dream of a new capital.

The first structure built on the city site, overlooking Lake Paranoá, was a small marble pyramid commemorating Bosco's vision. Brasília's most striking church, the **Ermida Dom Bosco** ❿ (open daily 8am–6pm) in 702 South, is a cubic chapel with walls made entirely of blue-and-violet stained glass.

Brasília also enjoys a reputation as "The Capital of the Third Millennium," by virtue of the 400-plus contemporary cults that flourish here. Further south, at 915, is the extraordinary **Templo da Boa Vontade** (Temple of Goodwill; open daily, 24 hours). Built in the form of seven pyramids in 1989 (seven is said to be the number of perfection), it is crowned with one of the world's largest crystals.

Valley of the Dawn

Several "new age" communities have been founded on the outskirts of Brasília. The largest and most accessible is the **Vale do Amanhecer** (Valley of the Dawn), south of Planaltina. Every Sunday, several hundred worshipers come here to be initiated into the commune established by "Aunt Neiva," a retired woman truck driver. The weekly parade of initiates, dressed in multicolored cloaks and veils, around a pond adorned with astrological symbols, is an eerie sight.

Parks and gardens

A short drive away from the Dom Bosco church, to the southeast of the city, is the **Jardim Botânico** ❑ (Setor de Mansões D. Bosco, Conjunto 12, Lago Sul; open Tues–Sun 9am–5pm), a pleasant place to look at the flora of the *cerrado*. To the north of the city is a 30,000-hectare (74,000-acre) nature reserve operated by the botanical

A cloaked worshiper in the new age community in the Valley of the Dawn.

BELOW: the empty roads of Goiás seem far removed from the capital.

gardens, the **Parque Nacional de Brasília** (open daily 8am–4pm). This is an area of savanna *(cerrado)* and low forest where birds, wolves, monkeys, and armadillos find refuge. There are forest trails, natural swimming pools, and a visitor center.

Goiás state

The state of **Goiás** is an area of savanna and large rivers that attract growing numbers of keen fishermen and ecotourists. The river banks are densely forested and rich in wildlife. Much savanna land is being taken over by plantations of soybeans, and the state is now the center of a campaign to protect the *cerrado*.

The principal attractions of the state are the sister hydrothermal resorts of **Caldas Novas,** 172 km (107 miles) from Goiânia, and **Rio Quente**, 43 km (17 miles) away, plus its colonial towns and its national parks. **Pirenópolis** ❷, a picturesque town 137 km (85 miles) from Brasília, was founded in the 18th century to house gold miners. Its cobbled streets and fine baroque houses make it well worth a visit. In the Pireneus mountain range, in which the town is set, blocks of quartz and sandstone have been sculpted by time and weather into spectacular shapes, on which grow lichens, moss, and cacti.

About 265 km (165 miles) north of Brasília is the **Parque Nacional da Chapada dos Veadeiros** ❸, a nature reserve with numerous beautiful waterfalls, rock formations, and natural swimming pools.

Goiás ❹ (also known as Goiás Velho), 340 km (212 miles) from Brasília, was the state's capital until 1937. It is interesting for its colonial architecture, with many well-preserved 18th-century churches and houses. In 2001 it became UNESCO-listed, after a comprehensive restoration program.

Along the Araguaia River

Forming Goiás's western border is part of a river whose valley is described by Durval Rosa Borges, author of *Araguaia, Heart and Soul,* as "the Garden of Eden." The Araguaia River is, in fact, 2,630 km (1,634 miles) long, cutting Brazil in two, from the wetlands of the Pantanal across the *cerrado* or central plains to the Atlantic Ocean at Belém. When the muddy floodwaters shrink in August to reveal immense white-sand beaches, 200,000 vacationing Brazilians descend on the river at **Aruanã** ❺, 530 km (330 miles) west of Brasília, and **Barra do Garças** ❻, both in western Goiás state, to establish lavish campsites and sound systems for all-night parties. Even so, their presence is dwarfed by the Araguaia's vast scale.

The source of the river in southern Goiás is in the **Parque Nacional das Emas** ❼, from which it flows northward, forming a barrier between the states of Mato Grosso, Goiás, Tocantins, and Pará, dividing to form the fluvial **Ilha do Bananal** ❽. To the north of the island is the **Parque Nacional do Araguaia** ❾. During the low-water season, floating hotels operate on the river's tributaries. ❑

Many of the herbs and plants growing in the Pireneus range have medicinal properties, and have been used by the local population for generations.

BELOW: the weather-beaten face of a Goiás farmer.

RESTAURANTS

Addresses in Brasília look a bit odd if you are not used to them, but are quite straightforward: *Bloco* means block, *Casa* means house, *Conjunto* means a group of buildings, and *Loja* means a unit.

Alice
QI 11, Conjunto 9, Casa 17, Lago Norte
Tel: 61-3368 1099/3577 4333
Open: D Fri–Sat.
French bistro that is considered by many to be the best restaurant in Brasília. $$

Bargaço
405 Sul, Bloco D, Loja 36
Tel: 61-3443 8729
Open: L&D Mon–Sat, L Sun.
Also at Pontão do Lago Sul, QI 10
Tel: 61-3364 6090
Open: L&D daily.
This good seafood restaurant is also represented in six other Brazilian cities, and all of them are equally reliable. $$$

Carpe Diem
104 Sul, Bloco D, Loja 1
Tel: 61-3325 5300
Open: L&D (until 2am) daily.
There's a varied and well-priced menu, but Carpe Diem is best known for its *feijoada* on Saturday, which has become an institution in Brasília. $$$

Dom Francisco
Setor de Clubes Esportivos

Sul (SCES),Trecho 2, Conjunto 3
Tel: 61-3224 8429/3323-5679/3226 2005
Open: L&D Mon–Sat, L (until 5pm) Sun.
Serves both exotic and regional dishes. At the main address *(above)* there is an excellent wine cellar, with more than 15,000 bottles. There are three other branches in town. $$

Feitiço Mineiro
306 Norte, Bloco B, Lojas 45/51
Tel: 61-3272 3032
Open: L&D (until last client) Mon–Sat, L (until 5pm) Sun.
Excellent regional cuisine from the state of Minas Gerais, hence the name. $$

Piantella
202 Sul, Bloco A, Loja 34
Tel: 61-3224 9408
Open: L&D Mon–Sat, L Sun.
Eat in pleasant and comfortable surroundings, in a venue that is popular with politicians. And there's a good wine list to accompany dishes. $$$

Porção
Setor de Clubes Esportivos Sul (SCES), Trecho 2, Conjunto 35, next to Pier 21
Tel: 61-3223 2002
Open: L&D daily.
The largest and best-known barbecue restaurant in the city (it seats 900), set beside Lake Paranoá. There are more than 20 different

cuts of meat, a generous buffet, and Japanese food as well. There are unlimited salads, to which you help yourself, and meat served from skewers at your table, all at a set price. There's a good wine selection, too. (There are several other branches of Porção in Rio.) $$$

Trattoria da Rosario
Fashion Park, Bloco H, Loja 215 Lago Sul
Tel: 61-3248 1672
Open: L&D Mon–Sat, L (until 5pm) Sun.
The owner and chef Rosario Tessier is keen to point out that this is a "regional Italian restaurant," and not simply an "Italian

restaurant," which means that there are specialties from all over Italy. And very good they are, too. $$$

Vila Borghese
Comércio Local Sul 201 Sul, Bloco A, Loja 33
Tel: 61-3226 5650
Open: L&D (until last customer) daily.
The Vila Borghese serves excellent Italian food, including delicious home-made pasta with tasty sauces. $$$

> **PRICE CATEGORIES**
>
> Prices for a two-course meal for two. Wine costs around US$20 a bottle.
> $= under $40
> $$ = $40–70
> $$$ = $70–100

RIGHT: lunch in the sun.

THE PANTANAL

The Pantanal is an extraordinary place. Not only
is the diversity of wildlife remarkable, but
the landscape and vegetation make it easy
to see a great deal of it on a brief visit

The highlight of any visit to western Brazil is the Pantanal ⑩, a vast natural paradise that is one of Brazil's major ecological attractions. Pristine and biologically rich, the area comprises 230,000 sq. km (89,000 sq. miles), shared unequally between Brazil, Bolivia, and Paraguay, of seasonally flooded territory, offering a density of tropical wildlife unknown outside Africa. The word Pantanal comes from the Portuguese *pântano*, meaning swamp or marshland, but the region is in fact an immense alluvial plain, comprising rivers, lakes, grassland, forest, and savanna. The Pantanal crosses two states, Mato Grosso and Mato Grosso do Sul, and access to it is from the major towns of Corumbá and Campo Grande in the south, and Cuiabá and Poconé in the north.

Protecting the Pantanal

Scarcely populated, the majority of the Pantanal is privately owned (only 135,000 hectares/333,000 acres is national park), and the region's economy is sustained by extensive cattle farming, agriculture (soy, rice, and corn are grown) and, increasingly, tourism. Hunting is prohibited (although fishing is permitted with a permit, and some restrictions), but because of the nature of the terrain and, until fairly recently, lack of government enforcement or support, this area has been poorly policed.

A hyacinth macaw egg can sell for more than US$10,000 and poachers, are still very active in the region.

Wildlife

It is the concentration, as well as the huge diversity, of wildlife that makes the Pantanal a naturalist's dream. Similar species are found here as in the Amazon, but owing to the lack of dense vegetation and, in the dry season, the collection of birds and mammals around feeding areas such as watering holes, they are far easier to spot. Film crews trying to capture

Main attractions
THE PANTANAL
CUIABÁ
CHAPADA DOS GUIMARÃES
CAMPO GRANDE
BONITO

LEFT: foliage on
the banks of the
Aquidauana River.
BELOW:
a dozy capybara.

TIP

Most of the Pantanal
lodges are open all year
round, and you can visit
the area at any season.

Amazon wildlife are frequently re-directed to the Pantanal, where their chances of sightings are far better.

The area is home to an estimated 650 bird species, the majority of which are wading birds such as the graceful jabiru stork, which stands at 1.4 meters (over 4 ft) tall, and the roseate spoon-bill with its distinctive beak. Although the Pantanal offers sanctuary for migratory geese and ducks moving between Argentina and Central America, most of the waterbirds found here are residents that follow the changing water levels inside the huge swamp, in pursuit of the 250 species of fish that support them in the food chain.

Especially delightful are the 15 won-derfully colorful species of parrot, including the majestic hyacinth macaw (the world's largest parrot, 1 meter/3 ft long), as well as an incredible prolifer-ation of toucans. These curious crea-tures, with their precise coloring and oversized beaks, often come to pick berries delicately from the fruit trees of your lodge as you sit at breakfast.

Glimpsing the mammals

You are more likely to catch a glimpse of the mammal inhabitants of the Pan-tanal during the dry season. The capy-bara is the world's largest rodent – an adult can weigh around 80 kg (175 lbs). These unusual-looking animals are dog-sized with the blunt snout of a

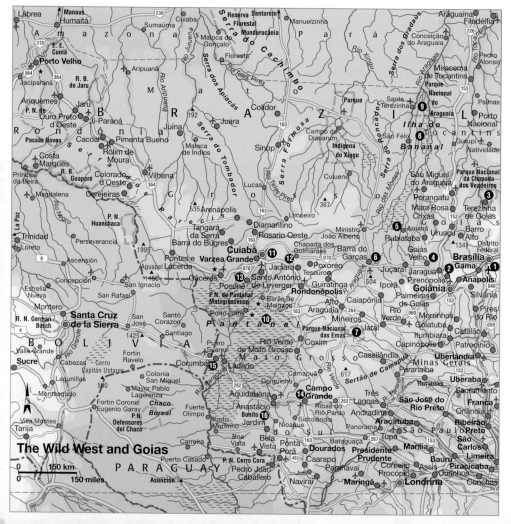

The Wild West and Goias

guinea pig. Capuchin and howler monkeys can often be seen and heard, and the extraordinary giant anteater, with its long, delicate nose and majestic gait, emerges to feed at dusk. Armadillos, marsh deer, and coatis are other common sights, but you would be very lucky to see the elusive jaguar and puma, which leave their paw prints in the dust.

The ubiquitous caiman lie open-mouthed, basking in the Pantanal sun, gorging themselves on fish, and waiting for the rains to come. And you may see the yellow anaconda, a greedy constrictor, which has been known to consume a whole capybara.

Rainfall cycles

Rainfall cycles are the key to the Pantanal: during the wet season – October to April – the River Paraguay and its tributaries burst their banks, spreading water into huge *baías*, or closed lakes where fish have been breeding. The waters activate ground vegetation and enable the overhanging trees to produce fruit on which the fish gorge themselves, before swimming through open canals to spawn in the rivers, and

attracting huge numbers of wading birds. Water levels can rise by up to 5 metres (16 ft), leaving many areas accessible only by boat or light aircraft. Mornings are usually dry and clear with a steady build-up of clouds throughout the day, and a sustained, heavy burst of rain in the evening. Temperatures are around 24°C (75° F), and mosquitoes can be fierce.

When the waters recede the landscape changes completely, and the Pantanal becomes dusty and arid. Many fish are retained in small ponds, providing a crucial food source for the mammal and reptile inhabitants, which congregate around the waterholes in the long dry season. In the heat trees lose their leaves, and wildlife becomes easier to spot. Temperatures can drop to 10°C (50° F) at night, but during the day the sun is hot and persistent.

Cuiabá

Cuiabá ⓫, in the center of Mato Grosso, was the west's first settlement, founded in 1719 by a group of slave-hunters from São Paulo who struck shallow gold and diamond deposits.

Giant otters can be seen in the Pantanal.

BELOW: an exhilarating ride through the waters.

The resulting rush of prospectors made Cuiabá the third-most important city in colonial Brazil. A century ago, the city found a new resource and acquired fame as a major supplier of exotic bird feathers to the milliners of Paris. Today, this prosperous city is a major starting point for trips into the Pantanal, and the capital of an immense logging, farming, and mining state. Little of colonial Cuiabá survives, but the city's Cathedral church of Bom Jesus de Lapa has a small adjoining museum of religious artifacts.

Cultural pursuits

The excellent **Museu do Indio Marechal Rondon** (open Mon–Fri 7.30–11.30am, 1.30–5.30pm, Sat–Sun 7.30–11.30am; admission charge) at the university entrance, 10 minutes' bus ride from the center, shows the artifacts and lifestyle of the Xingu tribes. Some of the items are on sale at a handicrafts shop run by FUNAI, the government Amerindian affairs bureau. Other landmarks are the Governor's Residence and the **Fundação Cultural de Mato Grosso** (Praça da República 151; open Mon–Fri 8am–5.30pm; admission charge), in a historic mansion which houses three interesting museums: Antropológica, História Natural, and Cultura Popular.

Fish is Cuiabá's culinary forte. Piranha may be deadly in the water, but legend has it that in soup they possess aphrodisiac powers – try the *caldo de piranha* (piranha broth).

After the lowland heat, relief is close at hand 70 km (45 miles) from Cuiabá. The **Chapada dos Guimarães National Park** is a rocky outcrop overlooking the flat plain of the Paraguay River and the Pantanal, 800 meters (2,600 ft) above sea level. In the misty cool of the Chapada's folded hills and jutting, monolithic rock formations are caves and stunning waterfalls. Local residents attest to the region's mystical qualities, and confirm frequent UFO sightings. These uplands provide one of the many water sources for the Pantanal marshlands.

Through the Gates of Hell

Later, the road curves through the **Portão de Inferno** (Gates of Hell) – a

vertical drop that marks the edge of the sandstone escarpment. Overhead tower pencil-like rock formations. Further on, visitors can admire the 86-meter (280-ft) **Véu da Noiva** (Bride's Veil) waterfall from above, or walk for half an hour down the thickly wooded canyon to reach its base.

Further into the Chapada is the Casa de Pedra – a natural cave-house capped by an immense stone shelf – and the Caverna Aroe Jari, on whose walls there are primitive paintings. You need a guide; they are easy to find locally, and will supply a torch.

Chapada dos Guimarães ⑫, with the 200-year-old church of Santana, is a historical town that grew up to provide Cuiabá's hungry miners with food. It is a good base for excursions into the surrounding countryside and the national park of the same name. Just outside town, a monument marks the geodesic center of South America.

Due south of Cuiabá on state highway 060 is **Poconé** ⑬, a dry area given over to farming; the swamps near by have all been disturbed by gold mining, wildlife poaching, and exces-sive fishing. However, this is another good jumping-off point for parts of the Pantanal.

Cowboy towns

For the southern Pantanal in Mato Grosso do Sul, the entry points are Campo Grande and Corumbá. **Campo Grande** ⑭, the state capital, began life in 1889, and is still an overgrown cowboy town. The **Museu Dom Bosco** (Rua Barão do Rio Branco 1843; open daily 8.30am–5pm; admission charge) has interesting Amerindian exhibits and a huge natural history collection.

Corumbá ⑮, on the Bolivian border opposite Puerto Suárez, was founded in 1778. From here there is access to the Pantanal by both road and river – even a brief boat tour gives a vivid impression.

Bonito

Crystal-clear rivers, waterfalls, and caves pepper the landscape of the Serra do Bodoquena, and **Bonito** ⑯ has become the center of nature tourism in the area. The town itself is not particularly interesting – a modern, friendly

A fisherman paddles his dug-out canoe during the wet season.

BELOW: the exotic red-necked tuiuiú.

Communications

From Poconé the Trans-Pantaneira Highway, which is in a poor state of repair, runs 145 km (90 miles) southward to Porto Jofre over 126 bridges. Begun in the 1970s, the Trans-Pantaneira highway was originally intended to link Luiabá with Corumbá, but local political wrangling and pressure from environmentalists cut it short. Because the road runs parallel to the rivers, huge bodies of water collect beside it, ensuring views of alligators and bird life even for those unwilling to get out of their cars.

There are also irregular cargo boats, usually transporting cattle, that ply the 185 km (115 miles) of the River São Lourenço to Corumbá, and which may take passengers if you are able to negotiate with the captain.

place with good bars, restaurants, and hostels – but it is a good spot to base yourself while exploring some of the natural attractions near by. The extraordinary clarity of the water here is due to the high concentration of carbonates, which bubble up from underwater springs from a limestone base; these calcify the impurities in the water, causing them to drop to the river bed, leaving the rivers breathtakingly clear.

Most of these natural sights are on private land and charge an entrance fee; it is a good idea to join an organized tour, since many of them are out of town. Bonito is a protected area, and the number of visitors to each site is limited. Places get booked up (and prices increase) in the Brazilian holiday season.

Rio da Prata is a stretch of almost transparent river water about 45 minutes' drive from Bonito. For the most part the river is only just over 1 meter (3 ft) deep, and floating downstream, brushing against sub-aqua flora, face to face with curious fish, makes you feel as if you have been dropped into a giant aquarium. When you do lift your head up out of the water you are likely to see capuchin monkeys and toucans in the trees above.

The Rio da Prata excursion includes river guides, and snorkel and wetsuit equipment. The Rio Sucuri trip is similar but shorter, and you are accompanied by a small boat. This is the better option for those who feel less comfortable in the water.

Pools and lakes

Balneiro Municipal is the local, natural swimming pool (a five-minute moto-taxi ride out of town) on the Rio Formoso. There are changing rooms and a café there, and the area is kept scrupulously clean.

At Estancia Mimosa (a 45-minute drive) you can hike through ciliar forest, stopping to bathe in waterfalls and natural pools.

Lagoa Azul is a lake inside a deep limestone cave that glows a brilliant blue when light from the cave's entrance is refracted in the limestone and magnesium. You can visit throughout daylight hours, but be careful: the descent can be slippery after rain. ❑

A gold prospector sifts his booty.

BELOW: coming up for air in the Caiman Ecological Reserve.

Tours and Lodges

Access to the Pantanal is usually from Corumbá, Campo Grande, or Cuiabá. Lodges are reached by a combination of paved and bumpy roads by four-wheel-drive in the dry season, or occasionally by light aircraft or boat in the wet months. Accommodation varies enormously, from hammocks slung beneath palapa roofs, to stylish, comfortable en suite cabins. Almost all lodges are full-board with three meals a day (but not drinks) and transport to and from the lodge included in the price. Two to three nights is recommended to make the most of the region, and lodges will include two tours a day, one early in the morning and the other late afternoon, when it is cooler and there is more chance of spotting wildlife. There is usually a jeep safari, a boat trip, a night safari, a horse ride, and a walk in the countryside.

Budget travellers can pick up a guide locally. On arrival at the airport or bus station in Corumbá, Campo Grande or Cuiabá there are usually people waiting to offer you a Pantanal tour. Be very careful what you pay for: standards vary hugely, and while you may not mind a few nights in a hammock, if your guide is not up to scratch your trip will certainly not be all it could be. To guarantee quality of accommodation and guides, your best bet is to find an all-inclusive trip at a reputable lodge. Some of the best are listed below.

From Campo Grande: **Pousada Aguape** is a delightful working cattle farm that has been in the family for 150 years. Lovely, simple cabins, a nice pool, fantastic food served buffet-style and friendly, English-speaking staff (tel: 67-3686 1036; www.aguape.com.br). **Refugio Ecologico Caiman** is a wildlife reserve, home to one of the most comfortable and tasteful lodges in the Pantanal, with immaculate cabins and great food. Tours are run by specialist bilingual guides. Thursday and Sunday pick-ups from Campo Grande (www.caiman.com.br). **Fazenda Rio Negro** is a traditional 1920s wooden farmhouse painted white and green. The simple, bright rooms are comfortable, and meals are taken on the back patio. The lodge is difficult to access by land, so you can expect to see richer, undisturbed wildlife here. Light aircraft fly from Campo Grande (one hour) (www.fazendarionnegro.com.br).

From Cuiabá: **Anaconda Tours**, in the town itself, at Avenida Isaac Póvoas 606, is very helpful for one- to three-day Pantanal tours, transportation, and airport transfers (tel: 65-3028 5990; www.anacondapantanal.com.br). The **Araras Lodge** is 132 km (82 miles) from Cuiabá (approximately two and a half hours by road, of which 32 km/20 miles is down a dirt track), and it has 19 lovely, rustic, en suite rooms in a fantastic setting (tel: 65-682 2800; www.araraslodge.com.br). **Hotel Porto Jofre** (245 km/152 miles from Cuiabá) is a more formal affair, with 26 comfortable concrete cabins, a good-sized pool and enclosed dining room. Access is by small plane or boat in the wet season, or by car. There are numerous motor boats for river trips and fishing (tel: 65-3637 1593; www.portojofre.com.br). **Pousada do Rio Mutum** comprises 16 neat, red-roofed chalets with en suite bathrooms and hot water, sheltered dining area and pool, set in relatively dense forest. The lodge is located at the point where the River Mutum merges with two lakes, so river otters are often seen (tel: 65-623 7022; www.pousadamutum.com.br).

From Corumbá: **Passo do Lontra** is a large lodge on stilts on the banks of the Miranda River, 120 km (75 miles) from Corumbá. Accommodation ranges from hammocks to simple rooms, and comfortable cabins with en suite bathrooms and hot water. There is a large indoor restaurant. The lodge specialises in river and fishing trips (tel: 67-3231 6569; www.passodolontra.com.br). ❑

RIGHT: taking it easy in a well-equipped lodge.

IGUAÇU FALLS

The Cataratas do Iguaçu are one of the natural wonders of the world, a place where you stand in awe of the power of nature, and they are high on the list of places most visitors to Brazil want to see

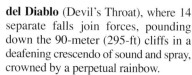

TIP
There are often touts waiting at the airport or the bus terminal, offering tours – so be careful what you pay for.

PRECEDING PAGES AND BELOW: the magnificent Iguaçu Falls.

Cataratas do Iguaçu ❶ (Iguaçu Falls) are one of the most powerful and extraordinary sights in the world. "Poor Niagara!" exclaimed Eleanor Roosevelt on first setting eyes on them. Indeed, the statistics are confounding: 275 individual falls – some of which are more than 80 metres (260 ft) high – plunge over a 3-km (2-mile) precipice in an unending wall of spray, discharging, at the peak, a cascade of more than 6.5 million litres (1.7 million gallons) of water per second. At the heart of this unforgettable scene is the **Garganta del Diablo** (Devil's Throat), where 14 separate falls join forces, pounding down the 90-meter (295-ft) cliffs in a deafening crescendo of sound and spray, crowned by a perpetual rainbow.

The falls are located on the Iguaçu River within a subtropical national park (a UNESCO World Heritage Site) on the Brazilian/Argentinian border, and can be reached from both countries. A half-day on the Brazilian side and a full day on the Argentinian side are recommended if you have the time.

Entrance to the Brazilian park is through a modern visitor center with a museum, shop, and ATM. From here, shuttle buses run to the falls (no cars are allowed within the park), making an initial stop at the **Macuco Safari** – an unmissable experience. Aboard sturdy, 20-seater inflatable boats you are able to see up close the incredible power of the water from the base of these majestic falls. You will inevitably get thoroughly drenched, so it is recommended that you wear a swimsuit, and take a plastic bag for your camera. The final stop on the shuttle bus takes you to the start of a 1-km (½-mile) wooden walkway, which gives a fantastic view of the Devil's Throat. When you reach the viewpoint at the end of the trail, you find yourself surrounded by the roaring water, the mist, and white foam that boils up all around the green of the jungle, and a 180-degree rainbow. It is an overwhelming (and extremely wet) experience.

Just before you reach the visitor center there's a helipad offering 10-minute rides over the falls for around US$60. Opposite is the Parque das Aves, an extensive bird park with huge aviaries housing, among others, the five species of toucan native to the region.

The Argentinian side

In order to cross to the Argentinian side – which you should certainly do – you must pass border control at Ponte Tancredo Neves (no visas required – passports compulsory). Though there may be short queues, the procedure is fairly painless. Over 80 percent of the falls belong to Argentina, and the tourist infrastructure there is more advanced. Trains leave every 15 minutes for two trailheads, both of which offer extraordinary close-up views of the falls. From the Lower Circuit – steeper and slightly longer than the Upper Circuit – you can take a boat to Isla San Martín, where a steep trail winds among some lesser-visited falls and pools. A second train continues to the Devil's Throat walkway for a look down into the pounding waters.

To see the full force of the falls, go to the park in January or February when the river is high. However, this is also when the humidity and heat are fierce, and the park is packed with tourists. From September to October, the water level is down but the temperature is pleasant and there are far fewer people. Whenever you go you are likely to get wet, so take a raincoat or poncho – many people just wear a swimsuit in the wet season.

Climate change is casting a worrying shadow over the region, however, and in July 2006 a continued drought saw the falls reduced to a trickle. Fortunately, rains brought water levels back to normal by late September.

Most hotels in **Foz do Iguaçu** ❷ can organise excursions or transport to and from the falls *(see page 350 for hotels, and page 366 for tour operators)*. Foz underwent a boom during the construction of the Itaipú dam and, because of its proximity to the falls, has a thriving tourist industry. The town is modern and uninspiring but has a good selection of medium-priced hotels and restaurants. ❑

TIP

There are parking facilities at the entrance to both visitor centers, and if you have your own transport you will simply have to pay the entrance fee to access the park.

BELOW: Foz de Iguaçu makes a good base for visiting the falls.

Itaipú Dam

Built between 1975 and 1984, the Itaipú dam was a joint construction project shared between Brazil and Paraguay, and is currently the world's largest hydroelectric plant. The dam itself is 8 km (5 miles) in length and produces in the region of 27 billion kwh each year, thus providing a quarter of Brazil's electricity (and 80 percent of Paraguay's). Despite this obvious benefit, the costs have been high, and not just in financial terms: the US$18-billion project has caused dramatic environmental damage, including the destruction of the homeland of indigenous people of the region, and a number of species of flora and fauna. Comprehensive, free tours of the dam are given Monday–Saturday, between 8am and 4pm.

THE SOUTHERN STATES

This subtropical, prosperous region of Brazil has some spectacular natural attractions, and a distinctive heritage, both European and gaucho

Map on page 324

The south of Brazil is different. Here, palm trees give way to pines, forested mountains are split by tranquil valleys, nature in general is more rugged, with roaring waterfalls and monumental canyons, and the temperate climate provides four distinct seasons, with cold weather, even snow, in the winter. The people, too, are different. Blue-eyed blonds replace the dark-featured types of the north and northeast, reflecting the deep European roots of the south.

The traditional breadbasket of Brazil, the south is a region of bounty. The farms and ranches of the states of **Paraná**, **Santa Catarina** and **Rio Grande do Sul** are the country's leading grain producers. Paraná is home to Brazil's most extensive pine forests, and it is one of the country's largest producers of soya and wheat. Across the flat pampas of Rio Grande do Sul wander Brazil's largest cattle herds. In recent years, the south has drawn from its agricultural wealth to invest in industry, and today the region is the center of Brazil's booming textile and footwear industries. Together, the south's rich earth and surging industrial power have given the inhabitants of its three states a standard of living second only to the state of São Paulo.

Paraná state and its capital

A combination of unleashed nature and pleasing urbanity are the trademarks of Paraná. It is here that you will find the wildly beautiful Iguaçu Falls *(see page 320)*.

Curitiba ❸, the capital of Paraná state, is an urban planner's dream, with ample green space, wide avenues, flower-decked pedestrian malls, and a relaxed and comfortable pace of life.

Founded by gold-seekers in the 17th century, Curitiba today is a bustling metropolis with a population of 1.7 million, located atop an elevated plateau at 900 meters (2,800 ft). In the latter half of the 19th century and the beginning of the 20th, Curitiba,

(see page 320)

Main attractions
CURITIBA
VILA VELHA STATE PARK
MORRETES
PARANAGUÁ
SANTA CATARINA
FLORIANÓPOLIS
PONTA DE GAROPABA
P. N. APARADOS DA SERRA

LEFT: Vila Velha rock formations.
BELOW: Florianópolis beach.

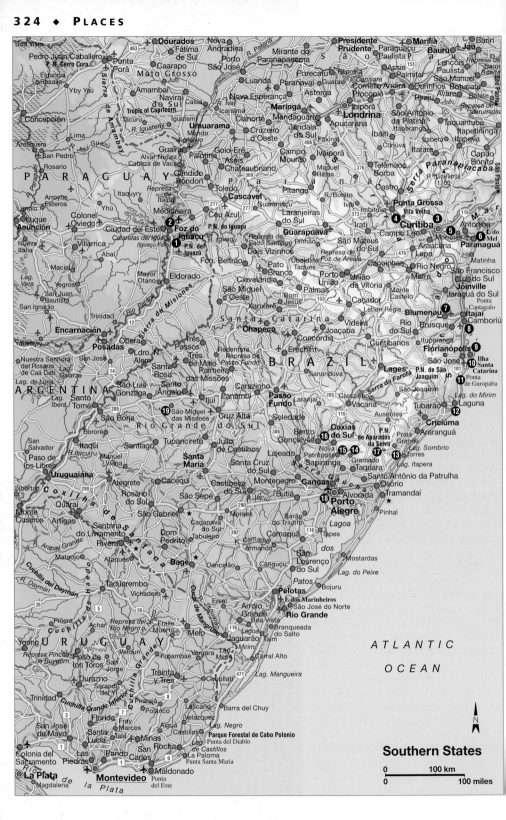

Southern States

| 0 | 100 km |

| 0 | 100 miles |

together with the state as a whole, received an infusion of immigrants from Europe (Italians, Poles, Germans, and Russians), which transformed the city into a European outpost in the heart of South America. The profusion of fair-haired people on the city's streets, together with Curitiba's annual ethnic festivals, are proof of the mixed origins of its citizens. The city's best-known ethnic neighborhood is **Santa Felicidade**, founded in 1878 by Italian immigrants and today home to Curitiba's finest *cantinas*, traditional, informal Italian eateries, among which Madalosso is the most popular.

Aside from its deserved reputation as Brazil's cleanest city, Curitiba is also a pedestrian's delight. A walking tour should begin at **Rua das Flores**, an extensive pedestrian mall in the city center, named after its beautiful flower baskets, and flanked by stores and boutiques as well as inviting cafés, restaurants, and pastry shops.

Near by is the historical center of Curitiba, concentrated in the blocks around Praça Garibaldi and the **Largo da Ordem**, the latter a cobblestoned square dominated by the **Igreja da Ordem Terceira de São Francisco das Chagas** (1737). This is the city's oldest church, known popularly as the Ordem Church. At night, the square comes alive with street musicians and outdoor cafés.

Every Sunday (9am–2pm) the historical center hosts a lively fair exhibiting good-quality local crafts, which is well worth a visit. There is more craftwork up the hill from the church in the **Garibaldi Mini Shopping**, which has handicrafts from all over Brazil, including woodcarvings, pottery, and leather and straw goods.

Back down the hill towards the Rua das Flores is the **Praça Tiradentes**, where Curitiba's neo-Gothic cathedral stands. Close to nearby **Praça Generoso Marques** is a walkway (with a glass roof) that is known as "Rua 24-Horas," where the shops, cafés, and bars stay open round the clock.

Rock formations

Some 80 km (50 miles) west of Curitiba is the area's second great natural attraction, the **Vila Velha State Park ❹** (open Wed–Mon 8am–4pm). Sited majestically atop the plateau, with the wind whipping around them, is a series of fantastical rock formations, carved over 350 million years by the wind and rain. There are 23 separate formations, each identified by the object, animal, or human form that it appears to represent. Close by is another of nature's mysteries: the Furnas Craters, two enormous holes sliced into the rocky ground to a depth of almost 100 meters (330 ft), half-filled with water. Take your swimsuit, because in one of these natural wells an elevator has been installed so visitors can descend 54 meters (180 ft) to water level.

A mini-train hustles among the formations, but most visitors find it hard to resist a long, contemplative walk through the near-mystical site, with its haunting mixture of shadows and rocks, made even more atmospheric by the sound of the wind.

TIP

A pleasant and easy way to see Curitiba is by hoping on and off the "Linha Turismo," a city bus that stops at 25 attractions spread across the city (Tues–Sun 9am–5.30pm). The first stop is at Praça Tiradentes, and the whole journey takes about 2½ hours.

BELOW: ornate glasshouse in Curitiba's botanical garden.

An unforgettable journey

Although Paraná is not known for its beaches, the train trip to the coast is one of the most breathtaking in Brazil. Completed in 1885, the railroad clings to the side of the mountains, at times threatening to march off into space as it passes over viaducts and through tunnels during the long, slow, three-hour descent to the coastal plain (for the best views sit on the left side of the train when going down). The trip offers an unmatched tour through the best-preserved section of Brazil's Atlantic rainforest, a richly green tangle of trees and undergrowth broken occasionally by waterfalls.

Two trains make this unforgettable journey. The conventional one leaves Curitiba station daily at 8.15am (Avenida Presidente Afonso Camargo 330; tickets from the office behind the bus station) and arrives three hours later in **Morretes ❺**, which is the best stop on the line (the final leg, Morretes to Paranaguá, does not have the same appeal as the rest of the journey and is only done by the Sunday train). The *litorina* (tourist train) leaves the same Curitiba station at 9.15am on weekends and holidays, and goes as far as Morretes. Reservations are highly recommended, especially in summer (Serra Verde Express, tel: 41-3323 4007; www.serra verdeexpress.com.br).

After such an adrenalin-packed journey, stomachs will be ready for a different sort of exploration, so it may be time to try the rich *barreado*, a local stew made of beef, pork, onions, and spices. The ingredients are mixed in a clay pot, which is then sealed with manioc flour and water, and cooked for 12 hours until the meat becomes very soft, and has a luscious and quite unique flavor. The traditional *barreado* is served with manioc flour and slices of bananas and oranges *(see margin note for recommended places to try this dish)*.

Paranaguá

Founded in 1648, **Paranaguá ❻** is one of Brazil's leading ports but, unfortunately, has preserved little of its historical past. What remains is located along **Rua XV de Novembro**, where

TIP

In Morretes the best *barreado* can be found at Armazem Romanus (Rua Visconde do Rio Branco 141), and in Paranaguá at Casa do Barreado (Rua José Antônio da Cruz 38) and Danubio Azul (Rua XV de Novembro 95).

BELOW LEFT: visiting Vila Velha.
RIGHT: the Paranaguá railroad.

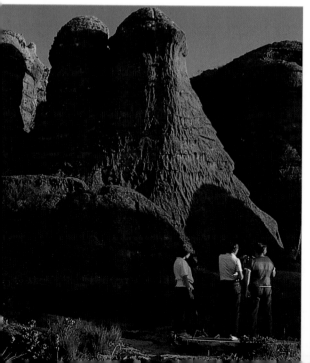

an **archeological museum** (open Tues–Fri 9am–noon, 1–6pm, Sat–Sun noon–6pm; admission charge) is housed in the town's grandest building (completed in 1755), formerly a Jesuit college. The museum contains a selection of indigenous artifacts and items from colonial life.

The area's primary attraction is the **Ilha do Mel**, an island paradise that is reached by a 20-minute boat ride from the town of **Pontal do Sul**, an hour's drive from Paranaguá (boats from Paranaguá also make the trip, but it takes two hours). The island is a nature reserve with natural pools, grottoes, and deserted beaches. It is also home to the ruins of an 18th-century fort and a 19th-century lighthouse. There are no cars on the island, and transportation is either by foot along the many paths or by fishermen's boats. Its primitive, unspoiled nature has made the Ilha do Mel a popular spot for campers, for whom a flashlight and insect repellent are essentials. Visitors may also stay in one of the rustic *pousadas* on the island. Pousada and Restaurant Fim da Trilha at Encantadas beach and Pousada das Meninas in Nova Brasília are both recommended for their location and charm.

The best option for the return trip to Curitiba is the **Graciosa Highway**, a winding road that cuts through the verdant forest with explosions of wild flowers along the route. From the viewpoints, you can catch glimpses of the old mule trail used by the original Portuguese settlers to climb the mountainside to Curitiba. Real adventurers can still make this trip.

Santa Catarina

Or you can continue down the coast from Paranaguá into Santa Catarina. The smallest of the southern states, **Santa Catarina** is also the most boisterous. Its German heritage is apparent in the Bavarian architecture in inland **Blumenau** ❼, home to South America's liveliest Oktoberfest, a three-week blow-out that attracts more

than a million visitors, making it Brazil's second-largest festival after Rio's Carnival.

Blumenau is also one of Brazil's main textile centers, and offers an excellent "direct-from-the-factory" opportunity for buying clothes and household linen. Try Hering factory store (Rua Bruno Hermann 1421) or the CIC shopping mall (Rua 2 de Setembro 1395).

But the state's real treasure is its coastline, with miles of unspoiled white-sand beaches. The northern coastal resort of **Camboriú** ❽ has a long crescent beach that is a near carbon copy of Rio's Copacabana, both for its landscape and its party atmosphere. During the summer holidays (December to February), Camboriú turns into a "Mercosul meeting point," where Argentinians, Paraguayans, and Uruguayans join Brazilians for weeks of sun, samba, and *caipirinhas*, the national drink.

Considered the capital that offers the best quality of life in the country, **Florianópolis** ❾ is the gateway to Santa Catarina Island. Before heading to the beaches, it is worth spending a

Cycling in the sun.

BELOW: participants in the Blumenau Oktoberfest.

TIP

The Ilha do Arvoredo, part of a biosphere reserve, has some of the best diving spots in the south of Brazil. Boats leave from Canasvieiras beach and take almost two hours to get to the island. Diving trips and courses can be arranged through the operators Acquanauta and Sea Divers in Canasvieiras.

BELOW: graceful Hercilio Luz Bridge, one of the largest suspension bridges in the world.

day or two exploring the island's history and culinary delights in Florianópolis. The best places to start are the old **Predio da Alfandega** (Customs Building; open Mon–Fri 9am–6.30pm, Sat 8am–12.30pm) on Avenida Paulo Fontes. Dating from 1875, it is now a craft market. The neighboring **Mercado Municipal** (open Mon–Fri 7am–7pm, Sat 7am–1.30pm) is where people meet to drink the excellent draft beer and eat *bolinhos de bacalhau* (salt-cod cakes) at Box 32.

Exploring the island

Ilha Santa Catarina ⑩ lies within an hour's drive from the city center, as it is linked to the mainland by the **Hercilio Luz Bridge**, one of the largest suspension bridges in the world. The island has 42 beaches, ranging from quiet coves to areas of roaring surf, and combines the aspects of a hectic capital with the delights of a laid-back fishing village. Here, life revolves around simple pleasures: swimming, sunbathing, eating, and drinking. The lifestyle, like the fish-based menu and

the accent of local people, is inherited from the Azorean immigrants who first arrived on the island in 1750.

It is a quick 17-km (10-mile) drive to **Santo Antônio de Lisboa**, the oldest and best-preserved Azorean village on the island. This is a great spot to watch the sunset, with the photogenic Hercilio Luz Bridge as a background.

Those in search of beach life during the day and a dance floor at night will find just what they want on the beaches to the north. They are well structured, with plenty of good hotels, restaurants, and shopping streets. Calm waters and a family atmosphere are found at Daniela beach or Lagoinha de Ponta das Canas. The most urbanized beaches are Jurere, Canasvieiras, and Ingleses, which are also favored by visiting Argentinians.

The northern shore is home to what is claimed to be the best beach resort in the country, the Costão do Santinho at **Praia do Santinho**. Good surf and beautiful people are to be found at Praia Mole and Joaquina, a world-famous surfing center that holds international competitions every year.

A few minutes away is the **Lagoa da Conceição**, a beautiful freshwater lake wedged between the island's mountain spine and the sea, with jet-ski and windsurfing facilities. Descendants of Azorean women still make lace in the traditional manner around the Rua das Rendeiras. There are lots of trendy stores, restaurants, and bars, some of them exceptional, such as the unpretentious **Um Lugar** (Rua Manuel Severino de Oliveira 371), which serves delicious, world-class gourmet seafood.

The island's southern beaches, such as Solidão, Naufragados and Lagoinha do Leste, are the most unspoiled and scenic. Many of them can be reached only by dirt roads or tracks that snake through some of the last stretches of preserved Atlantic forest left in the country. **Campeche** and **Armação** beaches are good choices for a day trip. Boats to Campeche Island leave from Armacão.

Near by is the colorful village of **Ribeirão da Ilha**, site of one of the first Azorean settlements on the island, and home to some of the best seafood restaurants. Ribeirão da Ilha's fishermen specialize in the cultivation of oysters, the highlight of local menus such as that at Ostradamus (Rodovia Baldicero Filomeno 7640) or its neighbor, Rancho Acoriano. After indulging the taste buds, take a walk round the village to enjoy the beautifully preserved Azorean architecture.

Southern beaches

Back on the mainland, the principal southern beaches are on the **Ponta de Garopaba ⓫** – Garopaba, neighboring Praia do Rosa (one of the most beautiful in the country), and Laguna. The largest concentration of cheerful, good-looking young Brazilians is found at Garopaba and Praia do Rosa. Surf shapes the local lifestyle, and the exceptional landscape of Praia do Rosa sets the scene for attractive little inns such as Quinta do Bucaneiro (Estrada Geral do Rosa s/n; www.bucanero.com.br), and Pousada Caminho do Rei (Caminho do Alto do Morro s/n; www.caminhodorei.com.br).

As Brazil's unofficial surfing capital, Garopaba became the headquar-

Porto Novo, at the southern end of Praia do Rosa, is the place to go fishing for tainhas (Brazilian mullet), which flourish in these waters.

BELOW: whale-watching trips can be very rewarding.

Whale-Watching

Between June and November the Garopaba and Praia do Rosa region takes on a distinctive role. It turns into a breeding site for hundreds of Southern Right Whales, which can be seen with their calves from the beach or upclose on a boat trip. Praia do Rosa is home to the conservation project Baleia Branca (White Whale; www.baleiafranca.org.br), created to study and to protect these special animals. The Vida Sol e Mar Resort in Praia do Rosa organizes whale-watching trips from Garopaba beach, as part of a package. Trips on 9-meter (30-ft) boats last about two hours and are accompanied by a biologist from the Institute. Check the Brazilian Incentive and Tourism website for more information: www.bitourism.com.

Wine Country

Although wine production came comparatively late to Brazil, it has taken a firm hold in the country – at least in the south. Brazil's wine industry is concentrated in the coastal mountains of Rio Grande do Sul, which is responsible for 90 percent of national production.

The grapes and the wines produced from them were first brought to Rio Grande by Italian immigrants, who began arriving in the 1880s. Since then, their descendants have carried on the tradition. Today, the cities and small farms of this area still retain an air of Italy about them. Cheeses and salamis hang from the ceilings of the prized wine cellars of the region's small farmers, many of whom make their own wine, cheese, and, of course, pasta. This culinary combination is also found in the area's restaurants, which are heavily dominated by Italian cuisine *(see page 335 for some recommendations)*.

The starting point for a visit to Brazil's wine country is **Caxias do Sul**, a booming industrial city tucked away in the mountains. Caxias hosts the region's Grape Festival, held every other year in February/ March. A long party during which the wine flows freely, this is well worth trying to catch if you are in the area at this time of year. The leading vineyard in Caxias is the **Château Lacave** (on the BR-116 Km 143; open Mon–Sat 9.30am–8.30pm, Sun 10am– 5pm), with its headquarters in a kitsch mock-European castle complete with drawbridge and towers.

The areas around the principal cities are scattered with *cantinas* – local wineries that offer visits to their vineyards (January to March), and to their wine-production and storage areas, along with tastings and sales of wine and local products. Some of the *cantinas* also have restaurants. Zanrosso and Tonet between Caxias do Sul and Flores da Cunha are highly recommended.

More wine country tasting treats are to be found in and around **Garibaldi** and **Bento Gonçalves**, the recognized capitals of the wine-growing region. On the main road, just outside Garibaldi, is **Maison Chandon** (guided visits Mon–Fri 8am–11.30am, 1–5.30pm, Sat 9.30am–3pm), Brazil's leading producer of *espumantes*, the local champagne regarded as the best product of the Brazilian viniculture. Do try to visit if you can.

Other important producers of *espumante* are Georges Aubert, Peterlongo, and De Lantier. Continue on to Bento Gonçalves for a visit to the **Cooperativa Vinícola Aurora** (Rua Olavo Bilac 500; open Mon–Sat 8.15am–5pm, Sun 8.30–11.30am). Bento is also home to several smaller, excellent producers, including **Salton**, **Vinícola Miolo**, and **Casa Valduga**. They all offer guided visits with generous tasting sessions at the end. Some, such as Casa Valduga (access via Km 216 of RS-470 Highway; www.casavalduga.com.br) have built attractive little hotels in the grounds of the vineyards to accommodate overly enthusiastic guests.

The leading Brazilian vineyards began to invest in quality in the mid-1970s because of the growing local demand for good wines. Using imported varieties of grapes, increasingly high-quality products started to appear on the market over the next 10 years. While the modernization process isn't yet complete, with most of the winemakers still adhering to the old tradition of oak barrels, some are stepping into the high-technology world of stainless-steel vats, which has substantially improved the quality of Brazilian wines, especially the whites. So marked is the improvement that several brands are now exported, mainly to the US, and it is expected that Brazil's wines will soon be challenging those of Chile and Argentina for pre-eminence in South America. ❑

LEFT: working in a Rio Grande do Sul vineyard.

ters of the top surf-gear manufacturers. One of the best is Mormaii, whose factory store can be found at the central Avenida João Orestes de Araujo.

The second-oldest town in the state, **Laguna ⑫** combines history, surf, and gorgeous beaches. Founded in 1676 as an outpost of the Portuguese crown, charged with protecting the region from the advance of Spanish forces, the little town continued to see bloodshed during the 1800s as a main center of the Revolucão Farroupilha, a Southern States revolutionary movement against Portuguese dominance.

The main beach of Mar Grosso is built up, but Farol de Santa Marta, 18 km (11 miles) out of town, is a really beautiful spot.

Gaucho state

The southernmost state of Brazil, Rio Grande do Sul is also the most distinct. Bordering Uruguay and Argentina, it has developed a culture of its own, a mixture of Portuguese and Spanish together with Italian and German. The unique gaucho culture is the trademark of Rio Grande do Sul. Here, cowboys roam the southern pampas with their distinctive flat hats and chinstraps, their baggy pantaloon trousers, red neckerchiefs and leather boots, and the symbol of gaucho-land, the *chimarrão*, a gourd of hot *mate* tea.

Machismo runs strong, and a man is definitely a man, a heritage of the state's violent history. More than any other in Brazil, Rio Grande do Sul has seen the ravages of war. In the 18th and 19th centuries it served as a battleground for warring armies, revolutionaries, adventurers, and Amerindians, who marched back and forth across its grasslands, leaving a bloody stamp that has been transformed into legend.

Proud and boastful, today's gauchos have re-channeled their warrior fury. Rio Grande is Brazil's leading manufacturer of leather footwear, and has recently been producing the country's finest wines. In addition, vast herds of cattle and sheep today graze on its former battlefields, providing wool for the south's textile factories and beef for the succulent *churrasco*, the traditional Brazilian barbecue.

The landscape of Rio Grande do Sul is as rugged and uncompromising as its inhabitants. The state's 450-km (280-mile) coastline is marked by pounding surf and rocky promontories, the best-known of which are located in the resort city of **Torres ⑬**.

The Serra Gaúcha

While Santa Catarina should not be missed for its beaches, Rio Grande's appeal is a few miles inland at its most famous mountain range, the **Serra Gaúcha**. Pine trees, lush green valleys, waterfalls, shimmering rivers, and awesome canyons distract the eyes of visitors as they wind their way through the *serra*. It was to this idyllic setting that thousands of German and Italian immigrants flocked in the late 19th century, establishing their homesteads along the valley floors. Today, many of the original stone and wood houses still stand as testimony to the hardy nature of the transplanted gauchos.

A watchful southerner and his gun.

BELOW: dancers wearing traditional gaucho clothes.

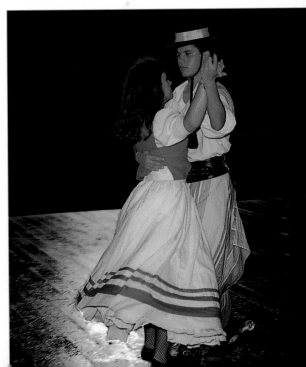

The crown jewels of the Serra Gaúcha are the twin cities of **Gramado**  and **Canela**. Both are slow-moving, Swiss-style mountain resorts where the residents of Brazil's non-stop southern cities escape the rush and indulge in upmarket shopping, fondue-based restaurants, copious amounts of chocolate, and cosy inns and chalets tucked away beneath the pines. Good choices are Casa da Montanha (Avenida Borges de Medeiros 3166; www.casadadamontanha.com.br) in Gramado, or Pousada Cravo e Canela (Rua Tenente Manoel Correa 144; www.pousadacravoecanela.com.br) located in Canela.

Signs to wineries in the Serra Gaúcha.

Gramado hosts a prestigious Brazilian and Latin American film festival every August, but the area's main attraction is the **Caracol State Park** (open daily 8.30am–5.30pm; admission charge), 9 km (5 miles) from Canela via Estrada do Caracol, where the dramatic **Caracol Falls** plunge 130 meters (400 ft).

BELOW: vines stretch out as far as the eye can see.

Some 30 minutes' drive away from Gramado and Canela is the small town of **Nova Petrópolis**, where the

area's German heritage is prominent. In addition to the Bavarian architecture of the community's homes and public buildings, Nova Petrópolis's roots are visible in the **Immigration Park** (Avenida 15 de Novembro; open daily 8am–7pm; free), highlighted by a reproduction of a German colonial settlement of the 19th century.

The park also contains a bandstand and *biergarten* that are the center of festivities in January, February, and July, when the small hotels and inns of Nova Petrópolis, as well as Gramado and Canela, fill up with tourists.

Bento Gonçalves, 48 km (30 miles) to the north, was founded in 1875 by Italian immigrants. The **Museu do Imigrante** (Rua Erny Dreher 127; open Tues–Fri 8–11.15am, 1.30–5.15pm, Sat 1–5pm, Sun 9am–noon; admission charge) documents its history. Today, Bento Gonçalves is the largest producer of fine wines in the country, as well as home to its only enology university. Tours and tastings are available at a number of *adegas* (vineyards) in and around Bento Gonçalves (*see page 330 for more*

information). There is an annual wine festival in February and March in the nearby city of **Caxias do Sul**.

Brazil's "Grand Canyon"

The area's premier attraction, located three hours' journey away from Bento Gonçalves, between the towns of Cambara do Sul and Praia Grande, is the **Aparados da Serra National Park** ⑰ (open Wed–Sun 9am–5pm; admission charge), about 120 km (75 miles) from Canela. The view is well worth the effort of getting there, for suddenly, in the midst of pasture and forest, the earth seems to open up, revealing the enormous **Itaimbézinho Canyon**. Some 700 meters (2,200 ft) deep, 7 km (4 miles) long and in places more than 2 km (1 mile) wide, the canyon is the largest in Latin America. There are walking trails and horseback riding tracks running through the beautiful national park.

Unlike North America's Grand Canyon, located in the dry southwest, Itaimbézinho impresses not simply because of its extraordinary size but also because of the varied shadings of green that mark it out, from the light-green pasture to the deep green of its forested cliffs. Waterfalls cascade down the canyon's sides.

Porto Alegre

The capital city of this southernmost state is **Porto Alegre** ⑱, a modern, commercial conurbation with a population of 1.4 million – the largest city of the south. Located near the coast at the northern end of the Lagoa dos Patos, the city can be used as a jumping-off point for sojourns into the state's other areas. Gramado and Canela, the wine country and Rio Grande do Sul's beaches can all be visited in day trips from the capital city. Trips to the missions region and the pampas, however, require two days at least *(see margin note for information)*. Porto Alegre is also a stopover on the land route from Brazil to Argentina and Uruguay.

As befits its status as the capital of a beef-producing state, Porto Alegre offers excellent leather goods sold in downtown boutiques, plus steak houses where you will be treated to the real

TIP

Missiotur at the Turis Hotel (Rua Antônio Manoel 726) in Santo Angelo organizes two-day tours of the Brazilian missions, and longer trips that include the Paraguayan and Argentinian ones. For more information visit www.rotamissoes. com.br.

BELOW: the enormous Itaimbézinho Canyon.

TIP

In the cities and the surrounding *estancias* (ranches) of the Campanha, Portuguese and Spanish are intermingled in the colloquial language of the frontier.

BELOW: some of the cattle that produce such excellent beef.

mouth-watering Brazilian *churrasco*. Although far removed from the gaucho lifestyle, Porto Alegre provides visitors with a close-up look at their traditional music and dances at a number of popular nightspots.

The missions

The area known as the missions lies due west of the Serra Gaúcha. Here, in the 17th century, with the authorization of the Portuguese and Spanish kings, Jesuit priests organized Guaraní tribespeople into a series of settlements. The Jesuit fathers controlled the region for nearly a century, establishing centers of sophisticated culture as well as religion, and overseeing the construction of Amerindian cities, some of which had 5,000 inhabitants.

In 1750 the Treaty of Madrid solved the dispute between Portugal and Spain regarding the limit of their respective domains, and Portugal received the missions region. The Guaraní did not recognize the treaty, and the relationship between the Jesuits and Portugal deteriorated fast. The Guaranitica War between the

Guaraní and Portuguese forces lasted until 1756, when the missions were attacked in force and overwhelmed. The Jesuits were expelled, and almost all the Amerindians were killed.

Today, the ruins of the missions, notably **São Miguel das Missoes** ⑲, designated a World Heritage Site, stand in dramatic solitude on the plain, all that is left of a once thriving Amerindian community. Visitors to the mission region should stay in the city of **Santo Angelo**, 53 km (32 miles) from São Miguel, from where day trips may be made to the ruins. Every evening São Miguel mission offers a spectacular sound-and-light show, portraying the history of the area.

Cowboy country

Across the windswept prairies of the **Campanha**, the legendary pampas, the gaucho cowboy still rides herd over the cattle and sheep that first brought wealth to Rio Grande do Sul. And *gaucho* tradition and culture are preserved in the southern cities that still seem to ring with the sound of cannon fire from the battles of the past. ❑

RESTAURANTS

Curitiba

Boulevard
Rua Voluntários da Pátria 539, Center
Tel: 41-3224 8244
Open: L&D Mon–Fri, D only Sat.
Boulevard is one of the city's top restaurants, offering a varied menu of reliably good international and Brazilian favorites. $$$

Capoani Café
Rua Comendador Araujo 906, Batel
Tel: 41-3018 6573
Open: L&D Tues–Sat, L only Sun.
Brazilian and international cuisine, always well-cooked and well-presented. $$

Durski
Avenida Jaime Reis 254, São Francisco
Tel: 41-3225 7893
Open: L&D Tues–Sat, L only Sun.
Durski serves a real Ukrainian feast – a cuisine that is well worth becoming familiar with. $$

Famiglia Caliceti Ristorante Bologna
Alameda Dr Carlos de Carvalho 1367, Batel
Tel: 41-3223 7102
Open: L&D Mon, Wed–Sat, L only Sun.
In a pretty house with a log fire and a winter garden, the Bologna has long been respected for its excellent pasta dishes. $$$

Madalosso
Avenida Manoel Ribas 5875, Santa Felicidade
Tel: 41-3372 2121
Open: L&D Tues–Sat, L only Sun.
This claims to be the largest restaurant in Brazil, and is a popular stop with visitors. Not surprisingly, given it can seat 4,800 and has 52 chefs. It offers a wide-ranging set menu with pasta, salads, chicken, liver, risotto, and fried polenta. Not for intimate dinners. $

Scavollo
Rua Emiliano Perneta 924, Batel
Tel: 41-3225 2244
Open: D only daily.
Excellent pizza and other Italian favorites, and very good value. $

Porto Alegre

Al Dente
Rua Mata Bacelar 210, Auxiliadora
Tel: 51-3343 1841
Open: D only Mon–Sat.
The best Italian food in town; the highlight is the home-made pasta, which comes in many varieties, and with many sauces. $$

Barranco
Avenida Protásio Alves 1578, Petrópolis
Tel: 51-3331 6172
Open: L&D daily.
An excellent, well-known barbecue house with an attractive outdoor area where tables are set under the trees. $$

Le Bateau Ivre
Rua Tito Livio Zambecari 805, Mont Serrat
Tel: 51-3330 7351
Open: D Mon–Sat.
The Mediterranean influence is strong here, in a restaurant that has recently been elected one of the best three in town. $$

Pampulhinha
Avenida Benjamin Constant 1641, Floresta
Tel: 51-3342 2503
Open: L&D Mon–Sat (closed Feb).
This is a top choice for fish and all kinds of seafood, with the *bacalhau* (salt cod) a particular favorite with local residents. $$

Steinhaus
Rua Coronel Paulino Teixeira 415, Rio Branco
Tel: 51-3330 8661
Open: D only Mon–Sat.
This is considered by many descendants of the German immigrant population to be the city's best German restaurant – and they should know. Regional and national Brazilian dishes are also on the menu. Good attentive service. $$

PRICE CATEGORIES
Prices for a two-course meal for two. Wine costs around US$20 a bottle.
$ = under $40
$$ = $40–70
$$$ = $70–100

RIGHT: enjoying a fish stew al fresco.

TRAVEL TIPS

TRANSPORTATION

GETTING THERE AND GETTING AROUND

Brazil is a very big country – larger than the continental United States, slightly smaller than Europe. The distance from top to bottom is similar to that from London to Central Africa. So even if places look close on the map – beware. Trying to fit in too much can mean spending your vacation on buses or in airport lounges.

Compounding your problem, moving around Brazil can be a slow business. Away from the main highways, bad road conditions can drag out journey times; and inside big cities, traffic can be a nightmare. São Paulo to Rio is just 430 km (270 miles), so it's four easy hours away on a good highway, but if you drive from the far side of one to the far side of the other at the wrong time of day, the urban crawl can almost double that time.

Most middle-class Brazilians insist on driving in town, even though some public transport may be quicker – for example, city Metro systems and buses that use priority lanes. Of course, public transport at rush hour is often impossibly crowded.

GETTING THERE

By Air

Many airlines offer international services to and from Brazil with a variety of routes (see page 340). Most incoming flights head for São Paulo and then stop at Rio de Janeiro, Brasília, Salvador, Fortaleza, and Recife on the northeastern coast, and the northern cities of Belém and Manaus on the Amazon River. Direct international flights link Brazil with both the east and west coasts of the United States, as well as with Florida and Canada, major cities in Europe, South America, Japan, and several African cities.

Flight time from the US is nine hours from New York, slightly less from Miami, and 12 hours from Los Angeles. Flights from Europe take 11–12 hours. Almost all international flights are overnight, so you arrive in the early morning.

There is a variety of special low-cost package deals, some of them real bargains. A travel agent will tell you what is available and make arrangements at no extra cost to you. See opposite for details on Brazilian air passes, which must be purchased outside Brazil.

Upon arrival, the airports have ATMS, currency-exchange facilities and information posts to help you find transportation or make a connecting flight.

By Ship

There is no regular ocean passenger service to Brazil, but it is possible to get there by boat. Costa (tel: 11-3217 8500) is a major operator that runs cruises up and down the Atlantic coast of South America during the European winter, and will take on transatlantic passengers when the ships return. You can cruise to Brazil from Europe with Island Cruises (UK tel: 0870 850 3927): two weeks from Mallorca via the Atlantic islands, then another week stopping at points along the coast to Rio. Several round-the-world cruise ships call at Brazilian ports, and reservations can be made for the trip to Brazil only. Special cruises travel up the Amazon River or visit Rio at Carnival time.

By Bus

Long-distance bus services run between a few of the larger Brazilian cities and major cities in neighboring South American countries, including Asunción (Paraguay), Buenos Aires (Argentina), Montevideo (Uruguay), and Santiago (Chile). The highway from Manaus to Caracas has recently been paved, allowing a regular daily bus service. While undoubtedly a good way to take in the landscape, remember that the distances are great, and you may find youself on a bus for several days and nights at a time. They are usually of a high standard, though, in many cases providing toilets, food, and even almost fully reclining seats.

Specialist Tours

A variety of individual and group tours to Brazil is available. Some are all-inclusive packages with transportation, food and lodgings, excursions, and entertainment all arranged for you; some include only air transportation and hotel accommodation. There are also special-interest tours that include international travel to and from Brazil. These include boat trips on the Amazon River, fishing, and wildlife (including birdwatching) tours to the Pantanal, Mato Grosso in the center-west, and Carnival tours to Rio, Salvador, or Recife.

If you aren't on a tour where everything is planned, you might want to go on one of the readily available city sightseeing tours, boat outings to nearby islands, day trips to mountain and beach resort areas, and evening entertainment tour groups that take in a show. If you ask your hotel reception to arrange a tour (best avoided) they will take a hefty commission, and often not give impartial advice.

Longer excursions can also be easily arranged once you are in Brazil – from Rio or São Paulo, for example, it is easy to get on a tour to the Amazon or Pantanal, take a day trip by plane to Brasília or the Iguaçu Falls, or join a tour of the northeast or the colonial towns of Minas Gerais. However, in the peak season there may be a wait, as these excursions do get fully booked. Ocean cruising up and down the coast has grown rapidly in recent years, with a number of companies offering a variety of destinations. CVC (www.cvc.com.br), a major Brazilian travel agent and tour operator, normally has a large selection available, though it is best to book ahead for peak seasons. Language may be a problem, so if booking a local cruise you may wish to inquire in advance about English-speaking staff on board (also see page 292).

ABOVE: Rio airport bus.

Some of the top-class hotels will send a driver to pick you up – it's best to arrange for this service when making your room reservation.

GETTING AROUND

On Arrival

At the airport, take a special taxi, for which you pay in advance at a fixed rate and can use credit cards. There are fewer communication problems, no misunderstanding about the fare, and if the driver takes you the "scenic route" you won't be charged extra. If you take a regular taxi, check out the fares posted for the official taxis so that you will have an idea of what is a normal rate.

An efficient special airport bus service will also take you into town. The route includes stops at the larger hotels. Inquire at the airport information desk.

River Trips

Local boat tours and excursions can be taken in coastal and river-side cities. There are also longer trips available. Amazon River boat trips may last a day or two, or a week or more (see page 288). These range from luxury floating hotels to more rustic accommodations. Boat trips can also be taken on the São Francisco River in the northeast and in the Pantanal marshlands of Mato Grosso, popular for the incomparable birds and wildlife. A lot of towns have local ferry services across bays and rivers and to islands.

Domestic Flights

Because Brazil is such an enormous country, it has a good network of domestic flights. The airline industry in Brazil has been going through significant reorganization in recent years. Varig has lost pride of place as the largest airline and went through a difficult bankruptcy process, but survived to resume operations with a smaller fleet. Main national operators are now TAM, Gol and Varig, with BRA, Ocean Air, and Pantanal offering budget or regional services. All of the larger lines fly extensive routes throughout the country and have ticket counters at the airports and ticket offices in most cities. At smaller airports in the more remote cities, these may only be manned shortly before a flight.

Tickets can also be purchased at travel agencies and often at hotels, and reservations can be made by phone or on the airlines' websites. Information is usually provided in English as well as Portuguese. Airlines used to offer a toll-free service, but most now charge a premium rate. When planning your route, you will find that it may be easier to travel in one direction than the other. In the case of Varig, most internal flights go clockwise around the country, especially in the Amazon. If you try to plan your itinerary anti-clockwise, you may find yourself having to use some very indirect routes, or being severely limited as to when you can travel.

Deregulation means that on some routes, flying is cheaper than

traveling by bus. Discounts of up to 60 percent can be obtained for most internal flights. Travel agents in Brazil can give you details (also see box on air passes below). The large airlines also operate shuttle services between Rio and São Paulo (with flights every half-hour), Rio and Brasília (flights every hour), and Rio and Belo Horizonte (usually about 10 flights per day). The Rio to São Paulo shuttle between the airports of Santos Dumont (Rio) and Congonhas (São Paulo) is not available on the air pass. On domestic flights checked baggage is limited to 20 kg (44 lb), and internationally accepted norms apply for hand luggage.

Brazilian Airlines

Two major Brazilian airlines currently operate both domestic and international flights: TAM and Varig. These, plus their subsidiaries and several budget airlines, are listed below.

Varig
Tel: 11-4003 7000
www.varig.com.br
Nordeste
Tel: 0800-992 004
www.nordeste.com
Rio-Sul
Tel: 11-3272 2590
www.rio-sul.com
Trip
Tel: 0300-789 8747
www.voetrip.com
BRA
Tel: 11-5090 9313/11-3017 5454
Gol
Tel: 0800-701213
www.voegol.com.br
TAM
Tel: 11-4002 5700
www.tam.com.br

Air Passes

Air passes are a good idea if you are going to be traveling around the country a great deal. Ask your travel agent about them, as they must be purchased outside Brazil. The cost depends on the number of flights, the season, and the region they cover. They are valid for 21 days and allow you to visit four or five cities (not including your starting point in Brazil). Each pass is only available for the flights of the issuing airline. Extra stops can be purchased. However, because bargain flights can be bought from the "no-frills" airlines now, air passes do not represent quite such good value as they used to be.

Flight Reconfirmation

You must *always* reconfirm your domestic and international flights by telephone, or in person at an airline office, at least 48 hours beforehand. If you don't, you risk being "bounced" onto a later flight.

You do not have to reconfirm with the major international carriers, but it is as well to arrive early at the airport for your flight during high season, as they have been known to be overbooked.

Ocean Air
Tel: 11-5090 9236
www.oceanair.com.br
Pantanal Linhas Aéreas
Tel: 11-5044 9070
www.voepantanal.com.br

International Airlines

Most of the major international airlines have headquarters in São Paulo. Main contact numbers are:
Aerolíneas Argentinas
Alameda Santos 2441, 14th Floor
Tel: 11-6445 3806
www.aerolineas.com.ar
Aeroperu
Rua da Consolação 293,
1st Floor – Centro
Tel: 11-257 4866
Air Canada
Avenida Paulista 949,
13th Floor
Tel: 11-3254 6630
Air France
Avenida Chedid Jafet 222,
Block B, 2nd Floor

Tel: 11-3049 0900/6445 2211/
0800-880 3131
Aeroporto de Guarulhos
Tel: 11-6445 2211
Alitalia
Avenida Paulista 777, 2nd Floor
Tel: 11-2171 7610/
3191 8706/0800-770 2344
Aeroporto de Guarulhos
Tel: 11-6445-3791
www.alitalia.com.it
American Airlines
Rua Araújo 216, 9th–10th Floors
Tel: 11-4502 4000/
6445 3568/6445 3508
www.avianca.com
Avianca
Avenida Washington Luis 7059
Tel: 11-2176 1111/2240 4413;
0800-724 4472
Aeroporto de Guarulhos
Tel: 11-6445 3798
www.aerolineas.com.ar
British Airways
Alameda Santos 745, 7th Floor
Tel: 11-3145 9700/
0800-176144
www.britishairways.com
Canadian
Avenida Araújo 216, 2nd Floor
Tel: 11-259 9066
Aeroporto de Guarulhos
Tel: 11-6445 2462
Continental Airlines
Rua da Consolação 247, 13th Floor
Tel: 0800-554 777
Aeroporto de Guarulhos
tel: 11-2122 7500
Delta Airlines
Rua Marquês de Itu 61, 12th Floor
Tel: 11-3225-9120/
0800-221 121
Aeroporto de Guarulhos
Tel: 11-4003 21221/6445 3926

Ibéria
Rua Araújo 216, 3rd Floor
Tel: 11-3218 7130/3218 7140
Aeroporto de Guarulhos
Tel: 11-6445 2060
Japan Airlines
Avenida Paulista 542,
3rd Floor – Paraíso
Tel: 11-2288 6121
Aeroporto de Guarulhos
Tel: 11-3175 2270/6445 2340
KLM
Avenida Chedid Jafat 222, Block B
tel: 11-309 0000/
0800-880 1818
Aeroporto de Guarulhos
Tel: 11-6445 2011
Korean Airlines
Avenida Paulista 1842, 5th Floor, Cj.
58 – Ed. Cetenco Plaza Torre Norte
Tel: 11-283 2399
Aeroporto de Guarulhos
Tel: 11-6445 2840
Lan Chile
Rua da Consolação 247, 12th Floor
Tel: 11-2121 9020
Aeroporto de Guarulhos
Tel: 11-6445 2824
Lloyd Aéreo Boliviano
Avenida São Luís 72, Centro
Tel: 11-258 8111
Aeroporto de Guarulhos
Tel: 11-6445 2425
Lufthansa
Rua Gomes de Carvalho 1356,
2nd Floor – Itaim Bibi
Tel: 11-3048 5800
Aeroporto de Guarulhos
Tel: 11-6445 3906
South African Airlines
Alameda Itú, 852, 1st Floor
Tel: 11-3065 5115/
0800-118 383
TAP
Praça José Gaspar 134
Tel: 11-2131 1200/0800-707 7787
Aeroporto de Guarulhos
Tel: 11-6445 2150
United Airlines
Avenida Paulista 777, 9th/10th Floor
Tel: 11-3145 4200/0800-162 323
Aeroporto de Guarulhos
Tel: 11-6445 3283

Trains

Except for crowded urban commuter railways, trains are not a major form of transportation in Brazil, and rail links are minimal. There are a few train trips, however, which are tourist attractions in themselves, either because they are so scenic or because they run on antique steam-powered equipment. Their schedules can be rather erratic, so check carefully before going to catch one of these trains.

In the southern state of Paraná, the 110-km (66-mile) Curitiba–

BELOW: : the São Paulo metro is efficient, but usually crowded.

Paranaguá railroad is famous for spectacular mountain scenery *(see page 326)*. The first part of the trip, to Morretes, is the most beautiful.

A return trip can be done in a day. Bear in mind that you may not see much on a cloudy day.

In the state of Minas Gerais, antique steam locomotives haul passengers the 12 km (7 miles) between São João del Rei and Tiradentes on a narrow-gauge railway from Friday to Sunday, and holidays *(see pages 212–13)*.

Long-Distance Buses

Comfortable, on-schedule bus services are available between all major cities, and even to several other South American countries. Remember that distances are great and bus rides can be long – in other words, several days. But you could break up a long journey with a stop along the way.

On most routes there are three classes available. You can take a regular bus, with upholstered, reclining seats; an executive bus, with more comfortable seats; or the top-rate sleeper *(leito)* bus, which has wider and fully reclining seats with footrests, as well as coffee and soft drinks on board.

On some routes, there may be just one bus per day (such as the Rio–Belém route, a 52-hour trip) or just one or two per week. Try to buy your ticket in advance through a travel agent or at the bus station.

There is a local bus service to the smaller, more isolated towns. This is quite a different experience and will leave you with no doubts that you are in a still developing country. Almost always overcrowded, buses bump along dirt roads, picking up passengers who wait along the roadside, often with large bundles

Daylight Robbery

Be on guard against robberies on crowded buses, which occur frequently, even in broad daylight. If you are bent on riding the regular city buses, try at least to avoid the rush hour, when passengers on certain lines are packed tighter than the proverbial sardines in a can.

Don't carry valuables, keep your shoulder bag in front of you, and your camera inside a bag. Avoid calling attention to yourself by speaking loudly in a foreign language. In other words, be discreet.

they are taking to market. Those who travel standing up – often for three to four hours or more – are charged the same as those who paid for a numbered seat. For the visitor, it may be a new experience, but you certainly have to admire the endurance and patience of the people for whom this precarious system is the only form of getting around.

South American Experience is a new service that allows visitors to arrange bus trips in advance or as part of a fly-drive package. A flexible pass allows you to get on or off at stops within Rio state. English-speaking staff will arrange accommodations and act as guides en route. The two main routes are "Costa Verde", taking in the islands of Angra do Reis and historic Parati before heading inland, and "Route Sol", which takes in the same sites, but with extra stops at Búzios and the surfing spot of Saquarema. Contact South American Experience, Rua Raimundo Correa 36A, Copacabana. Tel: 21-2548 8813; www.southamericaexperience.com.

City Buses

Since just a small percentage of Brazilians can afford cars, public transport is used a great deal. Some larger cities have special air-conditioned buses connecting residential areas to the central business district, including routes from airports and bus stations that swing by many of the larger hotels. You will be handed a ticket as you board. Take a seat and an attendant will come around to collect your fare, which will be extremely modest by North American and most European standards.

Your hotel may be helpful in providing information about bus routes, but most hotels discourage tourists from riding anything but special buses.

The regular city buses are very cheap. Get on (often quite a high step up) and after paying the "cobrador," who will give you change, move through the turnstile. Try to have your fare handy – several people may board at your stop and all have to get through the turnstile before they can sit down. This is also a favorite bottleneck for pick-pockets who can jump out the back door as the bus takes off, so be alert to what's going on around you.

If you travel standing up, be sure to hold on tight. Some bus drivers (especially in Rio) can be very inconsiderate, jamming on the brakes

(see page 326)

Travel Translated

Entrada = Entrance
Saída = Exit
Unitário = Single
Ida e volta = Return/Round trip

suddenly, careening around corners at full tilt, etc. Signal when you want to get off by pulling the cord (some buses have buttons).

The Metro

Rio de Janeiro and São Paulo have excellent, though not extensive, subway services, with bright, clean, air-conditioned cars. Maps in the stations and in each car help you find your way without needing to communicate in Portuguese.

Lines radiate from the city center, and the service is further extended by bus links, often with train-bus combination tickets. Subway extension bus lines are marked *integração*.

São Paulo has four lines, two of them crossing underneath the Praça da Sé at the city's heart. The north–south Line 1 (blue) connects Tucuruvi and Jabaquara; Line 2 (green) extends from Vila Madalena to Imigrantes; the east–west Line 3 (red) runs from Barra Funda to Itaquera; Line 4 (yellow) goes from Estação da Luz to Vila Sônia. They run from 4.40am–midnight and there are stops at the inter-city bus stations and bus link-ups to the Guarulhos International Airport.

Rio's two lines reach out from downtown as far south as Siqueira Campos station, and to the north as far as Irajá, with stops near the Sambódromo and Maracanã soccer stadium.

The Rio subway operates Monday–Saturday 5am–midnight and Sunday 7am–11pm.

Taxis

Taxis are probably the best way for visitors to get around in the cities. Of course, it's easy to get "taken for a ride" in a strange city. Whenever possible, take a taxi from your hotel, where a member of staff can inform the driver where you want to go.

Radio taxis are slightly more expensive, but safer and more comfortable. Although the drivers of the cabs you flag down on the street won't rob you, some occasionally try to overcharge or take you the long way around. Try to find out the normal fare for a given destination – most trips will be just a few dollars. Airport

ABOVE: checking bus times at Rio de Janeiro bus station.

taxis charge high rates by Brazilian terms, but you will probably still find fares relatively low compared to North America or Europe.

In the street, if possible get a cab at a *ponto*, an organized rank where the drivers are all known to each other. There is no standard colour for taxis in Brazil – in Rio they are yellow, in São Paulo they are white, but in other places they may look like regular cars with meters.

Radio taxis calculate a certain percentage above the meter rate (about 50 percent). If you hail a taxi at the curbside, be sure that the No. 1 tariff shows on the computerized display when the driver resets the meter. The No. 2 tariff indicates that the meter is set at a 20 percent higher rate – chargeable after 8pm and on Sundays and holidays, when going beyond certain specified city bounds or up steep areas. Cab drivers can also use the No. 2 rate during the month of December to earn the "13th-month salary" that Brazilian workers receive each year as a sort of a Christmas bonus.

Hitch-hiking

The basic rule about hitch-hiking is – don't. There is no real hitch-hiking tradition in Brazil, with the exception of a few very specific circumstances – police and army cadets in uniform, truck-stop girls, and perhaps students on one or two specific routes between campus and city center, etc. While it might sound like fun to try and "introduce a foreign custom," and it is a shame to mistrust the whole of humanity because of a warped minority, the bottom line is: not in Brazil. Be you single or a couple, male or female, you're asking for trouble. It is not worth the risk.

Private Transportation

Rental Car Services

Car rental facilities are available in the larger cities. Both **Avis** and **Hertz** operate in Brazil; www.avis.com, tel: 11-325-6868 (with a large number of outlets across Brazil) or www.hertz.com, tel: 11-32589229, fax: 11-4332 7158, São Paulo office open Mon–Fri 6am–11.45pm.

The three largest Brazilian national chains are: **Localiza** (www.localiza.com.br; 24-hour reservations, tel: 55-31 3247 762/ 0800-979 2000); **Nobre** (www.nobrerentacar.com.br/redenacional.htm); and **Unidas** (www.unidas.com.br, tel: 0800-121 121). Note that these websites are in Portuguese only. There are also good local companies. Rates vary depending on the type of car. Some companies bill a flat daily rate, while others bill by mileage. Major international credit cards are accepted by these companies. Some will charge extra if you rent a car in one city and hand it back in another. Check exactly what you're getting on your insurance – it's worth paying more to be covered for all eventualities.

Arrangements can be made at the airport as you arrive, through your hotel or at the agencies. An international driving license is helpful, but you can also rent a car with your own country's driving license. For a relatively modest additional fee you can hire a driver with the car.

Driving

Motoring in Brazil may seem chaotic compared to the rest of the world. Rio drivers are especially notorious for their erratic lane-changing, in-town speeding and disregard for

pedestrians and other drivers on the road. Be on the defensive and expect the unexpected. Speeding fines can be huge (several hundred dollars) even for going slightly over the limit, which can change erratically. There are speed cameras on many roads.

In the big cities, parking can be a difficult business downtown. A good solution in Rio is to park your car near the Botafogo subway station and take the underground into town. Wherever you park in Brazil, always lock your car. Never leave anything visible inside; even if you don't think of it as valuable, someone else might.

It seems wherever you park in the cities, within seconds a freelance car "guard" will appear, either offering to keep an eye on your car in the hope of receiving a tip or even demanding that you pay him in advance for his (dubious) vigilance. The fee is quite modest; a few coins will usually be enough. It's best to pay up or you risk finding some slight damage to the car upon your return.

In recent years licensed guards have been introduced in Rio and São Paulo; they will supply a receipt which covers a certain period of parking time.

The highways, especially the interstates, are generally quite good, but are crowded with more trucks than you will have ever seen. These huge vehicles bog down traffic on winding, climbing stretches of road in the mountains. Be aware that there are different rules of the road. It is polite to beep your horn when overtaking, and flashing your lights is a warning, for example.

If you plan to drive a lot in Brazil, buy the excellent Quatro Rodas (Four Wheels) *Guia Brasil* road guide, complete with road maps, city and regional itineraries, and hotel and restaurant listings (in Portuguese), which is available at most news-stands. The same company produces a more detailed *Guia Estradas*, with larger-scale road maps of the whole country, plus a range of individual state maps.

Road Safety

While they are at all other times a polite, decent people, something happens when Brazilians get behind the steering wheel, especially in Rio. Be cautious when driving or crossing streets, and be prepared to make a dash. Despite recent tightening of traffic regulations, most drivers expect pedestrians to watch out for themselves and move out of the way.

A CCOMMODATIONS

HOTELS, YOUTH HOSTELS, BED & BREAKFAST

Hotels

There is no shortage of excellent hotels in Brazil. The larger cities and resort areas, especially, have hotels run to international standards, with multilingual staff. Many have their own travel agencies, which can be very useful. At all grades, rooms are usually clean and the staff are polite. However, it's a good idea to see the room or, when booking in advance, look at photos on the website before deciding to take it. A Continental-style breakfast is usually included in the price.

In the Santa Teresa district of Rio there is a bed-and-breakfast association called Cama e Café (see next page), but this has not yet caught on elsewhere in the country.

It is always best to book well in advance, especially if you are visiting during Carnival or a major holiday. Hotels are then full of Brazilian tourists as well as visiting foreigners. Travelers from colder climates often come to Brazil to get away from the northern hemisphere winter, and Brazilians also travel more during school holidays in the summer months of January and February, and in July. Even if you are traveling to an area that you think is off the usual tourist route, local facilities may be saturated with Brazilian vacationers during these peak months. Hotels can also be unexpectedly full because of local festivals or events at various times of the year.

If you are traveling by car, you should be aware that motels may not be quite what you're used to at home: rooms, often garishly decorated, and outfitted with mirrors, private pools, and round beds are rented out by the hour for amorous trysts.

Budget Accommodations

Campgrounds

If you are interested in camping, contact the Camping Clube do Brasil. Its national headquarters is located at Rua Senador Dantas 75, 29th Floor, Rio de Janeiro; tel: 21-3479 4200 or 0800-227 050; www.campingclube.com.br.

Hostels

The Casa do Estudante do Brasil, located at Praça Ana Amelia 9, 8th Floor, Castelo, Rio de Janeiro; tel: 21-2220 7223, has a list of hostels in 10 Brazilian states that are registered with the International Youth Hostel Federation and charge just a few dollars. Despite the name, there is no age restriction. Another source of information for hostels is the Rio-based Hostel Brasil – part of Hostelling International - that has more than 80 hostels throughout Brazil on its books (www.hostel.org.br).

Hotel and Pousada Listings

The list on the following pages includes just a few of the best places to stay in the major tourism areas. Pousadas (inns) may be cheaper and simpler than hotels, although some are luxury boutique hotels. Note that room rates fluctuate greatly according to demand, so our price guide is therefore only a general approximation. (For the meaning of abbreviations used in addresses, see page 369.)

Charming Hotels

The Roteiros de Charme is a small group of hotels and pousadas. They are of a very high standard and

usually in historical buildings. Attractive, intimate, and with good food, these establishments are likely to offer the most memorable accommodation of your trip. For more information tel: 21-2287 1592; www.roteirosdecharme.com.br.

Top Touring Guide

If you are venturing away from tourist spots to places where no hotels are included in our listing, you will find the Quatro Rodas Guia Brasil road guide useful. Available at news-stands, it has road maps, and lists hotels, restaurants, and local attractions for more than 800 Brazilian towns and cities. It has a system of symbols with explanations in English and Portuguese.

Quatro Rodas also publishes specific guides and street maps to Rio de Janeiro, São Paulo, and a number of other cities and regions, as well as the Brazilian beaches.

Breakfast in Brazil

Breakfast in one of the larger Brazilian hotels can be a wonderful thing. Choices may include a vast range of fruit – grilled bananas are particularly decadent – and exotic fruit juices; ham, cheese, cereals (not a Brazilian food, but laid on for tourists), eggs prepared any way you can think of, including as omelettes, cooked before your eyes with a wide range of fillings. In smaller establishments the range will not be as great, but will invariably include a variety to suit every palate and preference. And, of course, there's always coffee.

RIO DE JANEIRO

Rio de Janeiro

Arpoador Inn
Rua Francisco Otaviano 177
Ipanema
Tel: 21-2523 0060
Fax: 21-2511 5094*
A small, simple hotel, but great value because it is situated in one of the most beautiful spots in Rio, right by the sea. Try and get a beach-front room as they are much quieter. **$$**

Caesar Park
Avenida Vieira Souto 460
Ipanema
Tel: 21-2525 2525
Fax: 21-2521 6060
www.caesar-park.com
Of a high international standard, the 23-floor Caesar Park has been considered the best hotel in Ipanema since opening in 1978. Well situated in the heart of Ipanema and on the beach-front. One of Rio's top business hotels. **$$$$**

Cama e Café
Rua Pascoal Carlos Mango 5
Glória
Tel: 21-2224 5689
Fax: 21-2221 7635
www.camaecafe.com.br
Cama e Café is not in itself a hotel, but a company that offers the option of bed and breakfast at a number of charming and historic buildings, mainly in and around the Santa Teresa area. The properties vary in the level of sophistication and facilities offered, but the website gives a very clear indication of what is on offer. **$–$$$**

Copacabana Palace
Avenida Atlântica 1702
Copacabana
Tel: 21-2548 7070
Fax: 21-2235 7330
www.copacabanapalace.com.br
An oasis of calm with superb restaurants and an excellent swimming pool. Good business facilities. Best afternoon tea in Brazil. Classic luxury at the heart of Copacabana beach. **$$$$**

Excelsior Copacabana
Avenida Atlântica 1800
Copacabana
Tel: 21-2195 5800
Fax: 21-2257 1850
www.windsorhoteis.com.br
This once traditional hotel has been totally refurbished, offering excellent value as a beach-front executive hotel. On the same block as the Copacabana Palace. **$$$$**

Glória
Rua do Russel 632*, Glória
Tel: 21-2555 7272
Fax: 21-2555 7282
www.hotelgloriario.com.br
Beautiful old building, with a convention center. Its downtown location makes it very convenient for those doing business in the city center. **$$$**

InterContinental Rio
Rua Prefeito Mendes de Morais 222, São Conrado
Tel: 21-3323 2200
Fax: 21-3322 5500
A good Inter-Continental hotel with full resort facilities. The nearest of the city's top-ranking hotels to Barra. **$$$$**

Ipanema Inn
Rua Maria Quitéria 27
Ipanema
Tel: 21-2523 6092
Fax: 21-2511 5092
A good low-priced hotel, well located for sight-seeing. The rooms are small but comfortable. Just round the corner from the beach. **$$**

Ipanema Plaza
Rua Farme de Amoedo 34
Ipanema
Tel: 21-3687 2000
Fax: 21-3687 2001
www.ipanemaplaza.com.br
Popular with regular visitors to Rio who appreciate its location in the heart of Ipanema, just one block from the beach. Modern and stylish. **$$$$**

Leme Othon Palace
Avenida Atlântica 656
Leme
Tel: 21-2122 5900

Fax: 21-2522 1697
www.othonhotels.com.br
Traditional beach-front hotel. Location at the Leme end of Copacabana makes it convenient for the city. **$$$**

Luxor Regente
Avenida Atlântica 3716
Copacabana
Tel: 21-2525 2070
Fax: 21-2267 7693
www.luxor-hotels.com
A good hotel well situated for the beach. **$$$**

Marina All Suites
Avenida Delfim Moreira 696
Leblon
Tel: 21-2172 1100
Fax: 21-2172 1010
www.marinaallsuites.com
Famous for its eight signature design suites, the result of a promotion for leading Brazilian interior designers. Modern and stylish, Marina All Suites is located on the beach-front at Leblon, and considered the area's best. **$$$$**

Méridien
Avenida Atlântica 1020
Leme
Tel: 21-3873 8888
Fax: 21-3873 8777
www.starwoodhotels.com/lemeridien
One of Rio's top hotels; excellent French restaurant, the Saint-Honoré, with great views. **$$$$**

Portinari Design Hotel
Rua Francisco Sa 17
Copacabana
Tel: 21-3288 8800
Fax: 21-3813-1773
www.hotelportinari.com.br
Each of the 11 floors is individually designed. No pool, and one block from the beach, but a great place to stay, and there are stunning views from the top-floor restaurant. **$$$**

Praia Ipanema
Avenida Vieira Souto 706
Ipanema
Tel: 21-2540 4949
Fax: 21-2239 6889
www.praiaipanema.com/
Well located beachfront hotel on the border of Ipanema and Leblon. **$$$$**

Rio Hostel Ipanema
Rua Barão da Torre 175,
Casa 14
Tel: 21-2247 7269
Fax: 21-2268 0565
www.geocities.com/hostelipanema
Friendly house with dormitory beds, two blocks from the beach. Lovely staff; tours offered. **$**

Rio Internacional
Avenida Atlântica 1500
Copacabana
Tel: 21-2546 8000
Fax: 21-2542 5443
www.riointernacional.com.br
Modern Copacabana beach-front hotel, popular with business and leisure travelers. Even standard rooms have balconies and sea views. Rooftop pool with great views. **$$$$**

Sheraton Barra
Avenida Lucio Costa 3150
Barra da Tijuca
Tel: 21-3139 8000
Fax: 21-3139 8085
www.sheraton-barra.com.br
Reflecting the growing importance of Barra da Tijuca, the Sheraton is the first of a number of hotels to open here in recent years. A beach-front resort; all rooms have sea views and balconies. Hotels in Barra are the closest to events at the Rio Centro convention center. **$$$$**

Sheraton Rio Hotel & Towers
Avenida Niemeyer 121
Leblon
Tel: 21-2274 1122
Fax: 21-2239 5643
www.sheraton-rio.com
Top resort hotel close to Leblon and Ipanema – offers excellent accommodation and facilities. **$$$$**

Sofitel Rio Palace
Avenida Atlântica 4240
Copacabana
Tel: 21-2525 1232
Fax: 21-2525 1200
www.accorhotels.com.br
Good conference and business hotel, with beautiful views and a standard, Sofitel style. **$$$$**

RIO STATE

Angra dos Reis

The hotels below are set in beautiful locations with sports facilities.

Club Med Village Rio das Pedras
BR-101 Norte Km 445
Tel: 21-2688 9191
Reservations, tel: 0800-2213 782
Fax: 21-2688 3333
www.clubmed.com
At the top of the range is this Club Med located in its own spectacular valley and on its own beach. $$$

Hotel do Frade Golf Resort
BR-101 Sul Km 123
Tel: 24-3369 2244
Fax: 24-3369 2254
www.frade.com
Features an 18-hole golf course and hosts international competitions in June and November. $$$*

Portogalo Suite
BR-101 Norte Km 71
Tel: 24-3361 1434
Fax: 24-3361 1461
www.redeprotel.com.br
Comfortable, with wide range of water-sports facilities. $$$

Búzios

Casas Brancas Boutique Hotel & Spa
Morro do Humitá 10
Tel: 22-2623 1458
Fax: 22-2623 2147
www.casasbrancas.com.br
A hip and charming all-white boutique hotel nestled in hills overlooking the bay of Búzios. Now has

BELOW: rooftop pool with a view.

a world-class spa for refreshing the weariest visitors. $$$$

Pousada Hibiscus Beach
Rua 1, 22 Quadra C
Praia de João Fernandes
Tel: 24-2623 6221
www.hibiscusbeach.com.br.
Beautifully designed rooms. Very relaxing. British-run. $$$

Pousada La Chimère
Praça Eugenio Honold 36
Praia dos Ossos
Tel: 24-2623 1460
Fax: 24-2623 1108
www.lachimere.com.br
Close to the beach. Has its own pool and a bar. $$$

Cabo Frio

La Plage
Rua dos Badejos 40, Peró
Tel/fax: 022-2647 1746
www.redebela.com.br
Cabo Frio's top beach-front property. $$$

Pousada Portal do Sol
Rua Francisco Paranhos 76, Algodoal
Tel: 22-2643 0069
www.portaldosolpousada.com.br
A well-located, cute, and moderately priced inn near the Municipal Theater and only 200 meters/yds from Praia do Forte. $$

Pousada Porto Peró
Avenida dos Pescadores 2002
Tel/fax: 22-2644 5568
www.portopero.com.br
A fairly basic inn. $$

Pousada Portoveleiro
Avenida dos Espardartes 129
Caminho Verde, Ogiva
Tel/fax: 22-2647 3081

www.portoveleiro.com.br
Comfortable hotel; facilities include pool and sauna. $$$

Ilha Grande

Pousada O Pescador
Vila do Abraão
Tel: 24-3361 5114
A simple little place, right on the beach, and absolutely charming. Breakfast is included; and it has one of the best restaurants in the area. $

Itacuruçá

Hotel do Pierre
Ilha de Itacuruçá
Tel: 21-2253 4102
www.hotelpierre.com.br
Twenty minutes by boat from the mainland. Restaurant, bars, sporting facilities. $$$

Itatiaia National Park

Hotel do Ypê
Parque Nacional Km 14
Tel/fax: 24-3352 1453
www.hoteldoype.com.br
Located high on the park road, with good meals included in the room rate. $$$

Hotel Simon
Parque Nacional Km 13
Tel: 24-3352 2214
Fax: 24-3352 1230
www.hotelsimon.com.br
In a beautiful setting, with an orchid garden attached. Helpful advice given on getting around the park. $$$

Nova Friburgo

Bucsky
Estrada Niterói–Nova Friburgo
Km 76.5,
Mury
Tel: 24-2522 5052
Fax: 24-2522 9769
www.hotelbucsky.com
A 4-star hotel a short distance from town. Meals included. $$$

Fazenda Garlipp
Estrada Niterói–Nova Friburgo
Km 71.5, Mury
Tel/fax: 24-2542 1330
German-run chalets, with meals included in the price. $$$

Pousada Vale das Flores
Rua Jacy Linhares Ramos 224, Braunes
Tel: 22-2526 3503
http://www.valedasflores.com
Very pleasant, medium-priced inn with a beautiful view, sauna, and pool. Book an off-road tour with owner Felipe. $$

Parati

Casa do Rio
Rua Antônio Vidal 120
Tel: 24-3371 2223
A youth hostel in a gorgeous house with a courtyard and hammocks next to the river. Boat-and four-wheel-drive trips can be organized. A real home-from-home. $

Pousada Corsário
Rua João do Prado 26
Tel: 24-3371 1866
Peaceful spot with riverside garden and pool. $$
www.pousadacorsario.com.br

Pousada do Ouro
Rua Dr Pereira 145
Tel: 24-3371 1378
www.pousadaouro.com.br
Centrally located, discreetly luxurious accommodation. $$$

Pousada do Sandi
Largo do Rosario 1
Tel: 24-3371 2100
Reservations, tel: 0800-232 100
Fax: 24-3371 2038
www.pousadadosandi.com.br
Considered by many to be Parati's top *pousada*. Has a very good restaurant. $$

Pousada Pardieiro
Rua do Comércio 74
Tel: 24-3371 1370
Fax: 24-3371 1308
www.pousadapardieiro.com.br
Traditional, attractive, and comfortable inn in the historic center of Parati with excellent pool and beautiful tropical gardens. $$$

PRICE CATEGORIES

Price categories are for a double room. Breakfast is usually, but not always, included:
$$$$ = over US$300
$$$ = US$200–300
$$ = US$100–200
$ = under US$100

Petrópolis

Casa do Sol
Avenida Ayrton Senna 115
Tel/fax: 24-2243 5062
www.casadosol.com.br
Comfortable, with a wide
range of facilities. **$$**
Locanda Della Mimosa
Alameda das Mimosas 30
Vale Florido
Tel/fax: 24-2233 5405
www.locanda.com.br
Luxury *pousada* on the

outskirts of Petrópolis (en
route to Vale Florido) which
has one of the region's
great restaurants. **$$$***
Pousada da Alcobaça
Rua Agostinho Goulão 298, Correas
Tel: 24-2221 1240
Fax: 24-2222 3162
One of the best *pousadas*
in town, housed in an old
building in lovely gardens,
with a great restaurant, a
swimming pool, sauna, and
a tennis court. **$$***

Teresópolis

Hotel Village Le Canton
Estrada Teresópolis-Friburgo Km 12,
Vargem Grande
Tel: 21-2741 4200
Freephone tel: 0800-285 4200
www.lecanton.com.br
Nestled in a green valley,
this is one of the most
traditional and well-equipped
resorts in the Rio de Janeiro
mountains. It has a
reputation for excellent

cuisine, smooth service,
and beautiful rooms. Top-
notch spa. **$$$$**
Rosa dos Ventos
Estrada Teresópolis–Nova
Friburgo Km 22.6
Tel: 21-2644 9900
www.hotelrosadosventos.com.br
This highly recommended hotel
is an interesting mix of alpine
and *fazenda*-style buildings. It
has extensive, attractive
grounds, a lake, and good
sports facilities. **$$$$**

SÃO PAULO CITY AND STATE

São Paulo

Blue Tree Towers Berrini
Rua Quintana 1012
Brooklin Novo
Tel: 11-5508 5000
www.bluetree.com.br
Close to Congonhas
airport. Great for short
business trips. **$$$**
Caesar Park São Paulo
Faria Lima
Rua das Olimpiadas 205
Vila Olimpia
Tel: 11-3848 6767
www.caesar-park.com
Top-ranking executive hotel.
$$$$
Estanza Paulista *
Alameda Jau 497*
Tel: 11-3016 0000
Reservations tel: 0800-726 1500
www.estanplaza.com.br
One of several Estanplaza
hotels in the city. Excellent
service, informal
environment. Close to
Avenida Paulista. **$$$**
Fasano
Rua Vitorio Fasano 88
Cerqueira Cesar
Tel: 11-3896 4000
www.fasano.com.br
Sophisticated elegance in
one of the best areas of
the city. **$$$$**
Hospedaria Mantovani
Rua Eliseu Guilherme 269
Paraiso
Tel: 11-3889 8624
hospedariamantovani@terra.com.br
Recommended budget
option in good
neighborhood. **$**
Inter-Continental São Paulo
Avenida Santos 1123
Cerqueira Cesar
Tel: 11-3179 2600
Reservations tel: 0800-118 003
www.intercontinental.com/saopaulo

One of the most luxurious
in town. Excellent service,
but very expensive. **$$$$**
L'Hotel
Alameda Campinas 266
Jardim Paulista
Tel: 11-2183 0500
Reservations tel: 0800-130 080
Part of the "The Leading
Small Hotels of the World"
group. **$$$$**
Pergamon
Rua Frei Caneca 80
Consolação
Tel: 11-3123 2021
Reservations tel: 0800-551 056
www.pergamon.com.br
Combines comfort with art
and design. Good value.
$$$
Pousada Dona Zilah
Alameda Franca, 1621/1633
Jardim Paulista
Tel: 11-3062 1444
www.zilah.com
Friendly and affordable
home-from-home in an up-
market part of town. **$$**
Radisson Faria Lima
Avenida Cidade Jardim 625
Itaim Bibi
Tel: 11-2133 5960
www.atlanticahotels.com
Has an exclusive women's
floor with fluffy robes. **$$$**
Renaissance
Alameda Santos 2233
Tel: 11-3069 2233
www.marriottbrasil.com/saobr
A large business hotel in a
great location. **$$$$**
Tryp Higienópolis
Rua Maranhão 371
Higienópolis
Tel: 11-3665 8200/ 3665 8201
www.tryphigienopolis.solmelia.com
Upmarket neighborhood,
a good-value option
for both business and
tourism. **$$$**

Atibaia

Estancia Atibainha
Via Dom Pedro I Km 55
Tel: 11-4597 3400
Fax: 11-4597 1155
Reservations tel: 11-3331 3114
www.hotelestanciaatibainha.com.br
Caters for business and
pleasure, with a business
center, health club, and 95
chalets. **$$$**
Village Eldorado
Rod. Dom Pedro I Km 75.5
Tel: 11-4411 0533
Fax: 11-4411 0300
www.hoteiseldorado.com.br
Well-equipped holiday hotel.
$$$$

Campos do Jordão

Grande Hotel Campos do
Jordão
Avenida Frei Orestes Girardi 3549
Capivari
Tel: 12-3668 6000
Reservations tel: 0800-770 0790
www.sp.senac.br/hoteis
A traditional casino turned
into hotel, combining luxury
and breathtaking natural
surroundings. **$$$$**
Hotel Frontenac
Avenida Dr Paulo Ribas 295
Capivari
Tel: 12-3669 1000
Reservations tel: 11-5505 9550
www.frontenac.com.br
Combines technology and
personalized service in a
classic European style.
$$$$
Toriba
Avenida Ernesto Diederichsen 2962
Tel: 12-3668 5000
www.toriba.com.br
Authentic alpine style with
local folkloric decor, and
panoramic views. **$$$$**

Caraguatatuba

Pousada da Tabatinga
Estr. Caraguatatuba–Ubatuba
Praia Tabatinga
Tel: 12-3884 6010
www.pousadadaportaldatabinga.com.br
Situated near the beach,
with all facilities. **$$$$**

Guarujá

Casa Grande Hotel Resort
& Spa
Avenida Miguel Stefano 1001
Praia da Enseada
Tel/fax: 13-3389 4000
www.casagrandehotel.com.br
A well-equipped, colonial-
style hotel with spa
facilities. The only Brazilian
resort in "The Leading
Hotels of the World." **$$$$**
Delphin Hotel
Avenida Miguel Stefano 1295
Praia da Enseada
Tel: 13-3386 2112
www.delphinhotel.com.br
Also on the beach but more
modest than the Casa
Grande. **$$$**

Ilhabela

Maison Joly
Rua Antônio Lisboa Alves 278
Tel: 12-3896 1201
www.maisonjoly.com.br
Favored by VIPs, this is one
of the most sophisticated
hotels of the coast. **$$$$**
Pousada Canto da Praia
Avenida Forca Expedicionaria
Brasileira 793,
Praia de Santa Teresa
Tel: 12-3896 1194
www.cantodapraiailhabela.com.br
Rustic elegance in a
converted fisherman's
house. **$$$$**

Santos

Avenida Palace
Avenida Presidente Wilson 10
Gonzaga
Tel: 13-3289 3555
Fax: 13-3289 5961
www.avenidapalace.com.br
The Avenida Palace is a
modest but pleasant,

comfortable hotel situated
on the beachfront. $$
Mendes Plaza
Avenida Floriano
Peixoto 42, Gonzaga
Tel: 13-3289 4243
Fax: 13-3284 8253
This is a central, upmarket
option, with a full range of
facilities. $$$

Ubatuba

Hotel Cassino Sol e Vida
Rua Domingo Della Monica
Barbosa 93,
Praia da Enseada
Tel: 12-3842 0188
Fax: 12-3842 0488
www.solevida.com.br
Situated on the beach, the

Sol e Vida has water-sports
facilities. $$$
Solar das Aguas Cantantes
Estrada do Saco da Ribeira s/n,
Praia do Lázaro
Tel: 12-3842 0178
www.solardasaguascantantes.com.br
This is an attractive hotel,
with gardens, pool, and a
good restaurant. $$$

MINAS GERAIS

Belo Horizonte

**Belo Horizonte Othon
Palace**
Avenida Afonso Pena 1050
Centro
Tel: 31-3273 3844
Fax: 31-3212 2318
Large and impersonal, but
it has spacious,
comfortable rooms, and all
facilities, plus a central
location. $$$$
Comodoro Tourist
Rua dos Carijós 508
Centro
Tel: 31-3201 5522
Fax; 31-3201 5843
A very simple hotel, but it's
central, and good value for
money. $$

Ouro Minas Palace
Avenida Cristiano Machado 4001
Tel: 31-3429 4001
Fax: 31-3429 4002
www.ourominas.com.br
The best hotel in town, with
a modern business
complex and health center.
Located 30 minutes from
the city center, 10 minutes
from the airport. $$$$

Diamantina

Diamante Palace
Avenida Sílvio Félicio dos Santos
1050
Tel/fax: 038-3531 1561
www.diamantepalacehotel.com.br
Comfortable hotel, with
restaurant and bar. $

Pousada do Garimpo
Avenida da Saudade 265
Consolação
Tel/fax: 038-3531 2523
www.pousadadogarimpo.com.br
Probably the area's best-
equipped *pousada*; basic,
pleasant with a pool. $$

Ouro Preto

**Estalagem das Minas
Gerais**
Rod. dos Inconfidentes Km 87
Tel: 31-3551 2122
Fax: 31-3551 2709
In its own grounds, with
panoramic views.
Restaurant and pool. $$$
**Grande Hotel de Ouro
Preto**

Rua das Flores 164
Tel: 31-3551 1488
Fax: 31-3551 5028
www.hotelouropreto.com.br
Oscar Niemeyer designed
this attractive, modern
hotel. Centrally located,
with a pool. $$
Luxor Pousada
Rua Dr Alfredo Baeta 16
Tel: 0800-165 322
Reservations tel: 0800-282 2070
Converted colonial mansion
in the historic center. $$$$
Pousada do Mondego
Largo de Coimbra 38
Tel/fax: 31-3551 2040/3551 3094
www.mondego.com.br
Attractive old building in the
colonial center, with well-
furnished rooms. $$

BAHIA

Arraial d'Ajuda
Ecoresort

**Hotel Pousada dos
Coqueiros**
Alameda dos Flamboyants 55
Tel: 73-3575 1229/3575 1373
www.pousadacoqueiros.com.br
A comfortable and pleasant
place to stay. $$
Ponta do Apaga Fogo
Arraial D'Ajuda
Tel: 73-3575 8500
Fax: 73-3575 1016
www.arraialresort.com.br
Not cheap, but offers
excellent upmarket
accommodation. $$$$
Pousada Etnia
Trancoso
Tel: 73-3668 1137
Fax: 73-3668 1549
www.etniabrasil.com.br
A small, exclusive *pousada*
in the delightful wooded
surroundings of the so-
called "global village" of
Trancoso. $$$$

Ilhéus

Cana Brava Resort
Rod. Ilhéus–Canavieiras Km 24
Praia de Canabrava
Tel/fax: 73-3269 8000
www.canabravaresort.com.br
Many sports facilities,
private beach, swimming
pool, sauna, and lake for
kayaking. $$$
**Transamérica Ilha de
Comandatuba**
Estrada P/Canavieiras Km 77, Una
Tel: 73-3686 1122
Fax: 73-3686 1457
www.transamerica.com.br
A top-class resort hotel
offering many amenities,
including a golf course and
the Spa L'Occitane.
Excellent location. $$$$

Lençóis

Hotel Canto das Águas
Avenida Senhor dos Passos 01
Tel: 75-3334 1154

Fax: 75-3334 1279
www.lencois.com.br
Delightful, comfortable
hotel in superb gardens.
Close to the historic
center. $$$
Hotel de Lençóis
Rua Altina Alves 747
Tel: 71-3369 5000
www.hoteldelencois.com.br
With a pleasant garden
and pool, this hotel is
good for families. Set
above the town. $$
Pousada Vila Serrano
Rua Alto do Bomfim 8
Tel: 75-3334 1486
Fax: 75-3334 1487
www.vilaserrano.com.br
Small and charming Swiss-
run *pousada* within walking
distance of town center.
Efficient and friendly. $$

Porto Seguro

Porto Seguro Praia
BR-367 Km 65,

Praia de Curuipe
Tel: 73-3288 9393
Fax: 73-3288 2069
www.portoseguropraiahotel.com.br
Set just 3.5 km (2 miles)
from Porto, this hotel has
excellent facilities. $$$
Poty Praia Hotel
Rua dos Ibiscos 140,
Praia de Taperapuan
Tel: 73-2105 1500
Fax: 73-2105 1515
www.poty.com.br
One of the best budget-
priced alternatives in
Porto Seguro. $$

PRICE CATEGORIES

Price categories are for a
double room. Breakfast is
usually, but not always,
included:
$$$$ = over US$300
$$$ = US$200–300
$$ = US$100–200
$ = under US$100

SALVADOR

Bahia Othon Palace
Avenida Oceânica 2456
Ondina
Tel: 71-203 2000
Fax: 71-245 4877
www.othon.com.br.
Comfortable rooms; good
ocean and city views. $$$$
Catherina Paraguaçu
Rua João Gomes 128
Rio Vermelho
Tel: 71-3334 0089
Family-run hotel in this
up-and-coming area. $$
Club Med Itaparica
Rodovia Bom Despacho, Nazaré
Km 13
Ilha de Itaparica, Vera Cruz
Tel: 71-3881 7141
Reservations, tel: 0800-707 3782
www.clubmed.com.br

On the magical
island of Itaparica, with
all facilities. $$$$
Convento do Carmo
Rua do Carmo 1
Pelourinho
Tel: 71-3327 8400
Fax: 71-3327 8401
Luxurious hotel in a
restored 16th-century
convent. $$$$
Pestana Bahia
Rua Fonte do Boi 216
Rio Vermelho
Tel: 71-2103 8000
Fax: 71-2103 8130
www.pestana.com
Comfortable hotel
on the seafront
with panoramic views.
$$$

Pousada Redfish
Ladeira do Boqueirão 1
Santo Antônio
Tel: 71-3243 8473/3241 0639
Fax: 71-3326 2544
www.hotelredfish.com
English-owned, attractively
designed *pousada* in
restored historic house.
Good breakfasts. $$$
**Solar dos Deuses –
Suítes de Charme**
Largo do Cruzeiro do São Francisco
12
Tel: 71-3320 3251
www.solardosdeuses.com.br
Another pleasant *pousada*
in the historic center. $$
Tropical da Bahia
Avenida 7 de Setembro 1537
Campo Grande

Tel: 71-2105 2000
Fax: 71-2105 2005
www.tropicalhotel.com.br
Close to the city center, good
location for Carnival. $$$$
Vila Galé Salvador
Rua Morro do Escravo Miguel 320
Praia de Ondina
Tel: 71-3263 8888
Fax: 71-3263 8800
www.vilagale.com.br
Pleasant beach hotel with
sea views. $$$
Villa Bahia
Largo do Cruzeiro do São Francisco
16
Tel: 71-3322 4271
www.lavillabahia.com
Small, new, boutique-style
hotel in the heart of the
historic old town. $$$$

SERGIPE AND ALAGOAS

Aracaju

San Manuel Praia
Rua Niceu Dantas 75
Atalaia
Tel: 79-3243 3404
Fax: 79-3243 3179
www.sanmanuelpraiahotel.com.br
Pleasant hotel one block
from beach. Wi-fi; pool. $
Pousada Mar e Sol
Avenida Santos Dumont 314

Atalaia
Tel: 79-243 3051
Simple budget hotel near
the beach. $

Maceió

Hotel Praia Bonita
Avenida Dr Antônio Gouveia 943
Pajucara
Tel: 82-2121 3700
Well located, overlooking

Pajucara beach. Ask for a
room at the front with sea
view. Close to restaurants
and artisan market. $$
Ritz Praia Hotel
Rua Eng. Mario de Gusmao 1300
Ponta Verde
Tel: 82-21214600
Pleasant rooms with air-
conditioning, TV and wi-fi.
50 meters/yds from beach.
English spoken. $

Porto de Pedras

Porto das Pedras
Rua Dr Fernandes Lima 28
Centro
Tel: 82-3298 1176
Beautiful colonial-style
pousada with well-kept
gardens. Large rooms with
DVD players; good service;
home-made breakfasts;
English spoken. $

RECIFE AND PERNAMBUCO

Olinda

Pousada do Amparo
Rua do Amparo 199
Tel: 81-3439 1749
Fax: 81-3429 6889
www.pousadadoamparo.com.br
Attractive, stylish hotel in
historic building. Luxury
rooms available on
request. $$$$
Pousada dos Quatro Cantos
Rua Prudente de Moraes 441
Carmo
Tel: 81-3429 0220
Fax: 81-3429 1845
www.pousada4cantos.com.br
Small and pleasant, in a
19th-century mansion in the
historic center. $$
Sete Colinas
Rua São Francisco 307
Tel/Fax: 81-3439 6055
www.hotel7colinas.com.br

In the historic heart of
town, with delightful
gardens and pool area. $$$

Porto do Galinhas

Hotel Armação
Lot. Merepe II, Quadra G1 Lote 1 A
Tel: 81-3552 1146
Fax: 81-3552 5200
www.hotelarmacao.com.br
Family-run hotel; three pools,
tennis, live entertainment.
Excellent value. $$$
Nannai Beach Resort
Access via Km 2 on PE-009
Praia de Muro Alto
Tel: 81-3552 0100
www.nannai.com.br
Upmarket resort, including
some bungalows with
private pools. $$$$
Pousada Tabapitanga
Access via Km 3 on PE-009

Praia do Cupe
Tel: 81-3552 1037
Fax: 81-3552 1726
www.tabapitanga.com.br
Comfortable bungalows.
$$$
Summerville Beach Resort
Gleba 6a, Praia de Muo Alto
Tel: 81-3302 5555
www.summervilleresort.com.br
Extensive grounds and pool
area. Good for families.
$$$$

Recife

Hotel Atlante Plaza
Avenida Boa Viagem 5426
Boa Viagem
Tel/fax: 81-3302 3333
www.atlanteplaza.com.br
One of the best hotels in
Recife, on the seafront.
$$$$

**Best Western Manibu
Recife**
Avenida Conselheiro Aguiar 919
Boa Viagem
Tel: 81-3084 2811
Fax: 81-3084 2810
www.hotelmanibu.com.br
A well-run hotel; excellent
value for money. $$$
Mar Hotel Recife
Rua Barão de Souza Leão 451, Boa
Viagem
Tel: 81-3302 4444
Fax: 81-3302 4445
www.marhotel.com.br
Rooms with balconies and
a superb pool area. $$$
Marolinda Residence Hotel
Avenida Conselheiro Aguiar 755
Tel: 81-3325 5200
www.marolinda.com.br
A hotel-cum-art gallery, with
an emphasis on local
culture. $$$

THE FAR NORTHEAST

João Pessoa

Caiçara
Avenida Olinda 235
Tambaú
Tel: 83-2106-1000
www.hotcaicara.com.br
An efficient hotel, part of
the Best Western chain; 10
minutes from center, one
block from the beach. $$

Littoral
Avenida Cabo Branco 2172
Praia de Cabo Branco
Tel: 83-2106 1100
Fax: 91-3241 0844
www.hotellittoral.com.br
Rooms with sea views;
small pool. The
Malagueta restaurant
offers Brazilian and
international dishes. $

Tropical Tambaú
Avenida Alm. Tamandaré 229
Praia de Tambaú
Tel: 0800 701 2670
www.tropicalhotel.com.br
Part of a small chain, the
Tropical offers comfortable
accommodation at a very
reasonable price. $

Natal

Manary Praia Hotel
Rua Francisco Gurgel 9067
Ponta Negra Beach
Tel/fax: 84-3204 2900
www.manary.com.br
Luxury beach-front hotel. Air-
-conditioning and internet
connection in rooms.
Swimming pool. $$$

Ocean Palace
Via Costeira Km 11
Ponta Negra Beach
Tel: 84-3220 4144
Freephone tel: 0800-844 144
Luxury five-star beach-front
hotel. Wi-fi internet in
rooms. $$

Praia Azul Mar
Rua Francisco Gurgel 92
Ponta Negra Beach
Tel: 84-4005 3555
www.praia-azul.com.br
Another beach-front hotel,
close to local restaurants.
Rooms have safe, cable TV,
internet access. $$

Tibau de Sul
Marinas Tibau Sul
Avenida Gov. Alusio Alves 301

Tel: 84-3207 0078
www.hotelmarinas.com.br
Luxury chalets with views
of the river and sand
dunes. Fishing and horse-
riding facilities. $$

Fortaleza

Praiano Palace
Avenida Beira Mar 2800
Meirelles
Tel: 85-4008 2200
Fax: 85-4006 2223
www.praiano.com.br
Recently refurbished,
modern four-star hotel;
Apartments and suites as
well as rooms. The Thames
restaurant serves regional
and international dishes.
$$$

Seara Praia Hotel
Avenida Beira Mar
Meirelles
Tel: 85-4011 2200
www.hotelseara.com.br
Excellent five-star hotel, all
rooms have a sea view. The
Azul de Prata restaurant
specializes in food with a

French influence. Access to
Olympic-size swimming
pool. $$$

São Luís

**Pousada Portas da
Amazonia**
Rua do Giz 129
Praia Grande
Tel: 98-3222 9937
www.portasdaamazonia.com.br
A pleasant *pousada*, well-
located in an attractive
19th-century colonial
building in the historic
center. $

Rio Poty Hotel
Avenida dos Holandeses s/n
Ponta D'Areia
Tel: 98-3311 1500
Fax: 98-3227-6576
www.riopotysaoluis.com.br
Large, modern hotel
located on Ponta D'Areia
beach. Rooms have
panoramic sea views.
Beauty salon,
hydromassage and saunas
on offer. Two restaurants
and three bars. $$

AMAZON

Belém

Beira-Rio
Avenida Bernardo Sayão 4804
Guamá
Tel: 91-408 9000
Fax: 91-249 7808
www.beirariohotel.com.br
Outside the town center,
with a pool and air-
conditioning. $$$

Hilton International Belém
Avenida Presidente Vargas 882
Praça da República
Tel: 91-4006 7000
Fax: 91-3241 0844
www.hilton.com
Rather run-down, but still
one of the best. $$$$

Regente
Avenida Governador José
Malcher 485
Nazaré
Tel: 91-3241 1222
Email: reserves@hregente.com.br
Modest but comfortable.
$$

Zoghbi Apart Hotel
Rua Ferreira Cantão 100
Tel: 91-3230 3555
Fax: 91-3230 2000

www.zoghbi.com.br
Clean and friendly modern
hotel, with small pool and
restaurant. Good value.
$$

Santarém

Santarém Palace
Avenida Rui Barbosa 726
Tel: 91-523 2820
Fax: 91-522 1779
Good rates and close to
center. Runs river tours. $

Manaus

Ana Cássia Palace
Rua dos Andradas 14
Centro
Tel: 92-3622 3637
Fax: 92-3234-4163
Email: hcassia@internext.xom.br
Faded but still charming,
with a pool and sauna. $$$

Best Western Lord Manaus
Rua Marcílio Dias 217
Centro
Tel: 92-3622 7700
Reservations, tel: 0800-761 5001
Fax: 92-3622 2576

www.bestwestern.com.br
Well located for the city
center. $$$

Holiday Inn Taj Mahal
Avenida Getúlio Vargas 741
Centro
Tel: 92-3633 1010
Fax: 92-3233 0068
Email: tajmahal@internext.com.br
Probably the best hotel in
the center. $$$$

Manaós
Avenida Eduardo Ribeiro 881,
Centro
Tel: 92-3633 5744
Fax: 92-3232 4443
Next to the Teatro
Amazonas, 39 rooms with
air-conditioning, which is
important in this heat. $$

Tropical
Avenida Coronel Teixeira 1320
Praia da Ponta Negra
Tel: 92-2123 5000
Fax: 92-3658 3034
www.tropicalhotel.com.br
Set in its own park 12 km
(7 miles) from the center,
on the banks of the
Amazon. Swimming pool
and tennis courts. $$$$

Macapá

Macapá
Avenida Eng. Azarias Neto 17
Centro
Tel: 96-217 1350
Fax: 96-217 1351
Good range of facilities and
pool; on the riverside. $$$

Pousada Ekinox
Rua Jovino Dinoá 1693
Tel: 96-3223 0086
www.ekinox.com.br
In the center. Very popular,
friendly, with an excellent
restaurant. Wi-fi. $$*

For Amazon jungle lodges,
see page 291.

BRASÍLIA

Brasília

Academia de Tenis Resort
Setor de Clubes Esportivo Sul
Trecho 04, Conjunto 05, Lote 1-B
Tel: 61-3316 6245/3316 6252
Fax: 61-3316 6264
www.academiaresort.com.br
Close to the lake, Excellent leisure facilities – pool, cinema, and 21 tennis courts. **$$$**

Blue Tree Park Brasília
Setor Hoteleiro Norte, Trecho 01, Conjunto 1B, Bloco C
Tel: 61-3424 7000
Fax: 61-3424 7001
www.bluetree.com.br
Modern hotel, by the lake. Excellent facilities,

convention center. One of the best in the city. **$$$$**

Blue Tree Towers Brasília
Setor Hoteleiro Norte, Trecho 01, Lote 1B, Bloco A–B
Tel: 61-3429 8000
Fax: 61-3429 8104
www.bluetree.com.br
Part of the same building as the Blue Tree Park, but it does not face the lake. All leisure facilities shared between the two hotels, including the marina and spa. Together they form the Blue Tree Alvorada complex. **$$$$**

Carlton
Setor Hoteleiro Sul, Quadra 5, Bloco G

Tel: 61-3224 8819
Fax: 61-3226 8109
www.carltonhotelbrasilia.com.br
A good business hotel with all the usual facilities. **$$$$**

Kubitschek Plaza
Setor Hoteleiro Norte, Quadra 2, Bloco E, Asa Norte
Tel: 61-3329 3333/3329 3655
Fax: 61-3329 3582
www.kubitschek.com.br
Very comfortable and well-situated hotel. **$$$$**

Meliá Brasília
Setor Hoteleiro Sul, Quadra 6 Bloco D
Tel: 61-3218 4700
Fax: 61-3218 4703/4705/4701
www.solmelia.com
Modern, international hotel, centrally located. **$$$$**

Nacional
Setor Hoteleiro Sul, Quadra 1, Bloco A
Tel: 61-321 7575
Reservations, tel: 0800-644 7070
Fax: 61-223 9213
www.hotelnacional.com.br
Old-fashioned but excellent. Weekend discounts. **$$$$**

Quality Suítes Lakeside
Setor Hoteleiro Norte, Trecho 01, Lote II
Tel: 61-3035 1445
Fax: 61-3035 2144
www.atlantica-hotels.com
Pleasantly situated by the lakeside, Has a marina where you can rent jet-skis and boats. Good value and good facilities. **$$$**

THE PANTANAL

Bonito

Muito Bonito
Rua Cel. Pilad Rebua 1448
Tel/Fax: 67-255 1645
reserves@muitobonito.com.br
Attractive hostel in a great location on main street. Comfortable rooms, a helpful English-speaking owner. Also have a tour agency and can arrange excursions. **$**

Zagaia Eco-Resort
Tel: 67-255 5601
vendas@zagaia.com.br
www.zagaia.com.br
Upmarket, a little way out of town, popular with Brazilian tourists. Apartments are modern and comfortable; large pool and good restaurant. **$$**

Campo Grande

Bristol Exceler Plaza
Avenida Afonso Pena 444
Tel: 67-3312 2800
exceler@bristolhoteis.com.br
www.bristolhoteis.com.br
Smart, comfortable high-rise with pool, tennis court, good breakfast, and friendly service. Located just out of town, and convenient for the airport. **$$**

Hotel Advanced
Avenida Calógeras 1909
Tel: 67-3321 5000
hoteladv@terra.com.br
www.hoteladvanced.com.br
Plain, uninspiring, soviet-style block, but it's good value, with comfortable rooms, nice bathrooms, and a big breakfast spread. Very central. **$**

International
Allan Kardec 223
Tel: 67-3784 4900
hotelint@terra.com.br
www.hotelintermetro.com.br
Good, modern hotel near the bus station. Small pool, comfortable, impersonal rooms, all conveniences. There is an incredible buffet breakfast. **$$**

Corumbá

Pousada do Cachimbo
Rua Alen Kardec 4
Bairro Dom Bosco
Tel: 67-3231 4833
cachimboresort@yahoo.com.br
www.pousadadocachimbo.com.br
A 5-minute drive from town, this traditional farmhouse has 14 comfortable apartments, a pool, and

views over the river. Friendly, helpful staff. **$$**

Santa Rita
Rua Dom Aquino Correia 860
Tel: 67-3231 5453
hsrita@terra.com.br
Simple, clean, and central. Air-conditioning, nice bathrooms, good breakfast. **$**

Cuiabá

Hotel Mato Grosso
Rua Commandante Costa 2522
Tel: 65-3614 7777
A clean modern hotel with comfortable rooms. **$**

Hotel Mato Grosso Palace
Rua Joaquim Murtinho 170
Tel: 65-3614 7000
www.hoteismattogrosso.com.br
Comfortable rooms and suites, very central. Great breakfast spread. **$$**

IGUAÇU FALLS

Bourbon Igaussu Golf Resort
Avenida das Cataratas 6845 Km 8.5
Reservations, tel: 0800-701 8181
www.bourbon.com.br
Accommodations in modern bungalows; 18-hole golf course. **$$$$**

Hotel Tropical das Cataratas
Rod. das Cataratas Km 25
Tel: 45-3521 7000
Fax: 45-3574 1688

reserves.iguassu@tropicalhotel.com.bt
www.tropicalhotel.com.br
Faded elegance in a colonial-style hotel, the only one in the Brazilian national park. **$$$$**

Internacional Foz
Rua Almirante Barroso 2006
Tel: 45-3521 4100
Fax: 45-3521 4101
mercurefoz@accorhotels.com.br
www.internacionalfoz.com.br
Modern hotel, with helpful

staff. Good location in the city center. **$$$$**

Nadai
Avenida República Argentina 1332
Tel/fax: 45-3521 5090
Reservations, tel: 0800-645 5090
www.hotelnadai.com.br
Air-conditioning, swimming pool, and sauna. **$$**

Nuevo Luz
Avenida Dobrandino da Silva 145
Tel/fax: 45-522 3535
luzhotel@luzhotel.com.br

A bit characterless, but it has large, comfortable rooms, and is next to the bus station. Good value. Home to Luz Tours, run by Antônio – an excellent guide to the falls. **$$**

Park Plaza
Tel: 45-523 1213
www.challengerhoteis.com.br
Modern, with spacious rooms and friendly service. A nice pool and sauna. **$$**

SOUTHERN STATES

Blumenau

Garden Terrace
Rua Padre Jacobs 45
Tel: 47-326 3544
Large hotel, with restaurant, bar, and travel agency. **$$**
Grande Hotel Blumenau
Alameda Rio Branco 21
Tel: 47-3326 0145
Fax: 47-3326 1280
www.hoteisbrasil.com/garden
Comfortable, modern hotel, with a good restaurant, bar, and pool. **$$$**
Plaza Blumenau
Rua 7 de Setembro 818
Tel: 47-231 7000
Reservations, tel: 0800-471 213
www.plazahoteis.com.br
A luxury hotel, the best in town, with business facilities. **$$$**

Canela

Pousada Quinta dos Marques
Rua Gravataí 200
Santa Teresinha
Tel: 54-3282 9812
www.quintadosmarques.com.br
Designed for pure indulgence, the *pousada* offers massages in the middle of the forest, among other delights. **$$$**

Curitiba

Bourbon Curitiba Hotel & Tower
Rua Cândido Lopes 102
Tel: 41-322 4001
Reservations, tel: 0800-701 8181
Wonderfully traditional hotel, enormous and very swish. **$$$$**
Four Points by Sheraton Curitiba
Avenida Sete de Setembro 4211
Batel
Tel: 41-3340 4000
Reservations, tel: 0800-555 855
www.starwood.com
Good, functional executive hotel, run to Sheraton standards. **$$$**
Grand Hotel Rayon
Rua Visconde de Nacar 1424
Centro
Tel: 41-2108 1100
Reservations, tel: 0800-7272 966
www.rayon.com.br
Located just by "Rua 24-Horas," this is considered the best hotel in town. **$$$**

Florianópolis and Beaches

Blue Tree Towers Florianópolis
Rua Bocaiuva 2304
Centro
Tel: 48-3251 5555
Reservations, tel: 0800-150 500
www.bluetree.com.br
Great sea views at a hotel conveniently located among bars, restaurants, and shopping centers in the town center. **$$$**
Costão do Santinho Resort & Spa
Rodovia Vereador Onildo Lemos 2505
Praia do Santinho
Tel: 48-261 1000
Fax: 48-261 1200
www.costao.com.br
This is considered the most comprehensive and luxurious resort in the southern region of Brazil. Sports facilities include tennis, canoeing, swimming, and soccer. **$$$$**
Intercity Hotel
Avenida Paulo Fontes 1210
Centro
Tel: 48-3027 2200
Reservations tel: 0800-703 7336
www.intercityhotel.com.br
Close to Florianópolis's historic, public market; rooms with bay views. **$$$**
Jurerê Beach Village
Alameda César Nascimento 646
Praia de Jurerê
Tel: 48-3261 5100
Reservations, tel: 0800-480 110
www.jurere.com.br
Good water-sports facilities. It is possible to rent chalets with one or two rooms; good for families. **$$$$**
Pousada da Vigia
Rua Con. Walmor Castro 291
Praia da Lagoinha*
Tel: 48-3284 1789
Tel: 48-3284 1108
www.pousadavigia.com.br
Built on top of a cliff, the *pousada* has privileged sea views. Delicious breakfast served until 11am, so you can sleep late without missing out. **$$$**
Pousada Penareia
Rua Hermes Guedes da Fonseca 207 Praia da Armação
Tel: 48-338 1616

www.pousadapenareia.com.br
Ideal for couples having an indulgent holiday. Some rooms have air-conditioning, hydro, and large verandas. **$$$**

Garopaba/Praia Rosa

Pousada Caminho do Rei
Caminho do Alto do Morro s/n
Tel: 48-3355 6062/3355 6071
www.caminhodorei.com.br
Lovely place, built in the 1980s by an idealistic young couple. Glorious views, and comfortable rooms furnished in bright, clean colors. **$$**
Quinta do Bucaneiro
Estrada Geral do Rosa s/n
(off BR-1-1)
Tel: 48-3355 6056
www.bucanero.com.br
Attractive, relaxing *pousada* close to the beach about 70 km (45 miles) from Florianópolis; with wooden balconies and a small pool. Glorious setting. **$$**

Gramado

La Hacienda Estalagem e Restaurante
Estrada da Serra Grande 4200
(access on RS-115 Km 37 to Taquara)
Tel: 54-3286 8186/3286 8027
Reservations, tel: 51-3388 4678
www.lahacienda.com.br
Sophisticated replica of the colonial farms established by European immigrants in the 1800s. **$$$$**
Varanda das Bromelias Boutique Hotel
Rua Alarisch Schulz 158–198
Planalto
Tel: 54-3286 0547/ 3286 6653
www.varandadasbromelias.com.br
Attractive and romantic, located at the highest point of Gramado. **$$$$**

Laguna

Laguna Tourist
Praia do Gi Km 4
Tel: 48-647 0022
Fax: 48-647 0123
www.lagunatourist.com.br
A large, modern hotel, well located on the beach. It has good views and great facilities. **$$$**

Taperoá

BR-101 Norte Praia de Itapirubá
Tel: 48-356 0222
Fax: 48-646 0294
Reservations, tel: 0800-480 222
Located on the beach. Good sports facilities. **$$**

Nova Petrópolis

Recanto Suiço
Avenida 15 de Novembro 2195
Tel/fax: 54-281 1229
Fifteen rooms with air-conditioning. There's a bar, a restaurant, and a swimming pool. **$$**

Porto Alegre

Deville Porto Alegre
Avenida dos Estados 1909
Anchieta
Tel: 51-3373 5000
Reservations, tel: 0800-703 1866
www.deville.com.br
Executive hotel, conveniently close to the airport. **$$$$**
Embaixador
Rua Jerônimo Coelho 354
Centro
Tel: 51-3215 6600
Reservations, tel: 0800-7016 610
www.embaixador.com.br
The Embaixador is very comfortable, with smooth, efficient service. **$$$**
Lido Hotel
Rua General Andrade Neves 150
Tel: 51-3228 9111
www.lidohotel.com.br
Combines value with comfort and a good location. **$**
Plaza São Rafael Hotel
Avenida Alberto Bins 514, Centro
Tel: 51-3220 7000
Reservations, tel: 0800-512 244
www.plazahoteis.com.br
A luxury hotel, the best in Porto Alegre, it also has the best convention center in the city. Some rooms overlook the river. **$$$$**

PRICE CATEGORIES

Price categories are for a double room. Breakfast is usually, but not always, included:
$$$$ = over US$300
$$$ = US$200–300
$$ = US$100–200
$ = under US$100

A CTIVITIES

The Arts, Nightlife, Festivals, Sports, Children's Activities, and Shopping

THE ARTS

Museums

Brazil's historical museums are unlikely to be at the top of most visitors' list of attractions. There are not enough resources available for proper upkeep and acquisitions – although there are exceptions. Those worth visiting are described in the Places section of this book, with their opening times. Temporary exhibitions are announced in the major Brazilian newspapers under the heading of *Exposições*.

Art Galleries

Those showing the work of contemporary artists abound in the larger cities, especially Rio de Janeiro and São Paulo. The art museums also organize periodic exhibits. Shows are listed in the papers under *Exposições*.

The Bienal or Biennial Art Exposition held in São Paulo every two years (2008, 2010, etc.) lasts from March–June and is Latin America's largest contemporary art show.

Music and Dance

Music is Brazil's forte. A variety of musical forms have developed in different parts of the country, many with accompanying forms of dance. While the Brazilian influence (especially in jazz) is heard around the world, what is known of Brazilian music outside the country is just the tip of an iceberg.

Take in a concert by a popular singer or ask your hotel to recommend a nightclub with live

Brazilian music: *bossa nova, samba, choro* and *serenata* are popular in Rio and São Paulo – each region has something different to offer. If you are visiting at Carnival, you'll hear and see plenty of music and dancing in the streets, mostly samba in Rio and *frevo* in the northeast. There are also shows all year long that are designed to give tourists a taste of Brazilian folk music and dance. *(For more on music, see pages 102–11.)*

A rock concert in Brazil is something not to be missed if that is your taste in music. The atmosphere is unimaginable, as the audience almost becomes part of the show, a seething, vibrant, ever-moving mass of enjoyment. The music is a magical blend; undeniably rock, yet at the same time Brazilian, with Latin rhythms pumped out by swollen percussion sections seamlessly and effortlessly merging with the power of electronic amplification.

The classical music and dance season runs from Carnival through mid-December. Besides presentations by local talents, major Brazilian cities (mainly Rio, São Paulo and Brasília)

Getting Tickets

Online ticket services:
Ticketmaster: Shows, concerts and sporting events in Rio, São Paulo, Belo Horizonte. www.ticketmaster.com.
Ingresso Fácil: Shows, concerts, and sporting events including football matches in Rio, São Paulo, Belo Horizonte. www.ingressofacil.com.br.
Ingresso.com: Good for advance purchase of movie tickets nationwide, also shows, and some theme parks. www3.ingresso.com.br.

are included in world concert tours by international performers. One of the most important classical music festivals in South America takes place in July each year in Campos do Jordão in the state of São Paulo.

If you want to attend a live music performance, check in the weekend section of the local paper, under the heading *Lazer* (leisure), which will give listings of clubs, theaters, bars and dance halls holding concerts.

Capoeira

A uniquely Brazilian activity, *capoeira* is a relic from slavery days, when fighting, and especially training for fighting, by the slaves had to be hidden. *Capoeira* is a stylized fight-dance, with its own accompanying rhythms and music, using the feet a great deal to strike out and requiring a graceful agility. This tradition has been kept alive chiefly in Salvador and Rio, where there are academies teaching *capoeira* (you can watch the classes free of charge). You can arrange to see a presentation or you may catch a street group performing on a beach or in a busy square *(also see page 106)*.

Theater

In order to enjoy the theater, you really do have to understand the language. Rio de Janeiro and São Paulo, especially, have busy seasons starting after Carnival and running through to November.

Movies

Most major international films are released on the principal Brazilian circuit more or less simultaneously with their release in Europe and the US. Recent years have seen a revolution in the movie-house business with the advent of modern, multi-screen venues often located in shopping centers, which means easy parking, more comfort and a wider choice. Prices in major cities are around US$9 for recent releases. People over 60 and students with the appropriate ID pay half.

Most foreign films are shown with original soundtrack and Portuguese captions *(legendas)*, but beware – some films, particularly those appealing to children, may also have dubbed versions *(dublado)* in some theaters. Good listings will indicate "L" and "D" or "Leg" and "Dub."

Some Brazilian cinema is very good. The country is slowly gaining prominence in the industry with films like Fernando Meirelles' *City of God* which received four Oscar nominations in 2004 *(see page 113)*. However, unless you understand Portuguese, it's better to see Brazilian movies abroad, where they may have subtitles.

There are various annual cinema festivals: the Rio festival takes place in September; São Paulo's in October; and Gramado – a small town in southern Brazil – hosts a major six-day event in August.

NIGHTLIFE

For information on nightlife in the main cities, see the relevant chapters in the Places section of this book. But beware, what is hot and happening one week can be deserted the following week. The legal drinking age in Brazil is 18, and some bars and clubs may ask young people for ID. Carry a photocopy of your passport rather than the real thing. Many nightclubs will not allow you to enter if wearing shorts. Prostitutes frequent many establishments – particularly those popular with tourists.

Major centers like Rio and São Paulo offer all kinds of after-hours activity, including restaurants, bars, and clubs that regularly stay open into the early hours. Brazilians love partying so even in smaller towns there is often a club staying open later at weekends, but beware – away from the tourist routes, people tend to go to sleep earlier, particularly during the week.

Some bars with live music charge for entry, typically US$5–10 for a competent attraction, while others may set a similar minimum spending limit per person *(consumação mínima)*. This is technically illegal

and object of a constant battle by consumer protection agencies. Live music in bars is most frequently some strain of Brazilian – samba, *choro, frevo, pagode, sertanejo* (country music), and the ubiquitous MPB, the latter standing for Popular Brazilian Music, and covering a host of styles including "tropicalized" rock'n'roll. As befits a global melting pot São Paulo offers a wide variety from jazz and electronic music to venues specializing in sound-alike "cover bands" from the 1960s and 1970s, such as The Doors, Led Zeppelin, and Pink Floyd. There are numerous bars and small restaurants with food and music from other Latin American countries, and many offering Arabic food and shows.

FESTIVALS

Besides national holidays, many religious or historical events are commemorated locally. Each city celebrates the date on which it was founded and the day of its patron saint. Many villages and neighborhoods stage their own regional folk celebrations – usually with music, dancing, and stalls selling food and drinks traditionally associated with the event. Some of the most important festivals are listed below *(also see Public Holidays, page 363)*.

January
1 New Year's Day
National holiday. Bom Jesus dos

ABOVE: all dressed up for Carnival.

Navegantes. A four-day celebration in Salvador starts with a spectacular boat parade.
6 Epiphany
Regional celebrations, mostly in the northeast.
3rd Sunday – Festa do Bonfim
One of the largest in Salvador.

February
2 Iemanjá
Festival in Salvador. The Afro-Brazilian goddess of the sea corresponds with the Virgin Mary *(also see New Year's Eve)*.

February/March
Carnival
National holiday celebrated all over Brazil on the four days leading up to

What's On

Major city newspapers have daily listings: *Folha de São Paulo* and *Estado de São Paulo* in São Paulo; *O Globo* and *Jornal do Brasil* in Rio. The *Veja* national newsweekly has regional supplements with good listings of restaurants. Also, the Friday edition of the *Folha de São Paulo* has a handy comprehensive booklet covering the week ahead, listing cinemas, theater performances, shows, concerts, etc, with selected restaurants. It's all in Portuguese, but not too difficult to get the gist of.

Websites
Boca a Boca (Mouth to Mouth) is a what's-on guide with separate weekly printed editions for Rio, São Paulo and Brasília, with an excellent website to match, where you can check city listings for films,

shows, concerts and exhibitions by title or venue (Portuguese only); www.bocaboca.com.br.
Guia da Semana (Weekly Guide) offers listings and reviews for cinema, shows, theater, and more in São Paulo, Rio de Janeiro, Belo Horizonte, Salvador, Porto Alegre, Brasília, Curitiba and Florianópolis (Portuguese only); www.guiadasemana.com.br
Guia Metropole has cinema and theatre listings for Recife. (Portuguese only); www.guiametropole.com.br
Samba & Choro lists dozens of bars and dancehalls throughout Brazil that have live shows of samba and *choro*, two essential musical styles. Separate pages for Rio and São Paulo. Listings include some traditional old establishments (Portuguese only); www.samba-choro.com.br.

and including Ash Wednesday. Dates vary depending on the date of Easter. Most spectacular in Rio, Salvador and Recife/Olinda.

March/April

Good Friday
National holiday. Colonial Ouro Preto puts on a procession; passion play staged at Nova Jerusalem.

April

21 Tiradentes Day
National holiday in honor of the martyred hero of independence. Celebrations in his native Minas Gerais, especially Ouro Preto.

June

15–30 Amazon Folk Festival
Held in Manaus.

June/July

Bumba-Meu-Boi
Processions and street dancing in Maranhão are held in the second half of June and beginning of July.
Festas Juninas
Street festivals in June and early July in honor of saints John, Peter and Anthony, featuring bonfires, dancing and mock marriages.

August

Festa do Peão Boiadeiro
In Barretos, São Paulo state. The world's largest annual rodeo, also country music.
Festival Literaria Internacional Parati (FLIP)
International literature festival in Parati on the coast southwest of Rio. This event attracts international

authors for a laid-back, long weekend of discussion in idyllic surroundings.

October

Oktoberfest
In Blumenau, staged by descendants of German immigrants.
Cirió
Religious procession in Belém.
12 Nossa Senhora de Aparecida
National holiday honoring Brazil's patron saint.

December

31 New Year's Eve
Millions gather on Rio de Janeiro beaches to watch spectacular firework displays, and to offer gifts to the goddess Iemanjá.

SPORTS

Participant Sports

Aquatic Sports

A large variety of aquatic sports can be enjoyed in Brazil. Almost any coastal town has boat rental facilities and many resort hotels rent sailboats, fishing tackle, jet-skis, diving gear and surf and windsurf boards. Sailboats, speed boats or schooner-like Brazilian *saveiros*, can all be rented complete with equipment and crew. In Rio go to the Marina da Gloria.

Excursion clubs arrange white-water canoeing, kayaking and sailing outings. Rapids-shooting rafting excursions can be arranged through hotels in Rio.

Diving
Diving equipment and tuition are available. Some of the more spectacular places to dive include Fernando de Noronha island, off Brazil's most northeastern point, and the coral Abrolhos archipelago off the coast of southern Bahia. More accessible are the Sun Coast, east of Rio de Janeiro (Cabo Frio, Búzios), and the Green Coast between Rio and São Paulo (Angra dos Reis, Parati).

Surfing
Brazil's seemingly endless coastline offers good opportunities for surfing. Saquarema, in the state of Rio de Janeiro, is the site of international championships.

Swimming
Ocean swimming is a delight, especially in the north and northeast, where the water is warm all year round. Many hotels have swimming pools, as do the private clubs. Be aware that many city beaches, especially in Rio, are badly polluted.

Fishing
There is a large variety of fish, both ocean and freshwater varieties, all along the coast as well as in the rivers and the flooded Pantanal marshlands. Fishing equipment can be rented along with a boat and guide, and special fishing excursions are organized. The website www.brasil fishing.com.br is a useful resource.

Professional fishermen in the northeast will sometimes take an extra passenger or two on their *jangada* rafts. Luft Turismo (tel: 11-6979 5353) organizes fishing trips to the Pantanal.

Camping
If you want to go hiking and camping, contact the Camping Clube do Brasil, Rua Senador Dantas 75, 29° Andar, Rio de Janeiro, tel: 21-3479 4200 or 0800 227 050; www.campingclube. com.br. They have camping sites throughout the country and they organize treks in out-of-the-way parts of Brazil. If you prefer to backpack on your own, check the maps available from the IBGE – Brazilian Institute of Geography and Statistics – tel: 0800 218181; www.ibge.gov.br.

Climbing and Caving
There are plenty of peaks to climb in Brazil, if you enjoy rock climbing or mountaineering. In Rio, you can even climb the city's landmarks, Sugar Loaf mountain and Corcovado. There are excursion clubs that arrange outings to nearby mountainous

BELOW: the ever-popular Praia Ferradura (Horseshoe Beach).

regions and areas where you can go spelunking (caving). Contact one of the following organizations: **Centro Excursionista Brasileiro, Avenida Almirante Barroso** 2–8 Andar, Centro, Rio de Janeiro CEP230031, tel: 21-2252 9844 or 2262 6360; www.ceb.org.br; **Sociedade Brasileira de Espeleologia** Caixa Postal 7031, Campinas S.P., Cep 13076, tel: 19-3296 5421; www.sbe.com.br

Cycling

Since the 1992 environment conference in Rio, good cycling facilities have been developed, including a cycle lane running the length of the Copacabana, Ipanema, Leblon, São Conrado and Barra beaches, and on into the city center.

ABOVE: one of the world's best-known venues for soccer, Rio's Maracanã Stadium.

Eco-tourism

This term is frequently used to describe any kind of nature or adventure tourism, and does not necessarily mean any consideration has been given to the environment. There are genuinely ecologically concerned tours on offer, but others may involve anything from catching caiman in the Amazon to fishing for piranha in the Pantanal, neither of which are sustainable activities.

Golf

Golf is not a big sport in Brazil and is played mostly in Rio, São Paulo, and Búzios. There are only a couple of public golf courses in Brazil and although country clubs are quite exclusive, you can arrange (through your hotel) to play as a visitor.

Hang Gliding

Hang gliding is popular, especially in Rio, where modern Daedaluses leap off the mountains and soar on air currents before landing on the beach below. Inexperienced flyers can go tandem with an instructor. In some places paragliding is available. Contact Riotur (tel: 21-3322 2286) or Rio Gliding (e-mail: konrad@globo.com; www.riogliding.com).

Horseback Riding

The Pantanal, home of Brazilian cowboys, is a popular place for horseback riding, and a good way to see local wildlife. The old gold trails in the mountains in the southern states offer scenic rides. The country's long, open beaches are ideal for galloping along the surf.

Hunting

Hunting is illegal in Brazil. The only shooting of wildlife permitted is the kind done with a camera.

Jogging

Joggers have a beautiful place to keep in shape while in Rio: the in-town beaches have wide sidewalks, with the distance marked in kilometers along the way. In São Paulo, Ibirapuera Park is a favorite spot for runners.

The biggest races are the Rio Marathon in June (tel: 21-2132 8888) and the São Paulo Marathon in April or May (tel: 11-3763 4294).

Motor Racing

Brazil is a rarity in that it is on both the Formula One and ChampCar racing circuits. The Formula One Grand Prix takes place in October at São Paulo's Interlagos circuit while Rio plays host to the ChampCar race and also the motorbike Grand Prix. Brazilian drivers are prominent in all categories.

Tennis

Some of the larger hotels have tennis courts. There are a few public courts, but the game is played mostly at clubs. Since the charismatic "Guga," Gustavo Kuerten, won the French Open and became a top player, interest in tennis in Brazil has definitely been on the increase.

Trekking

There are lots of places to trek in the country, whether hiking through lush forest trails, exploring scenic national parks, or climbing through mountainous regions. A local guide is usually advisable.

Volleyball

On the beaches, especially in Rio, you can spend many hours being entertained by the skill of volleyball players (Brazil has won both world and

Olympic titles). The atmosphere is relaxed, though the games are often skilful, and you may be able to join in.

Spectator Sports

Soccer (futebol)

This is Brazil's national sport and a passion that unites all ages and classes. During World Cup season, the country grinds to a halt as everyone tunes in to watch the matches on television.

If you're a soccer fan, arrange through your hotel to see a professional game – there are organized tours. The boisterous fans are often as interesting to watch as the actual game itself.

Especially exciting are the games between top rival teams in Rio's giant Maracanã Stadium, which squeezes in crowds of up to 95,000; or in São Paulo's Pacaembu Stadium. There is rarely any violence, but it is recommended that you get a reserved seat rather than sit in the packed bleachers (uncovered stadium seating). Many hotels can book tickets and transport – a worthwhile extra to avoid the crush.

Most weekend afternoons, or in the early evening, you can see a fast and furious "sand lot" match taking place between neighborhood teams on the beaches or in the parks of Brazil.

Horse Racing

Horse racing is popular, and several cities have tracks. The top prize event, called the Grande Premio do Brasil, is held in the first half of August at the Rio de Janeiro track (tel: 21-2512 9988). In São Paulo, contact the Jockey Club (tel: 11-2161 8300).

ABOVE: choosing a bikini from a vast array on offer.

The value of a gemstone is determined largely by its color and quality, not necessarily by size. When choosing a gem look for color, cut, clarity and cost. The stronger the color, the more valuable the stone. Buy from a reliable jeweler, where you will get what you pay for and can trust their advice. The two leading jewelers operating nationwide are H Stern and Amsterdam Sauer, but there are other reliable smaller chains. Top jewelers have shops in the airports and shopping centers, and in many hotels.

There are also some good modern jewelry designers working in Rio, whose pieces are worth seeking out. Flavio Guidi (tel: 21-2220 7285) and Pepe Torras (tel: 21-2274 5046) are among the best.

CHILDREN'S ACTIVITIES

Brazilians love children. What's more, they tolerate them to an extent that can occasionally exceed limits expected by some other cultures. If you go to a restaurant that caters to families at a weekend lunchtime, for example, don't be surprised to have children wander up and say hello, or run around shrieking.

Major cities have children's theater and cinema – see listings in *What's On* – but these will be Portuguese only, and expect foreign films to be dubbed.

Theme parks are popular. Three in or around São Paulo are:
Hopi Hari, Bandeirantes Highway SP-348, exit Km 70.5. Large fun park 70 km (44 miles) north of São Paulo. There are things for all ages: magic castles stuffed with Brazilian folklore and legends, carousels, Wild West shows, and a Rio Bravo raft ride. Current cost is US$19 per day for entry and most rides. Closed Mon and some weekdays; times vary. Tickets from tel: 0300-789 5566, or online at www.uol.com.br/hopihari.
Wet'n'Wild, Bandeirantes Highway SP-348, Km 72, 72 km (45 miles) north of the city. Water fun park. Entry US$27, additional charge for some attractions. Open Tues–Sun in summer 10am–6 pm. Tickets available online, at www.wetnwild.com.br, or on tel: 11-4496 8000.
Playcenter, Rua José Gomes Falcão 20, Barra Funda (with parking). Free shuttle bus from Barra Funda metro station. Traditional amusement park in São Paulo city includes a roller coaster, looping, and tower drop. Open weekends and holidays only 9am–2pm and 5–9pm. Tickets at the door or online at www.playcenter.com.br. Entry US$11 per session (2007); additional charge for some rides.

SHOPPING

What to Buy

Gemstones and Jewelry

One of the major attractions of shopping for gemstones in Brazil, besides the price, is the tremendous variety. Brazil produces amethysts, aquamarines, opals, topazes, and many colors of tourmalines, as well as the more precious diamonds, emeralds, rubies and sapphires.

Some 65 percent of the world's colored gemstones are produced in Brazil, which is also one of the world's major gold producers. Brazil today is one of the top jewelry centers in the world and costs are attractive because the operation is 100 percent domestic, from the mining of the gems to the cutting, crafting and designing of jewelry.

Regional Crafts

Ceramics are a particularly good purchase in the northeast, where clay bowls, water jugs, and other items are commonly used in the home. Also from the northeast come primitive clay figurines depicting folk heroes, customs and celebrations. Marajoara ceramic pieces, decorated with geometric patterns, come from the island of Marajó at the mouth of the Amazon River.

Beautiful handmade lace and embroidered clothing are produced mostly in the northeast, especially in the state of Ceará, while Minas Gerais is a traditional producer of handmade weavings and tapestries.

Also in Minas Gerais, soap-stone items are on sale every-where. Both decorative and utilitarian objects – cooking pots, toiletry sets, quartz and agate

Leather Goods

Shoes, sandals, bags, wallets and belts are all good buys. Although found throughout the country, some of the finest leather comes from the south. Shoes are plentiful, and hand-made leather items can be found at street fairs or covered markets.

Wooden Objects

Brazil has beautiful wood. Gift shops sell items such as salad bowls and trays, and wood carvings can be found at craft fairs. The grotesque *carranca* figureheads are difficult to fit into your suitcase but very unusual, being unique to São Francisco riverboats. Do be aware, though, that items may be made from endangered tropical hardwoods. It is not illegal to export them, but the industry is contributing to the mass deforestation of the Amazon.

bookends and ashtrays – can be found in many souvenir stores.

Straw and natural fibers (banana leaves, palm bark) are fashioned into baskets, hats, bags, mats, etc. especially in the northeast.

Indian handicrafts are mainly made in the northern Amazon region and include adornments (necklaces, earrings), utensils (sieves, baskets), weapons (bows, arrows, spears) and percussion instruments (like the "rain sticks" that imitate the sound of falling rain) made out of wood, fibers, thorns, teeth, claws, colorful feathers, shells and seeds.

Cotton hammocks are popular all over Brazil, but the best place to buy them is in the north and northeast, where they are used extensively instead of beds. They are sometimes finished with lacy crocheted edgings.

Musical Instruments and CDs

A fun thing to take home are the peculiar percussion instruments that you hear samba bands playing, usually on sale at street fairs. From Bahia comes the *berimbau*, a simple instrument consisting of a wire-strung bow and a gourd sound-box. It has a characteristic sound, but is surprisingly difficult to master. If you enjoy Brazilian music, buy CDs, too.

Fashion

Boutiques in most cities are clustered in certain districts, and shopping malls enable you to visit many shops in less time.

If you want something uniquely Brazilian, buy lace or embroidery from the northeast, or a tiny bikini or a beach cover-up which can be wrapped around in various ways.

T-shirts are everywhere in Brazil. From beautifully designed and expensive ones for the evening to humble but colorful screen-printed day-wear, they are excellent value and usually of good quality.

Paintings

These can be bought at galleries as well as crafts fairs and markets. Brazilian primitive, or naïve, paintings are popular *(see page 122)*.

Religious Articles

Popular amulets include the *figa* (a carved clenched fist with the thumb between the index and middle fingers) and the Senhor do Bonfim ribbons (to be wrapped around a wrist or ankle and fastened with three knots) from Salvador.

Also from Salvador come bunches of silver fruits, which Brazilians hang in their homes to ensure there is always plenty of food on the table.

Coffee

Ground and roasted Brazilian coffee can be found at any supermarket or bakery. You can get coffee packaged in a handy carton at the airport.

Where to Buy Crafts

Handicrafts shops and markets are plentiful throughout Brazil. In most of the larger towns in the northeast and in the Amazon there is a central craft market or a craft center. A few of them are listed below.

Rio de Janeiro

Pé de Boi
Rua Ipiranga 55, Botafogo
Tel/fax: 21-2285 4395.
Eskada, Avenida Gen. San Martín 1219, Leblon.

Gaia Jóias
Rua Fernando Mendes 28c
Copacabana
Tel: 21-2255 9646.
The Hippie Fair
Praça General Osório, Ipanema.
Lively, touristy, handicrafts market that attracts artisans from across Brazil. Sunday.

São Paulo

Amoa Konoya Arte Indígena
Rua João Moura 1002
Tel: 11-3061 0639.
Fabulous collection of Indian handicrafts from the Amazon and other parts of Brazil. Baskets, bows and arrows, feather, wood, and clay objects, and CDs of Indian music.
Arte Nativa Aplicada
Rua Dr Melo Alves 184
Tel: 11-3088 1811.
Textiles, table mats, and lamps in interesting tribal patterns.
Casa do Amazonas
Alameda dos Jurupis 460, Moema
Tel: 11-5051 3098.
Large variety of Indian art and crafts.
Cariri
Rua Francisco Leitão 277, Pinheiros
Tel: 11-3064 6586.
A wide range of Brazilian crafts – basketware, painted clay folkloric figures, wooden sculptures, and hammocks.
Jacques Ardies Gallery
Rua do Livramento 221
Tel: 11-3884 2916.
Primitive, naïve art.
São Paulo Craft Fairs
Praça de Republica: Saturday. Paintings, clothes, jewelry, gemstones.
Liberdade: Sunday. Plants, crafts, food, and clothes, in the Japanese district of the city.

Bookshops

Rio de Janeiro
FNAC
Barra Shopping, Avenida das Americas 4666, Loja B, 101–116.
General bookstore.
Livraria Argumento
Rua Dias Ferreira 417, Leblon.
Art and travel; also literature and children's books.
Nova Livraria Leonardo da Vinci
Avenida Rio Branco 185, Loja 2.
Wide selection of books about Brazil, also art and photography.
Jamer Books and Things
Rua Marques Sao Vicente 124, Loja 101.
Specializes in children's books.
São Paulo
FNAC
Avenida Paulista 901.
Good selection of books and music.
Livraria Cultura Editora
Avenida Paulista 2073, Conjunto Nacional.
Wide selection of books on all topics, including many about Brazil; the best in Latin America.
Livraria e Papelaria
5a Avenida Paulista 2239.
Wide selection of books.
Recife
Livro 7
Rua Sete de Setembro 329.
Foreign language books.

Praça Benedito Calixto: Saturday. Hippie Fair, with crafts, Indian clothes, pottery, and jewelry.
MASP: Sunday. Under the MASP art museum. Antiques.
Embu: Sunday. In a small town southwest of the the city. Arts, crafts, food, and plants, plus live music.

BELOW: naïve art for sale at the Hippie Fair, Ipanema.

A – Z

A HANDY SUMMARY OF PRACTICAL INFORMATION, ARRANGED ALPHABETICALLY

A dmission Charges

Museums and galleries normally charge a small entrance fee, typically US$1.50–7. There may be reductions for students, but this cannot be relied upon, and there are some free days. Churches are free but usually appreciate a donation.

Airport Taxes

Domestic flights carry an embarkation tax of roughly US$4–9, depending on the size of the airport. On international flights out of Brazil you pay roughly US$36. In addition, some companies may have fuel and security surcharges. Check with your travel agent when buying your ticket to find out if all these are included.

B udgeting for Your Trip

Allow US$80 upwards per day for two people for accommodation, starting at the hostel or "cheap and cheerful" level; US$20 per person per day upwards for basic meals in snack bars and inexpensive restaurants, without alcohol; obviously meals in better

restaurants cost a lot more *(see Restaurant sections at the end of relevant chapters for a guide).* Allow around US$25 per person per day for getting around Rio or São Paulo, based on one taxi ride and the rest by bus or Metro.

Business Hours

Business hours for offices in most cities are Monday–Friday 9am–6pm, sometimes with a very long lunch hour. Banks open Monday–Friday 10am–4pm. *Casas de câmbio* (currency exchanges) usually operate 9am–5pm.

Most stores are open Monday–Friday 9am–6.30pm or 9am–7pm, and Saturday until 12.30 or 1pm. They may stay open much later depending on their location. The shopping centers are open Monday–Saturday 10am–10pm as a rule (many are also open on Sunday), although not all the shops inside keep the same hours. Large department stores are usually open Monday–Friday 9am–10pm and 9am–6.30pm on Saturday. Most supermarkets are open 8am–8pm. Some stay open 24 hours, seven days per week.

Service station hours vary, but some stay open 24 hours a day, seven days a week.

Post offices are open Monday–Friday 9am–5pm and 9am–1pm on Saturday. Some larger cities have one branch that stays open 24 hours a day. Many pharmacies stay open until 10pm, and larger cities will have 24-hour drugstores.

The 24-hour and 12-hour clocks are both in common usage.

C limate

Almost all of Brazil's 8.5 million sq. km (3.3 million sq. miles) of territory lies between the Equator and the Tropic of Capricorn. Within this tropical zone, temperatures and rainfall vary from north to south, from coastal to inland areas, and from low areas (the Amazon River basin and the Pantanal, as well as along the coast) to higher altitudes. If you are coming from the Northern Hemisphere, you should remember that seasons are inverted (i.e. Brazil's summer is your winter), although at this latitude seasons are less distinct than they are in temperate zones.

CLIMATE CHART

Brasilia

Manaus

Rio de Janeiro

☐ Maximum temperature
■ Minimum temperature
— Rainfall

The North

In the Amazon River basin jungle region, the climate is humid equatorial, characterized by high temperatures and humidity, with heavy rainfall all year round. Although some areas have no dry season, most places have a short respite between July and November, so that the rivers are highest from December through June. Average temperature is 24–27°C (75–80°F).

The East Coast

The Atlantic coast from Rio Grande do Norte to the state of São Paulo has a humid tropical climate, also hot, but with slightly less rainfall than in the north, and with summer and winter seasons. The northeastern coast, nearer to the equator, experiences little difference in summer/winter temperatures, but more rainfall in winter, especially April–June. The coastal southeast receives more rain in summer

(December–March). Average temperature is 21–24°C (70–75°F), being consistently warm in the northeast, but fluctuating in Rio de Janeiro from summer highs of more than 40°C (104°F) down to 18°C (65°F), with winter temperatures usually around the 21°C (70°F) mark.

The Interior

Most of Brazil's interior has a semi-humid tropical climate, with a hot, rainy summer (December–March) and a drier, cooler winter (June–August). Year-round average temperature is 20–28°C (68–82°F). São Paulo, at an altitude of 800 meters (2,600 ft) above sea level, and Brasília, over 1,000 meters (3,300 ft) above sea-level on the Central Plateau, as well as mountainous Minas Gerais, can get quite cool: although the thermometer may read a mild 10°C (50°F), it will not feel so balmy indoors if there is no heating.

The mountainous areas in the southeast have a high-altitude tropical climate, similar to the semi-humid tropical climate, but rainy and dry seasons are more pronounced and temperatures are cooler, averaging from 18–23°C (64–73°F).

Part of the interior of the northeast has a tropical, semi-arid climate – hot with sparse rainfall. Most of the rain falls during three months, usually March–May, but sometimes the season is shorter, and in some years there is no rainfall at all. The average temperature is 24–27°C (75–80°F).

The South

Brazil's south, below the Tropic of Capricorn, has a humid, subtropical climate. Rainfall is distributed regularly throughout the year, and temperatures vary from 0–10°C (32–50°F) in winter, with occasional frosts and a rare snowfall, to 21–32°C (70–90°F) in summer.

Crime and Safety

Personal crime, in the form of pick-pocketing and theft from hotel rooms, is sadly common in parts of Brazil, particularly in bigger cities. But, with a little caution and common sense, most visitors manage to avoid trouble.

When traveling, always carry valuables and money in a money-belt, worn out of sight underneath clothing, and don't wear a flashy watch or expensive jewelry. Be especially alert in crowded places, such as rush-hour subway stations, city buses, beaches, and markets. Seek advice from your hotel about local areas to avoid at

night. A good general rule is to avoid the beach after dark.

Thieves often operate in teams, and are masters at diversionary tricks. If carrying expensive camera equipment, never let it out of sight, and be wary of strangers telling you, for instance, that you have stepped in something smelly, and offering to assist you.

Leave valuables in your hotel safe if available, but check to see that they are actually put away, and ask for a list of items deposited. Make sure that you can get access to them at all hours, if checking out very early or late.

Take photocopies of your passport and important documents and, if traveling with a friend, keep copies of each other's documents.

Always report any losses or injuries to the police and ask for a written report of the incident for insurance purposes. Tourist police (delegacia de proteção ao turista) can be contacted in the following cities:
São Paulo: tel: 11-3107 5642.
Aeroporto de São Paulo, Congonhas: tel: 11-5090 9032.
Aeroporto Internacional de São Paulo, Guarulhos: tel: 11-6445 2221/6445-2214.
Rio de Janeiro: tel: 21-2511 5112.
Salvador: tel: 71-3176 4200.
Santos: tel: 0800-173 887.

Customs and Duty Free

You will be given a declaration form to fill out on the plane before arrival. Customs officials spot-check some incoming "nothing to declare" travelers. If you are coming as a tourist and bringing articles obviously for your personal use, you will have no problem. As with most countries, food products of animal origin, plants, fruit, and seeds may be confiscated.

You can bring in US$500-worth of anything brought from abroad, except liquor, which is limited to one bottle (each) of wine and spirits.

If you are coming on business, it's best to check with the consulate as to what limitations or obligations you are subject to. Professional samples may be brought in as long as the quantity does not lead customs inspectors to suspect that they are, in fact, for sale.

Electronic devices worth no more than US$500 can be brought in on a tourist visa and need not leave the country with you – they can be left in the country as gifts.

There is a Duty Free shop at all major airports receiving international flights. Arriving passengers have a US$500 limit, but the shops are a one-chain monopoly and most prices are not wonderful.

Emergency Numbers

National (free) numbers:
Ambulance: 192
Police: 190
Fire: 193
Civil Defense: 199
São Paulo
Women's police station
(specializing in crimes against
women, staffed by female
officers): 11-3976 2908;
State highway police: 11-3327
2727
Rio de Janeiro
Women's police station: 21-3399
3690
Coastguard (Salvamar) 21-2253
6572
State highway police: 21-3399
4857/2625 1530.

Disabled Travelers

Airlines provide free wheelchair
reception for passengers with
disabilities who request it in
advance. Laws in Brazil require public
places to be wheelchair-friendly, but
not all are. Many major city centers
are gradually equipping all crossings
with curbramps, and some more
modern city buses can accommodate
wheelchair entry and exit. Some
elevators in more modern buildings
have Braille numbering for buttons.
Travelers with disabilities should
expect difficulties, but can also
expect friendly help.

Electricity

Voltage is not standard throughout
Brazil, but most cities use 127V
electricity; Brasília, Florianópolis,
Fortaleza, Recife, and São Luís
use 220V electricity; Manaus uses
110V electricity.
   If you can't do without your electric
shaver, hairdryer or personal computer, inquire about the voltage when
making hotel reservations. If you plug
an appliance into a lower voltage
than it was made for, it will function
poorly, but if you plug it into a much
stronger current it can overheat and
short-circuit. Many appliances have
a switch so they can be used with
either a 110-v or 220-v current
(110-v appliances work normally
on a 127-v current). Many hotels
have adapters, and some even have
more than one voltage available.

Embassies and Consulates

Australia
19 Forster Crescent, Yarralumla,
Canberra, ACT 2600

Tel: 612-6273 2372
Fax: 612-6273 2375
www.brazil.org.au
Canada
77 Bloor Street West, 1109 and
1105, Toronto, Ontario, M5S 1M2
Tel: 416-922 2503
Fax: 416-922 1832
www.consbrastoronto.org
New Zealand
10 Brandon Street – Level 9
PO Box 5432
Wellington
Tel: 644-473 3516
Fax: 644-473 3517
www.brazil.org.nz
Ireland
Harcourt Centre, Europa House,
Block 9, Harcourt Street, Dublin 2
Tel: 1-475 6000
Fax: 1-475 1341
UK
32 Green Street, London W1K 4AT
Tel: 020-7399 9000
Fax: 020-7399 9100
www.brazil.org.uk
US
Washington DC: 3009 Whitehaven
Street NW, DC 20008
Tel: 202-238 2828
Fax: 202-238 2818
www.brasilemb.org
Houston: 1233 West Loop South
1450A, TX 77027-3006
Tel: 713-961 3063
Fax: 713-961 3070
Los Angeles: 8484 Wilshire Blvd,
Suites 730–711, Beverly Hills,
CA 90211
Tel: 213-651 2664
Fax: 213-651 1274
www.brasilian-consulate.org
Miami: 2601 Bayshore Drive
Suite 800, FL 33131
Tel: 305-285 6200
Fax: 305-285 6232
www.brazilmiami.org
New York: 1185 Avenue of the
Americas, 21st Floor, New York,
NY 10036
Tel: 917-777 7777
Fax: 212-827 0225
www.brazilny.org
   There are Brazilian consulates in
Boston, Chicago, and San Francisco.
American citizens must contact one
of these to obtain a visa before
traveling to Brazil.

Foreign Embassies and Consulates In Brazil

Embassies are found in Brasília,
where consulates are located, and
also in Rio and São Paulo and some
other cities. Many countries also
have diplomatic missions in several
cities. Call before visiting because
they frequently keep unusual hours.
If you're coming to Brazil on
business, remember that your

consulate's commercial sector can
be of great help.
Australia
Brasília:
SES, Avenida das Nações, Qd. 801,
Conj. K, Lote 7
Tel: 61-3226 3111
Fax: 61-3226 1112
São Paulo:
Alameda Santos 700, 9th floor
Tel: 11-2112 6200
Fax: 11-3171 2889
Canada
Brasília:
SES, Avenida das Nações,
Qd. 803,
Lote 16, s1. 130
Tel: 61-3424 5400
Fax: 61-3424 5490
São Paulo:
Avenida Nações Unidas 12901,
16th Floor, Torre Norte
Tel: 11-5509 4321
Ireland
Brasília:
SHIS, Qd. 12, Conj. 5, Casa 09
Tel: 61-3248 8800
Fax: 61-3248 8816
São Paulo:
Avenida Paulista 2006, Conj. 514
(Cerqueira Cesar)
Tel: 11-3287 6362
New Zealand
Alameda Campinas 579
15th Floor
Tel: 11-3148 0616
South Africa
Avenida Paulista 1754
São Paulo
Tel: 11-3265 0449
UK
Brasília:
SES, Avenida das Nações, Qd. 801,
Conj. K, Lote 8
Tel: 61-3329 2300
Fax: 61-3329 2369
Rio de Janeiro:
Praia do Flamengo 284, 2nd Floor,
Flamengo
Tel: 21-2555 9600
Fax: 21-2555 9672
São Paulo:
Rua Ferreira de Araújo 741,
2nd Floor
Tel: 11-3094 2700
Fax: 11-3094 2717
US
Brasília:
SES, Avenida das Nações Unidas,
Qd. 801, Lote 3
Tel: 61-3312 7000
Fax: 61-3225 9136
Rio de Janeiro:
Avenida Pres. Wilson 147, Centro
Tel: 21-3823 2000
São Paulo:
Rua Henri Dunant 500
Chácara Santo Antônio
Tel: 11-5186 7000
Fax: 11-5186 7199

Entry Regulations

Visas

Tourist visas used to be issued routinely to all visitors upon arrival, but Brazil now has a reciprocity policy: if Brazilians need a visa in advance to visit your country, you will need a visa in advance to visit Brazil. US citizens need to apply for a visa in advance; European Union citizens do not. Your airline or travel agent should be able to tell you if you need a visa; or contact a Brazilian consulate or embassy.

If you do not need a visa in advance, your passport will be stamped with a tourist visa upon entry. This permits you to remain in the country for 90 consecutive days. If you apply for a visa in advance, you have up to 90 days after the issue date to enter Brazil. Upon entry, you will get a tourist visa allowing you to stay in Brazil for up to 90 days.

If you are traveling to several countries and not going straight to Brazil, the entry visa needn't be issued in your home country, but it's still a good idea to allow for enough time so as to avoid surprises and hassles. The 90-day tourist visa can be renewed once only for another 90 days. To get an extension, go to the immigration section of the federal police.

Temporary visas for foreigners who will be working or doing business in Brazil allow a longer stay than a tourist visa. If you are a student, journalist or researcher, or employed by a multinational company, contact the Brazilian consulate or embassy in your country well before you plan to travel. It is usually difficult or even impossible to change the status of your visa once you are in the country. If you come with a tourist visa, you will probably have to leave the country to return on another type of visa.

Permanent work visas and residency visas normally require the applicant to have a job offer from a Brazilian company in a senior position, or in a small group of professions determined by the government. Application must be made from outside Brazil and the process is lengthy and bureaucratic.

Etiquette

Generally speaking, social customs in Brazil are not vastly different from those you will find in "Western" countries, but Brazilians can be both awkwardly formal and disarmingly informal.

Surnames are little used. People start out on a first-name basis, but titles of respect – *senhor* for men

and most frequently *dona* for women – are used not only to be polite to strangers but also to show respect to someone of a different age group or social class. In some families, children even address their parents as *o senhor* and *a senhora* instead of the Portuguese equivalent of "you."

While handshaking is a common practice at introductions, it is also customary to greet friends, relatives, and even complete strangers to whom you are being introduced with hugs and kisses. The "social" form of kissing consists usually of a kiss on each cheek. However, in most circles men do not kiss each other, rather shaking hands while giving a pat on the shoulder with the other hand. If they are more intimate, men will embrace, thumping each other on the back. Although this is the general custom in Brazil, there are subtleties about who kisses whom that are governed by factors such as social position. Brazilians are incredibly kind people in general. You will encounter offers of help wherever you go. Ask for directions and you are likely to be taken there in person.

Brazilians are also generous hosts, ensuring that guests' glasses, plates, or coffee cups are never empty. Besides the genuine pleasure of being a gracious host, there is the question of honor. Even poor people like to put on a good party.

Although Brazil is definitely a male-dominated society, machismo takes a milder and more subtle form than is generally found in neighboring Hispanic America.

Expect schedules to be more flexible than you may be used to. It's not considered rude to show up half an hour late for a social engagement.

Except in the larger cities, even business appointments are often leisurely when compared with the US or Europe. Don't try to include too many in one day, as you may well find your schedule badly disrupted by unexpected delays.

 G ay and Lesbian Travelers

Brazil is a generally tolerant country, and both Rio and São Paulo have Gay Parades that have become major annual events with a Carnival atmosphere, attracting people of all kinds of minorities. Gay and lesbian travelers will not feel discriminated against in major city centers. However, as in most countries, the more remote rural areas tend to be conservative.

H ealth

A yellow fever certificate may be required if you are arriving from certain South American and African countries. This is subject to change, so check with the Brazilian embassy. If you plan to travel in areas outside of cities in the Amazon region or in the Pantanal in Mato Grosso, however, it is recommended that you have a yellow fever shot. This protects you for 10 years, but is effective only after 10 days, so plan ahead. Be sure to get a certificate for any vaccination. It is also a good idea to protect yourself against malaria in these same jungle areas: there are drugs that will provide immunity, and most need to be taken for several days before visiting the area. Consult your doctor or local public health service.

Don't drink tap water in Brazil. The

BELOW: always wear a hat to protect yourself from the fierce sun.

water in the cities is treated and is sometimes quite heavily chlorinated, but people filter water in their homes. Any hotel or restaurant will have inexpensive bottled mineral water, both carbonated *(com gas)* and uncarbonated *(sem gas)*. If you are out in the hot sun, make an effort to drink extra fluids. Coconut and other fruit juices or mineral water are good for replacing lost fluids.

Don't underestimate the tropical sun. There is often a pleasant sea breeze, and you may not be aware of how the sun is baking you until it's too late. Use an appropriate sunscreen or *filtro solar* – there are several brands on sale in Brazil.

Prescription drugs are available in abundance – frequently without a prescription – and you may even find old favorites that have been banned for years in your country. Bring a supply of any prescription drugs that you take regularly, but simple things like aspirin, antacids, plasters, sunscreen, and suchlike, are easy to obtain. However, there have been cases of falsification of medicines, so it's best to buy drugs in larger chain stores or in the big cities. Drugstores also sell cosmetics; sanitary protection can be purchased in any drugstore or supermarket.

Some US health insurance plans cover any medical service you may require while abroad, but you should check with the company, and if not, ensure you have private medical insurance before traveling, which is something visitors from the UK and elsewhere must always do.

Medical Emergencies

Should you need a doctor while in Brazil, your hotel should be able to recommend reliable professionals who often speak several languages. Many of the better hotels have a doctor on duty. Your consulate will also be able to supply you with a list of physicians who speak your language.

Internet

Brazil is now one of the most web-savvy countries on the planet and has helped make Portuguese the second-most used language on the Internet after English. Twenty-five

Left Luggage

This is *guarda volumes* in Portuguese. It is available at most major airports and bus stations, normally of the rent-a-locker variety, sometimes with a store-room option for larger items.

ABOVE: news-stands in the cities are always well-stocked.

million people in Brazil use the internet. Internet cafés are found throughout the country, although service can be slow in smaller beach resort areas. Many larger hotels offer internet facilities free to their guests. It also means it is easy to stay in touch via e-mail.

The importance and size of the Brazilian internet market is reflected by Yahoo! and Google setting up Portuguese-language search engines for Brazil.

While a lot of the web content on Brazil is in Portuguese, major websites tend to offer pages in English.

Lost Property

Lost and found in Portuguese is *achados e perdidos*. There is an *achados e perdidos* point at most major airports and bus stations. However, remember that Brazil is a country with widespread poverty, and most valuables lost in the street or on public transport are gone for good. Your documents may be returned, depending on your luck, but it is sensible to leave your passport in your hotel safe and carry a simple photocopy.

The Brazilian mail service – Correios – runs a nationwide document-return service, and people who find lost items can simply drop them in a public mailbox. There is an online service to check if your documents have been handed in: http://www.correios.com.br/servicos/achadoseperdidos/.

Maps

The Quatro Rodas publisher (part of the Abril group) has a nice range of state maps, and various national

guide books. The IBGE (Brazilian National Geographical Institute) sells more detailed maps in its own shops.

Media

Newspapers and Magazines

The *Miami Herald*, the Latin America edition of the *International Herald Tribune,* and the *Wall Street Journal,* are available on many news-stands in the big cities, as are news magazines like *Time and Newsweek*. At larger news-stands and airport bookshops you'll find other foreign newspapers and a large selection of international publications, including German, French, and English magazines.

You may want to buy a local paper to find out what's on in town. Besides the musical shows, there are always many foreign movies showing in the original language with Portuguese subtitles. Entertainment listings appear under the headings of *cinema, show, dança, música, teatro, televisão, exposições,* etc. *Crianças* means "children."

If you do know some Portuguese and want to read the Brazilian newspapers, the most authoritative and respected include: São Paulo's *Folha de São Paulo, Estado de São Paulo,* and *Gazeta Mercantil,* and Rio's *Jornal do Brasil* and *O Globo*. There is no nationwide paper, but these wide-circulation dailies reach a good part of the country. The colorful weekly magazine *Epoca*, along with *Veja* and *Isto E,* are also good sources of information.

Television and Radio

Brazilian television mostly features light entertainment programs, like quiz shows, comedies, and soaps. It is big business – with Brazil exporting programs around the world. There are a staggering 170 million viewers in the country.

There are six national and several hundred local networks, which bring television to nearly all parts of Brazil. Only one network, for educational television, is government-controlled. Brazil's giant TV Globo is the fourth-largest commercial network in the world. With over 40 stations in a country with a high illiteracy rate, it has great influence over the information many people have access to *(see the TV feature on page 115).*

Only about a third of all television programs in Brazil are imports, and these are mostly from the US. Foreign series, specials, sports coverage, and movies are dubbed in Portuguese, except for some of the late-night movies and musical shows.

Most hotels and many middle- and upper-class homes in the cities receive cable television offering close to 100 channels, including most of the global favorites such as CNN, BBC World and ESPN. It is even possible to watch American breakfast television while in Brazil. At present, cable television is the fastest-growing media industry in the country.

There are several thousand radio stations around Brazil which play international and Brazilian pop hits, as well as a variety of Brazilian music reflecting regional tastes. A good deal of American and British music is played; classical music programs are also popular, including Sunday afternoon operas in some areas.

The Culture Ministry station often has some interesting musical programs. All Brazilian broadcasts are in Portuguese.

Money

The currency is the *real* (plural, *reais)*, which is made up of 100 *centavos*. For exchange purposes, US$1 is currently (spring 2007) about R$2.2 and £1 about R$4.2, but this is subject to a great deal of fluctuation.

The use of commas and decimal points in Portuguese is the opposite of what you may be used to. In Portuguese, one thousand *reais* is written R$ 1.000,00.

ATM machines are found throughout Brazil, including airports, and major shopping areas usually accept Visa and MasterCard/Cirrus cards. The two major banks which provide this service are HSBC and Banco do Brasil. There will usually only be one international machine at a branch. Using ATMs is the easiest way to obtain foreign currency. You

Photography Tips

Digital photography has taken over Brazil, just like the rest of the world, and there are places to print photos or record them onto a CD in most shopping centers and downtown areas of larger cities. Additional memory cards are available in larger cities for most common international standards. Thirty-five-mm film is still available in larger centers, although it is increasingly difficult to find. The same goes for developing.

Light can be very strong, and during the middle of the day the near-vertical sun can result in strong contrasts. Better results are often obtained earlier in the morning, or toward the end of the afternoon.

Don't walk around with your camera hanging around your neck or over your shoulder; it is an easy target for a snatcher. Carry it discreetly and never leave it unattended on the beach. If you have expensive equipment, it's a very good idea to have it insured.

can exchange dollars, yen, pounds, and other currencies at accredited banks, hotels, and tourist agencies. If you can't find one of these, some travel agencies will exchange your currency, although this is, strictly speaking, an illegal transaction. The few hotels that exchange travelers' checks give a poor rate.

Banks will not exchange *reais* or travelers' checks into foreign currency. The only exception to this is the Banco do Brasil, which has branches at international airports. As you leave the country, they will exchange back, at the official rate, 30 percent of the currency you exchanged at a similar airport branch bank on your way into Brazil, if you show the receipt for the initial exchange. You cannot get travelers' checks cashed into dollars.

Most hotels will accept payment in travelers' checks or most major credit cards. Many restaurants and shops take credit cards; the most frequently accepted are American Express, Diners Club, MasterCard and Visa, which all have offices in Brazil. You can also pay with dollars. Hotels, restaurants, stores, taxis, and so on, will usually quote an exchange rate.

P ost

Post offices are generally open Monday–Friday 9am–5pm and 9am–1pm on Saturday, and are

closed on Sunday and holidays. In large cities, some branch offices stay open until later in the evening. The post office in the Rio de Janeiro International Airport is open every day from 7am–8pm. Post offices are usually designated with a sign reading *Correios* or sometimes ECT (for Empresa de Correios e Telégrafos – Postal and Telegraph Company).

An airmail letter to or from the US takes about a week to arrive. To the UK, it may take at least two weeks. In the more densely populated areas, domestic post is usually delivered a day or two after it is mailed. National and international rapid mail service is available, as well as registered post and parcel services (the post office has special boxes for these). Stamps for collectors can be also be purchased at the post office.

You can have mail sent to you at your hotel. Although some consulates will hold mail for citizens of their country, they tend to discourage this practice.

Public Holidays

January 1 New Year's Day.
February/March Carnival. Dates vary, depending on date of Easter.
March/April Good Friday.
April 21 Tiradentes Day.
May 1 Labor Day.
May/June Corpus Christi. Date varies: ninth Thursday after Easter.
September 7 Independence Day.
October 12 Nossa Senhora de Aparecida – Brazil's patron saint.
November 2 All Souls' Day.
November 15 Proclamation of the Republic.
November 20 Black Consciousness Day.
December 25 Christmas Day.

Public Toilets

Toilets are always found in shopping centers, hotels, restaurants, airports, bus stations, the better snack bars, better gas stations, and the like. You won't find any in the street and other public places, except for a few along Copacabana beach.

R eligious Services

Catholicism is the official and dominant religion in Brazil, but many people follow religions of African origin. Of these, *candomblé* is the purest form, with deities (the *orixás*), rituals, music, dance, and even language very similar to those practiced in the parts of Africa from which it was brought. *Umbanda* involves a syncretism with Catholicism in which each *orixá* has a corresponding Catholic saint. Spiritualism, also widely practiced in Brazil, contains both African and European influences. Many Brazilians who are nominally Catholic attend both Afro-Brazilian and/or spiritual and Christian rites.

Candomblé is practiced most in Bahia, while *umbanda* and spiritualism seem to have more mass appeal. In Salvador you can arrange through your hotel or a local travel agency/tour operator to see a ceremony – visitors are welcome so long as they show respect for the belief of others. Ask permission before taking any photographs.

If you wish to attend a service at a church of your faith while in Brazil, many religious groups can be found in the larger cities, and, besides the ever-present Catholic churches, there are many Protestant churches throughout Brazil. In recent years, evangelical churches have expanded their presence dramatically. Because of the diplomatic personnel in Brasília, there is a large variety of churches and temples. Rio de Janeiro and São Paulo both have several synagogues, as well as churches with services in foreign languages, including English.

Your hotel or your country's consulate should be able to help you find a suitable place of worship.

S tudent Travelers

There are Student Travel Bureaux in Rio (Rua Visconde de Pirajá 550, loja 201; tel: 11-2512 8577) and São Paulo (Avenida Brigadeiro Faria Lima 1713, 16th floor; tel: 21-3038 1500). The law says that students can buy cinema and theater tickets half-price, but most places insist on seeing ID issued by a local student union. By all means try a foreign student ID, but don't bank on success.

T elecommunications

Telephone

Brazil's once creaky telephone service has improved dramatically since privatization in the 1990s. Virtually all parts of the country are covered, and virtually all numbers have been standardized on an eight-digit format, plus an area code.

Dialing intercity requires the use of a two-digit "operator code" to select the carrier. Embratel, a national carrier uses code 21 and can connect between most cities, but depending on where you're calling from and to, there may be cheaper options.

When dialing intercity the order is: "0" to indicate intercity, then operator code (21 or other), then city code, then number. So to call, say, São Paulo from Rio (where 11 is the São Paulo city code) using Embratel, you dial 0 21 11 xxxx xxxx.

This is not the case with every phone, however, as some companies and hotels have already built the long-distance code into their system so you would dial as before, 011 + phone number.

The access code for Embratel's rival, Intelig, is 23. For Telemar dial 31; for Telefônica, 15.

So, accepting that the obvious is not always obvious, if you have to call long-distance within Brazil ask hotel staff or the owner of the phone which is the best – and cheapest – long-distance server.

Payphones in Brazil use phone cards, which are sold at newsstands, bars or shops, usually located near the phones. The phone card, *cartão de telefone*, comes in several values. The most common is a 30-unit card, but 90-unit cards can also be bought.

The sidewalk *telefone público* is also called an *orelhão* (big ear) because of the protective shell which takes the place of a booth – yellow for local or collect calls, blue for direct-dial, long-distance calls within Brazil. You can also call from a *posto telefônico*, a telephone company station (at most bus stations and airports), where you can either use a phone card, or make a credit card or collect call.

For international calls, country codes are listed at the front of telephone directories. For long-distance domestic calls, area codes within Brazil are listed on the first few pages of directories.

Domestic long-distance rates go down 75 percent 8pm–6am and are half-price weekdays 6–8am and 8–11pm, Saturday 2–11pm and Sunday and holidays 6am–11pm.

Brazil has national coverage for mobile phones (cell phones), in major urban centers, and the centers of more affluent smaller towns. However, not all operators or systems cover all regions.

Phones from other countries may be used temporarily in Brazil provided they can operate on 1800-Mhz using GSM or TDMA. Before leaving home, check with your operator to find out if your phone and payment plan will allow you to use international roaming in Brazil. It's also advisable to check out what charges will apply – for example, if a local call in Brazil will be billed at an international rate.

Another option if you plan phoning much within Brazil is to buy a prepaid phone and keep charging it up. Phones can be purchased in shopping centers and some larger supermarkets. There is a national register of prepaid cell phones, to try and prevent their use by criminals, so be prepared to show your passport. Credits can be bought in many places – the ubiquitous

Useful Telephone Numbers

International calling and enquiries:
Direct dialing – 00 + country code + area code + phone number.
000333 or 0800-703 2100 – information regarding long-distance calls (area codes, directory assistance and complaints).
0800-703 2111 – international operator, to place person-to-person, collect and credit-card calls. Operators and interpreters who speak several languages are available.
000334 or 0800-703 2100 – information regarding rates. International rates go down 20 percent 8pm–5am (Brasília time) Monday–Saturday and all day Sunday.
To access your US phone company: Connect: **000-8012**; Sprint: **000-8016**; AT&T: **1-800 437 0966 ext 60330** (English); **1-800 541 5281 ext 59859** (Spanish).

Domestic calling and inquiries:
Direct dialing (IDD) – 0 + operator code + area code + phone number. (Embratel's code is 21, Intelig's is 23, Telemar is 31; Telefônica, 15).
Direct-dial collect call – 90 + operator code + area code + phone number. A recorded message will tell you to identify yourself and the city from which you are calling after the beep. If the party you are calling does not accept your call, you will be cut off.
107 – operator-assisted collect calls from payphones (no token needed).

Other service numbers:
102 – local directory assistance.
area code + 102 – directory assistance in that area.
108 – information regarding rates.
0800-55135 – telegrams (local, national, and international).
138 – wake-up service.
130 – correct time.

lottery shops are a favorite, also gas stations and news-stands.

Fax

A fax can be sent from some post offices, and most hotels have telex and fax services for their in-house guests. Fax services are also widely available at travel agents, office-services bureaux, and many other outlets. The prices charged for sending and receiving faxes vary widely.

Gas-station attendants, the men who shine your shoes, etc. should be tipped a small amount, again, depending on the level of service.

If you are a house guest, leave a tip for any household help (who cooked or laundered for you while you were there). Ask your hosts how much would be appropriate to give them. A tip in dollars will be especially appreciated. A small gift brought from home will certainly be welcome, and may even be better.

ABOVE: an innovative phone box.

Time Zones

There are four time zones in Brazil. **Two hours behind GMT:** The archipelago of Fernando de Noronha, 350 km (220 miles) off the Atlantic coast.
Three hours behind GMT: The western extension of Brazil's main time zone – in which 50 percent of the country lies – is a north–south line from the mouth of the Amazon River, going west to include the northern state of Amapá and the entire southern region. Rio de Janeiro, São Paulo, Belém, and Brasília are all located in this zone.
Four hours behind GMT: Another large zone encompassing the Pantanal states and most of the north.
Five hours behind GMT: The far western state of Acre, and the westernmost part of Amazonas.
Daylight-saving time has been used in recent years, with clocks being set ahead in October and back to standard time in March. This, confusingly, means that time differences do not remain the same. Daylight-saving is only used in certain parts of Brazil, and takes place in the other half of the year in the Northern Hemisphere. Therefore, the time in Rio de Janeiro, for example, is often only two hours behind GMT.

Tipping

Hotels and the more expensive restaurants will automatically add a 10 percent service charge to your bill, but this doesn't necessarily go to the individuals who served you and were helpful to you. Don't be afraid of overtipping – most employees earn a pittance and rely on the generosity of tourists.

Tipping taxi drivers is optional; most Brazilians don't. Again, if your driver has been especially helpful or waited for you, reward him appropriately. At the airport, tip the last porter to help you – what you pay goes into a pool.

A 10–20 percent tip is expected in barber shops and beauty salons.

Tourist Offices

Each state has its own tourism bureau, as do the major cities like Rio and São Paulo. Addresses for some of these offices in the main cities are listed below.

If you would like the address for a tourism board in an area not listed here, you can obtain it through the national tourist board, Embratur, which will also send information abroad on request.
Embratur
Rua Uruguaiana 174, 8th Floor, 20050-092,
Rio de Janeiro
Tel: 21-2509 6017
Fax: 21-2509 7381
www.embratur.gov.br
Belém
Paratur, Praça Waldemar Henrique
Tel: 91-3212 0575
Fax: 91-3223 6198
Belo Horizonte
Belotur, Praça Rio Branco 56, Centro
Belo Horizonte, M6
Tel: 31-3277 6907
Fax: 31-3272 5619
Brasília
Setur, Setor de Divulgação Cultural, Centro de Convenções, Cetur, 3rd Floor
Tel: 61-3327 0494
Information Center: Airport
Florianópolis
Mercado Público 3rd booth from Rua Arcipreste Paiva
www.guiafloripa.com.br
Tel: 48-224 5822
Fortaleza
Setur, Centro Adm. Governador Viríglio Távora, Cambeba, Ed. Seplan, 60839-900 CE
Tel: 85-3101 4688
Manaus
Avenida 7 de Setembro 157
Tel: 92-3233 1517
www.visitamazonas.com.br
Information Center: Airport
Porto Alegre
Sindetur, Rua Vigário, José Inacio 368, 90020110, RS
Tel: 51-3224 9228
www.turismo.rs.gov.br
Information Center: Airport

Recife
Empetur, Complexo Rodoviário de Salgadinho, s/n, 5311 1970
Tel: 81-3463 3621/3425 8149
www.empetur.pe.gov.br
Information Centers: Airport, Bus Station, Casa da Cultura
Rio de Janeiro
Rio Convention and Visitors Bureau
Rua Visconde de Pirajá 547
Tel: 21-2259 6165
www.rioconventionbureau.com.br
rcvb@rcvb.com.br
Riotur
Runs an efficient over-the-phone service called **Alô Rio**
Tel: 21-2542 8080/0800-707 1808.
City only.
TurisRio
Rua da Ajuda 5, 6th floor, Downtown
Tel: 21-2215 0011
Everything outside the city limits.
City information Centers:
International Airport, Bus Station, Corcovado, Sugar Loaf, Cinelândia Subway Station, Marina da Glória
Salvador
Bahiatursa, Jardim Armação s/n, Historical Centre, BA
Tel: 71-3370 8400
www.bahiatursa.ba.gov.br
Information Centers: Airport, Bus Station, Mercado Modelo, Porto da Barra
São Paulo
Setur, Praça Antonio Prado 9, 6th Floor, 01010-904

ABOVE: a tip is always appreciated by those who look after you.

Tel: 11-3289 7588
Fax: 11-3107 8767
www.spcvb.com.br
Information Centers:
Praça da República, Praça da
Liberdade, Praça da Sé, Praça
Ramos de Azevedo, Avenida Paulista
in front of Top Center and at corner of
Rua Augusta, Shopping Morumbi,
Shopping Ibirapuera

Travel Agents and Tour Operators

Rio de Janeiro

Brazilian Incentive & Tourism
Barão de Ipanema 56, 5th floor,
Copacabana
Tel: 21-2256 5657
www.bitourism.com
Comprehensive program of tours that
covers the whole of Brazil.
Just Fly
Tel/fax: 21-2268 0565
Cell phone: 9985 7540
www.justfly.com.br
justfly@justfly.com.br
Hang-gliding over Rio, jeep tours of
Tijuca National Park, and bicycle hire.

São Paulo

Freeway
Rua Cap. Cavalcanti 322
Tel: 11-5088 0999
www.freeway.tur.br
freeway.adventures.com.br
Trips to Fernando de Noronha, Bahia,
and the Amazon. Ecotourism, trekking,
climbing, and diving expeditions.

Salvador

Kontik Operadora
Avenida Tancredo Neves 969,

10th Floor, Sala 1004/1005
Tel: 71-3271 8686/3251 8690
www.kontik.com.br
Specialized tours in the state of
Bahia, including climbing, trekking,
and sailing; folklore and city tours.
Tatar Turismo
Avenida Tancredo Neves 274,
Centro Empresarial Iguatemi, Bloco
B, Salas 222–224
Tel: 71-3450 7216
Fax: 71-3450 7215
www.tatur.com.br
tatur@tatur.com.br

Lençóis

Luck Adventure
Praça Horácio de Matos
Tel: 75-3334 1925
www.luckreceptivo.com.br
reservas@luckchapada-bahia.com.br

Natal

Manary Ecotours
Rua Francisco Gurgel 9067, Praia de
Ponta Negra
Tel: 84-3219 2900
www.manary.cam.br
Cultural and ecological trips in the
northeast and to Fernando de
Noronha. "Soft" adventure and
archeology.

Cuiabá (Pantanal)

Anaconda
Avenida Isaac Póvoas 606
Tel: 65-3028 5990
www.anacondapantanal.com.br
Trips in the northern Pantanal.

Manaus (Amazon)

CVC Travel Agent
www.cvc.com.br

Swallows and Amazons
Rua Quintino Bocaiuva 189, Suite 13
Tel/fax: 92-3622 1246
www.swallowsandamazonstours.com
American/Brazilian company offering
good Amazon tours.

Recife

Luck Adventure
Rua Jacana 105
Imbiribeir
Tel: 81-3302 3880
www.luckreceptivo.com.br
luckrec@luckviagens.com.br

Iguaçu

Iguassu Falls Tour
Floriano Peixoto 614, Foz do Iguaçu
Tel: 45-9104 7001
www.iguassufallstour.com,
contact@iguassufallstour.com
Offers a comprehensive set of
packages to the falls, as well as
excursions to Paraguay and the Itaipú
Dam.
Luz Tour
Avenida Gustavo Dobrandino
da Silva 145, Foz do Iguacu
Tel: 45-3522 3535
www.luzhotel.com.br luzhotel@luzhotel.com.br
Based in the Luz Hotel, next to the
bus station, Luz Tur provides good
one- and two-day trips to the falls.
Antônio, the owner, speaks good
English, and they have a
comfortable, air-conditioned mini-van.

W ebsites

Below is a list of some Brazilian
websites likely to be useful for
travelers, and if you are looking for
the obvious in Brazil, remember to try
".com.br" rather than ".com":
Brazilian Government
www.brazil.gov.br
Brazilian Embassy
(Washington)
www.brasil.emb.nw.dc.us
Brazilmax
(Self-styled "hip guide")
brazilmax.com
Embratur
(Brazilian Tourist Board)
www.braziltour.com
Estado de São Paulo
(Newspaper/links)
www.estado.com.br
Google
(Search engine)
www.google.com.br
O Globo
(Newspaper/links)
www.oglobo.com.br
Rio Tourist Board
www.rio.rj.gov.br/riotur
Salvador Tourist Board
www.emtursa.com.br
São Paulo Tourist Board
www.spguia.com.br

Bikini Rules

Don't forget to pack your swimsuit! Or buy a tiny local version of the string bikini, called a *tanga*, for yourself or someone back home – there are stores that sell nothing but beachwear. New styles emerge each year, in different fabrics and colors, exposing this part or that. The tiniest are called *fio dental*, or dental floss.

Topless sunbathing on Brazil's beaches has never really caught on. Women should avoid exposing their breasts on the beach; for most

Brazilians, this is regarded as offensive behavior. Despite their open attitude towards sex, it is worth remembering that Brazilians are a deeply Catholic and often conservative people.

Decently dressed women get ogled, too. Brazilian men don't go in for catcalls, but they draw their breath in sharply between clenched teeth, and murmur comments as the women pass by. Brazilian women certainly don't let this cramp their style.

Veja
(News magazine)
www.uol.com.br/veja

Weights and Measures

The metric system is used throughout Brazil, and temperature is measured on the centigrade or Celsius scale (°C). Other measuring units are used in rural areas, but people are familiar with the metric system.

What to Bring

Brazilians are very fashion-conscious, but are casual dressers. What you bring will depend on where you will be visiting and your holiday schedule. São Paulo tends to be more dressy, while in small inland towns people are more conservative. If you are going to a jungle lodge, you will want sturdy clothing and perhaps boots. If you are in Brazil on business, however, a suit and tie for men, and suits, skirts or dresses for women are the office standard.

Although some restaurants in the downtown business districts of the larger cities require a tie at lunch, other restaurants have no such regulations. Generally speaking, suits and ties are used less the further north you go in Brazil, even by businessmen, and the opposite holds true as you go south. Bring a summer-weight suit for office calls: linen is smart and cool, although liable to crease.

If you like to dress up, there are plenty of places to go to in the evening in the big cities. But avoid ostentation and expensive or flashy jewelry. There are many desperately poor people in Brazil, and unwitting foreign tourists make attractive targets for both pickpockets and purse-snatchers.

Shorts are acceptable for men and women in most areas, especially near the beach or in resort towns, but they

are not usually worn in the downtown areas of cities. Most churches, and some museums, do not admit visitors dressed in shorts, and the traditional *gafieira* dance halls will not admit those dressed in shorts, especially men. Jeans are acceptable and are often worn, but can be too hot.

If you come during Carnival, remember that it will be very hot, and you will probably be in a crowd and dancing non-stop. Anything colorful is appropriate. If you plan to go to any of the balls, you will find plenty of costumes in the shops – you might want to buy just a feathered hair ornament, flowered *lei* (garland) or sequined accessory to complete your outfit. Many women wear no more than a bikini and make-up. Most men wear shorts – with or without a shirt – or sometimes a sarong. There are fancy-dress balls with themes such as "Hawaii" or "Arabian Nights."

If you are traveling in the south or

in the mountains, or to São Paulo in winter, it can be quite chilly. Even in the areas where it is hot all year round, you may need a light sweater, jacket, or sweatshirt, if not for the cooler evenings, then for the chilly air-conditioning in hotels, restaurants, and offices. Rain gear is always worth taking with you – Brazilians tend to use umbrellas more than raincoats. Seaside hotels will usually provide you with sun umbrellas and beach towels.

As on any trip, it is sensible to bring a pair of comfortable walking shoes – there is no better way to explore than on foot. Sandals and beach thongs (flip-flops) are comfortable in the heat, and even if you don't plan to wear them for walking around the streets, they're very convenient for getting across the hot sand from your hotel to the water's edge. If there's one thing that gives Brazilians the giggles, it's the sight of a *gringo* going to the beach in shoes and socks. But as Brazil produces the popular Havaianas flip-flops, and sells them very cheaply, you may as well wait until you get there to buy them.

There is nothing better for the summer heat than cotton, and since Brazil produces linen and exports cotton you might want to pack the bare essentials, and acquire a new wardrobe.

When buying clothes, remember that some natural fabrics will shrink. *Pequeno* = Small; *Médio* = Medium; and *Grande* = Large (often marked "P", "M", and "G"). *Maior* means larger; *menor* means smaller.

BELOW: tour operators can arrange buggy hire, a good way to explore beaches.

LANGUAGE

UNDERSTANDING THE LANGUAGE

Although Portuguese, not Spanish, is the language of Brazil, a knowledge of Spanish will go a long way. You will recognize many similar words, and some Brazilians will understand you if you speak in Spanish. You will, however, find it difficult to understand them. Although many upper-class Brazilians know at least some English or French and are eager to practice on foreign visitors, don't expect people on the street to speak your language. An effort by a foreigner to learn the local language is always appreciated. Pronunciation can be confusing. For example, "R" is pronounced "H," so that "Rio" sounds like "Hee-o."

At most large hotels and top restaurants you can get by in English with very few problems. But if you like to wander around on your own, you might want to invest in a good dictionary; the *Berlitz Pocket Dictionary* is a useful one, light and easy to carry around.

Addressing People

First names are used a great deal in Brazil. In many situations in which English-speakers would use a title and surname, Brazilians often use a first name with the title of respect: *Senhor* for men (written *Sr* and usually shortened to *Seu* in spoken Portuguese) and *Senhora* (written *Sra*) or *Dona* (used only with first name) for women.

There are three second-person pronoun forms in Portuguese. Stick to *você*, equivalent to "you," and you will be all right. *O senhor* (for men) or *a senhora* (for women) is used to show respect for someone of a different age group or social class, or to be polite to a

stranger. As a foreigner, you won't offend anyone if you use the wrong form of address. But if you want to learn when to use the more formal or informal style, observe how others address you, and be guided by that. In some parts of Brazil, mainly the northeast and the south, *tu* is used a great deal. Originally, in Portugal, *tu* was used among intimate friends and close relatives, but in Brazil, it is equivalent to *você*.

If you are staying for some time and are serious about learning the language, there are plenty of Portuguese courses for non-native speakers. Meanwhile, here are some of the most essential words and phrases.

Greetings

Tudo Bem, literally meaning "all's well," is one of the most common forms of greeting: one person asks, *"Tudo bem?"* (or *"Tudo bom?"*) and the other replies, *"Tudo bem"* (or *"Tudo bom"*). This is also used to mean "OK," "all right," "will do," or as a response when someone apologizes, as if to say, "That's all right, it doesn't matter." "Ta legal" is a formal slang expression commonly heard. It means "OK" or "That's cool." Other forms of greetings are:

Good morning (good afternoon)
Bom dia (boa tarde)
Good evening (good night) *Boa noite*
How are you? *Como vai você?*
Well, thank you *Bem, obrigado*
Hello (to answer the telephone) *Alô*
Hello (common forms of greeting) *Bom dia, boa tarde, etc.*
Hi, hey! (informal greeting also used

to get someone's attention) *Oi*
Goodbye (very informal and most used) *Tchau*
Goodbye (literally "until soon") *Até logo*
Goodbye (similar to "farewell") *Adeus*
My name is (I am) *Meu nome é (Eu sou)*
What is your name? *Como é seu nome?*
It's a pleasure *É um prazer*
Pleasure (used in introductions as "Pleased to meet you") *Prazer*
Good! Great! *Que bom!*
Health! (the most common toast) *Saúde*
Do you speak English? *Você fala inglês?*
I don't understand (I didn't understand) *Não entendo (Não entendi)*
Do you understand? *Você entende?*
Please repeat more slowly *Por favor repete, mais devagar*
What do you call this (that)? *Como se chama isto (aquilo)?*
How do you say...? *Como se diz...?*
Please *Por favor*
Thank you (very much) *(Muito) Obrigado (or obrigada, if a woman is speaking)*
You're welcome (literally "it's nothing") *De nada*
Excuse me (to apologize) *Desculpe*
Excuse me (taking leave or to get past someone) *Com licença*

Pronouns

Who? *Quem?*
I (we) *Eu (nós)*
You (singular) *Você*
You (plural) *Vocês*
He (she) *Ele (ela)*
They *Eles (Elas)*
My (mine) *Meu (minha)* depending on gender of object
Our (ours) *Nosso (nossa)*

Addresses

The following will help you understand Brazilian addresses and place names:

Al. or *Alameda* = lane
Andar = floor, story
Av. or *Avenida* = avenue
Casa = house
Centro = the central downtown business district, also frequently referred to as *a cidade* (the city)
Cj. or *Conjunto* = a suite of rooms, or sometimes a group of buildings
Estr. or *Estrada* = road or highway
Fazenda = ranch, also a lodge
Lgo or *Largo* = square or plaza
Lote = lot
Pça or *Praça* = square or plaza
Praia = beach
Rio = river
Rod. or *Rodovia* = highway
R. or *Rua* = street
Sala = room

Your (yours) *Seu (sua)*
His (her/hers) *Dele (dela/deles)*
Their, theirs *Delas*

Getting Around

Where is the...? *Onde é...?*
beach *a praia*
bathroom *o banheiro*
bus station *a rodoviária*
airport *o aeroporto*
train station *a estação de trem*
post office *o correio*
police station *a delegacia de polícia*
ticket office *a bilheteria*
marketplace *o mercado*
street market *feira*
embassy (consulate) *a embaixada (o consulado)*
Where is there a...? *Onde é que tem... ?*
currency exchange *uma casa de câmbio*
bank *um banco*
pharmacy *uma farmácia*
(good) hotel *um (bom) hotel*
(good) restaurant *um (bom) restaurante*
snack bar *uma lanchonete*
bus stop *um ponto de ônibus*
taxi stand *um ponto de taxi*
subway station *uma estação de metrô*
service station *um posto de gasolina*
news-stand *um jornaleiro*
public telephone *um telefone público*
supermarket *um supermercado*
department store *uma loja de departamentos*
boutique *uma boutique*

jeweler *um joalheiro*
hairdresser (barber) *um cabeleireiro (um barbeiro)*
laundry *uma lavanderia*
hospital *um hospital*
doctor *um médico*
A ticket to... *Uma passagem para...*
I want to go to... *Quero ir para...*
How can I get to...? *Como posso ir para...?*
Please take me to... *Por favor, me leve para...*
Please call a taxi for me *Por favor, chame um taxi para mim*
I want to rent a car *Quero alugar um carro*
What is this place called? *Como se chama este lugar?*
Where are we? *Onde estamos?*
How long will it take to get there? *Leva quanto tempo para chegar lá?*
Please stop here (Stop!) *Por favor, pare aqui (Pare!)*
Please wait *Por favor, espere*
What time does the bus (plane, boat) leave? *A que horas sai o ônibus (avião, barco)?*
Where does this bus go? *Este ônibus vai para onde?*
Does it go by way of...? *Passa em...?*
Please let me off at the next stop *Por favor, deixe-me na próxima paragem*
Airport (bus station) tax *Taxa de embarque*
I want to check my luggage (on a bus, etc.) *Quero despachar minha bagagem*
I want to store my luggage (at a station) *Quero guardar minha bagagem*

Shopping

Do you have...? *Você tem...?*
I want... please *Eu quero... por favor*
I don't want... *Eu não quero...*
I want to buy... *Eu quero comprar...*
Can you help me please? *Pode ajudar-me, por favor?*
It's not quite what I want *Não é bem o que quero*
Where can I buy... *Onde posso comprar...?*
cigarettes *cigarros*
film *filme*
a ticket for... *uma entrada para...*
a reserved seat *um lugar marcado*
another the same *um outro igual*
another different *um outro diferente*
this (that) *isto (aqui)*
something less
expensive *algo mais barato*
postcards *cartões postais*
paper (envelopes) *papel (envelopes)*
a pen (a pencil) *uma caneta (um lápis)*

soap (shampoo) *sabonete (xampu or shampoo)*
toothpaste *pasta de dente*
sunscreen *filtro solar*
aspirin *aspirina*
How much? *Quanto?*
How many? *Quantos?*
How much does it cost? *Quanto custa? Quanto é?*
That's very expensive *É muito caro*
a lot, very (many) *muito (muitos)*
a little (few) *um pouco (poucos)*
handbag (purse) *bolsa/saco*
money purse *porta-moedas*
wallet *carteira*

At the Hotel

I have a reservation *Tenho uma reserva*
I want to make a reservation *Quero fazer uma reserva*
A single room (A double room) *Um quarto de solteiro (Um quarto de casal)*
With air-conditioning *com ar condicionado*
I want to see the room *Quero ver o quarto*
suitcase *mala/bolsa*
room service *serviço de quarto*
key *chave*
the manager *o gerente*

At the Restaurant

waiter *garçon*
maître d' *daitre*
I didn't order this *Eu não pedi isto*
The menu (the wine list) *O cardápio (a carta de vinhos)*
breakfast *café da manhã*
lunch *almoço*
supper *jantar*
the house specialty *a especialidade da casa*
carbonated mineral water *água mineral com gás*
uncarbonated mineral water *água mineral sem gás*
coffee *café*
tea *chá*
beer (bottled) *cerveja*
beer (draft) *chope*
white wine (red wine) *vinho branco (vinho tinto)*
a soft drink (juice) *um refrigerante (suco)*
an alcoholic drink *um drink*
ice *gelo*
salt *sal*

Emergencies

I need... *Eu preciso de...*
a doctor *um médico*
a mechanic *um mecânico*
transportation *condução*
help *ajuda*

TRANSPORTATION

ACCOMMODATIONS

ACTIVITIES

A – Z

LANGUAGE

Forms of Transport

taxi *taxi*
bus *ônibus*
car *carro*
Plane *avião*
train *trem*
boat *barco*

pepper *pimenta*
sugar *açúcar*
a plate *um prato*
a glass *um copo*
a glass of wine *uma taça de vinho*
a cup *uma xícara*
a napkin *um guardanapo*
bread *pão*
egg *ovo*
fish *peixe*
crab *caranguejo/aratu*
herrring *arenque*
lobster *lavagante*
seafood *marisco*
meat *carne*
beef *carne de boi*
chicken *frango*
ham *presunto*
lamb *borrego*
liver *fígado*
mutton *carneiro*
pork *porco*
stew *guisado*
vegetables *legumes*
potatoes *batatas*
aubergine (eggplant) *beringela*
avocado *abacate*
beans *feijãos*
broad beans *favas*
carrots *cenouras*
garlic *alho*
ginger *gengibre*
lettuce *alface*
well done *bem passado*
medium rare *ao ponto*
rare *mal passado*
baked *cocido no forno*
home-made *caseiro*

BELOW: it helps to be able to speak the language.

fumado *smoked*
I'm a vegetarian *Eu sou
vegetariano/a*
I don't eat meat/fish *Eu não como
carne/peixe*
The bill, please *A conta, por favor*
Is service included? *Está incluído o
serviço?*
I want my change, please *Eu quero
meu troco, por favor*
I want a receipt *Eu quero um recibo*

Money

bank *banco*
cash *dinheiro*
Do you accept credit cards? *Aceita
cartão de crédito?*
Can you cash a travelers' check?
Pode trocar um travelers' check?
(*cheque de viagem*)
I want to exchange money *Quero
trocar dinheiro*
What is the exchange rate? *Qual é
o câmbio?*

Time

When? *Quando?*
What time is it? *Que horas são?*
Just a moment please *Um
momento, por favor*
What is the schedule? (*bus, tour,
show, etc.*) *Qual é o horário?*
How long does it take? *Leva quanto
tempo?*
hour *hora*
day *dia*
week *semana*
month *mês*
At what time...? *A que horas...?*
At one o' clock (two, three) *A uma
hora (duas, três)*
An hour from now *Daqui a uma hora*
Which day? *Que dia?*
yesterday *ontem*
today *hoje*
tomorrow *amanhã*

this week *esta semana*
last week *a semana passada/*
next week *a semana que vem*
the weekend *o fim de semana*
Monday *segunda-feira (often 2a)*
Tuesday *terca-feira (often 3a)*
Wednesday *quarta-feira (often 4a)*
Thursday *quinta-feira (often 5a)*
Friday *sexta-feira (often 6a)*
Saturday *sábado*
Sunday *domingo*

Numbers

Ordinal numbers are written with °
i.e. a degree sign after the numeral,
so that 3° *andar* means 3rd floor.
BR followed by a number refers to
one of the federal interstate highways, for example BR-101, which
follows the Atlantic coast.

1 *um*
2 *dois*
3 *três*
4 *quatro*
5 *cinco*
6 *seis*
7 *sete*
8 *oito*
9 *nove*
10 *dez*
11 *onze*
12 *doze*
13 *treze*
14 *quatorze*
15 *quinze*
16 *dezesseis*
17 *dezessete*
18 *dezoito*
19 *dezenove*
20 *vinte*
21 *vinte um*
30 *trinta*
40 *quarenta*
50 *cinquenta*
60 *sessenta*
70 *setenta*
80 *oitenta*
90 *noventa*
100 *cem*
101 *cento e um*
200 *duzentos*
300 *trezentos*
400 *quatrocentos*
500 *quinhentos*
600 *seiscentos*
700 *setecentos*
800 *oitocentos*
900 *novecentos*
1,000 *mil*
2,000 *dois mil*
10,000 *dez mil*
100,000 *cem mil*
1,000,000 *um milhão*
half a dozen *meia*

Commas and periods in numbers
take an inverted form in Portuguese:
1,000 is written 1.000 and one and
a half (1.5) is written 1,5.

FURTHER READING

General Reading

Brazil since 1980, by Francisco Luna and Herbert Klein. CUP, 2006.
The Brazilians, by Joseph A. Page. Perseus, 1996.
The Brazil Reader, by Robert M. Levine and John J. Crocitti (eds). Latin American Bureau, 1999.
The Cloud Forest, by Peter Matthiessen. New York, 1987.

History and Travel

A Concise History of Brazil, by Boris Fausto. CUP, 1999.
Brazilian Adventure, by Peter Fleming. Putman, 1983. Account of a 1925 expedition.
Ninety-Two Days: A Journey in Guiana and Brazil, by Evelyn Waugh. Penguin, 1995.

Fiction

Brazil, by John Updike. Penguin, 1995.
City of God: A Novel, by Paulo Lins, Grove Press, Black Cat, 2006. The book on which the award-winning film was based – life and violence in a Rio slum.
Dom Casmurro, by Machado de Assis. New York, 1999.
Dona Flor and Her Two Husbands, by Jorge Amado. Serpent's Tail, 1999.
The Emperor of the Amazon, by M. Souza. Hypermass, 1983.
Soulstorm, by Clarice Lispector. New Directions, 1989. Short stories by writer noted for her blend of suspense and romance.
The War of the Saints, by Jorge Amado. Serpent's Tail, 1994.
The Brothers, by Milton Hatoum. Bloomsbury, 2000. Set in Manaus during the Rubber Boom, a fictional story of twin brothers.
Turbulence, by Chico Buarque. Bloomsbury, 1992. A nostalgic account of Rio de Janeiro.

Civilization and Society

Amazon Frontier: The Defeat of the Brazilian Indians, by J. Hemming. London, 1995. Chronicles the first 150 years from the time the Europeans first explored Amazonia.
At the End of the Rainbow? Gold, Land and People in the Brazilian Amazon, by G. Macmillan. Earthscan, 1995.
The Fate of the Forest, by S. Hecht and A. Cockburn. Penguin, 1990.
Fazendas: The Great Houses and Plantations of Brazil, by Fernando Tasso Fragosa Pires and Nicholas Sapieha. A picture book that traces the development of Brazil's sugar and coffee plantations and cattle ranches.
Futebol: The Brazilian Way of Life, by Alex Bellos. Bloomsbury, 2002. A wonderful, entertaining combination of history and anecdote that will fascinate even those who have no interest in football.
Disinherited Indians in Brazil, Survival International, 2001.

Feedback

We do our best to ensure the information in our books is as accurate and up-to-date as possible. The books are updated on a regular basis, using local contacts, who painstakingly add, amend and correct as required. However, some mistakes and omissions are inevitable and we are ultimately reliant on our readers to put us in the picture.

We would welcome your feedback on any details related to your experiences using the book "on the road". Maybe we recommended a hotel that you liked (or another that you didn't), as well as interesting new attractions, or facts and figures you have found out about the country itself. The more details you can give us (particularly with regard to addresses, e-mails and telephone numbers), the better.

We will acknowledge all contributions, and we'll offer an Insight Guide to the best letters received.

Please write to us at:
Insight Guides
PO Box 7910
London SE1 1WE
United Kingdom
Or send e-mail to:
insight@apaguide.co.uk

Murder in the Rainforest, by Jan Rocha. LAB, 1999.
Rio de Janeiro, by Ruy Castro, Bloomsbury USA (Writer and the City series), 2004. Well-known Brazilian essayist reveals his personal Rio de Janeiro, with fascinating anecdotes and neighborhood descriptions.
Tropical Truth, by Caetano Veloso. Bloomsbury. The John Lennon of Brazil tells how tropicalismo revolutionized Brazilian culture as well as its politics.
Travelers' Tales Brazil, by Annette Haddad and Scott Doggett. Travelers' Tales Inc., 1997. Fifty travel essays, varying in quality, on the country's commingling of cultures.

Race and Black Culture

Benedita da Silva, an Afro-Brazilian woman's story of politics and love. Benjamin and Mendança. LAB, 1998.

Other Insight Guides

Apa Publications has more guidebook titles than any other guidebook publisher. There are over 200 *Insight Guides* covering the countries, regions and cities of the world, all using Apa's well-known formula of expert writing and beautiful photography.

There are also more than 100 *Insight Pocket Guides*, which have recommended itineraries designed for the short-stay visitor.

A third series comprising 120 titles, *Compact Guides* are concise mini-encyclopedias to use on the spot.

Major *Insight Guides* are available to *Latin America, Rio de Janeiro, Chile, Ecuador, Peru, Venezuela, Argentina, Buenos Aires, Guatemala, Belize & Yucatán*, and *Amazon Wildlife*.

Insight City Guide: Rio de Janeiro takes a closer look at what many have called the most beautiful city in the world, focusing on the culture of Rio's people – the *cariocas*.

Insight Guide: South America is the perfect companion for those taking a tour of the whole South American continent. From the lost cities of the Incas to the nightclubs of Rio, it's all here.

ART & PHOTO CREDITS

INDEX

Numbers in italics refer to photographs

INSIGHT GUIDES
The classic series that puts you in the picture

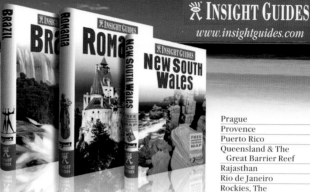

INSIGHT GUIDES
www.insightguides.com

**Greater
Rio de Jan**

0   10
0   100